Vogue Knitting

The Ultimate Knitting Book by the editors of Vogue Knitting Magazine

Vogue Knitting

Pantheon Books, New York

Editorial Concept and Development
Lola Ehrlich

Art Director and Designer
Karen Salsgiver

Project Director
Martha Moran

Magazine Editors
Joni Coniglio, Carla S. Patrick, Nancy J. Thomas

Book Editor
Cherie Gillette

Illustrations
Kate Simunek, Chapman Bounford and Associates (UK)

Copyeditors
Debbie Conn, Liza Wolsky

Editorial Coordinator
Catherine Quartulli

Design Assistant
Susan Carabetta

Contributing Writers
Kaffe Fassett, Barbara Walker, Elizabeth Zimmermann, Margaret Bruzelius, Mari Lynn Civelek

Photography
Jack Deutsch, Torkil Gudnason (fashion)

Charts and Schematics
Roberta Frauwirth, Timothy McGrath, Marie Schoeff

Consultants
Mike Brecher (In-the-Can Company Ltd), Michael Harkavy (Harkavy Publishing Service)

Contributors
Trevor Bounford, Berta Carela-Harkavy, Ann Clue, Carol Covington, Sandy Daniels, Roger Eaton, Lillian Esposito, Mary Ann Esposito, Elsie Faulconer, Maureen Fitzpatrick, David Frederickson, Joe Marc Freedman, Norah Gaughan, Kathy Grasso, Ilisha Helfman, Chris Jones, Sylvia Jorrin, Teri Leve, Hugh Mac-Donald, Elizabeth Malament, Nancy Marchant, Margarita Mejia, Annie Modesitt, Deborah Newton, Kay Niederlitz, Susan Olsen, Lisa Paul, Rose Ann Pollani, Dorothy Radigan, Mick Rivers, Cindy Rose, Emma Scott, Jessica Shatan, Karen Sisti, Joe Vior

Yarns and Tools
Westminster Trading Corp., Anny Blatt, Berger du Nord, Plymouth Yarns, Susan Bates, Inc., Boye Needle Co., Patternworks

Typesetting
The Sarabande Press

Separations
Acolortone Limited (UK)

Preparation and Film
Reflex Reprographics (UK)

Printer
Kingsport Press

President and Chief Executive Officer, Butterick Company, Inc.
John Lehmann

Consultant, Book Publishing
Mike Shatzkin

Director, Butterick Publications
Art Joinnides

Without the knowledge that came before us, this book and all the techniques included would not have been possible. The editors are indebted to the following: Barbara Walker, Elizabeth Zimmermann, Meg Swansen, Corinne Shields, Claudia Manley, Montse Stanley, Mary Thomas, Sally Harding, Margery Winter

Library of Congress Cataloging-in-Publication Data

Vogue knitting : the ultimate knitting book / by the editors of
   Vogue knitting magazine.
      p.   cm.
   ISBN 0-394-57186-X
   1. Knitting.   I. Vogue knitting international.
TT820.V624   1989
746.9′2—dc19   89-42555

Grateful acknowledgment is made for permission to use the following photographs: Page 2, by courtesy of the Board of Trustees of the Victoria & Albert Museum. Page 3, Hamburger Kunsthalle. Pages 4 and 5, by courtesy of the Board of Trustees of the Victoria & Albert Museum. Page 6, photographs by Cynthia LeCount; (bottom), from the collection of Jeff Appleby. Page 7 (top right), Leeds City Art Galleries, Leeds, England; (bottom), by courtesy of the Board of Trustees of the Victoria & Albert Museum. Page 12 (bottom), Albany International Research Company. Page 80 (top), Real Ireland Design Limited; (bottom), Peter Dressler.

Manufactured in the United States of America

First Edition

Table of Contents

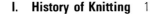

When the editors of *Vogue Knitting Magazine* were asked to create the ultimate book on knitting, they embarked on a three year course toward the completion of this book.

In researching literally hundreds of knitting books, some long out of print, they learned that not only did no one book cover knitting in a comprehensive way, but that a knitter would need to own dozens of books to cover the field. Using their expertise and years of experience in the industry, they developed the blueprint for the ultimate knitting reference, one that would cover every aspect of knitting in clear concise language partnered by vivid, accurate step-by-step visuals.

Over fifty specialists, directed by the editors of *Vogue Knitting Magazine,* participated in the making of *Vogue Knitting.* Every single technique in this book was meticulously researched, written and tested by the editors. Every word, swatch, photograph and illustration was created specifically for this book.

Nancy J. Thomas contributed the book's chapter on design and also much of the technical writing in its other sections. In addition she directed all of the knitting used for the book, managing dozens of knitters who worked from her precisely prepared instructions and keeping track of hundreds of swatches and photographs.

Carla S. Patrick, the book's primary technical expert and writer, also created the computer format for organizing and writing the book, the computer-generated symbolcraft library, the modular sweater concept and patterns, and coordinated and supervised all photography.

Joni Coniglio wrote and edited copy and directed illustration of the book. She painstakingly prepared sketches, notes and knitted samples for each illustration and worked with the illustrators throughout the process to assure the clarity and accuracy of each illustration.

Special Features of This Book

This book was written with great attention to both detail of content and organization of material. An understanding of a few of its features will greatly increase its usefulness and value to you.

A glance at the table of contents will show you that the book's chapters are *color-coded*. For example, the color bar for chapter XI (Designing) is blue. Simply look for the section of the book that is barred in blue—and there you are. All *chapter openers* are correspondingly *color-coded* and clearly mark the beginning point of each chapter. *Chapter openers* also show quick comprehensive overviews of techniques contained in the chapters.

Most pages display a running *cross-reference* at the bottom. This allows the reader quick and easy access to more detailed explanations pertinent to the task at hand, without having to spend time searching through the book or index to find them.

The *color boxes* highlight charts, lists and "tricks of the trade." *Symbolcraft,* an internationally recognized alternate system of expressing knitting instructions through the use of symbols and charts, is used throughout the book and is completely explained in chapter IV (pages 69-70). Comprehensive glossaries of *Knitting Terminology* and *Abbreviations Explained* are also found in chapter IV.

Vogue Knitting is designed to be a reference for all levels of knitter. The book is arranged by subject, not by advancement of technique. There is, therefore, something for every knitter, from beginner to professional, *in each chapter.* Skip around—see what you find. It is not necessary to learn *all* the techniques—simply the ones most useful for you. As you advance, as your needs change or become more specific, *Vogue Knitting* will continue to provide alternative solutions to your knitting needs and creative opportunities.

Enjoy yourself!

I. History of Knitting

The History of Knitting

This fragment from Egypt, dated 1200–1500 A.D., is an early example of Egyptian stranded knitting.

No one really knows how knitting was invented. Even its definition has been uncertain, for a wide range of fabrics, ranging from ancient Peruvian tapestries to metal wire decorations, have a knitted structure but are not produced with knitting needles. Many fabrics which seem to be knitted are actually made by various netting techniques using a type of sewing needle. A meticulous examination of the knitted textile itself can often, but not always, tell us how it was created, but many old textiles are too frail to be examined carefully.

Although we have no written record, knitting was undoubtedly invented when people who had been fiddling with loops of yarn discovered that they could make a strong and flexible fabric by continuing to loop the yarn through itself. Originally, like most methods of textile production, knitting was probably practiced mainly by men, while women produced the yarn. Although certain New World Indian tribes developed their own indigenous knitted fabrics, the Mediterranean seems to have been the cradle of knitting, and traders and sailors spread the craft throughout Europe and to the rest of the world.

In the absence of facts, knitters have used their imaginations to create colorful histories for their craft. Knitters have claimed that Penelope in Homer's *Odyssey* must have been unravelling her knitting, not her weaving, to avoid her unwanted suitors, and that Christ's seamless garment was a type of tunic knit in the round. Patterns typical of Fair Isle knitting are said to have been learned from Spanish sailors who survived the shipwreck of the Armada, and the traditional gansey patterns knit for English sailors were supposed to have served as a means of identifying bodies washed up on the shore. In fact, there is no evidence to support the existence of knitting until around the 13th century A.D. and none to substantiate any of these tales, which can be traced back to 19th century knitting historians who loved a good yarn (in both senses of the word).

No one can say if the earliest knitting was round or flat, or worked with straight or hooked needles. Historians presume that all knitting was originally worked in the round and that flat knitting developed later, simply because round knitting is simpler. It requires only one method of making loops, a knit stitch, while flat knitting requires two, the knit stitch and the purl stitch. It is not at all certain, however, that the knitting method that seems easiest and most logical to contemporary textile historians is necessarily the one devised by the first knitters.

The earliest surviving knitted fabrics are socks discovered in Egypt, where the dry climate has preserved them. These fragments are fairly common and can be found in many textile collections, including those of the Victoria and Albert Museum in London and the Detroit Institute of Arts in Michigan. These early socks were worked in the round in two-color stranded knitting and are dated from 1200 to 1500 A.D. It is certainly no accident socks were the earliest application of knitting since the flexibility of knitted fabrics is ideal for the contour of the foot. And in addition to being comfortable, these socks demonstrate that the first knitters thought not only of the needs of the body, but also those of the spirit; all are decorated in designs ranging from zigzags and other simple geometrics to inscriptions and complicated lozenge patterns reminiscent of carpet borders.

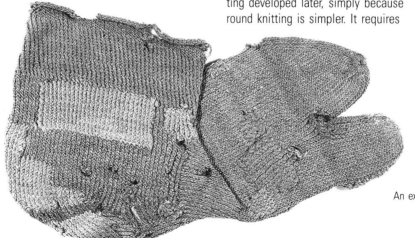

An exquisitely mended Egyptian sandal sock.

One of the earliest depictions of knitting, this 15th century painting shows the Madonna knitting circularly.

Unfortunately, until the establishment of knitting guilds during the Renaissance in Europe, the history of knitting is documented only by the survival of the occasional knitted fabric. Most of these knits are found in tombs or in church treasuries; we know nothing more about their history than what the pieces themselves reveal. Without written documentation, there is no way to tell whether knitting was widespread or the specialized province of a few highly skilled workers.

Two of the most extraordinary finds are a pair of knitted cushions preserved in 13th century Spanish tombs, each covered with different and highly elaborate two-color patterning at a gauge of 20 stitches to the inch. The patterning reveals a strong Arabic influence, not surprising in Moorish-influenced Spain. Perhaps these were knitted by nuns, who have labored over so many beautiful and elaborate fabrics. Many surviving medieval knitted artifacts are associated with the church—elaborate purses for relics in Switzerland and liturgical gloves found throughout Europe. As with the pillows, we can only marvel at their survival and their workmanship, and speculate about their makers.

One theory suggests that knitting was known to some early Renaissance painters. Several altar pieces from the 14th century depict the Virgin knitting a garment for the Christ child; she is usually pictured knitting a shirt in the round on four needles. But these paintings cannot tell us if the painter chose to show the Madonna knitting because it was an attribute of a fine lady, or one associated with ordinary people— they only demonstrate that knitting was known to the artists.

Aside from these largely ecclesiastical survivals, the earliest knitted garments were caps (which were felted), stockings and sleeve pieces. The so-called Monmouth cap, a felted knit hat, was first produced in the 13th century in Coventry, England, and a version of it was still being made in the 19th century for soldiers to wear in the Crimean War. Some of these survive in British museums and are recognizably the same kind of cap that appears in some of Holbein's portraits. The earliest cap knitters were licensed by the government and their prices were controlled to prevent profiteering. These cappers were certainly not occasional home knitters but were employed full time. Their tools—knitting needles— were difficult to manufacture and therefore both scarce and precious.

With the development of better metalworking technologies in the beginning of the 17th century, it gradually became possible to produce uniform knitting needles in quantity. This led to an enormous increase in all kinds of knitting, and was linked to the development of knitting guilds, some of which survived into the 18th century. These guilds were exclusively male and were spread throughout continental Europe (the only English knitting guilds were specifically for cap knitters).

The training process for a guild knitter was long and elaborate. It took six years to become a master knitter, three as an apprentice and three as a journeyman. After this service the aspiring master knitter was required to produce a felted cap, a pair of stockings or gloves with embroidered decoration, a shirt or waistcoat, and a knitted carpet

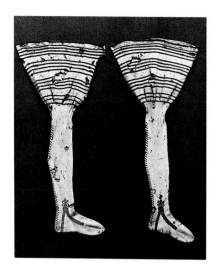

An Englishman's socks, from the mid-17th century, which were worn with the flared cuff over the top of the boot.

about six feet by five feet covered with flowers, foliage and animals—all in the space of 13 weeks. A few of these "masterpiece" carpets (which were meant not as floor coverings but as tablecloths or wall hangings) have survived. They are spectacular feats of knitting, with non-repeating floral motifs in the background and central medallions that imitate woven carpet design. Their complexity suggests that they may have been worked not on needles but on a knitting frame. With their increasing skills, knitters gradually supplanted the makers of fabric hose. During the 16th century fashion changed and very short, full pants became popular; knitters began to supply men with fancy stockings to show off

their legs. Henry VIII is said to have worn only cloth hose, but during the reign of Elizabeth I, patterned silk stockings imported from Spain became a luxury item for the queen and other aristocratic men and women.

The first knitting machine was invented during the reign of Elizabeth I by William Lee to increase the production of hose. Legend has it that Lee invented the machine to help his wife after watching her hard at work knitting stockings. Supposedly he was refused a patent by Queen Elizabeth because the machine would throw so many handknitters out of work. Lee was the first to attempt to mechanize knitting, the first step in a process which has today turned handknitting into a craft pursued almost exclusively for pleasure. And whether or not the Queen denied him a

patent, it is certainly true that Lee's machine could scarcely find favor in an area where so many depended on handknitting for their livelihood.

Queen Elizabeth's taste for elegant stockings has passed into knitting folklore in another story as well. A famous lace stitch, still known as Mrs. Montague's pattern, was supposedly invented by the Queen's "silk woman," Mrs. Montague. Unfortunately, as with many knitting stories, this one appears to have little basis in fact.

Elegant patterned stockings have survived from this era, some with fancy embroidery called "clocks" running up the side, and others with elaborate allover lace and knit-purl stitches. Expensive hose became so fashionable that it

Intricate pin cushions and purses, knitted by English ladies in the 18th and 19th centuries.

In this cap, Kashmiri knitters reinterpreted the paisley motif used in traditional woven shawls.

was railed against by the Puritans as a shamelessly expensive indulgence. A 16th century Swedish king, Erik XIV, owned 27 pairs—an almost unimaginable extravagance.

As the demand for their products grew, knitters began to produce other types of garments. An elaborately patterned pair of short knitted pants (called trunk hose) from the mid-16th century survives in Dresden, East Germany. They are decorated with both lace and knit-purl patterns. Slashes were knitted in to reveal the underclothing, and the codpiece is highly embellished with rows of garter stitch alternated with bands of moss stitch. During the 17th century, King Charles I of England is said to have been beheaded while wearing a fine gauge silk knit shirt, which is now preserved in the Museum of London. It is covered with an intricate damask pattern formed with purl stitches. Other garments of roughly the same era were made with metallic thread in elaborate two-color patterns, in imitation of woven jacquard fabrics. This patterned knitting was constructed in rectangular panels, which were later joined to form jackets, shaped with sections of plain stockinette. The most extraordinary example of 18th century knitting must surely be the Dutch damask-knit white wool petticoat that survives in the Victoria and Albert Museum in London. This garment measures 125 inches around and 30 inches deep and is entirely covered with animals and birds—

cows, rhinoceroses, alligators, geese, peacocks, dogs, wild boar, to name only a few—formed solely from alternating knit and purl stitches. As with the masterpiece carpets, it has been suggested that the petticoat must have been made on a knitting frame. No matter how it was made, it is a tour de force, at a gauge of 22 stitches to the inch and approximately 2,750 stitches to each round, without any repetition of motifs.

During the same period, a cruder if more practical knitting was being practiced in the countryside. Since knitting was easy to learn, readily transportable and conveniently picked up at any odd moment, it allowed rural people to produce articles (usually socks) which could be sold for ready money. This trade was by no means confined to women; the entire family—men, women and children—all participated. Each was expected to turn out at least one pair of stockings per week by knitting whenever possible—while herding cattle, tending sheep, or walking to market. In the winter, when farm work was slower, production increased as families knit at night by firelight. To find their yarn when it rolled into dark corners, knitters wound "yarn rattles" into the center of their balls of wool. Some of these 19th century devices still survive.

Despite the skill and speed that the knitters must have acquired, they performed this work mainly as a sideline, as the income it produced was not enough to make a living. Writers such as Samuel Johnson, Daniel Defoe, Joseph Addison and Adam Smith all mention knitting, generally as a trade practiced by the lower classes. And indeed, in Jane Austen it is only the poorest women who knit, while those of higher classes pursue other kinds of fancy needlework.

As Britain and other European nations colonized the world, the practice of knitting spread to the far reaches of the globe. The earliest American settlers established schools where boys and girls learned to knit, both to keep them out of mischief as well as to produce much needed socks and mittens. The craft was so well established by the time of the American Civil War that middle-class women on both sides organized efforts to provide knitted comforts for the troops. This was probably the first time that knitting was linked to patriotism, a public service a woman performed for the common soldier, and not simply for members of her own family. In the South, knitting became an economical way of replacing clothing as the war closed down harbors to imports of woven cloth.

The English also spread knitting to India, where certain areas became famous for their cotton stockings. Missionaries took the craft to China and Japan, which are now centers of knitting expertise, even though they have no indigenous knitting traditions.

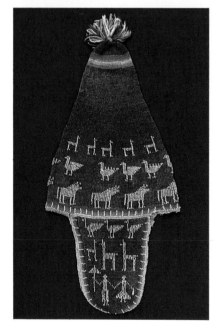

Bolivian chullos.

At the end of the 18th and the beginning of the 19th century, the quality and quantity of yarns improved enormously. High quality cotton yarn became available for the first time, and new, softer woolen yarns were developed from the fleece of Merino sheep. As knitting machines improved, handknitting ceased to be the craft of the rural poor. Advances in printing and the availability of knitting pattern books accelerated the spread of knitting as a leisure activity among the middle classes. The explosion of knitted artifacts created by the industrious ladies of the 19th century still boggles the imagination—from muffatees (mufflers) to pen wipers, from beaded purses where each bead had to be strung in exact order and laboriously knitted in one by one, to airy lace shawls that could be pulled through a wedding ring. In England, the Great Exhibition of 1851 contained some examples of this knitting fever, including a lace dress knit from white sewing cotton which is reputed to contain 1,464,859 stitches.

It was also during the 19th century that knitting was incorporated into many kinds of ethnic dress, usually in imitation of expensive and rare fabrics. Prosperous peasants in the Old and New Worlds developed their own knitting traditions. The most famous types of traditional knitting (many of them from the British Isles), such as Fair Isle,

Aran, Shetland lace and Scandinavian "lice" patterns, are not ancient but date from the 19th century.

Looking at ethnic knitting, we can see the fervor and ingenuity with which these knitters exploited its every possibility. Swedish farmers' wives knit themselves fancy short jackets in two-color stranded knitting, while Austrian women worked on complex knit-purl vests for their menfolk. Lithuanians excelled in complex many-colored mittens, which were exchanged as wedding tokens. South American Indians of the Andes adapted knitting to their own traditions and made themselves caps and leggings which imitated their traditional woven clothing. The Aran islanders produced their first highly embossed pullovers, and the Shetlanders their first lacy shawls. In India, displaced Kashmiri weavers adapted their traditional paisley patterns to create intricate knit caps. In Leo Tolstoy's novels we read of Russian servants knitting; most remarkably Anna Makarovna, the nanny in War and Peace, who knits two socks together, one inside the other. Everywhere knitting spread, men and women adapted it to their local costume, making the articles and designs most satisfying to them.

During the 19th century efforts were made to use knitting to improve both the morals and the finances of the poor. English reformers repeatedly suggested that street urchins be taught to knit socks to keep them from the workhouse. This tradition continues in the 20th century as philanthropists have organized knitting into an industry for the rural poor. Members of the artistocracy encouraged the Scottish knitters of the far north by fostering their craft and helping to create a demand for it

among the leisured classes. In the New World, a Scottish missionary's wife began the handknitting industry of the Cowichan Indians, who produce bold Fair Isle–type sweaters. In a similar vein, environmentalists were looking for a way to preserve the Alaskan musk ox and to provide cash for native Alaskans. They started a handknitting cooperative, Oomingmak, to produce articles from qiviut, yarn made from the wool of musk oxen. The Maryknoll sisters currently run a knitting cooperative in Cochibamba, Bolivia, which seeks to help the Andean Indians market their knitting skills.

One of the most famous examples of the marriage of social purpose with knit design was the Bohus Stikning business of Sweden. It was begun by Emma Jacobsson, the wife of the governor of the province of Bohuslan, to provide work for the wives of unemployed stone-cutters and farmers. Bohus Stikning produced fine gauge handknit garments of unequalled beauty and refinement inspired by, but not limited to, traditional patterns. The Swedish government used to give their products to visiting dignitaries; Nikita Khrushchev received one during a state visit in the '50s. With the arrival of post-war prosperity and the retirement of Mrs. Jacobsson, the business gradually faded away, and Bohus Stikning finally closed its doors in 1969.

The 20th century has seen an unparalleled explosion in the variety of knitting supplies and design. Handknitting has waxed and waned in popularity, but the handknit sweater remains a cherished part of the wardrobe of every person who is lucky enough to

Two sweaters knitted by the wives of stone-cutters in the Bohus cooperative in Sweden during the 1930s.

This portrait of the Prince of Wales made Fair Isle pullovers and vests immensely popular.

Elsa Schiaparelli's butterfly-bow trompe l'oeil pullover, made with a complex stranded technique.

own one. Handknits have been part of high fashion in the collections of Schiaparelli and Chanel, and, currently, Perry Ellis and Jean-Paul Gaultier. They have been made for soldiers at war and children at peace. They have been photographed clinging to curvaceous sweater girls of the '50s and on proper golfers for decades. Fiber artists have explored handknits as a means of creating wall hangings and other decorative objects. During the '70s English designers produced an extraordinary flow of knit design, leading all knitters to rediscover the possibilities in texture and color that had been ignored by the less adventurous. Bulky or fine, well wrought or awkwardly misshapen, handknitting has spread across national and class lines to become part of the texture of our lives.

The colorful borders on these socks, knitted by the Amish of Pennsylvania, were hidden under their somber clothing.

II. Knitting Supplies: Yarns and Tools

Yarns

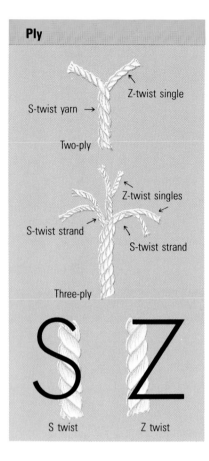

Ply

S-twist yarn →
Z-twist single

Two-ply

Z-twist singles

S-twist strand
S-twist strand

Three-ply

S
Z

S twist
Z twist

Equivalent weights

¾ oz = 20g	1¾ oz = 50g
1 oz = 28g	2 oz = 60g
1½ oz = 40g	3½ oz = 100g

Yarn is the essential element of knitting—after the needles and instructions have been put away, the knitted yarn is the finished product. Whatever qualities are in the yarn will appear in the final product—and no amount of fancy knitting can put into a garment a quality that the yarn does not possess.

Once very few kinds of yarn were on the market, and knitters knew the general properties of most of them. But the yarn marketplace has expanded enormously: new fibers have been developed to supplement the traditional triad of wool, cotton and silk; new treatments have been developed for traditional fibers; and innovative methods of spinning and combining fibers are constantly producing new and exciting yarns. Knowing the fibers used for knitting yarns and the ways in which they are processed will help you determine which yarn is right for a project.

Understanding yarns

All yarns are spun from fiber, but the fiber content alone does not determine how the yarn will look. The methods by which fibers are spun into yarn and the treatments the fibers receive also affect the final product.

Fibers are either filaments or staple fibers. Filaments are continuous strands of fiber which may be miles long; staple fibers are shorter and are measured in inches. Silk is the only natural filament yarn. All synthetic fibers are formed originally as filament, although they may later be cut into staple lengths from 1½ to 6½ inches and spun into yarn. In general, yarns spun from filament fibers are smooth and shiny. Filament yarns for knitting are usually multifilament; that is, they are spun from many filaments twisted together.

All the other natural fibers come in various staple lengths. Yarns spun from staples are composed of many short strands. The longer the staple of the fiber, the smoother and more lustrous is the yarn spun from it, which is why long-haired Merino sheep and long-stapled Egyptian cottons are both prized.

All staple fibers are carded to help clean and untangle the fibers. For coarser yarns, the fibers are formed into a thick, loose rope that is then made into yarn by drawing and spinning. For finer yarns, the fiber is combed after carding. Combing removes the short fibers, cleans the longer ones and puts them in parallel position before spinning.

Spinning twists yarns together. When the twisted yarn's spiral runs upwards to the left, it is called an "S" twist; when it runs upwards to the right, it is called a "Z" twist, which is considered standard. Some yarns with a "Z" twist are spun from individual strands which are themselves spun with an "S" twist. Finer yarns are usually more tightly twisted than heavier ones, as they need more twist for strength. The longer the staples are within the yarn, the less twist it needs to hold together.

A single is a strand of spun yarn. Plied yarn is formed from singles twisted together: a two-ply yarn is formed of two singles, a three-ply yarn of three, and so on. Yarns are plied to increase their strength, uniformity, and diameter, but an increase in the number of plies does not necessarily make a yarn heavier. A four-ply yarn formed of tightly twisted plies may well be thinner than a loosely spun single or two-ply yarn. Novelty yarns are formed either by plying two different yarns together or by plying strands of the same yarn together at different speeds.

Bouclé yarns are formed by allowing one yarn to form loops around another and holding them together with a third yarn (the binder). Nubbed or slubbed yarns can be formed either by incorporating tufts of fiber into the yarn in the spinning process or by regularly increasing the twist of the spinning so that the yarn curls into itself. Chenille yarn is not spun. It is made of fabrics woven specifically for this purpose, of which the weft is made of soft, twisted yarns. The fabric is then cut lengthwise into narrow strips which unravel slightly to give the yarn its pipe cleaner effect. Other novelty yarns are created by plying very different textures of yarns together for an unusual effect.

Yarns spun from wool are divided into worsted and woolen. Worsted yarn is spun from longer fibers combed to lie parallel, which creates a smoother, firmer feel. In American knitting terminology worsted generally refers to a readily available, medium weight yarn rather than to the way the yarn is spun. Perlé is a generic name for tightly spun, fine weight worsted yarns.

Woolen yarn is carded, but not combed. It is spun from shorter fibers, has a fuzzier surface, and is not as strong as an equivalent worsted weight yarn. Two well-known types of woolen yarn are Icelandic yarn, a medium weight woolen single, and Shetland yarn, a lighter weight two-ply woolen.

Yarns are available in many different thicknesses (commonly referred to as weight), from very fine to bulky. The names used to describe the various weights may once have had specific equivalents, but are now only guidelines, and different spinners often use the same term for different weights of yarn. To add to the confusion, spinners from different countries have their own ways of describing their yarns. Finger-

Structure

Spiral. A thick yarn wound around a thinner yarn.

Gimp. Two threads twisting in opposite directions, holding a thick yarn.

Slub. A yarn which is alternately thick and thin, frequently plied with another single or slubbed single.

Flake. Two singles plied together holding soft pieces of roving at frequent intervals.

Nub (knop). Two threads plied in such a way as to allow one strand to overwind at certain intervals to make bumps.

Bouclé. Two threads plied at different tensions, held in place with a binder thread.

Vrillé. A spiral structure with one strand allowed to overspin every so often, twisting upon itself to make a short stem.

Chenille. A yarn made from two thin strands tightly plied to hold a short velvety pile.

ing, or baby yarn (called two- or three-ply in Britain), is a fine yarn suitable for fitted clothing and garments for babies. Sport weight (four-ply in Britain) is a somewhat thicker yarn, suitable for cardigans and indoor clothing. Worsted, slightly thicker than sport weight, is the most commonly used weight in the United States; it is suitable for both indoor and outdoor wear. The British equivalent is DK (or double knitting) yarn, which is slightly finer than the American worsted. Fisherman, or Aran yarn, is slightly thicker than worsted and is often featured in Aran-type designs. Bulky, or chunky yarns are the thickest available.

Many different finishes may be applied to yarns. Wools and mohairs can be brushed, which makes the longer hairs stand out from the central core. It increases their loft and gives them a hairy appearance. Superwashed wools are treated so that they can be machine washed and dried without shrinking. Some wool yarns have been treated to be moth-resistant; this is usually noted on the label. Mercerization gives added strength and luster to cotton yarn.

Natural yarn colors range from off-white and beige to browns and black.

Yarns are dyed to give them other colors. Dying generally produces a solid color. To create multicolored yarns, the simplest method is to ply two yarns of different colors together. A multicolored yarn may also be made of two strands of different fibers which take dye at different rates. Space-dyed yarns are randomly dyed in different colors. Print-dyed yarns are stamped with different colors at set intervals. The knitted appearance of multicolored yarns will vary depending on the width of the piece being knitted, so it is impossible to predict the patterning from a small swatch. Narrow sleeve pieces may also look quite different from broader body pieces.

Many yarns are now available that are made from unconventional materials and processes, such as paper-like yarns, string, ribbon and shoelace-type yarns.

Yarns can be wound or held together in various ways. A hank is a loosely wound coil of yarn that is twisted around itself. A string tied in several places keeps it from tangling. A hank of yarn must be wound into a ball before it can be used. Skeins and balls come already wound and are available in a variety of shapes. A skein has been wound so that the inner strand can easily be pulled out from the cen-

ter. Some yarns are wound around a cardboard or foam core. Spools and cones hold a great quantity of yarn and are generally sold for machine knitting.

The ball band
Most handknitting yarns are packaged with paper labels that contain essential information, such as fiber content, any special processing the fiber may have had (mercerization, moth proofing, superwash, etc.), and washing instructions. The label may also suggest an appropriate gauge and needle size and give you the approximate length of the yarn in yards or meters. It will have the name and/or number of the color as well as the dye lot number stamped on it. Yarn is dyed in batches or lots which can vary from one to another. It is a good idea to buy all your yarn at one time, buying a little more than the instructions call for. If you must buy additional yarn to complete a project, be sure that it is from the same dye lot.

In some instances, yarn information and the brand name of the fiber (in the case of synthetic yarns) are given in the language of the country of origin.

Skein

Spool

Ball

Hank

Skein

Skein

Yarn Label Symbols

Needles and hooks

3½-4mm (5-6)
Manufacturer's suggested knitting needle size in metric and/or US sizes.

F/4mm
Manufacturer's suggested crochet hook size in metric and/or US sizes.

Gauge/tension

4×4″ (10×10cm) **30 M or S** **40 R**
The manufacturer's suggested gauge/tension with the suggested needle size. This block of knitting stitches can be translated to read: In stockinette stitch, 30 stitches (S) [in French—mailles (M)] and 40 rows (R) will equal 4 × 4″ (10 × 10cm).

Washing

Note: Washing symbols vary. Some yarns labeled with the tub and temperature are not necessarily machine washable.

DO NOT WASH BY HAND OR MACHINE

Washing by Hand

hand washable in lukewarm water only

hand washable in warm water at stated temperature

Washing by Machine

6
machine washable in warm water at stated temperature, cool rinse and short spin; more delicate handling

7
machine washable in warm water at stated temperature, short spin

40°C
machine washable in warm water at stated temperature

Bleaching

NO BLEACHING

or

CL
bleaching permitted (with chlorine)

Pressing

DO NOT PRESS

press with a cool iron

press with a warm iron

press with a hot iron

Dry cleaning

DO NOT DRY CLEAN

F
may be dry cleaned with fluorocarbon or petroleum based solvents only

P
may be dry cleaned with perchlorethylene or fluorocarbon or petroleum based solvents

A
may be dry cleaned with all solutions

Note: Ask your dry cleaner which solutions are used to clean your knitwear.

Fibers

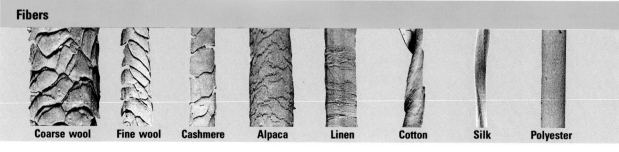

| Coarse wool | Fine wool | Cashmere | Alpaca | Linen | Cotton | Silk | Polyester |

Fibers

Fibers are divided into two basic categories, natural and synthetic. Natural fibers are themselves divided into animal fibers, which are formed of proteins—wool, mohair, alpaca, cashmere, vicuña, camel hair, angora and silk—and vegetable fibers, formed of cellulose—cotton, linen, ramie, sisal, hemp and jute. All animal fibers are susceptible to moths, whose larvae feed on the protein in the fiber. Synthetic fibers were developed after World War II and are derived from various mineral sources. The only exception is rayon, which was developed earlier and is made from the waste products of wood and cotton manufacturing. Rayon fibers are a cross between natural and synthetic; they are man-made, but from a natural (cellulose) material.

Animal fibers (protein)

Wool

Of the natural fibers, wool is preeminent—so much so that some knitters simply refer to all yarns as wool, no matter what their fiber content. Wool, spun from the fleece of sheep, is warm, elastic, durable, and very receptive to dye. Wool has excellent insulating properties—it provides warmth when the temperature is cold and coolness when the temperature is warm—which is why Bedouins, who live in the desert, traditionally weave their robes from wool. Wool fibers have a natural crimp that prevents them from packing together, creating dead air spaces which form an insulating barrier. Wool can absorb up to one-third its weight in water before it feels wet to the touch. This capacity to absorb (and release) moisture slowly adds to its insulating properties. And wool's absorbency makes it easy to dye. In addition, wool fibers can be bent again and again without breaking; they spring back to their original shape, so that wool fabric not only wears well but also resists wrinkles.

The surface of a wool fiber is covered with thin, scaly cells that overlap like the shingles on a roof. As a result of heat, moisture or friction, these scales will interlock and fuse, causing felting and—ultimately—shrinkage.

Each variety of sheep produces wool with different properties. Lambswool, from the first shearing of the sheep, is the warmest, softest hair. Shetland wool was once spun from the fleece of sheep bred on the Shetland Islands, whose hair was never shorn but combed throughout the year. The name is now used to describe a loosely twisted, two-ply wool yarn, usually used in Fair Isle-type patterns. Merino wool is spun from the fleece of Merino sheep, which have exceptionally long and soft coats. Botany wool is a fine wool spun from Merino sheep in Botany Bay, Australia; like Shetland, it has become a generic name for especially fine and soft yarns. Icelandic wool is a medium weight, fuzzy yarn traditionally used for Icelandic round-yoked sweaters.

Mohair

Mohair, an extremely lightweight and warm fiber, is spun from the fleece of the angora goat. These goats were traditionally raised in the Ankara (formerly Angora) region of Turkey, but now Texas is the largest producer of mohair. Kid mohair is spun from the fleece of kid angora goats, and is softer and finer than the fleece of the adult goat. Mohair has many of wool's properties, such as insulation, receptivity to dyes, and ease of care, but is somewhat less resilient. Mohair is generally blended with wool or nylon which help the mohair fibers cling together.

Alpaca

The alpaca is a member of the camel family found in South America. Its fleece is used to make alpaca yarn. Alpaca fibers are long and lustrous, and spin into a soft and warm yarn. Because the fleece itself is naturally beige to brown in color, alpaca must first be bleached before it can be dyed. Suri alpaca is considered to be the finest.

Cashmere

Cashmere yarn is synonymous with luxury. Cashmere fibers are not shorn but combed once a year from the bellies of the cashmere goat, which lives only in the mountains of China and Tibet. The yarn spun from this fiber has extraordinary softness, resilience and receptivity to dye. Because it is quite expensive and the fiber itself is somewhat weaker than wool, it is often found in combination with other fibers, particularly wool.

Camel hair

Camel hair is spun from the hair of the Asian or Bactrian camel. It is not shorn, but collected as it falls off the camel. It is both strong and warm—hence its use in camel hair coats. One hundred percent camel hair yarn is usually only available in natural shades because this fiber is not very receptive to dye.

Angora

The angora rabbit provides an extremely soft, fluffy and warm fiber. Angora is difficult to spin by itself because some of the hairs are so short, so it is often combined with other fibers. This shortness also accounts for angora's tendency to shed. The highest quality angora is combed from the rabbit, not shorn, and is less likely to shed. Since each animal can only produce a small amount of fiber, angora is extremely expensive.

Bulky

Worsted

Double knitting

Sport

Fingering

Tweed

Shetland

Cabled

Alpaca

Mohair

Angora

Other animal fibers

Other fibers are used either alone or in combination to produce specialty yarns. Alaskan musk oxen have a fine hair which is spun for qiviut, a very warm and delicate wool. The vicuña, cousin to the alpaca, also produces a warm, soft fleece; however, vicuña are nearly extinct, and vicuña wool is scarce. Yak, mink, chinchilla, reindeer and beaver hair have all been used for yarn. Enthusiastic spinner/knitters have even spun yarn from the hair of pet dogs.

Silk

Although silk is not a hair, it is grouped among the animal fibers since it has a protein structure. The silkworm spins two thread-like filaments around itself (which are cemented together by the air to become one filament) in order to form its cocoon, extruding a thread-like, protein resin through the spinnerets in its head. Each filament can be as long as 1,600 yards (1,500 meters). After the silkworm has spun its cocoon, it is killed, its cocoon is unwound and the filaments from many cocoons are spun together to create silk yarn. Silk has a wonderful luster, drape and a crisp yet soft hand (or feel).

Silkworms may be wild or cultivated: the wild produce a coarser fiber than the cultivated, which are fed exclusively on mulberry leaves in a controlled environment to produce the finest and smoothest filament.

Like wool, silk does not conduct heat, and is therefore a good insulator. It takes dye well, but is more susceptible to fading. It is quite strong and can be spun into very fine yarns. Silk yarns used in knitting are not resilient and tend to stretch as they are worn.

Because the silkworm requires a great deal of care, silk is expensive and is frequently blended with other fibers.

Vegetable fibers (cellulose)

Cotton

Cotton is one of the oldest known textile fibers, and is certainly the most widely available. It is grown in hot climates all over the world. Cotton is available in many grades, the finest and smoothest of which are Egyptian and Sea Island, and a cross between them called Pima. All cotton is non-allergenic. It absorbs moisture quickly and dries quickly, which gives it a cooling effect. Since it is stronger wet than dry, cotton is also easy to wash, needing none of the care necessary for animal fiber yarns. However, cotton is not as elastic as wool, and especially in heavy garments can tend to stretch out. Because of its lack of resilience it shows flaws in knitting tension.

Mercerized cottons (named after John Mercer, who invented the process) are treated with caustic soda and then stretched, which makes them smoother, more lustrous, stronger, and less prone to shrink than untreated cotton yarns. French mercerized yarns are labeled "fil d'écosse" (Scottish thread), as Mercer was a Scotsman. Cotton is also available in an unmercerized string-like yarn often called matte cotton, which comes in all weights, and in very loosely twisted yarns (usually spun around a strong core thread). These yarns are softer than mercerized cottons but do not wear as well. Unlike protein fiber yarns, cotton has no attraction for moths, but it can mildew.

Some cotton yarns are mixed with small amounts of synthetic fiber to increase elasticity and decrease weight. Cotton is also blended with wool for a softer and warmer yarn.

Linen

Evidence suggests that prehistoric man was spinning linen in 8,000 B.C. Linen fiber is derived from the stem of the flax plant, which grows in temperate climates. It requires a great deal of processing before it can be spun into yarn: the outer husk of the plant must be soaked and then broken down before the inner, usable fibers can be extracted. Once spun it forms a lustrous, strong yarn. Like cotton, linen is both extremely washable and comfortable to wear in hot weather, as it draws moisture quickly away from the body. It lacks resilience, and so wrinkles easily, although this is not as noticeable in knit fabrics.

There are few 100 percent linen handknitting yarns available. Because pure linen yarns tend to be stiff until they have been worn a few times, they are frequently blended with cotton or other fibers to soften them. Because linen's fiber is heavy, it is usually spun into very fine yarns.

Ramie

Ramie is a linen-like fiber which has long been used in the Orient, especially in China and Japan. It has recently become more available in other parts of the world as well. Ramie shares many qualities with linen; it is strong, lustrous and washes well, but is somewhat stiff and has little resilience. In knitting yarns it is usually found in combination with other fibers.

Sisal, hemp, jute, raffia

The stems of the hemp and jute plants produce fibers of the same names; sisal is derived from the leaves of the agave plant. In general, these three fibers are coarser and heavier than linen or ramie and have traditionally been used for twines and sacking. Raffia is a type of straw generally used in basket-making. Synthetic raffia, made from rayon, is a similar yarn available in small hanks in many bright colors. It is quite stiff and inflexible. The yarns made from these plants can be used for knitting decorative items. Since they are coarse, they may be rough on the knitter's hands; an inexpensive pair of cotton knit gloves can help to prevent chafing. The stiffness of these yarns also makes them difficult to knit evenly.

Synthetics

The disruption in trade and the shortages caused by World War II encouraged an enormous increase in the production and improvement of fibers derived from coal and petroleum products. The first of these was nylon, originally introduced by the Du Pont corporation in 1938. A number of synthetic fibers have since been developed, most notably acrylic and polyester. Many synthetics are marketed under brand names such as Orlon, Dacron or Kodel, which are promoted by the corporations which own their trademarks (Dacron, Fiberfill, Fortrel, Kodel and Vycron are all trademarked brands of polyester). All synthetic yarns are manufactured as filament, but most synthetics available for handknitters are then cut into staple lengths and spun into yarn to resemble the texture of natural fibers.

Synthetic yarns have had a rather uneven reputation among knitters. They are appreciated because they are easy to care for (many can be machine washed and dried), they do not stretch, and are inexpensive. On the other hand, synthetics can be uncomfortable (since

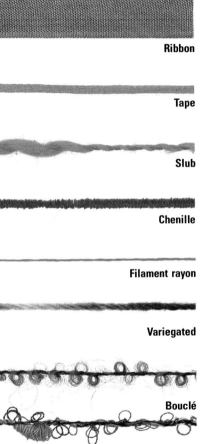

Silk

Matte cotton

Mercerized cotton

Ribbon

Tape

Slub

Chenille

Filament rayon

Variegated

Bouclé

Bouclé/knop

Knop

Metallic

Elastic thread

they absorb very little moisture they can feel hot and clammy), they are prone to pill, and once a stain has set in, it is almost impossible to remove. However, synthetic yarns are constantly being improved and are becoming more accepted as their hand and performance are enhanced. Yarn manufacturers are also combining natural and synthetic fibers to create new yarns that share the best properties of both fibers.

Polyamide

Nylon is the original Du Pont brand name for the polyamide fiber, and is now accepted as a generic noun. Nylon is the strongest textile fiber (which explains why it is so hard to break nylon yarns) and is durable, lightweight and elastic. Since synthetic fibers are created to obtain specific properties, it is difficult to generalize for all polyamides; some may be crimped for texture, others treated to create stretch yarns. However, all are heat sensitive and must be blocked with extreme caution—once the fiber has been overheated it may lose its body and sag. Static cling can also be a problem with yarns containing a high percentage of nylon, as with all synthetics. Nylon is often added to other fibers to reinforce them.

Acrylic

This family of synthetic fibers was created to obtain a softness and bulk not readily available in polyamide fibers. Acrylic fibers imitate wool, although they lack its insulating properties. One hundred percent acrylic yarn can be found in all weights and colors. Like nylon, it is frequently found in combination with natural fibers. Two brands of acrylic are Orlon and Dralon. Acrylic is

heat sensitive and must be pressed or steamed with caution. Spun Orlon has a softness which can be compared to cashmere.

Polyester

Polyesters are generally found in combination with other fibers. Polyester has outstanding wrinkle resistance even when wet, so that polyester blends hold their shape well. When used in combination with other fibers, polyesters provide strength and stability to the yarn.

Polypropylene

This is the newest of the synthetic fibers and is also produced from a petroleum base. Polypropylene fiber is extremely inexpensive to produce, is light and has good insulating properties. It can easily be spun into wool-type yarns and has less tendency to develop static than other synthetics.

Rayon

Although rayon is man-made, it is not a synthetic fiber. Developed in 1910, rayon is the oldest man-made fiber and is considered the most versatile. It is spun, either as a filament or staple, from cellulose obtained from cotton lint and wood chips. Two types of rayon are on the market: viscose rayon, commonly called viscose, and cuprammonium rayon, referred to as rayon. Their properties are the same, but their chemical and manufacturing techniques differ.

Rayon has a higher luster and softer hand than cotton, and can be dyed to brilliant colors. Rayon yarns are not resilient, so that ribbings knit in 100 percent rayon yarn will not hold, and heavier garments may stretch from their own weight. Rayon ribbons are widely available in many brilliant colors, and

rayon/cotton blends are common. Unlike coal-based synthetics, rayons will not melt when pressed at too high a heat, but will scorch like cotton.

Metallic fibers

There are two types of metallic yarns. One is made from very thin metallic foil, coated with plastic film and cut into narrow strips. The other, Mylar, is a form of polyester treated with vaporized metal and then bonded on both sides with a film. Different coloring agents are added to the metallic foil or to the bonding film. Modern metallic yarns do not tarnish, but neither type is very strong, and they are often blended with other fibers for strength. As with all synthetics, knitters must be cautious in applying heat to metallic yarns. Some types are too scratchy to be worn next to the skin, although some newer metallics are quite soft.

Elastic thread

Elastic thread is always used with another yarn. It can be worked with the yarn as you knit or woven into the fabric when the piece is complete. It helps less resilient yarns to keep their shape and is mainly used at edges.

Substituting yarns

Sometimes the yarn specified in a pattern or the yarn you had in mind for a design is not available, and you need to make a substitution. Substituting yarn is not simply a matter of replacing one ball for another, even when they are the same weight or length. It is also difficult to substitute one texture for another. The only way to make sure the substitution is accurate is to knit a swatch and compare its gauge with the gauge given for the original yarn.

Tools

Needles

The basic tool of knitting is a pair of needles. Knitting needles are available today in a wide variety of materials and styles. The most important fact to remember is that the needles you choose are meant to serve you—if you find a particular kind difficult to use, give them away and try something else. Your needles should help you knit comfortably and quickly, so that you enjoy not only the end product, but the process as well.

Needles are usually an afterthought—after you choose your pattern and the yarn, you try to remember if you have the right size needles at home. Besides size, however, you'll want to consider other factors too.

Knitting needles can be divided into basic categories, straight or circular. Straight needles are used for flat knitting, in which the knitter works back and forth, creating pieces of knitting that are later sewn together. Circular needles allow the knitter to work in a

continuous round, shaping tubular pieces that form the entire garment.

Single-pointed straight needles have one pointed working end and a permanently attached knob on the other. Double-pointed needles are straight needles with two pointed working ends and are used for circular garments. Single-pointed needles are packaged in pairs, while double-pointed needles come in sets of four or five depending on the manufacturer.

1   Oversized aluminum needles

2,3 Plastic needles

4   Bamboo needles

5   Teflon-coated aluminum needles

6   Aluminum needles

7   Double-pointed, aluminum needles

8   Aluminum-tipped circular needle

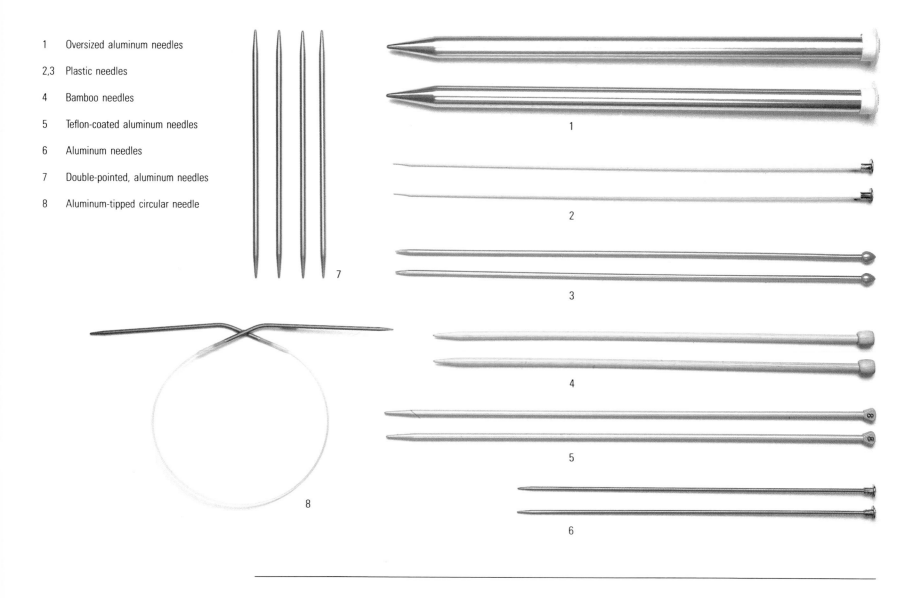

Circular needles have two working ends joined by a thin nylon wire. You can also buy circular needles with separate sets of needle points and wires that can be attached to them, allowing you to form several different lengths of needles from the same set. Jumper needles are circulars with only one pointed end and a knob at the end of the flexible wire.

Circular needles offer several advantages. They are more balanced than straight needles, which require you to shift your work back and forth between the needles. Circulars allow the weight of your work to rest in your lap, a great advantage with heavy garments. Because circular needles are flexible, you can work more comfortably in constricted spaces such as wing chairs, bus or subway seats without waving the ends of your needles around, and you can easily tuck them into your knitting bag. Even if your pattern calls for flat knitting, you can use circular needles and just turn the work at the end of each row as though you were using straight needles.

All needles, whether straight or circular, come in a standard range of diameters and lengths. The size of the needle is based on its diameter, and this can be expressed in the American or metric standard.

American needle sizes range from 0 to I5, with the diameter increasing as the number gets larger. Some needles called jumbos come in sizes as large as 17, 19 and even larger. For lace knitting, very fine steel needles are available in sizes 0 down to 0000.

Metric needles are also sized by numbers, ranging from 2 to 10mm. Again, the needle's size increases as its number does.

In the United States, most needles sold are marked with both the American size and its metric equivalent. The chart shows how these two standards compare. Some sizes have no direct equivalents. Knitters who have inherited needles should be aware that older British needles were once marked by yet another standard, and they will have to use the sizing holes which are on most stitch gauges (see Accessories) to determine the metric or American equivalent. The crucial fact to remember is that it is the gauge you obtain that determines which needle size you must use; the size given in pattern-directions is only a suggestion, not a command.

The most common needle lengths are: for single-pointed needles, 10 and 14 inch (25 and 36cm); for double-pointed needles, 7 and 10 inch (18 and 25cm); for circulars, 16, 24, 29 and 36 inch (40, 60, 80 and 90cm); and for jumpers, 18 inch (45cm). It is also possible to find 7 inch (18cm) single-pointed needles and 14 inch (36cm) double-pointed needles, 11 inch (29cm) circulars and longer jumpers as well, but these are generally available only from specialized sources. In the past, the smaller sizes of double-pointed needles were made in 5 inch (13cm) lengths for gloves, and these can sometimes still be found.

The gauge of your work determines what size needle you will use, but the right length will depend on practicality and your own preference. When choosing circular needles for a sweater knit in the round, you should consider its circumference. As a general rule, a sweater that is 22 inches (56cm) around should be knit on 16 inch (40cm) needles; a sweater with a 40 inch (I02cm) chest measurement can be knit on 24, 29 or 36 inch (60, 80 or 90cm) needles

You can find 11½ inch (29cm) circular needles for very small areas such as cuffs, but they are awkward to use, so you may prefer double-pointed needles.

Straight needles can be made of aluminum, plastic, bamboo, wood, steel or bone, and can be coated with Teflon or plastic. Circulars are available with plastic, aluminum, bamboo or wooden tips, and plastic wires.

Aluminum and plastic needles are the most widely available. Both materials are light and smooth, although aluminum is thought to make the fastest and smoothest needles. Plastic needles are quieter and warmer to the touch than aluminum. The plastic and teflon coatings that are applied to both plastic and aluminum needles are designed to increase their smoothness so stitches will glide on the needles.

Bamboo and wooden needles have reappeared recently in response to the trend for natural materials; both are smooth, light and warm to the touch. With constant use, they will develop a patina from the natural oils in your hands. Since these materials are not as hard as plastic or aluminum, always check that the points are smooth and undamaged. Knitting on bamboo or wood is slower than on aluminum or plastic. However, this may be an advantage for the beginning knitter, as the stitches will stay more firmly in place.

Bone needles are no longer manufactured and have become a collector's item, although a synthetic bone-like needle is now available. Steel needles (which are really nickel-plated) are also hard to find, although they are still being made. They come mostly in the smaller sizes and in double-pointed sets and are favored by lace knitters who need very fine and rigid needles.

The tip of the needle is its most important part, as it does all the work. Needle tips differ depending on the manufacturer and the material they are made of. Examine the ends of your needles: a very slender, sharp tip may cause you to split stitches; a very dull tip may make it hard to insert the needle at all. You may need to try a different needle if you feel that the tips on yours are not working well for you. Never try to knit with needles that have damaged tips. In addition to slowing you down, they can make your work uneven and will snag your yarn.

Knitting needles

US	Metric	UK
0	2mm	14
1	2¼mm	13
	2½mm	
2	2¾mm	12
	3mm	11
3	3¼mm	10
4	3½mm	
5	3¾mm	9
	4mm	8
6		
7	4½mm	7
8	5mm	6
9	5½mm	5
10	6mm	4
10½	6½mm	3
	7mm	2
	7½mm	1
11	8mm	0
13	9mm	00
15	10mm	000

Accessories

Stitch gauge

This is a flat piece of metal or plastic with either a ruler marked on one side or a window cut out in the center to help you determine gauge, and a graduated row of holes to measure needle size. If your stitch gauge has a window, it should be at least two inches (5cm) long.

A stitch gauge is easier to use than a tape measure for determining gauge. To figure your gauge, place your work on a flat surface and place the stitch gauge on top of it, lining up the bottom of the window evenly along one row of stitches. Count the number of stitches and rows revealed by the opening and divide by the number of inches marked on the side of the window to calculate the number of stitches in one inch (2.5cm). Some stitch gauges have windows that will allow you to measure both stitch and row gauge.

Most stitch gauges have a range of holes for measuring needle sizes. These are helpful since some needles are not true to size and others may not be marked at all. The most useful stitch gauges show both American and metric needle sizes. Some stitch gauges are made of plastic which protects the finish on Teflon-coated needles. To determine needle size, just slip the needle into each hole. The number of the first hole that allows the entire needle—tip and shaft—to move through easily is the size of your needle.

Cable needles

These are short needles, pointed at both ends, that are used to hold stitches while you work a cable. They can be shaped with a bend in the middle, or look like the letter "U," with one arm of the U longer than the other. These shapes prevent the stitches from falling off the needle while you work the cable. Like regular needles, cable needles are available in a variety of materials and sizes.

Crochet hooks

Crochet hooks, like knitting needles, are available in a variety of materials. They can be designated in numbered or lettered sizes. Even knitters who don't crochet will find crochet hooks useful for picking up dropped stitches and for working edges. You may want to buy a set of crochet hooks in a variety of sizes to keep with your knitting supplies.

Crochet Hooks

US	Metric	UK
14 steel	.60mm	
12 steel	.75mm	
10 steel	1.00mm	
6 steel	1.50mm	
5 steel	1.75mm	
B/1	2.00mm	14
C/2	2.50mm	12
D/3	3.00mm	10
E/4	3.50mm	9
F/5	4.00mm	8
G/6	4.50mm	7
H/8	5.00mm	6
I/9	5.50mm	5
J/10	6.00mm	4
	6.50mm	3
K/10½	7.00mm	2

1 Stitch gauge

2 Stitch markers

3 Plastic-head pins

4 Knitting spool

5 Bobbins

6 Row counter

7 Pompom maker

8 Tape measure

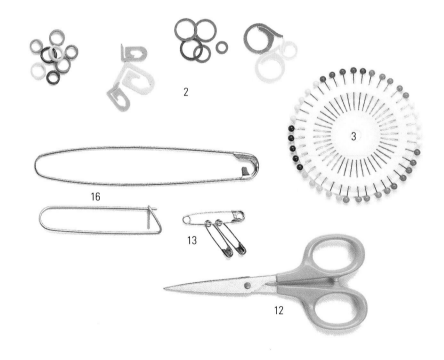

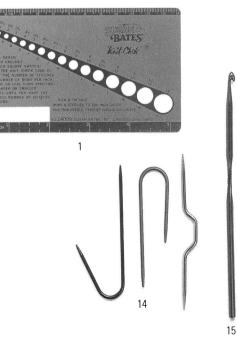

Stitch markers

These are used to keep track of places in your knitting where increases, decreases or other kinds of patterning occur, or to keep your place at the beginning of each round in circular knitting. They slip from needle to needle along with the stitches, and they must be smooth in order not to catch on your work or your hands.

Stitch markers can be solid rings or split coils, and come in a wide variety of shapes and colors. An advantage to split coils is that you can attach them directly to the knitted stitches and remove them easily at a later time. Fishermen's split rings, available in various sizes at sporting goods stores, make good plain, smooth markers. If you have no markers, you can use a simple loop of thread or yarn in a contrasting color.

Stitch holders

These are used to hold stitches that will be bound off or worked in some other way at a future point in your knitting. There are many varieties of stitch holders, from simple elongated safety pins to more elaborate versions with springs in them. They range in length from about 1½ to 10 inches (4 to 10cm). In general, the smaller sizes are the most useful. If you must hold a great number of stitches, it is sometimes easier simply to thread them onto a length of yarn in a contrasting color and tie the ends.

Row counters

These little gadgets keep track of each row while you work. You can find several kinds, such as a cylinder that fits on the needle (and must be the right size for the needles you are using), a larger version that includes a push button to click each number forward, and one that looks like a tiny cribbage board with moveable pegs that can keep track of shaping and stitch patterns at the same time. The cylindrical models also come with two dials if you need to count both individual rows and the total number of rows in a pattern piece.

No row counter is automatic, so you must remember to register each row as you complete it.

Point protectors

These are small rubber caps which slip over the pointed ends of the needles to protect the knitter as well as the needles. They also protect your work by keeping stitches from falling off the needles. Point protectors come in a variety of sizes to fit your needles.

Sewing needles

These can be used for duplicate stitch (also called Swiss darning), sewing pieces together and for weaving in the ends of your knitting. The best sewing needles for knitters are blunt-tipped darning or tapestry needles made of metal or plastic. Metal needles are usually smoother and faster. Blunt needles are preferable to sharp ones because they don't split stitches. For sewing bulky knits there are plastic needles with small balls at the tips instead of points. The needle's eye should be big enough to accommodate your yarn easily.

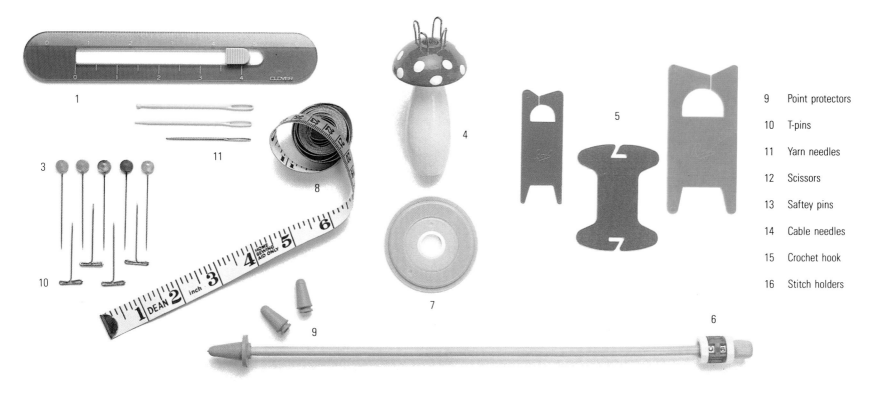

9   Point protectors

10   T-pins

11   Yarn needles

12   Scissors

13   Saftey pins

14   Cable needles

15   Crochet hook

16   Stitch holders

Pins

Every knitter needs a supply of straight pins, T-pins and safety pins. Straight pins are used for pinning knitted pieces together to be sewn. The best ones have colored heads so they do not get lost in your work.

T-pins are good for pinning together heavier knits. They are also essential for blocking, because they are easy to insert and remove, and hold down the knitted pieces firmly.

Safety pins are especially versatile. You can use them as holders, either for a small number of stitches or for a dropped stitch that you discover too late to hook up. They are handy to mark your place in a row, and if you have a pattern that makes it difficult to distinguish between the right and wrong sides of your work, you can mark the right side with a safety pin.

Bobbins

Knitters who are working intarsia or stranded patterns wind their contrasting yarns around small pieces of plastic called bobbins. Most bobbins have two small arms that just touch on one end to keep the yarn from unwinding. They are available in two sizes—one for lightweight and average yarn, one for bulky.

Tape measures

No knitter should ever be without a tape measure. A good tape measure should be flexible but not stretch. Fiberglass tape measures are the best because, unlike plastic tapes, they do not expand and contract in reaction to the temperature. Many tape measures are marked with both centimeters and inches, and some very handy ones are retractable. You should discard a tape measure at the first sign of distortion or wear.

Scissors

The handiest scissors for knitters are small and sharply pointed. If you carry them with your knitting, be sure to use a case or put a point protector over the tip to keep them from damaging your work.

Graph paper

Standard square graph paper is extremely useful for charting patterns and developing your own schematic drawings for sweater designs. If, however, you plan to create your own color patterns, you should use knitters' graph paper, which has grids that represent different gauges. For example, graph paper for the gauge of five stitches and seven rows to the inch would have five squares to every horizontal inch and seven squares to every vertical inch. This enables you to design directly on the graph paper without having to allow for the distortion that would result if you knitted a pattern developed on ordinary graph paper.

Yarn swift and ball winder

These tools can take much of the tedium out of winding balls from yarn packaged in hanks.

The swift is an umbrella-like device that is raised to hold a hank of yarn. When you pull the yarn end to wind a ball, it spins freely. Some yarn swifts have a small crank at the top that allows you to reverse the process and wind a hank of yarn from a ball.

A ball winder is a small machine that allows you to wind yarn into a ball by cranking a handle.

Magnetic ruler

This is a boon to anyone following complicated pattern directions or trying to keep a place on a graph. It is simply a metal sheet accompanied by a magnetic ruler. The pattern sheet or graph goes over the metal sheet, and the ruler sits on top. As you progress through the pattern, you simply move the ruler along to keep your place.

Wool brushes

These stiff bristled brushes will fluff out fuzzy yarns such as mohair or brushed wool that may get flattened during the process of knitting. They often come with two brushes back to back, each with a different degree of stiffness.

Organizing your work

Notebook

Every knitter should have a notebook to record comments about the work in progress. Many knitters make a copy of their pattern directions and clip these into a notebook instead of carrying around the originals. The truly meticulous will keep their swatches in a notebook, each with the label of the yarn it was knit from, the needle size used, and any other pertinent information.

Bags and baskets

The container you use to store your knitting must be completely smooth inside. It should be large enough to hold your current project comfortably, and should have an interior pocket for small items such as measuring tape, holders and pins.

You could also keep a separate box inside your knitting bag to hold these small items.

If you plan to carry your work, it should have comfortable handles. Some bags have a wooden inner structure that opens out so you can stand the bag beside you as you knit, and fold it with your work inside when you want to carry it.

Light-colored yarn can be difficult to keep clean while you work with it. A good solution is to keep it in a small plastic box made for this purpose—it has a slot or a hole in its top to thread the yarn through.

Care of your knitting tools

Knitting equipment needs to be kept clean and free of dust. Various kinds of storage cases for your needles are available, from fabric holders with slots for different sized needles, to hard plastic cases with lift-off tops.

If your needles get dirty, wipe them with a damp cloth and dry them thoroughly. If the yarn seems to stick on them, take heavy waxed paper and rub it vigorously up and down all over the needles. If you use steel needles and they rust, clean them with a rag dipped first in kerosene, wash them and rub them with waxed paper. They can also be polished with the finest steel wool.

Trim accessories

Pompom makers

These are plastic disks with their centers cut out. You wind yarn around them to make pompoms.

Knitting spools

These are used to make lengths of knitted braid. Knitting spools are available in molded plastic or in decorative shapes such as the mushroom pictured.

III. Basic Techniques

The Structure of Knitting

Interlocking of
knit stitches.

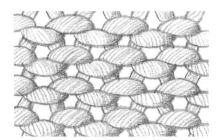

Interlocking of
purl stitches.

Knitting is the process of forming a fabric by making interlocking loops from a continuous strand of yarn using two or more needles. Each loop is called a "stitch." Each new stitch is formed when one needle is used to pull a loop of yarn through the existing stitch on another needle. A horizontal series of loops becomes a "row" and is completed by working stitches from one needle to the other. Each row links together with the row below, and each stitch is attached to its neighbor to create a fabric that is interdependent and will unravel if even one stitch is cut. This structure makes a fabric that is pliable, resilient and porous and, therefore, comfortable to wear.

A knitted fabric has many advantages over a woven one that is made of two independent sets of yarn or thread of a set length running perpendicular to each other. This produces a firmer cloth without the elasticity of a knitted fabric. Another benefit of knitting is that garments such as socks and mittens can be knit in a circular fashion, eliminating undesirable and uncomfortable seams.

The first row of knitting is called the "cast-on" row. This is the foundation upon which rows of stitches can be built. Once the knitted piece is complete, the loops must be finished to prevent unraveling. This final row is called the "bind-off" (or "cast-off") row.

The basic stitch is appropriately called a "knit" stitch. When worked on every row, it is called "garter stitch." The right side of this fabric looks exactly like the wrong side. Garter stitch creates a dense fabric that stretches more lengthwise than crosswise.

The second basic stitch is the "purl" stitch. When a row of knit stitches is alternated with a row of purl stitches, it is called "stockinette stitch" (or stocking stitch or jersey). When working in stockinette, the knit stitch resembles a V. The knit side is the right side of the work. On the reverse side (the purl side or wrong side), each stitch is a horizontal rounded structure. When working in the round on circular needles, a tubular fabric in stockinette stitch is formed by working continuously in a knit stitch. Stockinette stitch has more crosswise than lengthwise stretch.

These two stitches, the knit and the purl, are the basis of all knitting and can be worked in unending combinations.

Shape of a knit stitch

The shape of a single knit stitch (in stockinette) is not square but elongated. In most gauges the number of stitches per inch is less than the number of rows per inch. (For example, in one gauge, five stitches equals one horizontal inch, whereas six rows equals one vertical inch.) Most color charts in instructions are drawn on a square grid, as in the sample, top right. The image below was drawn on "knitter's graph paper," where the squares are the same proportion as the knitted gauge (five stitches and six rows). The image on the square graph is elongated, but the image on the knitter's graph shows exactly how the finished knitted piece will look.

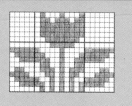

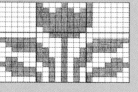

circular knitting **75-78**   right/wrong sides **67-68**   color charts **87-89**

stockinette **22, 34**   gauge **18-19, 57-59**

Holding Yarn and Needles

Watch other people knit and you'll notice that everyone has a different way of holding the yarn and knitting needles. This is the most difficult thing to master when learning to knit, and it's important that you find a method that works for you.

The way you hold the yarn and needles will partly depend on which of two basic ways you choose to knit. If you use the English method, you hold the yarn in your right hand; with the Continental method, you hold it in your left. If you're a left-hander, and you cannot master either the English or Continental method, you can use an alternate technique which will be discussed later in the chapter.

Your own preferences will also affect your holding position. For example, you may find it easier to knit close to the tip of the needles, or you may prefer to work with the stitches further back on the shafts. You may use only one finger to control the yarn, or you may use several fingers to obtain the same control. Any method is correct as long as the yarn flows evenly and the tension is consistent. Just work in the way that is easiest for you. Once you become comfortable with holding your needles, you will automatically increase your knitting speed.

Two traditional methods of holding yarn and needles are shown below.

English

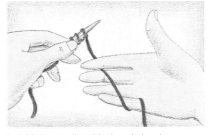

1 Hold the needle with the stitches in your left hand as shown. Wrap the yarn around your little finger and then around the index finger on your right hand.

2a Hold the working needle with your right hand as shown, controlling the tension with your right index finger.

2b An alternate method is to place the working needle between the thumb and index finger of your right hand as if your were holding a pencil.

Continental

1 Hold the needle with the stitches in your right hand. Wrap the yarn around your little finger and then around the index finger of your left hand. Transfer the needle back to your left hand.

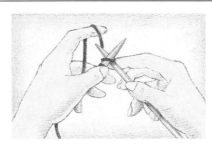

2 Hold the working needle with your right hand as shown, controlling the tension with your left index finger.

Casting On

Before you begin to knit, you must first make a foundation row called a cast-on. You can choose from a wide variety of cast-on methods, some worked with one needle and others with two. Several methods presented here are basic, multipurpose cast-ons; some are decorative cast-ons serving special functions. You may want to try all methods, but if you are like most knitters, you will probably use one or two cast-ons for most purposes.

The cast-on row affects all the rows which follow, so it is essential to create the neatest edge possible. If you are a beginner, choose a basic cast-on and practice keeping the tension of the loops even before you begin to knit. If your cast-on stitches are too tight, you may have difficulty working the first row. Try casting on with two needles held together, and removing one of them before you begin to knit or try using a larger needle. If your cast-on stitches are too loose, the edge will stretch out. You can tighten your cast-on by using a smaller needle and changing to the correct size on the first row.

Once the loops are on the needle, you must decide which will be the right and wrong side of your work. Many cast-on methods form a loopy edge on one side (much like that of a purl stitch), while the other side is flatter and smoother. Pick the one you like best. Make a mental note of whether cast-on tail is on the right or left side of your work to help you keep track of right and wrong sides.

Slip knot

The first stitch of any cast-on method is a slip knot. For both double cast-on methods, you must leave a predetermined length of yarn free before working the slip knot. A general guide is to allow a length of approximately three times the planned width of the cast-on edge. For the other methods only an 8-10 inch (20-25cm) length is necessary.

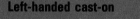

1 Hold the short end of the yarn in your palm with your thumb. Wrap the yarn twice around the index and middle fingers.

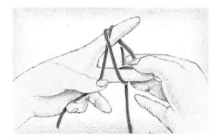

2 Pull the strand attached to the ball through the loop between your two fingers, forming a new loop.

3 Place the new loop on the needle. Tighten the loop on the needle by pulling on both ends of the yarn to form the slip knot. You are now ready to begin one of the following cast-on methods.

Left-handed cast-on

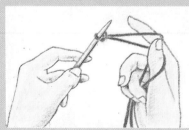

1 Make a slip knot on the left needle, leaving a long tail. Wind tail end around right thumb from front to back. Wrap yarn from the ball over your index finger and secure both ends between palm and fingers.

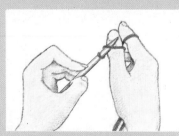

2 Insert the needle upwards into the loop on your thumb.

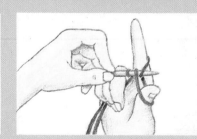

3 Insert the needle downwards into the loop on your index finger and draw it through the loop on your thumb. Continue in this way until all stitches are cast on.

right/wrong sides **67-68**

Double cast-on

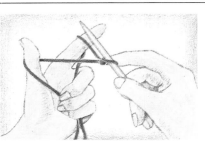

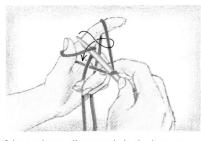

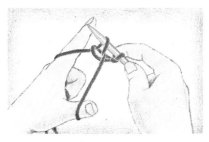

The double cast-on method provides a firm yet elastic edge and is frequently recommended for beginners.

1 Make a slip knot on the right needle, leaving a long tail. Wind the tail end around your left thumb, front to back. Wrap the yarn from the ball over your left index finger and secure the ends in your palm.

2 Insert the needle upwards in the loop on your thumb. Then with the needle, draw the yarn from the ball through the loop to form a stitch.

3 Take your thumb out of the loop and tighten the loop on the needle. Continue in this way until all the stitches are cast on.

Double cast-on—thumb method

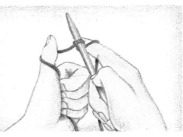

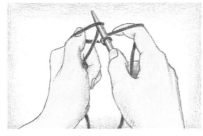

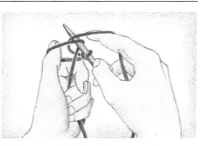

The thumb method has the same finished look as the double cast-on shown above.

1 Make a slip knot on the right needle, leaving a long tail. Wind the tail end around your left thumb, front to back. Wrap the yarn from the ball over your right index finger and secure both strands in your palms.

2 Insert the needle upwards through the loop on your thumb.

3 Using your right index finger, wrap the yarn from the ball over the needle knitwise. Pull the yarn through the loop on your thumb to form a stitch. Tighten the loop on the needle by pulling on the short end. Continue in this way until all the stitches are cast on.

Single cast-on

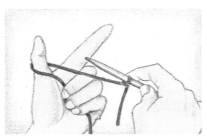

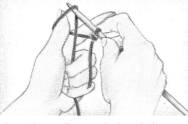

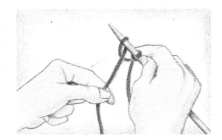

This is the simplest but not the neatest method of casting on. It is a good technique to use for teaching children.

1 Place a slip knot on the right needle, leaving a short tail. Wrap the yarn from the ball around your left thumb from front to back and secure it in your palm with your other fingers.

2 Insert the needle upwards through the strand on your thumb.

3 Slip this loop from your thumb onto the needle, pulling the yarn from the ball to tighten it. Continue in this way until all the stitches are cast on.

Knitting-on

With the knitting-on method you use two needles and one length of yarn.

1 Make a slip knot on the left needle. *Insert the right needle knitwise into the stitch on the left needle. Wrap the yarn around the right needle as if to knit.

2 Draw the yarn through the first stitch to make a new stitch, but do not drop the stitch from the left needle.

3 Slip the new stitch to the left needle as shown. Repeat from the * until the required number of stitches is cast on.

Cable cast-on

The cable cast-on forms a sturdy yet elastic edge. It is perfect for ribbed edges.

1 Cast on two stitches using the knitting-on cast-on described above. *Insert the right needle between the two stitches on the left needle.

2 Wrap the yarn around the right needle as if to knit and pull the yarn through to make a new stitch.

3 Place the new stitch on the left needle as shown. Repeat from the *, always inserting the right needle in between the last two stitches on the left needle.

Alternate cable cast-on

This cast-on creates a firm edge for knit one, purl one rib. After casting on, knit the knit stitches through the back loops on the first row only.

1 Cast on two stitches using the knitting-on method. *Insert the right needle from back to front between the two cast-on stitches.

2 Wrap the yarn around the left needle as if purling and pull the yarn through.

3 Place the new stitch on the left needle as shown. Cast on a new stitch using the cable cast-on. Repeat from the *, always inserting the right needle between the last two stitches on the left needle.

knitwise **66**   ribbing **34-35, 172-73**   as if to purl **32**

as if to knit **30**   front/back loops **37**

Tubular cast-on: version A

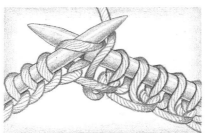

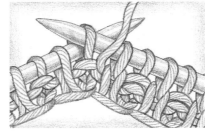

The tubular cast-on method produces a neat edge for knit one, purl one rib. However, this cast-on is not recommended for bulky yarns because the edge may tend to flair.

1 With a contrasting yarn, cast on half the required stitches (plus one extra, if an odd number of stitches) using the single cast-on. Cut the yarn. With the main color yarn at the back, knit one, *with yarn at front, knit one; repeat from the * to the end of row.

2 *Knit one, bring yarn to front, slip next stitch purlwise, bring yarn to back through needles; repeat from the *, end knit one. On next row, bring yarn to front, *slip one, bring yarn to back, knit one, bring yarn to front; repeat from the * to last stitch, slip last stitch.

3 Work the two rows in step 2 once more. Then work in knit one, purl one rib. After ribbing a few rows, remove the contrasting yarn.

Tubular cast-on: version B

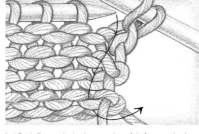

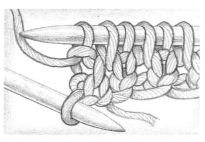

This tubular cast-on produces a similar look to version A.

1 With a contrasting waste yarn, cast on half the number of stitches required using the single cast-on method. Cut the waste yarn. With the main color yarn, purl one row, knit one row. Repeat these two rows once.

2 *Purl first stitch. Insert tip of left needle into first main color loop, between first two contrasting yarn loops of cast-on row, as shown. Slip this loop onto left needle and with yarn at the back, knit it through back loop. Repeat from the * to the last stitch.

3 Purl the last stitch, pick up the half-loop of the main color at the very edge and knit it through the back loop. Remove the waste yarn and work your ribbing.

Invisible cast-on

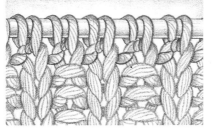

This cast-on creates a rounded edge and is best used when elasticity and strength are needed. You will need two pairs of needles, one pair the size recommended for the yarn and one pair two sizes smaller.

1 With the larger needles and a contrasting color, cast on half the number of stitches required. Work knit one, purl one rib for three or more rows. Cut the yarn. With the smaller needle and the main color, knit one, purl one in each stitch, doubling the cast-on stitches.

2 Knit the knit stitches and slip the purl stitches with the yarn in front of the work. Repeat for four rows more, then work in ribbing for required length. Remove the contrasting yarn.

main color yarn/MC **62**	(bring) with yarn in	slip a stitch **46**	knit **30**
front/back loops **37**	front/back **35**	ribbing **34-35**	purl **32**

Open cast-on

The open cast-on is used when stitches are to be picked up and worked later, such as hems.

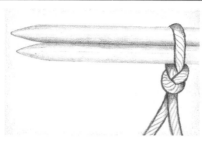

1 Cut a strand of contrasting waste yarn about four times the required width. With the working yarn, make a slip knot and place it on two needles, or one needle which is three sizes larger than the size you are using.

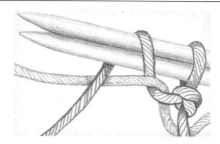

2 Hold the waste yarn beside the slip knot and take the working yarn under it and over the needles from front to back. Bring the working yarn in front of the waste yarn.

3 Repeat step 2 until all the stitches are cast on. Take out one needle before knitting the first row. Remove the waste yarn only when the piece is finished and you are ready to pick up stitches along the edge.

Picot cast-on

The picot cast-on can be used to form a decorative edging for cuffs, gloves or baby clothes.

1 Cast on two stitches using the knitting-on method. *Place yarn to the front of the work to make a yarn over and slip the first stitch purlwise. Holding the yarn over with your left thumb so that it does not cross the slip stitch, knit the next stitch as shown.

2 Lift the slip stitch over the knit stitch and off the needle. Turn the work and repeat from the * until the picot chain has the required number of loops. Repeat the steps once more but without the yarn over. One stitch remains on the needle.

3 Working from right to left, pick up a stitch in each picot loop along one side. Then continue knitting in the usual way.

Guernsey cast-on

This decorative cast-on was traditionally used for Guernsey sweaters.

1 Make a slip knot and, using the single cast-on method, cast on one stitch. With a second needle, lift the slip knot over the cast-on stitch and off the needle.

2 Cast on two more stitches and lift the first stitch over the second stitch as shown. Repeat this step until you have cast on all the stitches.

picking up **106-8**   slip a stitch

yarnovers **63**   purlwise **46**

Chain cast-on

In this cast-on method, a crochet hook is used to cast the stitches onto the needle. The edge resembles the edge produced by the cable cast-on.

1 Make a slip knot on the crochet hook. Hold the needle and yarn in your left hand with the yarn under the needle. Wrap the yarn around the hook as shown. Pull the yarn through the slip knot.

2 Bring the yarn to the back under the needle, wrap the yarn as before and pull it through the loop on the hook. Repeat this step until you have cast on the desired number of stitches minus one.

3 Bring the yarn to the back. Slip the loop from the hook to the needle as shown.

Chain cast-on for knit one, purl one rib

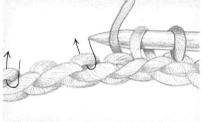

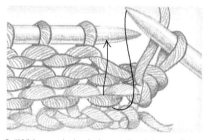

This cast-on is used for knit one, purl one rib and made with a contrasting waste yarn that is later removed.

1 With a contrasting yarn and a crochet hook, chain an even number of stitches. With the knitting needle and the main color, pick up and knit one stitch in the first two loops at back of the chain as shown, then in every other loop to the end.

2 Purl one row, knit one row. With the purl side facing, and the yarn in front, insert the right needle purlwise into the first stitch on the left needle, and into the first main color loop from the first main color row as shown. Purl these stitches together.

3 *With yarn in back, insert the right needle into the next main color loop and knit this stitch. With yarn in front, purl the next stitch on the needle; repeat from * to the last stitch. Knit the last stitch together with the last main color loop. Continue ribbing as usual.

Tips for casting on

A cast-on edge should be firm, but not tight. If the cast-on is too tight, it will eventually snap and unravel.

If you tend to cast on too tightly, use a larger needle than the suggested size, or use two needles held together. After casting on, remember to switch back to the correct needle size.

The cast-on should not be too loose, or the edge will flair out unattractively.

To create a firmer edge, cast on with a double strand of yarn.

A firmer cast-on should be used with yarns that have less resilience, such as cottons and silks. You can also use smaller needles, or cast on fewer stitches (increasing to required number after the last row of ribbing or edging) when using these yarns.

It is best to use longer needles when casting on a large number of

stitches. Also, use a stitch marker after every tenth stitch to help in counting.

Leave a 12 to 16 inch (30 to 40cm) tail to use for sewing seams. To keep it out of the way, bundle up the tail while working on your piece.

crochet chain **210**	picking up **106-8**	purl **32**	ribbing **34-35**
main color/MC **62**	knit **30**	purlwise **46**	markers **18**

The Basic Knit Stitch

The first stitch you will learn to make is called a knit stitch. You can work this stitch in two basic ways (or use an alternate method for left-handers).

The most common technique in English-speaking countries is known as the English or American method. The second method, which has always been associated with European countries, is called the Continental or German method. Each has its merits.

If someone taught you to knit, you probably learned the method used by your teacher. If you are learning now, you can try both methods and decide which is best for you. Usually the first technique you learn will be the easiest for you. (If you learn both methods, however, you will be able to knit color-work patterns using both hands.)

In the English method, your right hand controls the tension of the yarn and wraps it around the needle. The right needle usually rests on your lap or under your arm while you knit. (At one time, knitters used long double-pointed needles and wore a belted pouch around their waist, resting the right needle in a hole in the pouch.)

With the Continental method, you hold the yarn stationary in your left hand, and use the right needle to pull the strand through to create a stitch. Although many consider this to be the quickest way to knit, the resulting fabric can sometimes be looser than fabric worked by the English method.

When you're a beginner, learning to knit is awkward no matter which hand you favor, and left-handers might just as well learn one of the above two methods. However, if you find that both of those methods are too difficult, you can use a technique especially for left-handers. Just remember that knitting instructions are written for Continental and English knitting, and left-handers will have to reverse most pattern directions.

To learn the knit stitch, you must prepare by casting on a row of stitches. The directions at the right show you how to knit into each cast-on stitch on your needle, thus completing the first row (this row is always a little trickier to work since the tension has not yet been established). The yarn is always held to the back when knitting. After working the first row, switch the needle with the stitches to your opposite hand, and either work a second row of knit stitches to form garter stitch or go on to the purl stitch.

English

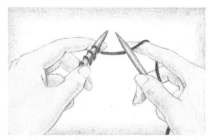

1 Hold the needle with the cast-on stitches in your left hand. The first stitch on the left needle should be approximately 1" (2.5cm) from the tip of the needle. Hold the working needle in your right hand, wrapping the yarn around your fingers.

Continental

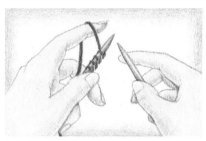

1 Hold the needles in the same way as the English method above, but wrap the yarn around your left hand rather than your right.

For left-handers

1 Hold the needle with the cast-on stitches in your right hand and the working needle and yarn in your left.

cast on **24-29**   with yarn in   garter **22, 34**
purl **32**   front/back **35**

2 Insert the right needle from front to back into the first cast-on stitch on the left needle. Keep the right needle under the left needle and the yarn at the back.

3 Wrap the yarn under and over the right needle in a clockwise motion.

4 With the right needle, catch the yarn and pull it through the cast-on stitch.

5 Slip the cast-on stitch off the left needle, leaving the newly formed stitch on the right needle. Repeat these steps in each subsequent stitch until all stitches have been worked from the left needle. One knit row has been completed.

2 Insert the right needle from front to back into the first cast-on stitch on the left needle. Keep the right needle under the left needle, with the yarn in back of both needles.

3 Lay the yarn over the right needle as shown.

4 With the tip of the right needle, pull the strand through the cast-on stitch, holding the strand with the right index finger if necessary.

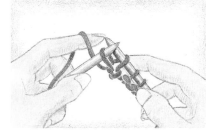

5 Slip the cast-on stitch off the left needle, leaving the newly formed stitch on the right needle. Continue to repeat these steps until you have worked all of the stitches from the left needle to the right needle. You have made one row of knit stitches.

2 Insert the left needle from front to back into the first cast-on stitch on the right needle. Keep the left needle under the right needle and the yarn at the back.

3 Wrap the yarn under and over the left needle in a counterclockwise motion.

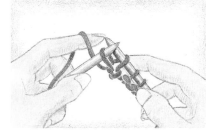

4 With the left needle, catch the yarn and pull it through the stitch on the right needle.

5 Slip the cast-on stitch off the right needle. The left needle holds a new stitch. Continue to repeat these steps until you have worked all of the stitches from the right needle to the left one. This completes one row of knit stitches.

The Basic Purl Stitch

You are ready to learn the second essential stitch—the purl stitch. The purl stitch is the reverse of the knit stitch. If you purl every row, your fabric will look the same as if you had knit every row. This is called garter stitch. If you alternate one row of purl stitches and one row of knit stitches, you create stockinette stitch, the most commonly used stitch. When you work stockinette stitch, the knit rows are the right side of the work and the purl rows are the wrong side. When you work the knit stitch and the purl stitch in the same row, you can create stitch patterns with dimension and texture.

When purling, the yarn and the needles are held in the same way as when knitting. The yarn, however, is kept to the front of the work rather than to the back and the right needle is inserted into the stitch from back to front.

Working a purl stitch may be a bit more difficult for those who knit using the Continental method.

English

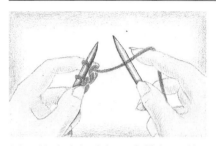

1 As with the knit stitch, you hold the working needle in your right hand and the needle with the stitches in your left. The yarn is held and manipulated with your right hand and is kept to the front of the work.

Continental

1 As with the knit stitch, you hold the working needle in your right hand and the needle with the stitches in your left. The yarn is held and manipulated with your left hand and is kept to the front of the work.

For left-handers

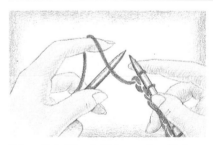

1 As with knitting, hold the needle with the stitches in your right hand and the working needle in your left. The yarn is held and manipulated with your left hand and is kept to the front of the work.

stockinette **22, 34**   with yarn in
right/wrong sides **67-68**   front/back **35**

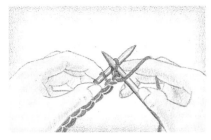

2 Insert the right needle from back to front into the first stitch on the left needle. The right needle is now in front of the left needle and the yarn is at the front of the work.

3 With your right index finger, wrap the yarn counterclockwise around the right needle.

4 Draw the right needle and the yarn backwards through the stitch on the left needle, forming a loop on the right needle.

5 Slip the stitch off the left needle. You have made one purl stitch. Repeat these steps in each subsequent stitch until all stitches have been worked from the left needle. One purl row has been completed.

2 Insert the right needle from back to front into the first stitch on the left needle, keeping the yarn in front of the work.

3 Lay the yarn over the right needle as shown. Pull down on the yarn with your left index finger to keep the yarn taut.

4 Bring the right needle and the yarn backwards through the stitch on the left needle, forming a loop on the right needle.

5 Slide the stitch off the left needle. Use your left index finger to tighten the new purl stitch on the right needle. Continue to repeat these steps until you have worked all of the stitches from the left needle to the right needle. You have made one row of purl stitches.

2 Insert the left needle from back to front into the back loop of the first stitch on the right needle.

3 Wrap the yarn clockwise over and under the left needle, holding the yarn taut with your left index finger.

4 Draw the left needle through the stitch, bringing the yarn with it, making a new stitch on the left needle.

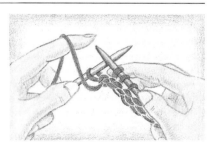

5 Slip the stitch off the right needle. You have made one purl stitch. Repeat these steps until you have worked all of the stitches from the right needle to the left one. This completes one row of purl stitches.

Basic Stitch Patterns

If you have knit or purled every row, you've made garter stitch. If you've worked alternate rows of knit and purl stitches, you've made stockinette stitch. If you turn the stockinette stitch fabric around so that the purl stitches are on the right side of the work, you have reverse stockinette stitch. These three stitches and the others on these two pages are simply different combinations of knit and purl stitches.

You will need to learn how to make ribbing before beginning your first garment. In ribbing, all the knits line up over the knit stitches and all the purl stitches line up over the purl stitches. You must be able to recognize the difference between knit and purl stitches.

Once you have mastered basic rib stitches, try some twisted ribbings which are made by working into the back loop of a stitch, which twists the stitch. In some twisted ribs, you work into the back loop of just the knit stitches, in others you work into the back loops of both the knit and the purl stitches.

Seed stitch is a textured stitch created by working a sequence of knit and purl stitches, usually alternated on every row. Unlike ribbing, you knit the purl stitches and purl the knit stitches.

The instructions for these stitch patterns have been spelled out for beginners to understand.

Garter stitch

Any number of stitches
Knit every row.

Stockinette stitch

Any number of stitches
Row 1 (right side): Knit.
Row 2: Purl.
Repeat rows 1 and 2.

Reverse stockinette stitch

Any number of stitches
Row 1 (right side): Purl.
Row 2: Knit.
Repeat rows 1 and 2.

Garter ridge stitch

Any number of stitches
Rows 1 and 3 (right side): Knit.
Row 2: Purl.
Row 4: Knit.
Repeat rows 1 through 4.

Knit one, purl one ribbing

An odd number of stitches
Row 1 (right side): Knit one, *purl one, knit one; repeat from * to end.
Row 2: Purl one, *knit one, purl one; repeat from * to end.
Repeat rows 1 and 2.

Knit two, purl two ribbing

Multiple of 4 stitches plus 2 extra
Row 1 (right side): Knit two, *purl two, knit two; repeat from * to end.
Row 2: Purl two, *knit two, purl two; repeat from * to end.
Repeat rows 1 and 2.

Seed stitch

An even number of stitches
Row 1 (right side): *Knit one, purl one; repeat from * to end.
Row 2: *Purl one, knit one; repeat from * to end.
Repeat rows 1 and 2.

Double seed stitch

An even number of stitches
Row 1 (right side): *Knit one, purl one; repeat from * to end.
Row 2: Repeat row 1.
Row 3: *Purl one, knit one; repeat from * to end.
Row 4: Repeat row 3.
Repeat rows 1 through 4.

---

right/wrong sides **67-68**

front/back loops **37**

Twisted knit one, purl one ribbing (half twist)

An odd number of stitches
Row 1 (right side): Knit one through the back loop, *purl one, knit one through the back loop; repeat from * to end.
Row 2: Purl one, *knit one, purl one; repeat from * to end.
Repeat rows 1 and 2.

Twisted knit one, purl one ribbing (full twist)

An odd number of stitches
Row 1 (right side): Knit one through the back loop, *purl one, knit one through the back loop; repeat from * to end.
Row 2: Purl one through the back loop, *knit one, purl one through the back loop; repeat from * to end.
Repeat rows 1 and 2.

Knit five, purl two ribbing

Multiple of 7 stitches plus 5 extra
Row 1 (right side): Knit five, *purl two, knit five; repeat from * to end.
Row 2: Purl five, *knit two, purl five; repeat from * to end.
Repeat rows 1 and 2.

Knit two, purl five ribbing

Multiple of 7 stitches plus 2 extra
Row 1 (right side): Knit two, *purl five, knit two; repeat from * to end.
Row 2: Purl two, *knit five, purl two; repeat from * to end.
Repeat rows 1 and 2.

With yarn at back; With yarn at front

When knitting a stitch, the yarn is always held at the back of the work. When purling a stitch, the yarn is always at the front. In ribbing, when you change from a knit to a purl stitch, you must be sure the yarn is in the correct position to work the next stitch. When you are moving the yarn from the back to the front, or vice versa, the yarn should go between the two needles, and not over them.

With yarn at back

With yarn at front

knit **30**   front/back loops **37**

purl **32**

Joining Yarns

Whenever possible, join new balls of yarn at the beginning or end of a row. When the garment is finished, you can easily untie the strands and weave them into the seams.

Sometimes, however, joining the yarn in the middle of the row is unavoidable, such as on garments that are knit in the round or with some colorwork patterns. Mid-row joinings, especially with flat yarn in flat stitches such as stockinette stitch, should be handled carefully. Join the yarn, whenever possible, in an inconspicuous place, such as at

the edge of a cable or in a textured stitch area. Wherever you join the yarn, it is essential to weave the ends in neatly during finishing. Always weave the strands into the wrong side of the fabric by untying any knots and working them in opposite directions. If you are using a thick yarn, you should untwist the strands and weave them in separately.

There are ways to avoid running out of yarn in mid-row. If you're almost to the end of the ball of yarn and you're not sure you can complete the next

row, lay your piece flat and fold the remaining yarn back and forth over the knitting. If you have at least four times the width of your piece, you will have sufficient yarn to work a row of simple stitch patterns (a row of stitches such as bobbles or cables may require more yarn). Another method is to fold the remaining yarn in half and make a slip knot about 6" (15cm) from the folded end. If you do not reach the knot when working the next row, you know that you will have enough yarn to work one more row.

Joining methods

To join a new yarn at the side edge, tie it loosely around the old yarn, leaving at least a 6" (15cm) tail. Untie the knot later and weave the ends into the seam.

1 To join a yarn in the middle of the row, insert the right needle into the next stitch to be worked, wrap the new yarn around the right needle and start knitting with the new yarn.

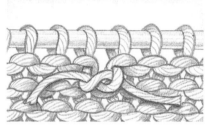

2 Work to the end of the row. Tie the old and new strands together loosely before continuing so they will not unravel.

1 To join the same color in the middle of a row, splice the two ends together by untwisting the ends of both the old and the new yarn. Cut away approximately 4" (10cm) from half of each set of strands as shown.

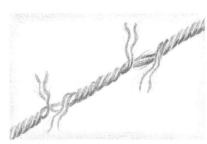

2 Overlap the remaining uncut strands and twist them together in the same direction as the yarn. Continue working with the twisted yarn, weaving in the loose ends later.

Increases

Increases are used to shape a piece of knitting by adding stitches to make it larger. Some increases are inconspicuous and do not interrupt the pattern, while others are meant to be visible and add a decorative touch. (Decorative increases are generally worked two or three stitches from the edge of the work.)

Most increases are worked on the right side of the work, for two reasons. First, you'll be able to see the finished look and placement of the increases. Also, it is easier to keep track of your increase rows when you work them at regular intervals, such as on every right-side row.

Often a knitting pattern may not specify the type of increase to be used. Increases that have a definite right or left slant can be placed to follow the slant of the increase. To choose an appropriate one, you should learn a variety of increases and note their characteristics. The symbolcraft symbol appears for each type of increase shown in this chapter. Use these as a reference when working with charts for patterns that are given in symbolcraft.

If you want to add one or two stitches use increases, but if you need to add several stitches at one time at the side edge, it is better to cast on the additional stitches.

Bar increase—knit side

The bar increase is a visible increase. A horizontal bar will follow the increased stitch on the knit side of the work, whether you work the increase on the knit or the purl side.

1 To increase on the knit side, insert the right needle knitwise into the stitch to be increased. Wrap the yarn around the right needle and pull it through as if knitting, but leave the stitch on the left needle.

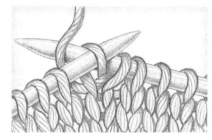

2 Insert the right needle into the back of the same stitch. Wrap the yarn around the needle and pull it through. Slip the stitch from the left needle. You now have two stitches on the right needle.

Working in front and back loops

The front of the stitch is the loop closest to you. Always work front loop unless otherwise stated. To knit into front loop, insert right needle, left to right into stitch on left needle. To knit into back loop (loop farthest from you), insert needle from right to left under left needle and into stitch. To purl into front loop, insert needle from right to left into stitch. To purl into back loop, insert needle from behind into stitch.

Knitting into the front loop

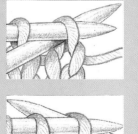

Knitting into the back loop

Purling into the front loop

Purling into the back loop

right/wrong sides **67-68** symbolcraft
knitwise **66** charts **69-70**

Lifted increase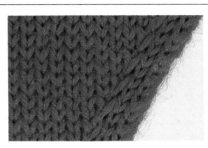

This increase is barely visible and can be used almost anywhere. However, since you are increasing by pulling up a loop from the previous row, the work may pucker if there are fewer than three rows between each increase.

The lifted increase, worked on the knit side.

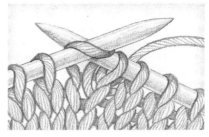

1 To work the increase on the knit side, turn the work on the left needle towards you so that the purl side of the work is visible. Insert the tip of the right needle from the top down into the stitch on the left needle one row below as shown.

2 Knit this stitch, then knit the stitch on the left needle.

The lifted increase, worked on the purl side but as it looks on the knit side.

1 To work the increase on the purl side, insert the left needle under the loop two rows below the last stitch on the left needle.

2 Insert the right needle purlwise into this stitch and purl it.

Working multiple increases

When making multiple increases across a row, it is best to space them as evenly as possible. First, subtract one from the number of stitches to be increased. Divide this number into the number of stitches on the needle. For example, if there are 59 stitches on the needle and you need to increase nine stitches; then $9 - 1 = 8$ and $59 \div 8 = 7$ with a remainder of 3. You would then have seven stitches between each in-crease with three remaining stitches to distribute over the ends.

If you are working the increase between the stitches, as in the make one increase, the instructions would be as follows: Work one stitch, [make one, work seven stitches] eight times, make one, work two stitches.

If you are using an increase that is worked into a stitch, such as the bar increase, then there are actually six stitches between each increase, as one of the seven stitches is being used for the increase. The instructions would be as follows: Work one stitch, [increase one stitch in the next stitch, work six stitches] eight times, increase one stitch in the next stitch, work one stitch.

Make one: version A

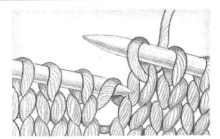

The make one increase is made between two stitches and is practically invisible. This one slants to the right on the knit side.

1 Insert the left needle from back to front into the horizontal strand between the last stitch worked and the next stitch on the left needle.

2 Knit this strand through the front loop to twist the stitch.

To make the increase on the purl side, insert the left needle from back to front into the horizontal strand and purl it through the front loop.

Make one: version B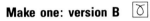

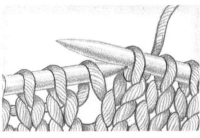

This make one method is similar to version A above, but it slants to the left on the knit side.

1 Insert the left needle from front to back into the horizontal strand between the last stitch worked and the first stitch on the left needle.

2 Knit this strand through the back loop to twist it.

To make the increase on the purl side, insert the left needle from front to back into the horizontal strand and purl it through the back loop.

Make one: version C

This decorative version of the make one increase creates a small hole because the stitch is not twisted.

On the knit side, insert the left needle from back to front into the horizontal strand between the two needles, and knit it through the back loop.

On the purl side, insert the left needle from front to back into the horizontal strand between the two needles and purl it through the front loop.

Median increase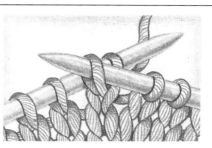

The median increase is a decorative one that can be used on either the left or right side of the work.

This photo shows the knit increase on the right side.

1 To work the increase on the knit side, knit the stitch to be increased but do not drop the old stitch from the left needle.

2 Knit one stitch in the row below the same stitch you have just knit and drop the top stitch from the left needle.

The purl median increase looks the same as the knit increase on the knit side.

1 To work the increase on the purl side, purl the stitch to be increased but do not drop the old stitch from the left needle.

2 Purl one stitch in the row below the same stitch you have just purled and drop the top stitch from the left needle.

Increasing into a pattern

When shaping, it is fairly simple to increase stitches in a simple pattern such as stockinette stitch. However, increasing stitches in a more complex stitch pattern may require some planning, especially in patterns with repeats of two or more stitches.

Usually the new stitches are worked in stockinette (or another specified stitch) until you have enough stitches to continue the pattern. An easy way to keep track of the increase stitches is to place a marker before the first increase. Keep this marker in the same place on each row until you

have enough stitches to continue the pattern, then move the marker back to the edge. Continue in this way until you have increased all of the stitches.

Right edge increase on the knit side

This increase is worked at the beginning of a knit row and at the end of a purl row.

1 On the knit side, knit the first stitch. Insert the left needle into the left-hand loop of the stitch one row below the stitch you have just knit.

2 Knit this stitch through the back loop.

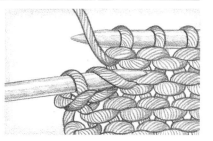

On the purl side, work until one stitch remains on the left needle. Insert the left needle into the purl stitch one row below the last purl stitch on the right needle. Purl this stitch. Purl the last stitch on the left needle.

Left edge increase on the knit side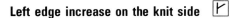

This increase is worked at the end of a knit row and at the beginning of a purl row.

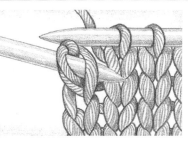

1 On the knit side, work until one stitch remains on the left needle. Insert the left needle into the loop of the stitch one row below the stitch on the left needle.

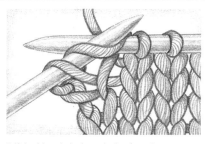

2 Knit this stitch through the front loop as shown. Knit the last stitch on the needle.

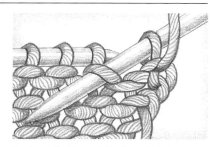

On the purl side, purl the first stitch. Insert the right needle into the purl loop of the stitch one row below the next stitch on the left needle, slip to left needle and purl this stitch.

Charting increases into the pattern

Another way to help keep track of your pattern when increasing stitches is to draw it on a piece of graph paper, including increase stitches. Then you can see exactly how it will continue on new stitches.

In order to chart out the pattern, you will need symbolcraft, which is explained in Chapter IV. The example at right shows increases worked into a cable stitch pattern.

front/back loops **37**

symbolcraft **69-70**

Decreases

Decreasing is a method of reducing the number of stitches (usually one or two at a time) to narrow a piece of knitting.

As with increases, a variety of methods can be used, depending on the purpose they will serve. For example, decreases can slant to the left, right or be vertical. When shaping an armhole, you might want to work a left-slanting decrease on the right-hand side of the garment, and a right-slanting decrease on the left-hand side of the garment, thus emphasizing the slope of the shaping. If placed one or two stitches in from the edge, the decreases become a decorative detail. This type of visible decreasing is called "full-fashioned" decreasing. Placing the decreases away from the edge also makes it easier to seam the pieces together.

Of course, the decreases do not have to be visible. A simple decrease (such as knitting two stitches together) can be placed at the edge of the knitting so that it will be invisible once the pieces are sewn together.

Most decreases are worked on the right side of the knitting, but sometimes it is necessary to decrease stitches on the wrong side (such as when the decreases are worked on every row). For this reason, we have included in this chapter decreases that can be worked on the purl side of the work.

Basic single left-slanting decrease ◩

Knitting (or purling) two stitches together through the back loops is a decrease that slants the stitches to the left on the knit side of the work. It is abbreviated as k2tog tbl (or p2tog tbl).

With the right needle behind the left needle, insert the right needle through the back loops of the next two stitches on the left needle. Knit these two stitches together.

With the right needle behind the left needle, insert the right needle into the back loop of the second stitch, and then into the back loop of the first stitch on the left needle, which twists the two stitches. Purl these two stitches together.

Basic single right-slanting decrease ◪

Knitting (or purling) two stitches together is the easiest technique and one that every beginner must learn. This basic decrease slants to the right on the knit side of the work. It is abbreviated as k2tog (or p2tog).

Insert the right needle from front to back (knitwise) into the next two stitches on the left needle. Wrap the yarn around the right needle (as when knitting) and pull it through. You have decreased one stitch.

Insert the right needle into the front loops (purlwise) of the next two stitches on the left needle. Wrap the yarn around the right needle (as when purling) and pull it through. You have decreased one stitch.

seaming **98-101**   front/back loops **37**

right/wrong sides **67-68**

Single left-slanting decrease: version A

This decrease slants the stitches to the left on the knit side of the work. It is abbreviated as SKP or sl 1, k1, psso (slip one stitch, knit one stitch, pass slip stitch over knit stitch).

1 Slip one stitch knitwise, then knit the next stitch. Insert the left needle into the slipped stitch as shown.

2 Pass the slipped stitch over the knit stitch and off the right needle.

Single left-slanting decrease: version B

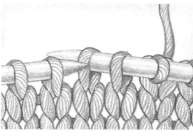

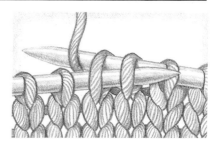

This decrease slants the stitches to the left on the knit side of the work. It is abbreviated as ssk (slip one, slip one, knit two together).

1 Slip two stitches knitwise, one at a time, from the left needle to the right needle.

2 Insert the left needle into the fronts of these two slipped stitches as shown and knit them together.

Single left-slanting decrease: version C

This decrease, worked on the purl side, slants the stitches to the left on the knit side.

1 Slip two stitches knitwise, one at a time, from the left needle to the right needle. Return these two slipped stitches to the left needle as shown, keeping them twisted.

2 Purl these two stitches together through the back loops.

slip a stitch **46**   front/back loops **37**

knitwise **66**

Single right-slanting decrease: version A

This decrease slants stitches to the right on the knit side.

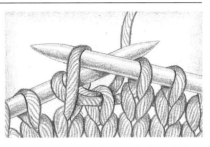

1 Knit one stitch, slip one stitch knitwise; return the slipped stitch (keeping it twisted) and the knit stitch (as shown) to the left needle.

2 Pass the slipped stitch over the knit stitch and off the left needle as shown. Slip the knit stitch purlwise to the right needle.

Single right-slanting decrease: version B

This decrease, worked on the purl side, slants stitches to the right on the knit side.

1 Slip the next stitch on the left needle purlwise, then purl one stitch as shown.

2 With the left needle, pass the slipped stitch over the purl stitch and off the right needle.

Double left-slanting decrease: version A

This method decreases two stitches and slants to the left on the knit side.

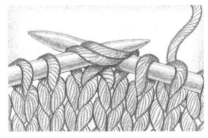

1 Slip the next stitch knitwise, then knit the next two stitches together as shown to decrease one stitch.

2 Pass the slipped stitch over the decreased stitch.

slip a stitch
knitwise/purlwise **46**

Double left-slanting decrease: version B

This method, worked on the purl side, decreases two stitches and slants to the left on the knit side.

1 Purl two stitches together and return this decreased stitch to the left needle as shown.

2 Pass the second stitch on the left needle over the decreased stitch and off the needle. Then return the decreased stitch to the right needle.

Double right-slanting decrease: version A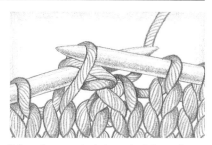

This method decreases two stitches and slants to the right on the knit side.

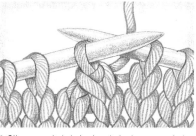

1 Slip one stitch knitwise, knit the next stitch, pass the slipped stitch over the knit stitch (SKP). Return this decreased stitch to the left needle.

2 Pass the second stitch on the left needle over the decreased stitch and off the needle. Return the decreased stitch to the right needle.

Double right-slanting decrease: version B

This method, worked on the purl side, decreases two stitches and slants to the right on the knit side.

1 Slip one stitch purlwise, then purl two stitches together as shown.

2 Pass the slipped stitch over the decreased stitch.

slip a stitch
knitwise/purlwise **46**

Double vertical decrease: version A

This method decreases two stitches and creates a vertical stitch.

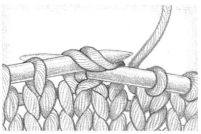

1 Insert the right needle into the next two stitches on the left needle as if you were knitting them together and slip them to the right needle.

2 Knit the next stitch on the left needle. With the left needle, pull both slipped stitches over the knit stitch as shown.

Double vertical decrease: version B

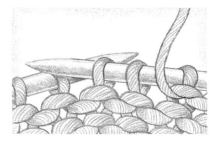

1 Insert the right needle into the next two stitches on the left needle one at a time as if you were knitting them. Slip them to the right needle. You now have two twisted stitches on the right needle.

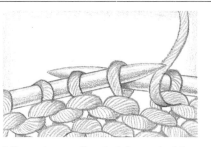

2 Return the two slipped stitches to the left needle, keeping them twisted.

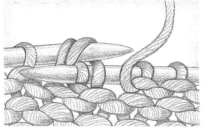

3 Insert the right needle through the back loops of the second and the first slipped stitches and slip them together off the left needle.

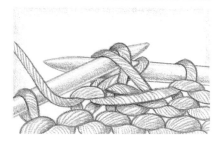

4 Purl the next stitch. With the left needle, pass the two slipped stitches over the purl stitch and off the right needle.

Slipping a stitch knitwise and purlwise

To slip a stitch is to pass it from one needle to another without working it. It is sometimes used when decreasing as well as when working color and stitch patterns. A stitch slipped purlwise, remains untwisted, but slipped knitwise, it will twist. If instructions do not specify which way to slip the stitch, slip it purlwise except when decreasing, in which case, slip knit stitches knitwise and purl stitches purlwise.

To slip one stitch purlwise, insert right needle into the next stitch on left needle as if you were purling the stitch. Pull this stitch off the left needle. The stitch is now on the right needle.

To slip one stitch knitwise, insert right needle into next stitch on left needle as if you were knitting the stitch. Pull this stitch off the left needle. The stitch is now on the right needle and twisted.

slip one
stitch
purlwise

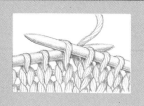

slip one
stitch
knitwise

Binding off

Binding off links stitches which are no longer to be worked and keeps them from unraveling. The resulting selvage can be connected to other pieces of knitting or it can stand on its own. The bound-off edge should be elastic, but firm—not too loose or too tight. Knitters often tend to bind off too tightly. A way to reduce this tendency is to use a larger needle to bind off. Unless otherwise stated, you should bind off in the stitch pattern used for the piece.

Binding off is not only used for finishing knit pieces, but also for shaping armholes, necks and shoulders. It can be the first row of a buttonhole, or it can be used to create three-dimensional stitch patterns.

Although several basic bind-offs are multipurpose, others serve special functions, such as the invisible bind-off which eliminates the edge in ribbing, and a variety of bind-offs that form decorative edges.

Some bind-offs are worked with two or more knitting needles while others require the use of one knitting needle along with a crochet hook or sewing needle.

If you bind off all the stitches in the row, pull the yarn through the last stitch to fasten off the piece.

Basic knit bind-off

This is the most common bind-off method and the easiest to learn. It creates a firm, neat edge.

1 Knit two stitches. *Insert the left needle into the first stitch on the right needle.

2 Pull this stitch over the second stitch and off the right needle.

3 One stitch remains on the right needle as shown. Knit the next stitch. Repeat from the * until you have bound off the required number of stitches.

Basic purl bind-off

  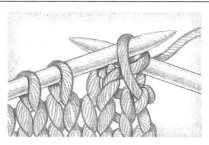 

The purl bind-off creates a firm edge and is used on purl stitches.

1 Purl two stitches. *Insert the left needle from behind the right needle into the back loop of the first stitch on the right needle as shown.

2 Pull this stitch over the second stitch and off the right needle.

3 One stitch remains on the right needle as shown. Purl the next stitch. Repeat from the * until you have bound off the required number of stitches.

selvages **194-95**   front/back loops **37**

ribbing **34-35, 172-73**

Suspended bind-off

  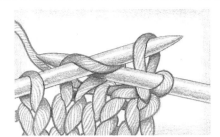 

The suspended bind-off is similar to the basic knit bind-off but is more flexible. You can use this method if you have a tendency to bind off too tightly.

1 Work the first two stitches. *Pull the first stitch over the second stitch, but do not drop it from the left needle.

2 Knit the next stitch on the left needle.

3 Slip both stitches off the left needle. Two stitches remain on the right needle, and one stitch has been bound off. Repeat from the * until you have bound off all the stitches.

Decrease bind-off

  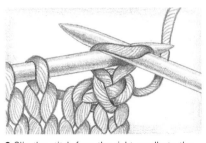

The decrease bind-off is a decorative one that is ideal for conspicuous edges such as pockets or trims.

1 *Knit two stitches together through the back loops as shown. One stitch remains on the right needle.

2 Slip the stitch from the right needle to the left needle, making sure it is not twisted. Repeat from the * until the required number of stitches are bound off.

One-over-two bind-off

 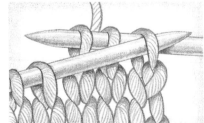 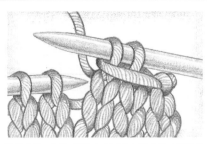 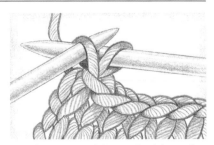

This bind-off pulls the stitches together for a gathered edge. It is used with pattern stitches that have a great deal of lateral spread, such as allover traveling cables or openwork stitches.

1 Work three stitches. *Insert the left needle into the first stitch.

2 Pull the first stitch over the next two stitches and off the right needle.

3 Work one more stitch onto the right needle, then repeat from the * until you have bound off the required number of stitches. If binding off every stitch, work the last two stitches using the basic knit bind-off as shown.

pockets **214-19**   front/back loops **37**

trims **231-38**

Single crochet bind-off

The crochet bind-off is good for yarns that are not resilient, such as cottons and silks, as it creates an elastic edge.

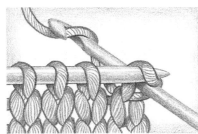

1 Use a crochet hook of comparable size to your knitting needle. With the yarn in your left hand, insert the hook knitwise into the first stitch on the needle. Pull the yarn through to make a loop on the hook and let the old stitch fall from the needle.

2 *Work the same way into the next stitch, but pull the loop through both the stitch on the needle and the loop on the hook. One loop remains on the hook. Repeat from the *.

Double crochet bind-off

The double crochet bind-off is decorative and should be used for open edges.

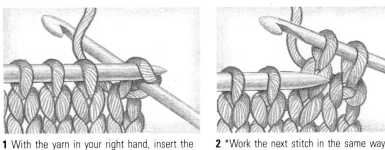

1 With the yarn in your right hand, insert the hook knitwise into the first stitch and wrap the yarn around the hook as if to knit. Draw a loop through and let the old stitch fall from the needle.

2 *Work the next stitch in the same way. You now have two loops on the hook.

3 Wrap the yarn around the hook as before and pull it through both loops on the hook. Repeat from the * until you have bound off the required number of stitches.

Graphing out neck and shoulder shaping

There are 68 sts on the needle. *Next row (RS):* Work 25 sts, join 2nd ball of yarn and bind off center 18 sts for neck, work to end. Working both sides at once, bind off from each neck edge 4 sts twice, 3 sts once. After all neck decs have been worked, bind off from each shoulder edge 4 sts once, 5 sts twice.

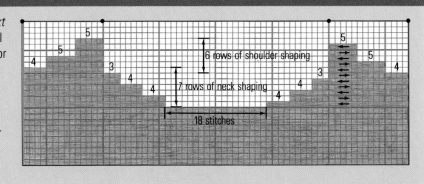

Picot bind-off

The picot bind-off creates a decorative edge you can use at open edges that will not be seamed, such as on afghans, baby clothes and blankets.

1 Using the basic knit method, bind off the first two stitches (or however many stitches you want between picots). *Turn the work and, using the cable cast-on method, cast on two additional stitches.

2 Turn the work. Bind off all but one of the cast-on stitches by passing the second over the first, and the third over the first. One stitch remains on the right needle.

3 Bind off two more stitches, then repeat from the * until you have bound off the required number of stitches.

Sloped bind-off

The sloped bind-off is ideal for shoulder and neck shaping. It avoids the stair-step edge that is formed by a series of bind-offs by making a smooth transition from one bind-off row to the next.

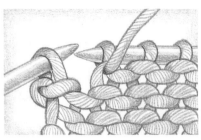

1 *One row before the next bind-off row, work to the last stitch of the row. Do not work this stitch. Turn the work.

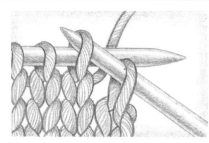

2 With the yarn in back, slip the first stitch from the left needle purlwise as shown.

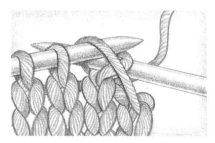

3 Pass the unworked stitch of the previous row over the slipped stitch. The first stitch is bound off. Bind off the desired number of stitches for that row. Work to the end of the row. Repeat from the *.

Bind-off tips

When working a pattern stitch, such as ribbing, you should keep to the pattern when binding off, unless otherwise stated. For example, to bind off knit one, purl one ribbing, knit the knit stitches and purl the purl stitches as you bind them off.

When binding off in a cable pattern, try to bind off the stitches just after a twist row. This will help to keep the stitches from stretching.

If an edge is bound off too tightly, the stitches can break with wear. If you have a tendency to bind off tightly, on the bind-off row, try using a needle two to three sizes larger than you used for knitting. Check the edge frequently as you bind off to be sure it is elastic enough. This will eliminate the need to redo the entire bind-off.

It is especially important that the bound-off edge of a neckband is loose enough so that you can easily pull the sweater over your head.

After you have finished binding off the last stitch, leave a long tail which can be used for sewing or weaving seams together.

---

shoulder and neck
shaping **178-80**

slip a stitch
purlwise **46**

Knit one, purl one bind-off

This method produces a subtle finish that is perfect for edges worked in single ribbing such as neckbands. A yarn needle is used in place of the right needle.

1 Cut the yarn three times the width of the ribbing. Insert the yarn needle purlwise into the first (knit) stitch. Pull the yarn through. With the yarn needle behind the knit stitch, insert it knitwise into the purl stitch as shown. Pull the yarn through.

2 *With the yarn needle, slip the first knit stitch knitwise and then insert the yarn needle into the next knit stitch purlwise as shown. Pull the yarn through.

3 With the yarn needle, slip the first stitch purlwise. Go behind the knit stitch and insert the yarn needle knitwise into the next purl stitch as shown. Pull the yarn through. Repeat from the * in step 2 until all the stitches are bound off.

Knit two, purl two bind-off

This method is used for finishing a knit two, purl two rib. A yarn needle is used in place of the right needle.

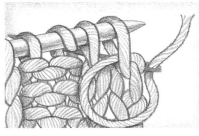

1 Cut the yarn three times the width of the ribbing. Insert the yarn needle purlwise into the first (knit) stitch. Pull the yarn through. With the yarn needle behind the two knit stitches, insert it knitwise into the first purl stitch as shown. Pull the yarn through.

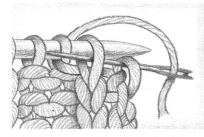

2 *With the yarn needle, slip the first knit stitch knitwise. Insert the yarn needle purlwise into the second knit stitch as shown. Pull the yarn through.

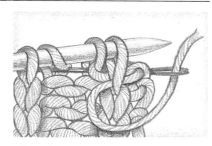

3 Take the yarn needle behind the knit stitch; insert it purlwise into the first purl stitch and knitwise into the second purl stitch as shown. Pull the yarn through.

4 With the yarn needle, slip the first knit stitch knitwise. Insert the yarn needle purlwise into the next knit stitch as shown. Drop the first purl stitch from the left needle. Pull the yarn through.

5 Insert the yarn needle purlwise into the first purl stitch as shown. Pull the yarn through. Drop the stitch from the needle.

6 Take the yarn needle behind the next two knit stitches. Insert it knitwise into the next purl stitch as shown. Pull the yarn through. Repeat from the * in step 2 until all the stitches are bound off.

Two-row bind-off

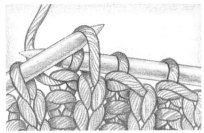

The two-row bind-off is one that leaves small eyelets along the edge. It is used at edges of afghans for attaching fringes, and with knit one, purl one ribbing.

1 *Knit one stitch, purl one stitch, then pull the knit stitch over the purl stitch as shown. Repeat from the * across the row, passing knit stitches over purl stitches, but leaving the purl stitches on the right needle.

2 Cut the yarn and turn the work. Slip the first two stitches purlwise.

3 Pass the first stitch over the second stitch. Continue binding off in this way, slipping the purl stitches before binding them off. Sew down the last loop.

Binding off two pieces together

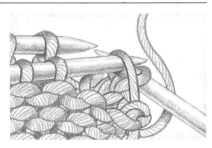

This bind-off is used to join two edges which have the same number of stitches, such as shoulder edges which have been placed on holders.

1 With the right side of the two pieces facing each other, and the needles parallel, insert a third needle knitwise into the first stitch of each needle, wrap the yarn around the needle as if to knit.

2 Knit these two stitches together and slip them off the needles. *Knit the next two stitches together in the same way as shown.

3 Slip the first stitch on the third needle over the second stitch and off the needle. Repeat from the * in step 2 across the row until all the stitches are bound off.

Neatening the last loop

When you have bound off all the stitches and only one stitch remains on the right needle, you must secure this stitch so that the row will not unravel. You can simply pull the yarn through the last stitch, but this often leaves a loose loop. You can tighten up this loose loop and complete the bind-off at the same time. Bind off until one stitch remains on the left needle. Slip this last stitch to the right needle. There are now two stitches on the right needle. With the left needle, pick up the left loop of the stitch one row below the slipped stitch as shown. Return the slipped stitch to the left needle and knit the picked-up loop and the slipped stitch together. Bind off the last stitch on the right needle and pull the yarn through the last stitch.

ribbing **34-35**

knitwise **66**

slip a stitch purlwise **46**

IV. Understanding Knitting Instructions

Understanding Knitting Instructions

Knitting instructions may vary in style but essentially all follow a basic order and sequence and use the same standard abbreviations and terms. Some of the terminology and abbreviations may seem confusing at first, especially if you have never worked from knitting instructions, but they are actually logical and simple to use once you are familiar with them. This chapter begins by discussing size selection, the meaning of knitted measurements, the selection of materials and how to work a gauge swatch. Later, abbreviations and special terms are explained, as well as symbolcraft. Even if you plan to design your own garments, you will find this chapter invaluable.

Before you begin to knit from knitting instructions, it is helpful to read them from beginning to end. Look carefully at any special notes, pattern stitches or materials that you will need to complete your pattern. Once you have a general idea of what the pattern

entails, you will know if it suits your technical ability and personal style. If you are a beginner, it is best to choose styles with simple patterns and shaping until you have enough experience to tackle more complicated projects.

Sizes

Knitting patterns are generally written in more than one size. The smallest is given first and appears outside of the parentheses. The larger sizes are given inside the parentheses in ascending order. As you read the instructions, your size will be in the same position throughout. For example, if your size is third in the sequence, subsequent figures for your size—indicating yarn amounts, number of stitches to be cast on, and so on—will always appear third in the sequence. If only one number is given, it applies to all of the sizes. It's always a good idea to highlight your size to make reading the pattern less confusing.

Sizes are expressed as bust or dress sizes. It's important to note that these sizes reflect actual body measurements

and not the finished measurements of the sweater. The sections below on finished measurements and the schematic drawing will help you determine the right fit.

Knitted Measurements

Knitted measurements are the dimensions of the garment after all the pieces have been knit and sewn together. These measurements, along with the schematic drawing, will help you to decide which size to select. The range of knitted measurements varies from sweater to sweater. If a sweater has simple shaping and a flexible pattern, it will have a wider range of sizes than a sweater with complicated shaping or with large pattern repeats that cannot be broken up.

Fit Chart

Body measurements	Fit captions & corresponding finished bust measurements				
bust sizes	very close fitting (body-hugging)	close fitting (body-contoured)	standard fitting (body-skimming)	loose fitting (straight-hanging)	oversized (full, roomy)
32″ (81cm)	30″ (76cm)	32-33″ (81-84cm)	34″ (86cm)	36″ (91cm)	37″ (94 cm) or more
34″ (86cm)	32″ (81cm)	34-35″ (86-89cm)	36″ (91cm)	38″ (96cm)	39″ (99 cm) or more
36″ (91cm)	34″ (86cm)	36-37″ (91-94cm)	38″ (96cm)	40″ (101cm)	41″ (104 cm) or more
38″ (96cm)	36″ (91cm)	38-39″ (96-99cm)	40″ (101cm)	42″ (106cm)	43″ (109 cm) or more
40″ (101cm)	38″ (96cm)	40-41″ (101-104cm)	42″ (106cm)	44″ (112cm)	45″ (114 cm) or more

gauge **18-19, 57-59**   measurements **166**

symbolcraft **69-70**

Knitting instructions usually give three measurements: the finished bust (or chest for a man or a child), the finished length and the sleeve width at upper arm.

The finished bust or chest measurement is the width around the entire sweater at the underarm. If you are making a cardigan, the width is determined with the front bands overlapped and buttoned.

The length measurement is the length of the sweater from the highest point of the shoulder to the bottom of the ribbing.

The sleeve width is measured at the upper arm, its widest point. This is after all the increases have been worked and before the cap shaping (if any). This width should fit comfortably around your upper arm.

Different measurements may be given for garments other than sweaters or jackets or those with unusual shaping. These include the waist, hip width, or the distance from sleeve cuff to sleeve cuff.

Ease is the amount of extra room you'll have when you wear your sweater. Ease is determined by subtracting your actual body measurements from the garment's finished measurements. Use the fit captions to find the ease that you desire for your size. For example, if you're making a size 36 (91cm) and the finished bust is 45½ inches (114cm), the ease of the sweater bust is 9½ inches (23cm) which makes the sweater oversized. If you wish to make this sweater, but with less ease, you may want to make the next smaller size, which has a finished bust of 41½ inches (106cm). The ease would then be 5½ inches (15cm).

Schematic drawing

A schematic is a line drawing of the finished pieces drawn to scale, which frequently accompanies knitting instructions. Schematics show the dimensions of the garment's pieces before they are sewn together or finished. Learning to use these drawings can be valuable as you learn more about fit and how to determine the best size for you. They are also helpful when making alterations.

Some instructions show full body pieces; however, when the front and back are similar in shape, only one schematic is given for both pieces. For cardigans, the back and only one of the front pieces are shown. In some instructions only one-half of each piece is shown.

The schematic drawing on the right shows the entire back piece of a cardigan. The numbers along the side indicate the measurement of each section between the dots. The schematic on the far right shows the left front piece of the cardigan.

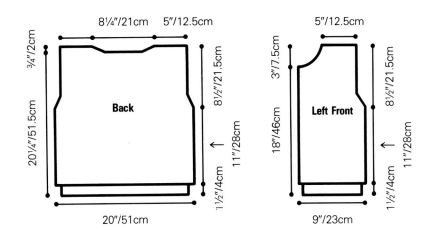

Carefully check the measurements given, as some instructions have drawings which show them from one point to the next, while others give incremental measurements.

Compare the finished bust/chest measurement to the figure on the schematic which shows the width of the piece. In most instructions for pullovers, this figure is one-half of the finished bust/chest measurement. To calculate the finished measurement of a cardigan, add the back width, double the width of the front piece and add the width of one front band.

When schematic drawings are not included, you can draw your own from calculations based on the gauge given in the instructions. Chapter XI explains how to do this.

Materials
All knitting instructions provide a list of materials and tools. Most include yarn types and needle sizes, but may not give you detailed information about the yarn or other accessories needed to complete your garment. Read the pattern carefully to determine what you will need.

Knowing as much as possible about the yarn suggested in the instructions is helpful whether you plan to use it or a substitute. The instructions will specify the amount needed to make your garment. It is wise to buy a little extra, and be sure that all the balls have the same dye lot number to ensure consistent color throughout your project. (The dye lot of a yarn is given on the ball band next to the yarn color number and signifies the "bath" in which that particular ball was dyed.) The weight of the yarn appears in ounces or grams or sometimes both. When planning to use a substitute yarn, information about the length of the yarn in yards or meters is essential. Make sure, since yarns of the same weight may have different lengths, that the total required amount of the substitute yarn equals the total yardage or meters of the original yarn.

Your instructions usually include the brand name of the manufacturer and the name of the yarn. Occasionally the name of the distributor is given, but you may not find it on the ball band of the yarn.

The color name and number of the yarn are also listed. Some instructions give a generic color rather than the specific color name printed on the ball band of the yarn. If more than one yarn or color is given, it is usually identified by a letter or letters shown in parentheses after the color. When only two colors are given, they are often referred to as MC (main color) and CC (contrasting color). When more than two yarns or colors are given, they are most likely expressed as A, B, C, and so on. The same letters will be used to identify these colors in charts. Other information about the yarn such as its type, content and size is sometimes included and is valuable for substitution.

Other than yarn, the next most important information given in your instructions is the suggested needle size. Needles may be expressed in American or metric sizing or sometimes in both. (See the needle conversion chart in Chapter II.) Occasionally, if a special needle length is desirable, it will also be noted. If you can't get the proper gauge using the needles suggested, you should try other sizes until you obtain the correct gauge.

Remaining information could include other tools you will need, such as circular needles, cable needles or bobbins. The instructions should also list any additional items required to finish your piece, such as buttons, tapes, ribbons or elastic. The size and amount of these additions are often specified.

gauge **18-19, 57-59**   yarn label symbols **12**   needle conversion chart **17**   circular needles **16-17**   bobbins **19-20, 85**

ball band **11**   color charts **87-89**   cable needles **18**

Gauge

Gauge (called tension in the UK) is the number of stitches and rows per inch, based on the size of a knitted stitch. The size of a stitch will vary depending on the yarn, the size of your needles and the way you control the yarn.

Controlling the yarn through your fingers is similar to setting the tension dial on a sewing or knitting machine to determine how tightly the thread feeds through the needle. Each knitter has a different way of controlling the yarn, which can further vary depending on the type of yarn and needles used (or

even the knitter's mood). Since no two knitters work alike, one knitter may have to use a different needle size (even as much as two or three times larger or smaller) than another to obtain the same gauge.

Another factor which affects gauge is yarn substitution. A different yarn can alter the gauge as well as produce a different texture. Gauges using the same quality yarns may differ from color to color. For example, a black yarn can have a different gauge than the same type of yarn in white.

Even the type of needle that you use can affect the gauge. You may obtain a slightly different gauge using aluminum needles than you would with plastic ones.

Make sure that you use the same type of yarn, color and needles throughout your project.

If you do not achieve the exact gauge, you will alter the size as well as the texture of your finished garment. That is why it is imperative to check your gauge before beginning every project.

Each swatch was made in stockinette stitch with the same number of stitches and rows, but using three different needle sizes, from smaller to larger. The smaller the needle, the smaller the swatch and the larger the needle, the larger the swatch.

Here are three different pattern stitches which were made using the same needle size and the same number of stitches and rows, but resulting in three different finished sizes.

How to make a gauge swatch

A gauge swatch is a small piece of knitting, made before beginning a garment, that is used to make sure you can obtain the gauge given in the instructions.

Normally the gauge is given for four inches (10cm) square. Your swatch should be at least this size to make measuring easier and to give a more accurate gauge. If the gauge is given for a smaller piece, you will have to calculate the stitches and rows needed to make four inches (10cm). For example, if the gauge is given for one inch, multiply the number of stitches and rows by four; if given for two inches, multiply by two.

Using the needles and yarn suggested, cast on the number of stitches required to get at least four inches (10cm). You may also add two garter stitches at each edge to make it easier to measure between them. (If so, be sure to add these extra stitches when you cast on for your swatch.) Or make a swatch that is four to six stitches and rows larger than the stated gauge and measure the correct number of stitches between pins you place in the work.

Frequently, the gauge is given in stockinette stitch. However, if the gauge calls for a specific pattern stitch, work this stitch for your swatch. It may not always be possible to obtain a four inch (10cm) square when working in a stitch pattern because the swatch has

to be a specific number of stitches. To determine your gauge you can either use the center four inches (10cm), or measure the entire swatch and divide that measurement by the number of stitches to get the number of stitches per inch.

If you are knitting several different stitch patterns in one garment, such as an Aran sweater, and the instructions give one gauge for all the patterns, make one large swatch, incorporating all the stitch patterns.

When working with lacy patterns or yarns that stretch, such as cottons or silks, make your swatch at least six to eight inches (15 to 20cm) square so that both horizontal and vertical stretch are taken into account. Block the swatch before measuring it.

If no pattern is given, you can assume that the gauge is in stockinette stitch.

Instead of binding off the last row of your swatch, place it on a stitch holder or simply cut the yarn and thread it through the stitches before you remove them from the needle. Binding off may pull in the stitches at the top and make measuring your swatch more difficult. However, if it is a lacy pattern or one that tends to spread, you should bind off the last row.

If your gauge matches the one given, you can proceed with your knitting. But if it does not match exactly, you must try another swatch until you can achieve the correct gauge. If your swatch is smaller than the stated

gauge, try larger needles. If it is larger, use smaller needles. Label each swatch with the needle size, number of stitches and gauge for future reference.

With some yarns, such as mohairs and bouclés, the stitches are difficult to count individually because they are less defined. You should therefore cast on the exact number of stitches given in the gauge, work the specified number of rows and measure the entire swatch. Or place stitch markers on either side of the stitches needed for the gauge, and measure between the markers.

You must use a different technique to make a gauge swatch for a garment that is knit in the round, especially if it is stockinette stitch. When you work stockinette in the round, you knit every row, never purling. Since knitting differs slightly from purling, the gauge for straight knitting will differ from that for circular knitting. It is possible to make a swatch without working in the round by knitting every row on a circular or two double-pointed needles as follows: After the first row, cut the yarn. Slide the stitches to the other end of the needle to begin a new row, without turning your work. Repeat at the end of each row.

How to check and measure gauge

It is easiest to measure stitches on a flat, even swatch. You may need to steam or wet block your swatch after taking it off the needles, unless the finishing instructions say not to block. Pin the swatch on a flat surface, such as an ironing board, and do not stretch it.

When the swatch is thoroughly dry, measure the gauge with a tape measure or stitch gauge. Be sure to count the stitches carefully because a variation of even half a stitch will make a significant difference in your finished piece.

On certain fabrics, such as ribs, you may have to stretch the fabric slightly to obtain an accurate gauge. (See Chapter XI on design for information about ribbed gauges.)

Your gauge may change from your swatch to your knitted piece, because your style of knitting may be different when you have only a few stitches on the needle. Check your knitting after working five or six inches (12 or 15cm) to be sure the gauge is accurate. If it has changed, you will have to knit the piece again using the next size needle, measuring again after several inches.

Importance of row gauge

Some knitters believe that the row gauge is not as essential as the stitch gauge. This is not necessarily true. In shaping pieces, such as sleeves, if you work the increases given in the instructions without getting the proper row gauge, you may alter the length.

When you work a sweater from a full body chart, you must work the exact number of rows on the chart. If you do not have the correct row gauge, your finished piece will be too long or too short.

Some sweaters are worked from side to side. In this case, the rows determine the width, making the row gauge essential for proper fit.

Uses for gauge swatches

Not only do gauge swatches help ensure the success of your projects, they can have many other useful purposes. Here are some suggestions:

Use them to practice borders, buttonholes, embroidery and finishes.

Sew squares together to make an afghan or blanket.

Put swatches in a notebook to keep for future reference.

Use them for patches or pockets.

Test the yarn's washability or colorfastness.

Measuring gauge

You can measure your gauge swatch between selvage stitches using a tape measure, as the first two photos show. Or you can use a stitch gauge in the center of your swatch and count the stitches and rows inside the two inch (5cm) right angle opening, as shown in the third photo.

Abbreviations Explained

A

alt—alternate; alternately

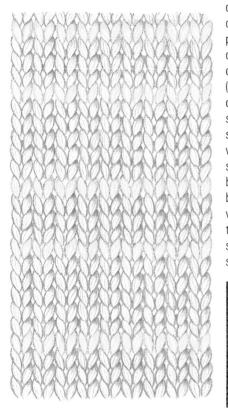

Alternate increases or decreases are used when shaping pieces to create an even slant. For example, in the illustration above, the increases or decreases (highlighted in yellow) are worked alternately every 4th and 6th row. This means the first increase or decrease is worked on the 4th row. Five rows are worked even and then the stitches are increased or decreased again on the next row (the 6th row after the first increase or decrease, or the 10th row from the beginning). Therefore every ten rows you work two sets of increases or decreases.

approx—approximately

B

BC—back cross; back cable (See cable.)

beg—begin; begins; beginning

BO—bind off

BO—bobble (See MB.)

C

C—cable; cross A cable (also called cross) is formed by using an extra needle, usually a cable needle or double-pointed needle, to hold stitches to be crossed either to the front (which crosses them to the left), or to the back (which crosses them to the right). The cable crossing is worked on the right side of the work. The extra needle should be thinner than those you are working with to avoid stretching the stitches. After you have worked the cable, be sure to pull the yarn firmly before working the next stitch to prevent gaps in your work. The illustrations below show examples of a six-stitch front (or left) cable and a six-stitch back (or right) cable.

Front (or left) cable

Back (or right) cable

Front (or left) cable

1 Slip the first three stitches of the cable purlwise to a cable needle and hold them to the front of the work. Be careful not to twist the stitches.

2 Leave the stitches suspended in front of the work, keeping them in the center of the cable needle where they won't slip off. Pull the yarn firmly and knit the next three stitches.

3 Knit the three stitches from the cable needle. If this seems too awkward, return the stitches to the left needle and then knit them.

Back (or right) cable

1 Slip the first three stitches of the cable purlwise to a cable needle and hold them to the back of the work. Be careful not to twist the stitches.

2 Leave the stitches suspended in back of the work, keeping them in the center of the cable needle where they won't slip off. Pull the yarn firmly and knit the next three stitches.

3 Knit the three stitches from the cable needle. If this seems too awkward, return the stitches to the left needle and then knit them.

increasing **37-41**	binding off **47-52**	slip a stitch	right/wrong sides **67-68**
decreasing **42-46**	needles **16-18**	purlwise **46**	

CC—contrasting color When two colors are used, the contrasting color is the yarn which is used as an accent.

ch—chain

cm—centimeter(s)

cn—cable needle

CO—cast on

cont—continue; continuing

cross 2 L—cross two stitches to the left (See cable.)

cross 2 R—cross two stitches to the right (See cable.)

D

dc—double crochet

dec—decrease; decreasing

decs—decreases

DK—double knitting

dp; dpn—double-pointed needle

dtr—double treble

E

EON—end of needle

F

FC—front cross (See cable.)

foll—follow; follows; following

G

g; gr—gram

grp; grps—group; groups

g st—garter stitch

H

hdc—half double crochet

hk—hook

I

in; ins—inch; inches

inc—increase; increasing

incl—including

incs—increases

K

k—knit

k-b; k 1 b—knit stitch in row below (Infrequently used for knit through back loop—see tbl.)

With the yarn at the back, insert the right needle from front to back into the center of the stitch one row below the next stitch on the left needle. Knit this stitch. Slip the top stitch off the left needle without working it.

kfb—knit into the front and back of a stitch

k tbl—knit through back loop

k2tog—knit two together

kwise—knitwise

L

LC—left cross (See cable.)

LH—left-hand

lp; lps—loop; loops

LT—left twist A left twist is formed by crossing one stitch over another. Work this as a two-stitch cable using a cable needle, or use any of the following three methods. All slant to the left.

From the knit side: version A

1 Skip the first stitch on the left needle. With the right needle behind the left one, insert the right needle into the back loop of the second stitch on the left needle. Wrap the yarn knitwise and pull it through.

2 Knit the skipped stitch through the front loop as shown and slip both stitches from the left needle.

From the knit side: version B

Knit the second stitch through the back loop as for version 1. Then knit the first and second stitches together through the back loops.

From the purl side

1 Skip the first stitch on the left needle and purl the second stitch through the back loop as shown.

2 Purl the skipped stitch through the front loop as shown and slip both stitches from the left needle.

M

m—meter(s)

MB—make bobble A bobble is a three-dimensional stitch made by working multiple increases in one stitch, sometimes working a few rows, and then decreasing back to one stitch. The following example is of a five-stitch bobble.

Make bobble

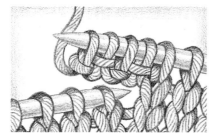

1 Make five stitches in one stitch as follows: [knit the stitch in the front loop and then knit in the back loop without slipping it from the left needle] twice, knit in the front loop once more. Slip the stitch from the left needle.

2 [Turn the work and purl these five stitches as shown, turn the work and knit five] twice.

3 With the left needle, pull the second, third, fourth and fifth stitches one at a time over the first stitch and off the needle. One bobble has been made.

MC—main color When two or more colors are used, the main color is the yarn which is dominant.

mm—millimeter(s)

m1—make one

N

no—number

O

oz—ounce

P

p—purl

pat; pats—pattern; patterns

p-b—purl stitch in the row below

1 With the yarn at the front, insert the right needle from back to front into the center of the stitch one row below the stitch on the left needle. Purl this stitch. Slip the top stitch off the left needle without working it.

pfb—purl into the front and back of a stitch

pnso—pass next stitch over

psso—pass slip stitch over

p tbl—purl through back loop

p2tog—purl two together

pwise—purlwise

R

RC—right cross (See cable.)

rem—remain; remaining

rep—repeat

rev St st—reverse stockinette stitch

RH—right-hand

rib—ribbing

rnd; rnds—round; rounds

RS—right side

RT—right twist A right twist is formed by crossing one stitch over another. Work this as a two-stitch cable using a cable needle, or use any of the following three methods. All slant to the right.

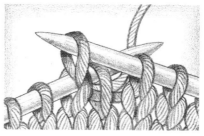

From the knit side: version A

1 Knit two stitches together through front loops. Do not slip them from the left needle.

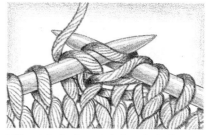

2 Then knit the first stitch through the front loop as shown. Slip both stitches from the left needle.

From the knit side: version B

Skip first stitch on left needle. Insert right needle into front loop of second stitch on left needle. Wrap yarn knitwise and pull it through, do not slip stitch off needle. Knit skipped stitch through front loop and slip both stitches from left needle.

From the purl side

1 Skip the first stitch on the left needle and purl the second stitch through the front loop as shown.

2 Purl the skipped stitch through the front loop as shown and slip both stitches from the left needle.

S

sc—single crochet

sk—skip

SKP—slip one, knit one, pass slip stitch over

sl—slip

sl st—slip stitch

sp; sps—space; spaces

ssk—slip, slip, knit

st; sts—stitch; stitches

St st—stockinette stitch

T

tbl—through back loop

tch; t-ch—turning chain

tog—together

tr—treble

trtr—triple treble

W

WS—wrong side

won—wool over needle

wrn—wool round needle

wyib—with yarn in back

wyif—with yarn in front

Y

yb (or ybk)—yarn to the back

yf (or yfwd)—yarn to the front (or forward)

yfon—yarn forward and over needle (See yarn overs.)

yfrn—yarn forward and round needle (See yarn overs.)

yo—yarn over   A yarn over is a decorative increase made by wrapping the yarn around the needle. There are various ways to make a yarn over depending on where it is placed.

yo twice; yo2—yarn over two times

yon—yarn over needle (See yarn overs.)

yrn—yarn round needle (See yarn overs.)

Yarn overs

Between two knit stitches

Bring the yarn from the back of the work to the front between the two needles. Knit the next stitch, bringing the yarn to the back over the right needle as shown.

Between a knit and a purl stitch

Bring the yarn from the back to the front between the two needles, then to the back over the right needle and to the front again as shown. Purl the next stitch.

Between a purl and a knit stitch

Leave the yarn at the front of the work. Knit the next stitch, bringing the yarn to the back over the right needle as shown.

Between two purl stitches

Leave the yarn at the front of the work. Bring the yarn to the back over the right needle and to the front again as shown. Purl the next stitch.

At the beginning of a knit row

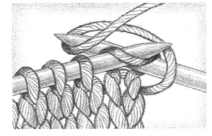

Keep the yarn at the front of the work. Insert the right needle knitwise into the first stitch on the left needle. Bring the yarn over the right needle to the back and knit the next stitch, holding the yarn over with your thumb if necessary.

At the beginning of a purl row

To work a yarn over at the beginning of a purl row, keep the yarn at the back of the work. Insert the right needle purlwise into the first stitch on the left needle. Purl the stitch.

Multiple yarn overs

1 In multiple yarn overs (two or more), wrap the yarn around the needle as for a single yarn over, then wrap the yarn around the needle once more (or as many times as indicated). Work the next stitch on the left needle.

2 Alternate knitting and purling into the multiple yarn over on the subsequent row, always knitting the last stitch on a purl row and purling the last stitch on a knit row.

---

wyib, yb, ybk **35**   purlwise/knitwise **66**   slip a stitch **46**   stockinette **22, 34**   right/wrong sides **67-68**

wyif, yf, yfwd **35**   SKP **43**   ssk **43**   front/back loops **37**

Knitting Terminology

A

above markers: Knitting worked after the point where stitch markers have been placed.

above rib: Knitting worked after the last row of ribbing.

after . . . number of rows have been worked: Continue working as instructed after completing the designated number of rows.

along neck: Generally used when picking up stitches at an unshaped, or straight, neck edge.

around neck: Generally used when picking up stitches at a shaped, or curved, neck edge.

as established: Continue to work the pattern as previously described.

as foll: Work the instructions that follow.

as for back (front): Work an identical piece to the back (or the front).

as to knit: Work the stitch as if you were knitting.

as to purl: Work the stitch as if you were purling.

AT SAME TIME: Work the instructions that immediately follow this term simultaneously with those that immediately precede it.

attach: Join a new strand of yarn.

B

back edge: Any edge on the back piece of the garment.

beg and end as indicated: Used when working with charts. Begin the row of knitting at the point on the chart which is indicated for your size by an arrow or straight line and the term "beg" (beginning). Continue working the chart as instructed, knitting the last stitch at the point indicated by another arrow or straight line and the term "end." (See chart knitting.)

bind off . . . sts at beg of next . . . rows: Often used in armhole and shoulder shaping. Stitches are almost always bound off at the beginning of a row. Therefore, after binding off the designated number of stitches, work to the end of the row, turn the work and bind off the same number of stitches at the beginning of the next row.

bind off center . . . sts: Determine the center stitches and place markers on either side of the center stitches, if desired, on the needles. Work the next row to the first marker, join a new ball of yarn and bind off the center stitches, then work to the end of the row with the new ball of yarn.

bind off from each neck edge: A term used when both sides of the inside neck edge are shaped simultaneously after binding off the center stitches. (See neck shaping.)

bind off in rib (or pat): Always bind off stitches as they appear. That is, knit the knit stitches and purl the purl stitches as you bind them off. (See binding off.)

bind off loosely: Do not pull the yarn too tightly when binding off. Or, you may use a needle one size larger on the bind-off row. (See binding off.)

bind off rem sts each side: A term usually used for the remaining stitches of each shoulder after shaping a neck. After you have completed all the shaping, bind off the stitches that remain on one side, then bind off the remaining stitches on the other side. (See binding off.)

block pieces: The process of laying flat completed pieces of knitting to even and smooth the stitches and to give them their permanent shape. (See blocking.)

body of sweater is worked in one piece to underarm: A term used when using a circular needle to knit a sweater with no side seams up to the underarm. (See circular knitting.)

both sides at once (or at same time): A term used after an opening has been made on a row, such as for a placket. When stitches have been bound off and you have two separate pieces on one needle, work both sides simultaneously with separate balls of yarn. That is, work one row on the first side, then work the corresponding row on the second side with the second ball of yarn. Then turn the work.

C

cap shaping: The shaped part of the sleeve above the armhole which will fit into the armhole of the sweater. (See sleeve shaping.)

carry yarn loosely across back of work: In color knitting, let the yarn not in use span loosely across the wrong side of the work until you need to use it again. (See color stranding.)

cast on . . . sts at beg of next . . . rows: When adding two or more stitches at the edges of a piece, cast on the designated number of stitches before beginning the row, work the cast-on stitches, then work to the end of the row. Turn the work and cast on the same number of stitches at the beginning of the next row. (See casting on.)

cast on . . . sts over bound-off sts: Usually refers to making buttonholes. Work to where the stitches from the previous row were bound off. Cast on the specified number of stitches, then work to the end of the row. (See buttonholes.)

center back (front) neck: The point that marks the center of the back (or front) neck.

change to smaller (larger) needles: Proceed with the work using smaller (or larger) needles than those used previously.

cont in pat: Continue to work the pattern as previously described.

cont in this way: Continue to work in the manner previously described.

D

directions are for smallest (smaller) size with larger sizes in parentheses: Many knitting instructions are written for more than one size. Usually, the number referring to the smallest (smaller) size is the number before the parentheses. The numbers indicating larger sizes appear inside the parentheses in ascending order.

discontinue pat: Stop working the pattern immediately preceding and continue as directed.

do not press: Do not use an iron to press or steam the knitted fabric. (See blocking.)

do not turn work: Keep the work facing in the same direction as the row you have just completed.

E

each end (side): Work designated stitches at both the beginning and the end of a row.

easing in any fullness: In seaming, gather in any extra fabric evenly. (See seaming.)

end last rep: After completing a full repeat of a pattern and not enough stitches remain to complete another repeat, end the pattern repeat as directed.

end with a RS (WS) row: The last row worked is a right side (wrong side) row.

every other row: When shaping, work one row between each increase or decrease row.

F

fasten off: When binding off, pull the yarn through the last loop on the needle to finish the piece and prevent unraveling. (See binding off.)

finished bust: The circumference of a garment at the bustline after the front and back have been sewn together.

finished bust (buttoned): A term usually used for cardigans or jackets to indicate the circumference at the bustline after the two fronts and the back have been sewn together and the fronts are buttoned.

from beg: A term used when measuring from the cast-on edge of the piece or beginning of the knitted piece.

front edge: Any edge on the front piece of the garment.

full-fashioned: A term used in ready-to-wear which means deliberately showing decreases worked in stockinette stitch a few stitches from the edge. (See decreasing.)

G

gauge: The number of stitches and rows per inch (centimeter). (See gauge.)

grafting: Weaving two edges together that have not been bound off, resulting in an invisible joining. (See seaming.)

H

hold to front (back) of work: A term usually referring to stitches placed on a cable needle which are held to the front (or the back) of the work as it faces you. (See cables.)

I

inc . . . sts evenly across row: Increase the stitches at even intervals across the row. (See increasing.)

inc sts into pat: When increasing, work the added stitches into the established pattern. (See increasing.)

in same way (manner): Repeat the process that was previously described.

it is essential to get proper row gauge: When instructions are written for a specific number of rows (such as in garments with large motifs), you must obtain the specified row gauge to get the correct length. (See gauge.)

J

join: When used in circular knitting, the process of uniting the first and last stitch of a round. (See circular knitting.)

join 2nd ball (skein) of yarn: A phrase used when dividing the work into two sections (such as for placket or neck shaping), where each section is worked with a separate ball (or skein) of yarn. (See joining yarns.)

join, taking care not to twist sts: When casting on in circular knitting, join the first and the last cast-on stitch to form a circle, making sure that the stitches are not twisted on the needle. (See circular knitting.)

K

k the knit sts and p the purl sts (as they face you): A phrase used when a pattern of knit and purl stitches has been established and will continue for a determined length (such as ribbing). Work the stitches as they face you: Knit the knit stitches and purl the purl stitches. (See shape of a knit or purl stitch.)

k the purl sts and p the knit sts: A phrase used when a pattern of knit and purl stitches will alternate on the following row or rows (such as in a seed stitch pattern). Work the stitches opposite to how they face you: purl the knit stitches and knit the purl stitches. (See shape of a knit or purl stitch.)

keep careful count of rows: Advice usually given with intricate patterns or shaping in which the row count is important. Keep track either by writing down each row as you complete it or by using a row counter. (See row counters.)

keeping to pat (or maintaining pat): A term used when new instructions are given (such as shaping), but the established pattern must be continued.

knitwise (or as to knit): Insert the needle into the stitch as if you were going to knit it.

L

left: Refers to the left-hand side of the garment as you are wearing it.

lower edge: The bottom edge of the piece, usually the cast-on edge.

M

matching colors: Work the stitches in the same color sequence as on the previous row.

multiple of . . . sts: Used when working a pattern. The total number of stitches should be divisible by the number of stitches in one pattern repeat.

multiple of . . . sts plus . . . extra: Used when working a pattern. The total number of stitches should be divisible by the number of stitches in one pattern repeat, plus the extra stitches (added only once).

N

next row (RS), or (WS): The row following the one just worked will be a right side (or wrong side) row.

O

on all foll rows: A direction that applies to all the rows that follow the row just worked.

P

pick up and k: Used in finishing to refer to pulling up loops through stitches and rows of a finished edge with the stated knitting needles and a ball of yarn to begin an edge or a new piece. (See picking up stitches.)

piece measures approx: A term used when a specified number of rows must be worked, as in shaping or pattern work. The piece should measure the stated amount within one-fourth inch (6mm) if you have the correct row gauge.

place marker(s): Slide a stitch marker either onto the needle (where it is slipped every row) or attach to a stitch, where it remains as a guide. (See stitch markers.)

preparation row: A row that sets up the stitch pattern but is not part of the pattern repeat.

pull up a lp: Often used in crochet, this term in knitting signifies drawing a new stitch (or loop) through the knit fabric. (See picking up stitches.)

purlwise: Insert the needle into the stitch as if you were going to purl it.

R

rep between *'s: Repeat the instructions which fall between the two asterisks.

rep from * around: In circular knitting, repeat the instructions that begin at the asterisk, ending at the joining.

rep from *, end . . . : Repeat the instructions that begin at the asterisk as many times as you can work full repeats of the pattern, then end the row as directed.

rep from * to end: Repeat the instructions that begin at the asterisk, ending the row with a full repeat of the pattern.

rep from . . . row: Repeat the pattern rows previously worked, beginning with the row specified.

rep inc (or dec): Repeat the increase (or decrease) previously described.

rep . . . times more: Repeat a direction the designated number of times (not counting the first time you work it).

reverse pat placement: A term used for garments such as cardigans where the right and left fronts have symmetrical patterns. Generally, the instructions for only one piece are given, and you must work patterns for the second piece in the opposite order.

reversing shaping: A term used for garments such as cardigans where shaping for the right and left fronts is identical, but reversed. The instructions for only one piece are given and you must work the shaping for the second piece in the opposite order.

right: Refers to the right-hand side of the garment as you are wearing it.

right side (or RS): Usually refers to the surface of the work that will face outside when the garment is worn.

row: A horizontal line of stitches formed by transferring all the stitches from one needle to the other. (See structure of knitting.)

row 2 and all WS (even-numbered) rows: A term used when all the wrong side or even-numbered rows are worked the same.

S

same as: Follow the instructions given in another section or piece of the garment.

same length as: A term used when two or more pieces of a garment are equal in length, and the measurement of one has already been given.

schematic: A scale drawing showing specific measurements of all the pieces of a garment before they are sewn together and finished. (See designing.)

selvage st: An extra stitch (or stitches) at the edge of a piece used either to make seaming easier or as a decorative finish. (See selvages.)

set in sleeves: Sew the sleeves into the armholes. (See finishing.)

sew shoulder seam, including neckband: A phrase used when seaming a shoulder before working a neckband. After the neckband is completed, sew the open shoulder seam along with the side edges of the neckband. (See finishing.)

sew top of sleeves between markers: A term generally used when the garment has no armhole shaping (such as for drop shoulders), and markers must be used to denote the depth of the armhole. Center the sleeve at the shoulder seam, with the ends of the sleeve top at the markers, and sew it to the front and back of the garment. (See finishing.)

short row: A technique, generally used in shaping, to add rows in one segment of a piece without decreasing the number of stitches on the needle. (See short rows.)

side to side: When a piece is worked horizontally from side seam to side seam instead of vertically from the lower edge.

sleeve width at upper arm: The measurement of the finished sleeve at its widest point, which, when seamed, fits around the widest part of the arm. (See sleeve shaping.)

slightly stretched: A term often used when measuring stitch patterns that tend to pull in, such as ribbing or cables. A more accurate gauge of the pattern is obtained when the stitches are pulled apart slightly. (See ribbing.)

slip marker: To keep the stitch marker in the same position from one row to the next, transfer it from one needle to the other as you work each row.

slip marker at beg of every rnd: In circular knitting, slip the marker from one needle to the other every time you begin a new round. (See circular knitting.)

slip sts to a holder: Transfer the stitches from the needle to a stitch holder. (See stitch holder.)

swatch: A sample of knitting used to check the gauge or to try out a stitch or colorwork pattern before knitting the garment. (See gauge.)

sweater is worked in one piece: Work all the parts of a sweater—the front, back and sleeves—as one piece.

sweater is worked in two pieces: Work the front half of the sweater (including the front half of the sleeves) in one piece and the back half in another.

T

through both thicknesses: A term usually used in seaming when working through two pieces of fabric at one time. (See seaming.)

through . . . row: Work up to and include the designated row. This term is usually used when knitting from a chart. (See chart knitting.)

to . . . row: Work up to but do not include the specified row. This term is usually used when knitting from a chart. (See chart knitting.)

total length: The length of a garment after finishing, including ribbing or edging and any shoulder shaping.

turning: The process of switching your knitted piece from right side to wrong side or vice versa to work a new or partial row.

turning ridge: A row of raised stitches (often purl stitches on stockinette stitch) which indicates where the piece will fold in or out, as in a hem. (See hems.)

twist yarns on WS to prevent holes: A term used in colorwork when changing from one color to the next across a row. Twist the old and the new yarns around each other to prevent a hole in your work. (See color knitting.)

U

use a separate bobbin for each block of color: When working intarsia (large color block patterns), where the yarn cannot be carried across large areas of color, use a bobbin for each separate block of color. (See color knitting.)

W

weave in ends: In finishing, loose ends must be worked in so that they will not unravel. (See finishing.)

when armhole measures: This term is used to denote the point in a sweater at which the neck, shoulder or placket shaping begins and is measured from the beginning of the armhole shaping.

weave or twist yarns not in use: In Fair Isle knitting, when you must carry yarns for more than a few stitches, weave or twist yarns that are not being used around the working yarn to avoid long, loose strands. (See color knitting.)

width from sleeve edge (cuff) to sleeve edge (cuff): When the body and sleeves of a sweater are knit in one piece, this term refers to the width measurement from the edge of one sleeve, across the shoulder and neck edges, to the edge of the second sleeve.

with RS facing: A term often used when picking up stitches. The right side of the work must be facing you and the wrong side facing away from you.

with WS facing: A term used when the wrong side of the work must be facing you and the right side facing away from you.

work across sts on holder: Work the stitches directly from the stitch holder, or transfer the stitches from the holder to a knitting needle and then work them.

work back and forth as with straight needles: When knitting on a circular needle, turn the work at the end of every row instead of joining it and working in rounds.

work buttonholes opposite markers: When markers for buttons have been placed on the button band, work the buttonholes opposite these markers on the other band so that they will correspond to the buttons. (See buttonholes.)

work even (straight): Continue in the established pattern without working any shaping.

working in pat: Follow the instructions for the pattern, whether written or graphed.

work in rounds: In circular knitting, the process of working a piece in which the ends have been joined and which has no seam. (See circular knitting.)

working needle: The needle being used to make new stitches.

working yarn: The yarn being used to make new stitches.

work rep of chart . . . times: When working a pattern from a chart, work the stitches in the repeat as many times as indicated. (See chart knitting.)

work to correspond: A term used when instructions are given for one piece, and a similar second piece must be made to correspond. There are usually some exceptions on the second piece such as reversing shaping or pattern placement.

work to end: Work the established pattern to the end of the row.

work to . . . sts before center: Work the row to a specified number of stitches before the center of the row, which is generally indicated by a stitch marker.

work to last . . . sts: Work across the row until the specified number of stitches remains on the left needle.

work until . . . sts from bind-off (or on RH needle): After binding off, work until the specified number of stitches remains on the right needle.

wrong side (or WS): Usually refers to the surface of the work that will face inside when the garment is worn.

Symbolcraft

Symbolcraft is a universal form of knitting instructions. Instead of writing out a stitch pattern with words and abbreviations, symbols are used.

Each symbol represents the stitch as it appears on the right side of the work. For example, the symbol for a knit stitch is a vertical line and the symbol for a purl stitch is a horizontal one. On right-side rows, you work the stitches as they appear on the chart—knitting the vertical lines and purling the horizontal ones. When reading wrong-side rows, work the opposite of what is shown; that is, purl the vertical lines and knit the horizontal ones.

In symbolcraft charts, each square represents one stitch and each line of squares equals one row. The rows are read from bottom to top. Usually, the odd-numbered rows are listed on the right-hand side of the chart. Unless otherwise stated, these are always right-side rows and read horizontally from right to left. The numbers on the left-hand side of the chart are wrong-

Symbolcraft chart

Selvage or edge stitch

St st: Stockinette stitch (knit on RS, purl on WS)

rev St st: Reverse stockinette stitch (purl on RS, knit on WS)

yo: Yarn over

twisted St st: Knit stitch through back loop on RS; purl stitch through the back loop on WS

twisted rev St st: Purl stitch through back loop on RS; knit stitch through back loop on WS

sl st knitwise: With yarn in back, slip stitch knitwise on RS; with yarn in front, slip stitch knitwise on the WS

sl st purlwise: With yarn in back, slip stitch purlwise on RS; with yarn in front, slip stitch purlwise on WS

sl st purlwise (to create a float): With yarn in front, slip stitch purlwise on RS; with yarn in back, slip stitch purlwise on WS

k1-b: Knit stitch in row below on RS; p1-b: purl stitch in row below on WS

p1-b: Purl stitch in row below on RS; k1-b: knit stitch in row below on WS

m1: Make one stitch as follows: on RS, insert left needle from front to back under horizontal strand between stitch just worked and next stitch on left needle. Knit this strand through the back loop. On WS, insert left needle from back to front under strand as before and purl it through back loop.

Make one stitch to form an eyelet as follows: on the RS, insert left needle from front to back under horizontal strand between stitch just worked and next stitch on left needle. Knit this strand. On WS, insert left needle from back to front under strand as before and purl it.

inc 1 st: Increase one stitch as follows: knit in front then in back of stitch on RS; purl in back then in front on WS

Increase one stitch to the right as follows: with right needle, pick up next stitch on left needle in row below. Place loop on left needle and knit it.

Increase one stitch to the left as follows: with left needle, pick up next stitch on right needle one row below and knit it

Increase three stitches in two as follows: insert right needle knitwise into next two stitches on left needle. Knit one, purl one, knit one. Drop loops off left needle.

k2tog: On RS, knit two stitches together. p2tog: On WS, purl two stitches together.

SKP: On RS, slip one stitch. Knit next stitch and pass slip stitch over knit stitch. On WS, slip next two stitches knitwise. Slip these two stitches back to left needle without twisting them and purl them together through the back loops.

ssk: On RS, slip next two stitches knitwise. Insert tip of left needle into fronts of these two stitches and knit them together. On WS, slip one stitch, purl one stitch, then pass slip stitch over purl stitch.

p2tog: On RS, purl two stitches together. k2tog: On WS, knit two stitches together.

p2tog tbl: On RS, purl two stitches together through the back loops. k2tog tbl: on WS, knit two stitches together through back loops.

k3tog: On RS, knit three stitches together. p3tog: On WS, purl three stitches together.

p3tog: On RS, purl three stitches together. k3tog: On WS, knit three stitches together.

sk2p: On RS, slip one stitch, knit two stitches together. Pass slipped stitch over two stitches knit together. On WS, slip two stitches to right needle as if knitting two together. Slip next stitch knitwise. Slip all stitches to left needle without twisting them. Purl these three stitches together through back loops.

k4tog: On RS, knit four stitches together. p4tog: On WS, purl four stitches together.

dot-knot stitch: Insert RH needle from front to back under horizontal strand between 1st and 2nd sts on LH needle, wrap yarn and draw through a loop loosely; insert RH needle between same sts above horizontal strand, draw through another loop loosely; bring yarn to front between needles and purl the first st on LH needle; with point of LH needle, pass the 1st loop over the 2nd loop and the purled st and off needle; pass the 2nd loop over the purled st and off needle.

peppercorn st: K next st, [sl st just knit back to LH needle and knit it again tbl] 3 times.

make bobble: [K1, p1] twice into next st, turn, p4, turn, k4, turn [p2tog] twice, turn, k2tog.

make bobble: [K1, p1, k1, p1, k1] in the same st, making 5 sts from one; then pass the 4th, 3rd, 2nd and first over the last st made.

make bobble: [K1, p1] 3 times, k1 in one st (7 sts made), then pass 2nd, 3rd, 4th, 5th, 6th and 7th st over last st made.

abbreviations explained **60-63**	selvages **194-5** yarn overs **63**	front/back loops **37** right/wrong sides **67-68**	slip a stitch knitwise/purlwise **46**	increasing **37-41** decreasing **42-46**	bobbles **62**

side rows, and are read from left to right. If you are working on a circular needle in rounds, you would read all the rows from right to left. (See chart knitting.)

Sometimes only a single repeat of the pattern is charted. But if the pattern is complex, more than one repeat will be shown so that you can see how the finished motif will look. Heavy lines are usually drawn through the entire chart to indicate the repeat. These lines are the equivalent of an asterisk (*) or brackets [ ] used in written instructions.

Symbolcraft: cables

2-st right twist: On RS rows, k2tog leaving sts on LH needle, k first st again, sl both sts from needle. On WS rows, wyif skip next st and purl the 2nd st, then purl skipped st, sl both sts from needle tog.

2-st left twist: With RH needle behind LH needle, skip the first st and k 2nd st tbl, insert RH needle into backs of both sts, k2tog tbl.

2-st right purl twist: Sl 1 st to cn and hold to back of work, k1, p1 from cn.

2-st left purl twist: Sl 1 st to cn and hold to front of work, p1, k1 from cn.

3-st right twist: Sl 2 sts to cn and hold to back of work, k1, then k2 from cn.

3-st left twist: Sl 1 st to cn and hold to front of work, k2, k1 from cn.

3-st right cable: Sl 1 st to cn and hold to back of work, k2, k1 from cn.

3-st left cable: Sl 2 sts to cn and hold to front of work, k1, k2 from cn.

3-st right purl cable: Sl 1 st to cn and hold to back of work, k2, p1 from cn.

 3-st left purl cable: Sl 2 sts to cn and hold to front of work, p1, k2 from cn.

4-st right cable: Sl 2 sts to cn and hold to back of work k2, k2 from cn.

4-st left cable: Sl 2 sts to cn and hold to front of work, k2, k2 from cn.

4-st right purl cable: Sl 1 st to cn and hold to back of work, p3, k1 from cn.

4-st left purl cable: Sl 3 sts to cn and hold to front of work, k1, p3 from cn.

4-st right purl cable: Sl 1 st to cn and hold to back of work, k3, p1 from cn.

4-st left purl cable: Sl 3 sts to cn and hold to front of work, p1, k3 from cn.

4-st wrap: Wyib sl 4, wyif sl same 4 sts to LH needle, wyib sl same 4 sts.

5-st right cable: Sl 3 sts to cn and hold to back of work, k2, sl purl st from cn to LH needle and purl it, k2 from cn.

 5-st right purl cable: Sl 2 sts to cn and hold to back of work, k3, p2 from cn.

5-st left purl cable: Sl 3 sts to cn and hold to front of work, p2, k3 from cn.

tie st: Sl 5 sts to cn and hold to back of work, wrap yarn around these 5 sts 3 times, return sts to LH needle, then work them as foll: K1, p3, k1.

6-st right cable: Sl 3 sts to cn and hold to back of work, k3, k3 from cn.

6-st left cable: Sl 3 sts to cn and hold to front of work, k3, k3 from cn.

wrapped sts: K2, p2, k2, sl the last 6 sts worked onto cn and wrap yarn 4 times counterclockwise around these 6 sts; then sl the 6 sts back to RH needle.

12-st right cable: Sl 6 sts to cn and hold to back of work, k6, k6 from cn.

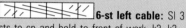

12-st left cable: Sl 6 sts to cn and hold to front of work, k6, k6 from cn.

V. Correcting Errors

Correcting Errors

Learning to correct mistakes is as necessary to knitting as learning to knit and purl—and most errors are easy to rectify. Some common problems for beginners include stitches that are backwards, unwanted, dropped or incomplete. If you are a beginner, check your work often because it is easiest to correct mistakes soon after you've made them.

How you fix a mistake will depend on how quickly you discover it. If you have worked only a row or two beyond the error, you can work back to it stitch by stitch. If you don't discover the error until you have worked many more rows, you must unravel to the mistake and rework from that point. However, you may be able to drop individual stitches above the error and unravel or "ladder" them back to the mistake, instead of unraveling several rows.

To unravel, use a contrasting yarn or stitch marker to mark the row with the error. Remove the knitting needle and pull out the stitches to that row. When working an intricate stitch pattern, keep track of the number of rows you unravel so that you won't lose your place.

After unraveling, put the stitches back onto a smaller needle—it will be easier to slip it into the loops. Make sure that the stitches are not backwards as you return them to the needle. Work the stitches on the next row with the correct needle size.

Remember that certain novelty yarns and mohair are not easy to unravel. Use scissors to gently snip the hairs of fuzzy yarns as you unravel.

Twisted stitches—knit and purl

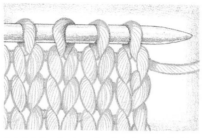

A twisted or backwards stitch is created either by wrapping the yarn incorrectly on the previous row or by dropping a stitch and returning it to the needle backwards.

To correct the backwards knit stitch, knit it through the back loop.

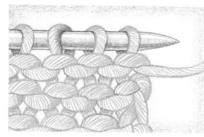

A backwards purl stitch looks different from a regular purl stitch in that the back loop is nearer the tip of the needle than the front loop.

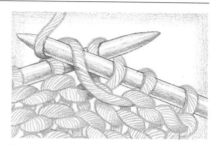

To correct the backwards purl stitch, purl it through the back loop.

Picking up a dropped knit stitch

1 This method is used when a knit stitch has dropped only one row. Work to where the stitch was dropped. Be sure that the loose strand is behind the dropped stitch.

2 Insert the right needle from front to back into the dropped stitch and under the loose horizontal strand behind.

3 Insert the left needle from the back into the dropped stitch on the right needle, and pull this stitch over the loose strand.

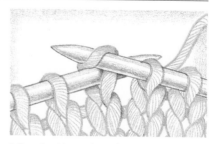

4 Transfer this newly made stitch back to the left needle by inserting the left needle from front to back into the stitch and slipping it off the right needle.

Picking up a dropped purl stitch

1 This method is used when a purl stitch has been dropped only one row. Work to the dropped purl stitch. Be sure that the loose horizontal strand is in front of the dropped stitch.

2 Insert the right needle from back to front into the dropped stitch, and then under the loose horizontal strand.

3 With the left needle, lift the dropped stitch over the horizontal strand and off the right needle.

4 Transfer the newly made purl stitch back to the left needle by inserting the left needle from front to back into the stitch and slipping it off the right needle.

Picking up a running knit and purl stitch

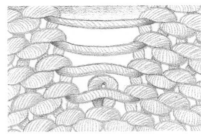

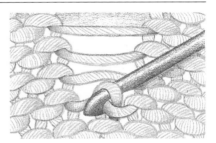

A running stitch is one that has dropped more than one row. It is easiest to pick it up with a crochet hook. For a knit stitch, be sure the loose horizontal strands are in back of the dropped stitch.

Insert the hook into the stitch from front to back. Catch the first horizontal strand and pull it through. Continue up until you have worked all the strands. Place the newest stitch on the left needle, making sure it is not backwards.

Before picking up a dropped purl stitch several rows below, be sure that the loose horizontal strands are in front of the stitch.

Insert the hook into the stitch from back to front. Pull the loose strand through the stitch. Continue up until you have worked all the strands. Place the newest stitch on the left needle, making sure it is not backwards.

Incomplete knit and purl stitches

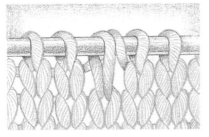

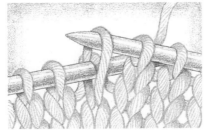

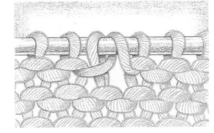

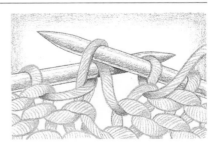

An incomplete knit or purl stitch is one where the yarn is wrapped around the needle but not pulled through the stitch. The illustration above shows an incomplete stitch from the previous purl row.

Work to the incomplete stitch. Insert the right needle from back to front into the stitch on the left needle and pull it over the strand and off the needle.

This illustration shows an incomplete stitch from the previous knit row.

Insert the right needle into the stitch on the left needle and pull it over the strand and off the needle.

An extra stitch at the edge

If you bring the yarn back over the top of the needle at the beginning of a knit row, the first stitch will have two loops instead of one, as shown.

To avoid creating this extra stitch, keep the yarn under the needle when taking it to the back to knit the first stitch.

At the beginning of a purl row, if the yarn is at the back, and then brought to the front under the needle, the first stitch will have two loops instead of one, as shown.

To avoid making these two loops, the yarn should be at the front before you purl the first stitch.

Unraveling stitch by stitch

Knit stitches Keep the yarn at the back. Insert left needle into the stitch one row below the stitch on right needle. Drop stitch and pull the yarn to undo it.

Purl stitches Keep the yarn at the front. Insert left needle into the stitch one row below the stitch on right needle. Drop stitch and pull the yarn to undo it.

Unraveling rows

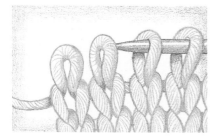  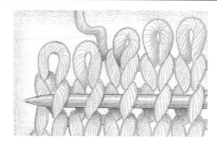 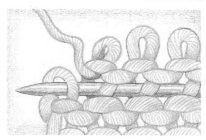

If you need to unravel one or more rows, you must put the stitches back onto the needle correctly. Make sure the working yarn is at the left side. Using a smaller needle, insert it from back to front into each stitch across the row.

To put purl stitches back on the needle after unraveling them, first make sure the working yarn is at the left side. Insert a smaller needle from front to back into each stitch across the row.

If you are concerned about dropping stitches, you can weave the right needle under the first loop and over the second loop of each knit stitch along the entire row. Pull the working yarn to unravel all the stitches above those on the needle.

You can also use this method with purl stitches. Insert the needle under the first loop and over the second loop of each purl stitch along the entire row. Pull the working yarn to unravel all the stitches.

VI. Circular and Double-Pointed Knitting

Circular and Double-Pointed Knitting

Although almost certainly preceded by back-and-forth knitting, circular knitting simply must have been around since prehistoric times. We know from the Bible that Jesus wore a seamless robe that many argue was knitted, and Penelope is said to be knitting in the *Odyssey*. The trail seems to lead back through Egypt, and from there it disappears from our history books. Knitting in the round was first documented in the Knitting Madonna paintings by various Italian artists in the mid to late 1300's. They depict Mary knitting around on four double-pointed needles.

Somewhere along the way, some intelligent knitter (and just show me an unintelligent knitter!) tumbled to the conclusion that purling back on every second row—in order to achieve a smooth surface—could be avoided by working *all* rows in *all* knit in the same direction, with smoothness on one side and bumps on the other. Almost certainly, the instinctive solution to this conundrum must have been to use three needles for holding the stitches in a convenient triangle from which they could be worked by a fourth needle, thus freeing needle number one to dig into the stitches on the second needle, and so on around and around. Eureka! No more purling; no more sewing up of seams; no more peering over the top of the needles to see where you are (the right side of the work always faces you). This solution must have held sway for literally thousands of years and produced all manner of

handsome and comfortable seamless circular caps, mittens and stockings, let alone the forerunner of our current sweaters. Knitting around on a multiple of "pins" (as they were called) naturally required a modest hedgehog of sharpish needles which had to be switched frequently on every round, with a tightening of the first stitch on each needle to prevent unsightly vertical areas. Large garments may have required as many as eight to 10 double-pointed needles. Often the sly needles would slip away into the depths of a chair—or worse, onto the forest floor, the hayfield or into the drink. They must have sighed patiently, all those knitters through all those thousands of years, and wished for one long flexible needle with points at either end. Possibly they were calmed down with soothing promises ... all the way to the 20th century. . . .

I rejoice to have been born just in time for the appearance of the circular knitting needle in my dear Auntie Pete's knitting bag on a sandy Cornish beach in 1918. My mother and her sisters could hardly believe their eyes, and I (aged eight) was privileged to knit a few stitches with it. The center section of the needle was cabled wire, of which one strand had freed itself so that the stitches caught on it. We soon solved this problem by resourcefully reversing the needle and holding the faulty bit in the other hand. And who cared about such a relatively slight blemish on such a magical tool? Imagine—all the advantages of seamless knitting without the sunburst array of needle points sticking out in all directions.

So, I grew up with circular needles. Perhaps I did not improve, but they certainly did. Their manufacturers have replaced the cabled wire with nylon, smoothed the joins, provided all necessary sizes, and, quite recently, all necessary lengths—from 11½ inches (29cm) for cuffs, socks and mittens to 60 inches (4.6m) for enormous lace tablecloths. I find the 16 inch (40cm) and 24 inch (60cm) lengths sufficient for my needs, and have had a Shetland wool shawl of 600 stitches fit happily and comfortably onto a 24 inch (60cm) needle.

Naturally, I do work garter stitch back and forth (but on a circular needle; no spare needle to lose, and no worry about poking fellow travelers in the ribs), but I can think of few hand-knitted objects which are not their most pleasant when knitted round and round. Just think of the joy and delight of working a Fair Isle or textured pattern with the right side always under the knitter's eagle eye. Forced to name a disadvantage, I can find only one: the current fashion for intarsia, or motif knitting, is not possible when worked in the round. However, I do not feel in the least deprived, as this type of color-pattern knitting has little appeal to me. I prefer the Scandinavian and Fair Isle techniques of carrying only two colors at a time, and no carry greater than five stitches. Following these edicts, one can fall into a soothing and beguiling knitting rhythm: manual and mental therapy. Also—not a disadvantage, but

a potential pitfall—when working a swatch to determine your gauge: If the garment is to be knitted in the round, the swatch should also be worked in the round. Very few knitters achieve an absolutely identical gauge in both knit and purl. Your circular swatch may take the form of a hat knitted on a 16 inch (40cm) needle; swatch caps, I call them!

As a knitter specializing in circular designs, I am accustomed to hearing about techniques and styles that "cannot be worked in the round"; that knitting in the round is "too limiting for a designer." Yes, it is easier to work certain stitch patterns back and forth—but very few of them—and, as for limited shaping, I have often been challenged but have not been stumped at coming up with a variety of sweater styles in seamless, circular versions: saddle-shoulder, shirt-back, set-in-sleeve, box-the-compass, hybrid, lap-shoulder ... at present I am up to 12 choices for seamless shoulder shaping, not to mention the classic Norwegian and Guernsey and dropped-shoulder circular styles. There was a period when knitting in the round was sneered at—even Mary Thomas refers to circular knitting as "peasant knitting"—but we seem to have come full circle (as it were!) in the 1970s and '80s, as the interest in traditional garments—knitted in the traditional seamless manner—has revived. And the best part is, as far as new discoveries and variations are concerned, there is no end in sight. Are we knitters not fortunate?

Elizabeth Zimmermann

Circular Needles

When knitting on circular needles, you can join the work to make tubular pieces, or work back and forth as with straight needles. Actually, many knitters prefer circular needles when knitting flat pieces, especially with a large number of stitches, since the stitches and the weight of the knitting are evenly distributed.

Circular needles are available in several lengths. The length that you use will depend on the number of stitches you will be working with and the stitch gauge. The needle should be short enough so that the stitches are not stretched when joined. The needle can accommodate up to four times the original number of stitches, so you may not have to change needle length when you increase stitches above the rib.

Circular needles are available with plastic, aluminum or teflon-coated tips, but all have plastic joining wires. If the plastic wire portion of the needle curls, immerse it in hot water to straighten it before you begin to knit.

When you join your work, make sure that the stitches are not twisted around the needle. A twisted cast-on can't be rectified once you have worked a round. To help you keep the stitches untwisted, keep the cast-on edge facing the center, or work one row before joining the stitches, then sew the gap closed later.

To identify the beginning of each new round, place a marker between the first and last cast-on stitches before joining. Slip the marker before each subsequent round.

Casting on and knitting

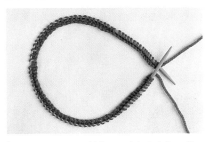

Cast on as you would for straight knitting. Distribute the stitches evenly around the needle, being sure not to twist them. The last cast-on stitch is the last stitch of the round. Place a marker here to indicate the end of the round.

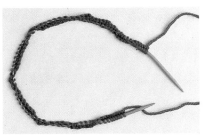

If the cast-on stitches are twisted, as shown, you will find that after you knit a few inches the fabric will be twisted. You will have to rip out your work to the cast-on row and straighten the stitches.

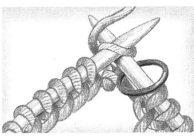

Hold the needle tip with the last cast-on stitch in your right hand and the tip with the first cast-on stitch in your left hand. Knit the first cast-on stitch, pulling the yarn tight to avoid a gap.

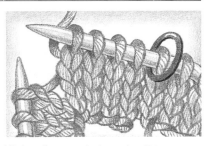

Work until you reach the marker. This completes the first round. Slip the marker to the right needle and work the next round.

Adapting stitch patterns

Most patterns are written for straight, single-pointed needles. However, you can often adapt them to circular knitting by making a few adjustments to the pattern.

The most important point to remember is that the right side of the work is always facing you. This means that if you knit every row, you get stockinette stitch. To work garter stitch you must alternate one knit row with one purl row.

If the existing pattern has stitches outside of the pattern repeat, you will have to add or subtract from the total number of stitches to come up with a multiple of the stitch repeat.

If the pattern is charted, read all the rows from right to left. If the pattern is written out, work the right-side rows as written, but reverse the wrong-side rows by reading them from right to left and working the opposite stitches. For example, for straight knitting the pattern reads: *Row 2 (WS):* K2, sl 1 wyib, k2, p3. For circular knitting the row should read: K3, p2, sl 1 wyif, p2. It is helpful to write out all the wrong-side rows before you begin.

Double-Pointed Needles

Double-pointed needles have points at both ends and come in sets of four or five needles in 7 inch (18cm) and 10 inch (25cm) lengths.

Unlike circular needles, they are used only for tubular pieces. Actually, the very first circular knitting was done on double-pointed needles. Since the invention of circular needles, double-pointed needles are used less often, usually to knit small items such as mittens, gloves, socks, hats and sleeve cuffs.

The stitches are divided evenly among three or four needles. An extra needle is used to knit the stitches.

When your work is joined on three needles, the needles form a triangle. When joined on four needles, a square is formed. Make sure that you keep an even tension when going from one needle to the next. If you find that your stitches slip off the needles as you work, choose longer double-pointed needles or switch to a circular needle.

On the first round, you can work the first few stitches with both the working yarn and the cast-on tail to create a neater joining. Another way to make a neat joining is to cast on one extra stitch on the last needle. Slip this stitch to the first needle and knit it together with the first cast-on stitch.

Just as for circular needles, you should mark the beginning of the round, and take care to make sure that the cast-on edge is not twisted.

On the last round, use the free needle to bind off the stitches on the first needle until one stitch remains. Drop the free needle and use the needle with the one remaining stitch to bind off the stitches on the next needle to the last stitch. Continue in this way to the last stitch on the last needle and fasten off this stitch.

Casting on and knitting

Cast-on with three needles.

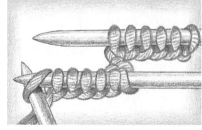

Cast on the required number of stitches on the first needle, plus one extra. Slip this extra stitch to the next needle as shown. Continue in this way, casting on the required number of stitches on the last needle.

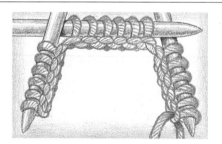

Arrange the needles as shown, with the cast-on edge facing the center of the triangle (or square).

Place a stitch marker after the last cast-on stitch. With the free needle, knit the first cast-on stitch, pulling the yarn tightly. Continue knitting in rounds, slipping the marker before beginning each round.

double-pointed needles **16-17**

cast on **24-29**

cast-on tail **29**

binding off **47-52**

VII. Color Knitting

Color Knitting

Inspiration for color knitting can come from various sources such as architecture, paintings, textiles and pottery.

It took years for me to understand why people were so astounded by my color-filled knitting. Coming from the world of painting, with a growing fascination for the decorative arts, lavish use of color and pattern seemed the only way to go when I started knitting. I had never been very moved by monotone canvases in the abstract painting world. Pierre Bonnard's blossom-packed garden scenes and Gustav Klimt's joyous use of pattern were the images that lit up my imagination. In the decorative arts I was more attracted to intensely detailed objects like mosaics and patchwork quilts than the pure lines of brown pottery.

So, when I learned to ride this bicycle called knitting (it was just that complicated and totally simple), I put 20 colors in my first effort—a busily striped cardigan. Only once in the 21 years that followed have I ever attempted a plain-colored jumper, and the effort nearly killed me with sheer boredom.

Following the rhythm of a geometric pattern or some great organic madness with many changing tones is the most highly motivating activity I've ever found. I must admit that geometric patterns held little fascination until it dawned on me what superb vehicles for color they were. Geometrics give the knitter an allover structure for a garment. Usually executed with too limited a scheme, they become repetitious and boring, but the simplest geometric pattern leaps to life when unexpected amounts of color are used. Stars, tumbling blocks, rows of circles or overlapping squares give endless joy to knitters interested in arrangement of color.

Once a knitter becomes involved in this world of tone, examples of structures and color schemes present themselves everywhere—mosaics, shop displays, aerial views or even piles of bricks in a builder's yard suggest infinite palettes. Insects or animal markings, lichens, shells, leaves and flowers supply us with constant surprises in subtle to startlingly bold colors.

The use of complex shading in design can be daunting to most people, who feel they need a specific art training to avoid serious mistakes. By pointing knitters towards the more primitive designs in the world, I have seen many break through their inhibitions into a joyous playfulness.

At first there seems to be a distinct color phobia in people attempting to knit more creatively. Fancy stitches are used with great confidence, but only recently have I found knitters casting off the constraints of technique to wallow in pools of color. I design most of my garments using only stockinette stitch to encourage this concentration on masses of color, and I am rewarded again and again with stunningly original results by knitters with no previous training or experience in design. By giving knitters helpful starting points like trying geometric forms, using many shades in each color and playing with textures such as mohair, silk, cotton, chenille and wool, I have seen even timid knitters produce a new richness in their work. Some first attempts can be crude, even vulgar, but once the ice is broken, refinements creep in.

After knitters abandon themselves to the sheer joy of color, they start to notice and collect examples of its more subtle or powerful uses. Suddenly museums and galleries have a new fascination. Color schemes lurk in corners of paintings, on enamelled buttons, on glorious decorated china, and in old tapestries. They abound in the ethnic world of textiles, jewelry, pottery and beadwork. Natural history collections of feathers, shells, butterfly wings and colorful stones and minerals can make the knitter's head spin with exciting possibilities. What is thrilling to me is the endless personal interpretations people make of this material. I never worry that knitters will use the same ideas I've developed, because we all approach them so differently. So many elements —scale, color, form—can be manipulated to make the same source material unique to each knitter.

I think it is now being demonstrated that knitting with a limited number of hues—say three or four—is quite a difficult task compared to arranging 20 to 40 colors in a garment. Most knitting patterns talk down to knitters by giving them only the simplest of ideas, and offering little to catch the eye. On the other hand, when knitters use many shades and textures, the resulting garments are anything but predictable. Knitters who produce this richness light up many a street with their moving tapestries of color.

I feel strongly that the great folk art tradition we value so deeply has surfaced again in the humble art of knitting. Long may it continue giving all us knitters that thrill of creation!

Kaffe Fassett

Fair Isle Knitting

Traditionally, Fair Isle knitting was defined as knitting with many colors, but never using more than two in a row. Most Fair Isle patterns were made up of small motifs which repeated across the piece. The term now refers to any color knitting where color changes are frequent, requiring the yarns to be carried across the wrong side of the work.

Most Fair Isle patterns are worked in stockinette stitch. Traditional Fair Isle sweaters were often worked circularly to avoid purling. Knitters would work the entire Fair Isle sweater or vest in the round and then cut in the armholes or neck shaping. One special kind of Fair Isle knitting from Sweden, called Bohus knitting, incorporates knit and purl stitches along with the color changes.

Some Fair Isle patterns have a square gauge, where the stitches and rows are the same size. Carrying yarns across the back of the pieces causes the rows to condense more than with solid-color knitting. Always work a swatch using your yarn and the Fair Isle pattern to check your gauge before you begin to knit.

You can carry the yarn in different ways, depending on how often the color changes occur.

Stranding is used for small, regular pattern repeats, usually with a maximum of four stitches. In stranding, the yarns are picked up alternately over and under one another across each row.

If you have never tried color knitting, it's a good idea to practice before you begin a sweater. You may find wool slightly easier and more forgiving for Fair Isle knitting than a yarn that has little resiliency, such as cotton.

The most difficult part of color knitting is keeping an even tension. If the yarn carried across the back of the work is pulled too tightly, the work will pucker.

When picking up a new color to knit, stretch the stitches on the needle farther than you intend to carry the yarn, so that the work will lie flat. The stranded yarn should be somewhat loose along the back and have the same give as the knitting itself.

You can strand with one or two hands. With two hands, you must know both the English and Continental knitting techniques. Hold the dominant color in the hand you are most comfortable knitting with and the second color in your other hand.

When you have more than four stitches between color changes, it is best not to leave long, loose floats that may sag and catch on fingers or jewelry. One way to avoid this is to weave the yarn not in use over and under the stitches until you use it again. The yarn can be woven every stitch or every few stitches. Hold the working yarn in your right hand and the woven yarn in your left. This extra strand creates another layer of fabric, making the sweater thick and warm.

Keeping an even tension in weaving is just as important as in stranding. If the woven yarn is too tight, it will pucker the fabric.

When weaving, the colors may show through to the front of the work. Therefore, you should not use high contrast colors such as black and white.

Another way to carry yarns across more than four stitches is to twist them around the working yarn every two or three stitches, rather than weaving them into every stitch. In Fair Isle patterns, this technique will cause the yarns to tangle quickly, so you should untangle them at the end of every row.

To keep the back of your work neat and to make finishing easier, learn how to join the yarns and weave in the ends at the same time. This is especially helpful when working garments with many colors.

Stranding: one-handed

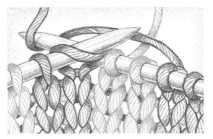   

1 On the knit side, drop the working yarn. Bring the new color (now the working yarn) over the top of the dropped yarn and work to the next color change.

2 Drop the working yarn. Bring the new color under the dropped yarn and work to the next color change. Repeat steps 1 and 2.

1 On the purl side, drop the working yarn. Bring the new color (now the working yarn) over the top of the dropped yarn and work to the next color change.

2 Drop the working yarn. Bring the new color under the dropped yarn and work to the next color change. Repeat steps 1 and 2.

Stranding: two-handed

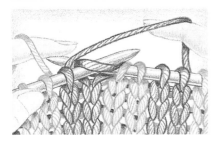 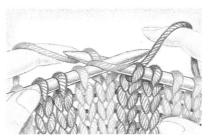  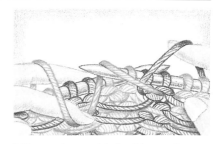

1 On the knit side, hold the working yarn in your right hand and the non-working yarn in your left hand. Bring the working yarn over the top of the yarn in your left hand and knit with the right hand to the next color change.

2 The yarn in your right hand is now the non-working yarn; the yarn in your left hand is the working yarn. Bring the working yarn under the non-working yarn and knit with the left hand to the next color change. Repeat steps 1 and 2.

1 On the purl side, hold the working yarn in your right hand and the non-working yarn in your left hand. Bring the working yarn over the top of the yarn in your left hand and purl with the right hand to the next color change.

2 The yarn in your right hand is now the non-working yarn; the yarn in your left hand is the working yarn. Bring the working yarn under the non-working yarn and purl with the left hand to the next color change. Repeat steps 1 and 2.

Correct and incorrect tension

  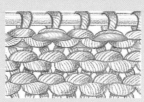 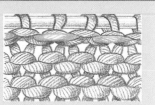

Correct stranding on the right side.

Incorrect stranding on the right side.

Correct weaving on the wrong side.

Incorrect weaving on the wrong side.

right/wrong sides **67-68**

Weaving

 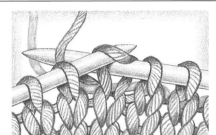  

1 Hold working yarn in right hand and yarn to be woven in your left. To weave yarn above a knit stitch, bring it over right needle. Knit stitch with working yarn, bringing it under woven yarn.

2 The woven yarn will go under the next knit stitch. With the working yarn, knit the stitch, bringing the yarn over the woven yarn. Repeat steps 1 and 2 to the next color change.

1 To weave the yarn above a purl stitch, bring it over the right needle. Purl the stitch with the working yarn, bringing it under the woven yarn.

2 To weave the yarn below a purl stitch, purl the stitch with the working yarn, bringing it over the woven yarn. Repeat steps 1 and 2 to the next color change.

Twisting

On the knit side, twist the working yarn and the carried yarn around each other once. Then continue knitting with the same color as before.

On the purl side, twist the yarns around each other as shown, then continue purling with the same color as before.

Tips on keeping colors from tangling

If your pattern has many different colors, you can use a bobbin for each one or try one of these home-made methods to keep the yarns from tangling:

Thread one strand of each color through the holes of a large button or punch holes in a stiff piece of cardboard.

Keep each ball of yarn in a separate container, like a box or jar. Move the containers around when the yarns begin to twist.

Divide a shoe box into compartments with cardboard or small boxes. Make holes in the lid to correspond to each section. Place the different yarns in the compartments and thread the

ends through the holes on the lid. Secure the lid and turn the box every time you turn the work.

For small sections of color, use short lengths (about one yard/one meter) of yarn for each color instead of bobbins. It will be easy to untangle them.

bobbins **19-20, 85**

Intarsia

Intarsia is a colorwork technique in which blocks of color are worked with separate balls of yarn or bobbins. The yarns are not carried across the back of the work between color changes and must be twisted around each other at each change to prevent holes in the work.

Intarsia knitting should not be worked circularly, because at the end of the round, the yarns would be in the wrong position. You would have to cut all the yarn and reattach it, leaving you to weave in hundreds of ends.

When changing colors in a vertical line, the yarn must be twisted on every row. When changing colors in a diagonal line, the yarns must only be twisted on every other row. If the diagonal slants to the right, twist the yarn only on the knit rows. If the diagonal slants to the left, twist the yarn only on the purl rows.

Changing colors in a vertical line

1 On the knit side, drop the old color. Pick up the new color from under the old color and knit to the next color change.

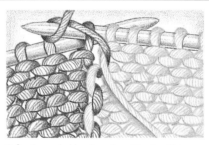

2 On the purl side, drop the old color. Pick up the new color from under the old color and purl to the next color change. Repeat steps 1 and 2.

Changing colors in a diagonal line

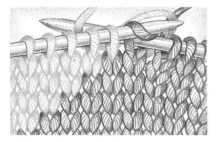

1 When working a right diagonal on the knit side, bring the new color over the top of the old color and knit to the next color change.

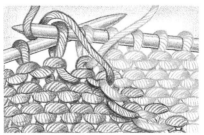

2 On the purl side, pick up the new color from under the old color and purl to the next color change.

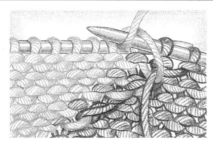

1 When working a left diagonal on the purl side, bring the new color over the top of the old color and purl to the next color change.

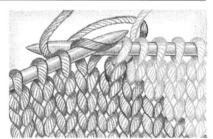

2 On the knit side, pick up the new color from under the old color and knit to the next color change.

bobbins **19-20, 85**

circular knitting **75-78**

Bobbins

When you knit with more than one color, whether you prefer the stranded or intarsia method, bobbins will help to keep the yarns from tangling.

You can purchase ready-made plastic bobbins in several sizes, or you can make your own out of cardboard. You can also wind your own, as described below. The type of bobbin you use will depend on your pattern or motif, the weight of the yarn and your own preference. If you're using a heavy yarn, a large bobbin will accommodate the extra bulk. Use a bobbin if you are working with only one or two colors at a time, but for numerous small areas of color, it is better to use short, manageable pieces of yarn—usually one or two yards (or meters) long.

The bobbin should accommodate an adequate supply of yarn, be lightweight and release the yarn easily as needed. It shouldn't have any rough ends that could catch on your work.

Hand-wound bobbin

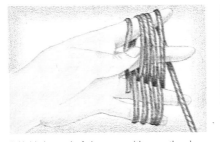

1 Hold the end of the yarn with your thumb. Bring the yarn around your forefinger and middle finger. Wrap it in the opposite direction around your ring finger and little finger. Continue wrapping the yarn in a figure eight until you have enough.

2 Cut the yarn, leaving about an eight inch (20cm) tail. Remove the yarn from your fingers, wrap the tail several times around the center and tie a knot as shown.

3 Pull the unknotted end of the strand to release the yarn as needed.

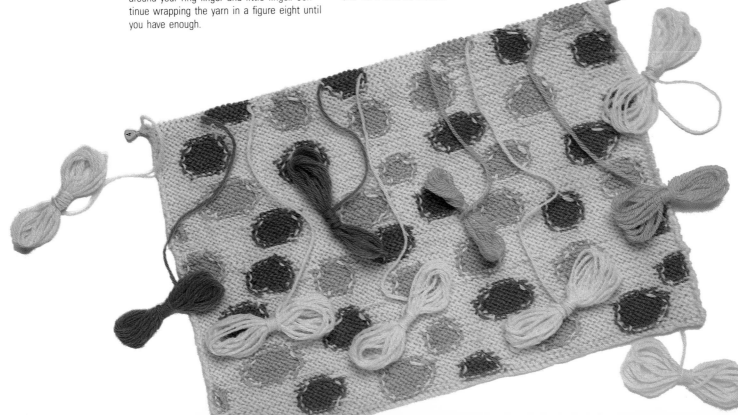

Joining a new color: version A

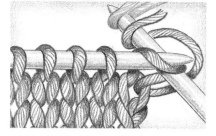  

1 Wrap first the old and then the new yarn knitwise and work the first stitch with both yarns.

2 Drop the old yarn. Work the next two stitches with both ends of the new yarn.

3 Drop the short end of the new color and continue working with the single strand. On the following rows, work the three double stitches as single stitches.

Joining a new color: version B

  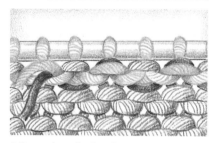

1 Cut the old yarn, leaving about four inches (10cm). Purl the first two stitches with the new yarn. *Insert the needle purlwise into the stitch, lay the short ends of both the old and new colors over the top of the needle and purl the next stitch under the short ends.

2 Leave the short ends hanging and purl the next stitch over them.

3 Repeat from the * until you have woven the short ends into the wrong side of the piece.

Joining a new color: version C

  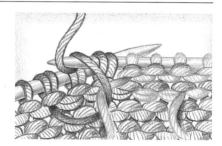

1 Work to three stitches before where you want to join the new yarn. Work these stitches with the yarn folded double, making sure you have just enough to work three stitches.

2 Loop the new yarn into the loop of the old yarn, leaving the new yarn doubled for about eight inches (20cm). Knit the next three stitches with the doubled yarn. Let the short end of the new yarn hang and continue knitting with one strand.

3 On the next row, carry the first yarn across the back of the work from where it was dropped on the previous row and twist it together with the second yarn. Work the doubled stitches as single stitches.

Charts

Colorwork patterns are usually charted on square graph paper instead of written in words. It is much easier to read a chart than written instructions, as a chart provides a visual guide to what the finished motif will look like. If the colorwork pattern is written out, you may want to transfer the design to graph paper to see how the pattern appears. If you draw the pattern on knitter's graph paper (where the grid is proportionate to the gauge), the pattern will look like the knitted piece. Motifs drawn on square graph paper will be slightly elongated, since stitches are not square.

Each square of the chart represents one stitch, and each line of squares represents one row. The right-side (or odd-numbered) rows are read from right to left, and the wrong-side (or even-numbered) rows are read from left to right, unless the instructions state otherwise. (If working circularly, however, read all the rows from right to left.) Read the rows of the chart from the bottom to the top. Unless otherwise stated,

color charts are worked in stockinette stitch.

The different colors are coded with symbols or shaded color, as in this book. If symbols are used, a color key will show what color each symbol represents. Many times, a box without a symbol will represent the main color. If you are substituting colors, you may want to create a new color key before you begin.

Most color charts have repeat lines through the chart to show the stitch repeat of the motif. The equivalent in written patterns is "rep from *," "rep between *'s" or [ ]. There are usually no repeat lines for the rows. In that case, work from row 1 to the top of the chart, then return to row 1 again.

Depending on the complexity of the pattern, you can knit each color change as it appears on the chart, or you can work large areas of the prominent colors and then go back and duplicate stitch the small areas of color. For example, the diamonds on the chart below were knit, and the single-stitch crosses were worked in duplicate stitch after the piece was completed.

To help you keep your place in the chart, place a ruler or straight edge under the row you are working and move it up as you progress. You may also want to check off or highlight each row as you complete it. If the symbols are so small that it strains your eyes, you can copy the pattern onto large-square graph paper, using either the same symbols or colored pencils. You can also enlarge the chart with a photocopy machine.

You should always make a sample swatch of the charted pattern to check the gauge and at the same time become familiar with the pattern. When working from a large chart, pick an area that is representative of the whole piece.

Color and symbol charts

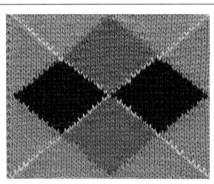

The knitted argyle pattern, shown here on the knit side, can be made by using either the color or symbol chart shown at the right.

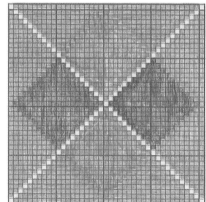

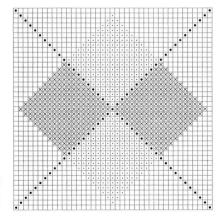

Charts with large repeats

If a chart has a large number of stitches in the repeat but no beginning or ending indications, you must decide where to begin the motif. If you start at the beginning of the repeat, you may end up with only a partial repeat at the end of the row, and the motif may not be centered on your sweater. To determine where to begin and end on the chart, find the center of your sweater. Count the number of stitches from the

center point to one edge. Then locate the center of the pattern repeat. Count the number of stitches from the center of the pattern to the repeat line and subtract it from the number of stitches that you counted on the sweater. Then continue subtracting full repeats as far as you can. Subtract the remaining number from the center of the motif (it may extend past the repeat line).

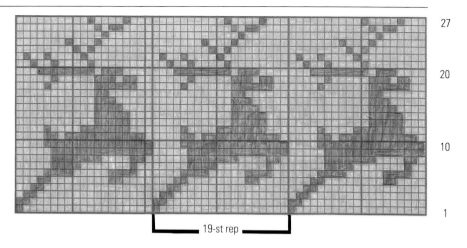

27
20
10
1

19-st rep

Charts with small repeats

When working charts with small repeats and no beginning or ending indications, it is not so important where you begin the row. In this case, you can usually start at the beginning of the chart. You may, however, want to check where the motif stops at the end of the row. If the number of stitches on your

piece is an exact multiple of the chart repeat, or just one or two stitches different, you don't have to worry where to begin. If it is any more than that, you may want to center the motif as with the large repeats, described above.

Charts with sizing lines

Some instructions will draw lines through the chart (aside from the repeat lines), which show you where to begin and end each size. In this case, the centering of the motif is done for you, and you only need to know how to read these lines. Begin the chart at the square indicated (usually with an arrow) for the size you are making. Work the

chart to the repeat line, then work full repeats as many times as you can. Continue working the squares to the left of the repeat line, ending at the square indicated for your size. If the same chart is used for both the body and the sleeves, take care to use the arrow for the correct piece.

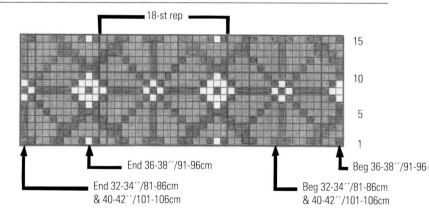

18-st rep

15
10
5
1

End 36-38″/91-96cm

End 32-34″/81-86cm
& 40-42″/101-106cm

Beg 36-38″/91-96

Beg 32-34″/81-86cm
& 40-42″/101-106cm

Multiple chart knitting

When a sweater has more than one charted pattern, and each pattern has different stitch and row repeats, each chart is usually drawn separately. If you are working with more than one chart at a time, as in our sample piece, you must keep track of where you are on each one.

Be sure that you work the stitches of all three charts across the row in the correct order. In this example, on right-side rows, begin with the first stitch of the small chart, work the medium chart, then the large chart. On wrong-side rows, begin with last stitch of the large chart, work the medium chart, then the small chart.

To make reading the charts easier, make several photocopies of each one and tape them together in the same way they are placed on the sweater, making one big chart to follow row for row.

Horizontal Stripes

Horizontal stripes are one of the easiest types of color knitting, since you do not have to carry yarns across the row as you work. You can cut the yarn as you finish each stripe, but this means weaving in many ends after the pieces are complete. To avoid this, carry the yarns you are not using along the side of the work.

If working a stripe pattern back and forth, you should have an even number of rows in each stripe, so that the yarn will be at the correct side of the work when you need it. If the pattern calls for odd-numbered stripes, you will have to cut the yarn and rejoin it on the opposite side. To avoid this, you can change the pattern to make an even number of rows in each stripe. You can also work the piece back and forth on a circular needle. If you complete a stripe and need to change to the new color, but the yarn is at the opposite side, go back to the beginning of the row you just finished, without turning the work, and pick up the color you need. If you are knitting the garment circularly, it does not matter how many rows are in the stripes, as you are always working right-side rows.

When you change colors on the right side of the work, and you purl with the new color on top of knit stitches in the old color, you will get a broken line. To avoid this, knit one row with the new color.

Carrying colors along the side

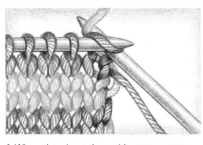

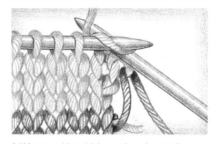

1 When changing colors with narrow, even-numbered stripes, drop the old color. Bring the new color under the old color, being sure not to pull the yarn too tightly, and knit the next stripe.

2 When working thicker stripes (generally more than four rows), carry the old yarn up the side until it is needed again by twisting the working yarn around the old yarn every couple of rows, as shown.

Different types of stripes

Four-row stripes in knit two, purl two ribbing.

Four rows of one color in stockinette stitch and two rows of another color in garter stitch.

Four-row stripes in stockinette stitch, shown on the right side.

Four-row stripes in garter stitch, shown on the right side.

circular knitting **75-78, 188-93**

right/wrong sides **67-68**

circular needles **16-17**

Vertical Stripes

When working vertical stripes, you must either carry the colors across the back of the work or use separate balls or bobbins for each stripe. If each stripe has four or less stitches, you can carry the yarns across the back. With more than four stitches, you should use bobbins for each color and twist the colors around each other on every row.

To make a vertical stripe of only one stitch in stockinette, it is neater to first knit the piece in the main color and then duplicate stitch the vertical stripe onto it.

If you want the stripes to start at the beginning of the piece, cast on with only one color, then start the stripes on the first row. Or you can cast on using the colors in the stripes, as shown below.

A corrugated rib is ribbing made of vertical stripes in knit and purl stitches. While it does make an interesting effect, it does not have the same give as solid-color ribbing and should be made slightly wider to compensate for its lack of resiliency. It is best worked in knit one, purl one or knit two, purl two ribbing. Remember to always twist the colors on the wrong side of the work to prevent holes.

Casting on for vertical stripes

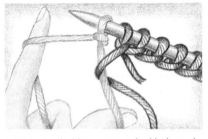

1 Using the double cast-on and with the end of the yarn coming from the skein over your thumb, cast on the first color. Make a slip knot on the needle with the second color. To cast on the second stitch, twist the old and new colors, as shown.

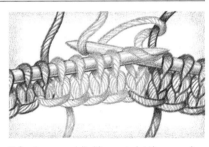

2 If working in stockinette stitch, purl the first row, twisting the yarns at each color change, as shown. Pull the yarn tightly to prevent gaps.

3 On the second (knit) row, twist the yarns by bringing the working yarn over the old yarn.

Corrugated ribbing

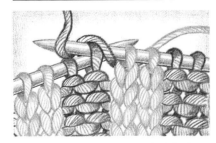

1 On the right side, before a purl stitch, drop the old color. Bring the working color under the old color and to the front of the work between the needles. Purl the next two stitches.

2 Before a knit stitch, bring the old color to the back of the work and leave it. Bring the working color under the old color and knit the next two stitches.

1 On the wrong side, before a knit stitch, drop the old color. Bring the working color over the top of the old color and to the back of the work as shown. Knit the next two stitches.

2 Before a purl stitch, drop the old color, bring the working color over the top of the old color and purl the next two stitches.

bobbins **19-20, 85**   duplicate stitch **233**   cast on **24-29**

main color/MC **62**   right/wrong sides **67-68**   ribbing **34-35, 172-73**

Mosaic Knitting

This form of colorwork requires no bobbins, no stranding and no changing of colors in the middle of a row. Color changes are made at the side edge every other row. You can work a mosaic motif either in stockinette, reverse stockinette or garter stitch. It is shown below in stockinette and garter stitch.

Only two colors are used in a motif. Each color is used alone for two entire rows. The first stitch of the chart is a guide to which color will be worked on that row. Reading the chart below, all

the stitches in the dark color are worked (either knit or purl) over two rows while the light color is slipped purlwise over the same two rows. In the next two rows, the light color is worked and the dark color is slipped. The first and last stitch of every row is always worked, never slipped.

Usually only the right-side rows are charted. When working wrong-side rows, you do not need to look at the chart. The colors are either slipped or worked exactly as they were in the preceding row.

When you slip stitches, always hold the working yarn to the wrong side of the work; that is, to the back on right-side rows and to the front on wrong-side rows.

When changing colors at the edge, drop the yarn you have just used and pick up the other yarn behind it.

This mosaic chart was used to make the two swatches to the right.

This swatch was made following the chart in stockinette stitch; that is, knitting the right-side rows and purling the wrong-side rows.

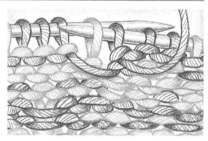

This swatch was made following the chart in garter stitch; that is, knitting every row.

Working mosaic knitting in stockinette stitch

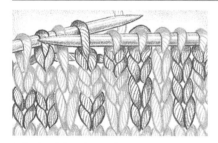

1 On the right-side row (here chart row 7), knit all the stitches in the light color and slip all the stitches in the dark color purlwise with the yarn at the back.

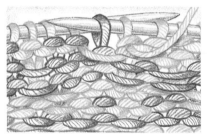

2 On the wrong-side row (here chart row 8), purl all the stitches in the light color and slip all the stitches in the dark color purlwise with the yarn at the front.

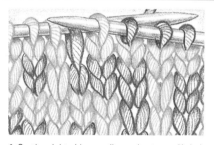

1 On the right-side row (here chart row 9), knit all the stitches in the dark color and slip all the stitches in the light color purlwise with the yarn at the back.

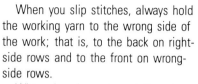

2 On the wrong-side row (here chart row 10), purl all the stitches in the dark color and slip all the stitches in the light color purlwise with the yarn at the front.

---

slip a stitch purlwise **46**   garter/ stockinette **22, 34**   right/wrong sides **67-68**

VIII. Blocking, Assembling and Finishing

Blocking, Assembling and Finishing

Large, flat, padded surface

Pins

Tape measure

Spray bottle with cool water

Steam iron or hand-held steamer

Press-cloth

Towels

Blocking is the process of wetting, pressing or steaming finished knit pieces to give them their permanent size and shape. You should give this process as much care and attention as you do to knitting the pieces.

Water or steam is an essential element in the blocking process. You can wet block by submerging the pieces in water or by spraying them, or you can steam press them with an iron or hand-held steamer.

Most pieces of knitting should be blocked before seaming. As you knit, the edges of the pieces may roll and become uneven—especially stitches such as stockinette. Blocking the pieces will flatten and smooth out their edges. Blocking also evens out the stitches.

In addition, you can lightly steam seams from the wrong side once they are sewn.

The only time you would block a completed sweater is when making a circular garment or when washing a sweater after wearing it.

Your decisions about how to block your pieces will depend on the content of the yarn and the type of stitch pattern. Understanding the properties of the yarns you use will help you decide on how to block. Always read the yarn's ball band carefully before you proceed. It will often give you important information about the care of the yarn. Synthetic yarns and textured stitches, for example, shouldn't be pressed. Some novelty yarns, such as lurex, or highly textured yarns with many different fibers should not be blocked at all. Long-haired yarns such as mohair and angora will become matted if you press them. You can lightly block ribbed patterns if you want a slightly stretched appearance. If you have any doubts about how the yarn will react to pressing or wetting, experiment with your gauge swatch before you actually block your pieces.

You can make some changes to the shaping and the size of the pieces as you block. The amount of change that you can achieve with blocking really depends on the type of yarn, how

tightly knit the pieces are and which blocking method you use. Wool yarns, when wet, are the best fibers to stretch and change. Care should be taken with cotton yarns, since they are not as resilient as wools and can lose their shape. It is difficult to change pieces worked with synthetic yarns. With many synthetics, the shape you form as you knit will be the permanent shape of the piece. Loosely knit pieces are easier to stretch out than those which are tightly knit. Pieces can be stretched more easily when they are wet blocked, especially when they have been submerged in water. It is also easier to enlarge pieces rather than to reduce their size. However, you shouldn't expect to enlarge pieces more than one size if you have achieved your correct gauge.

Some yarns are not colorfast, especially those that are dyed in very dark or rich colors. If you are in doubt about the colorfastness of a yarn, it is wise to test it before you begin to knit, and be wary of using it with other colors. High contrast yarns, such as very dark colors mixed with very light ones, should always

be tested carefully before using. To test your yarn, thoroughly wet a piece, wrap it tightly around a paper towel and allow it to dry. If the color does not bleed through the paper, it is colorfast. If it does bleed, then you should dry clean your garment.

right/wrong sides **67-68**   yarn label symbols **12**

ball band **11**   gauge swatch **18-19, 57-59**

When blocking cardigan fronts, place the pieces side-by-side on the blocking board.

Materials

The flat surface you choose for blocking should be large enough to hold one full piece of knitting. Since the average sweater is usually no more than 25 inches (63cm) wide and 30 inches (76cm) long, a blocking area 36 inches (91cm) square should be adequate. The surface should have a padded covering that can easily receive pins. This could be as simple as an absorbent cloth over a padded surface, or you can make a special blocking board. Start with a dressmaker's cutting board or any board made of porous material, such as cork. Cover it with a foam pad and an absorbent cloth. You can use a gingham fabric or, to help you with your measuring, use one with an even pattern of squares. If you do not have a special padded board for blocking, you can use a carpet or bed that is covered with plastic to protect it from moisture. An ironing board can be used for small pieces such as swatches, hats or scarves, but it is not large enough to hold sweater pieces.

If you can't find an out-of-the-way spot, you may wish to cover your pieces while they dry. Just make sure that the spot you choose will not require you to move the pieces before they are completely dry.

Always use rustproof pins that will not leave marks on wet pieces of knitting. T-pins are ideal for blocking, since they can be easily placed and are long enough so that they do not get buried in the knitting. You could also use glass- or plastic-headed pins. Longer pins are easier to work with.

Preparation for blocking

Before you begin to block your pieces, you should have all your equipment at hand as well as a schematic drawing or the written finished measurements. It is especially important to know one-half the finished bust/chest and length measurements as well as the sleeve width at the upper arm. If these measurements are not given, you can easily calculate them by dividing the number of stitches or rows by the stitch or row gauge for one inch (one centimeter). For example, if your bust/chest is 100 stitches and the stitch gauge for one inch is five stitches (two stitches for one centimeter), the piece should measure 20 inches (50cm) at the bust/chest.

T-pins **19**   measurements **166**
schematic **55**   gauge **18-19, 57-59**

It's a good idea to block pieces right-side up, so that you can see the results as you work.

To pin, begin at key areas such as the shoulders, the bust/chest just below the armhole and at lower-edge points. Keep all the pieces straight and even as you pin them, smoothing them from the center out. You may want to mark the center of each piece at its widest point. Then measure from this center point, placing the first crucial pins. Then make sure the width and length measurements are accurate before you place pins at closer intervals. Insert the pins at a slight angle, approximately one inch (2.5cm) apart.

Take care that the pins are close enough together so that you don't leave marks or create scalloped edges when the pieces dry. Do not pin ribbed areas that are intended to pull in.

If you have two matching pieces such as cardigan fronts or sleeves, you

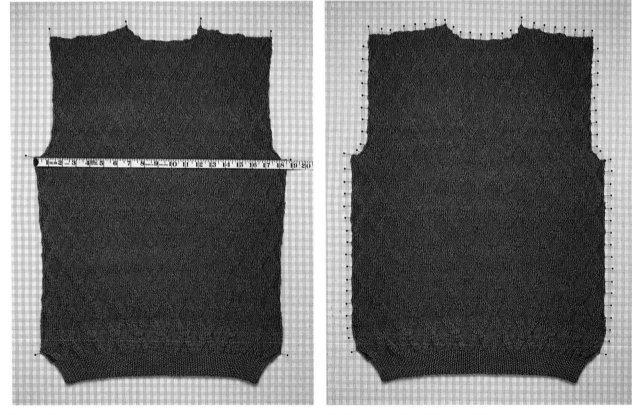

First, pin the key areas as shown.

Pin the piece evenly, omitting the ribbing.

can block them side by side to ensure that the measurements of both pieces are accurate. Block one piece first and then use a large piece of brown paper or non-woven interfacing to trace around it. Block the matching piece on the tracing. Or you can place the pieces one on top of the other. When the pieces are partially dry, remove the top one to allow for faster drying. To block a piece that has blouson areas above a tighter rib, pin it to a curved cushion, since it is impossible to lay the piece completely flat.

Wet blocking

Wet blocking is done without steaming or pressing. You can either completely submerge the pieces in cool water before laying them on your blocking surface, or you can first pin the pieces

down and then use a spray bottle to wet them thoroughly. You may find that it is slightly easier to work with dry pieces and dampen them once the pinning is complete. This method works especially well for heavy garments to shorten the drying time. No single method is correct—it really depends on your personal preference. Always allow the pieces to dry completely before beginning to seam them.

Steam pressing

You can steam press with an iron or a hand-held steamer. The important elements in blocking are heat and moisture, not the pressure of the iron, so take care when pressing. If you use an iron, never place it directly onto your knitted piece. Hold it above the piece and slowly work over the entire area. Let the steam dampen each piece completely.

It is a good idea to use a pressing cloth between the iron and the knitted piece to protect the surface from intense heat and keep it clean. You can steam press either by using a dry pressing cloth with a steam iron, or a wet pressing cloth with a dry iron.

Set the temperature of your iron carefully. Cottons can stand warmer temperatures than wools. Synthetics may need a very cool iron setting. Be especially careful with synthetic blends, as the wrong type of blocking or steaming could permanently damage the fibers.

Pressing guide

Because fibers react differently to heat, it is best to know what to expect before you press or steam them. Just remember that there are many combinations of fibers, and you should choose a process that is compatible with all the fibers in your yarn. If you are unsure about the fiber content of your yarn, test your gauge swatch before you block your sweater pieces.

Angora—Wet block by spraying.

Cotton—Wet block or warm/hot steam press.

Linen—Wet block or warm/hot steam press.

Lurex—Do not block.

Mohair—Wet block by spraying.

Novelties (highly textured)—Do not block.

Synthetics—Carefully follow instructions on ball band—usually wet block by spraying, do not press.

Wool and all wool-like fibers (alpaca, camel hair, cashmere)—Wet block or warm steam press.

Wool blends—Wet block by spraying, do not press unless tested.

Seaming

You can choose from many types of seaming techniques, depending on your personal preference. Each method has its own characteristics and may require different tools.

It is best to use your knitting yarn to sew the pieces together, unless you have used a novelty or untwisted, roving yarn. In that case, sew the seams with a flat, firm yarn in a compatible color. Be sure that it has the same washability as your knitting yarn.

Block your pieces before you sew them together to make the edges smoother and easier to seam. Pin or baste the seams before final seaming. Try the garment on and make sure that it fits properly.

Attach any small items, such as pockets or embroidery, before seaming, as it is easier to work with one piece than the entire garment.

Most knitters follow this sequence when seaming a garment: Sew one or both shoulder seams, depending on the type of garment and the method you'll use to add any neckband. Sew the sleeves to the body, and then sew the side and sleeve seams.

As you seam, try to keep an even tension. Pull the yarn firmly as you go but not so tightly that the edges will pucker.

Do not use too long a piece of yarn when seaming—no more than 18 inches (46cm). The constant friction of the yarn through the knitting can cause the yarn to break.

Be sure to keep the seam in a neat, straight line. Always insert your needle or hook in the same place along the seam. If necessary, run a contrasting thread through the stitches or rows to help you see the line more clearly.

If the two pieces you are seaming are slightly different lengths, you can compensate by picking up two rows or stitches on the longer side every few inches. This can only work if the difference is no more than one-half inch (1.5cm). If it is any more than that, you must rework one of the pieces.

Any edges that will be turned back, such as cuffs or a turtleneck, should be seamed from the opposite side so that the seam will not show when the edge is turned.

How to begin seaming

If you have left a long tail from your cast-on row, you can use this strand to begin sewing. To make a neat join at the lower edge with no gap, use the technique shown here. Thread the strand into a yarn needle. With the right sides of both pieces facing you, insert the yarn needle from back to front into the corner stitch of the piece without the tail. Making a figure eight with the yarn, insert the needle from back to front into the stitch with the cast-on tail. Tighten to close the gap.

Invisible vertical on stockinette stitch

The invisible vertical seam is worked from the right side and is used to join two edges row by row. It hides the uneven selvage stitches at the edge of a row and creates an invisible seam, making it appear that the knitting is continuous.

The finished vertical seam on stockinette stitch.

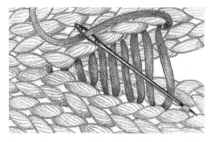

Insert the yarn needle under the horizontal bar between the first and second stitches. Insert the needle into the corresponding bar on the other piece. Continue alternating from side to side.

Invisible vertical on reverse stockinette stitch

As with stockinette stitch, this invisible seam is worked from the right side, row by row, but instead of working into the horizontal strand between stitches, you work into the stitch itself. Alternate working into the top loop on one side with the bottom loop on the other side.

The finished vertical seam on reverse stockinette stitch.

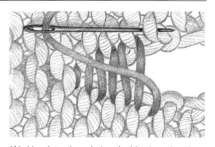

Working into the stitches inside the edge, insert the yarn needle into the top loop on one side, then in the bottom loop of the corresponding stitch on the other side. Continue to alternate in this way.

Invisible vertical on garter stitch

This invisible seam is worked on garter stitch. It is similar to the seam worked on reverse stockinette stitch in that you alternate working into the top and bottom loops of the stitches.

The finished vertical seam on garter stitch.

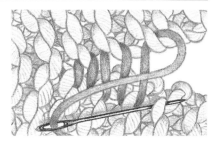

Insert the yarn needle into the top loop on one side, then in the bottom loop of the corresponding stitch on the other side. Continue to alternate in this way.

right/wrong sides **67-68**   top/bottom loops/structure of knitting **22**
selvages **194-95**

Invisible horizontal

This seam is used to join two bound-off edges, such as shoulder seams, and is worked stitch by stitch. You must have the same number of stitches on each piece. Pull the yarn tight enough to hide the bound-off edges. The finished seam resembles a row of knit stitches.

The finished horizontal seam on stockinette stitch.

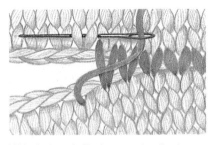

With the bound-off edges together, lined up stitch for stitch, insert the yarn needle under a stitch inside the bound-off edge of one side and then under the corresponding stitch on the other side.

Invisible vertical to horizontal

This seam is used to join bound-off stitches to rows, as in sewing the top of a sleeve to an armhole edge. Since there are usually more rows per inch (2.5cm) than stitches, occasionally pick up two horizontal bars on the piece with rows for every stitch on the bound-off piece.

The finished vertical to horizontal seam on stockinette stitch.

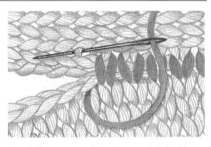

Insert the yarn needle under a stitch inside the bound-off edge of the vertical piece. Insert the needle under one or two horizontal bars between the first and second stitches of the horizontal piece.

Basting

Some knitters use basting as a seaming technique. However, it is rather unattractive and is not recommended for finished seams. Basting is best used as a preliminary step to seaming. Baste all of the pieces together with a contrasting yarn, try on the garment, then remove the basting yarn and seam the pieces together.

You should baste close to the edge, making the basted seam allowance as similar as possible to that of the finished garment. Use a yarn needle and yarn that is heavy enough to hold the pieces together. Do not use sewing thread, as it can easily break when you try on the sweater.

Run the thread in and out through both thicknesses.

binding off **47-52**

armhole shaping **176**

Backstitch

This is a strong seam which is worked from the wrong side and creates a seam allowance. Because it is not worked at the edge of the fabric, it can be used to take in fullness. The seam allowance should not exceed three-eighths inch (1cm).

The finished backstitch on stockinette stitch.

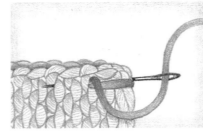

1 With the right sides of the pieces facing each other, secure the seam by taking the needle twice around the edges from back to front. Bring the needle up about one-fourth inch (.5cm) from where the yarn last emerged, as shown.

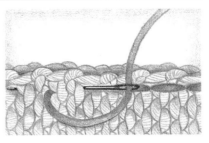

2 In one motion, insert the needle into the point where the yarn emerged from the previous stitch and back up approximately one-fourth inch (.5cm) ahead of the emerging yarn. Pull the yarn through. Repeat this step, keeping the stitches straight and even.

Overcasting

This seam is usually worked from the wrong side, but can also be worked from the right side with a thick yarn in a contrasting color to create a decorative, cord-like seam.

The finished overcast seam on stockinette stitch.

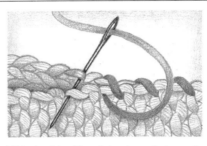

With the right sides of the pieces facing each other and the knots lined up, insert the needle from back to front through the strands at the edges of the pieces between the knots. Repeat this step.

Edge-to-edge

The edge-to-edge seam, being flat, is perfect for reversible garments. It is worked at the very edge of the piece. Because it is not a strong seam, it is best used with lightweight yarns.

The finished edge-to-edge seam on stockinette stitch.

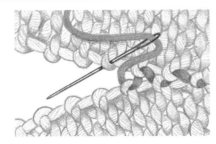

The finished edge-to-edge seam on reverse stockinette stitch.

With the purl sides facing you and the edges of the pieces together, insert the yarn needle into the knot on one side, then into the corresponding knot on the other side.

right/wrong sides **67-68**   reverse stockinette **34**

stockinette **22, 34**

Grafting

Grafting, also called weaving or kitchener stitch, joins two open edges stitch by stitch using a yarn needle. The grafted edges resemble a row of stitches and leave no seam. This makes grafting useful when a seam is undesirable, such as on mittens, hoods that may fold over, and the toes of socks.

Because you must follow the path of the stitches with the yarn needle, grafting is best used on simple stitches such as stockinette, reverse stockinette or garter stitch, which have been worked in flat, smooth yarns, making the stitches clearly visible.

You should graft stitches together while they are still on the knitting needle, slipping a few off at a time as you work. Be sure that the needles are pointing in the same direction when the wrong sides of your work are placed together. In order to do this, you will need to work one row less on one needle or reverse one of the needles.

When grafting garter stitch, it is important that the purl stitches of the front piece face the knit stitches of the back piece.

Grafting on stockinette stitch

A grafted seam on stockinette stitch.

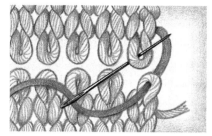

1 Insert the yarn needle purlwise into the first stitch on the front piece, then knitwise into the first stitch on the back piece. Draw the yarn through.

Grafting on garter stitch

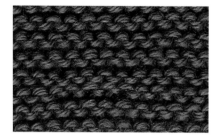

A grafted seam on garter stitch.

1 Insert the yarn needle purlwise into the first stitch on the front piece, then purlwise into the first stitch on the back piece. Draw the yarn through.

Grafting on knit one, purl one ribbing

A grafted seam on knit one, purl one ribbing. You will need four double-pointed or circular needles for this technique.

1 Separate the knit stitches from the purl stitches on each ribbed piece by slipping the knit stitches onto one needle and the purl stitches onto a second needle.

---

stockinette/reverse stockinette **22, 34**   garter **22, 34**   knitwise/purlwise **66**   circular needles **16-17, 188-93**   double-pointed needles **16-17, 78**

right/wrong sides **67-68**   ribbing **34-35**

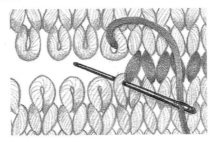

2 Insert the yarn needle knitwise into the first stitch on the front piece again. Draw the yarn through.

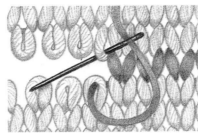

3 Insert the yarn needle purlwise into the next stitch on the front piece. Draw the yarn through.

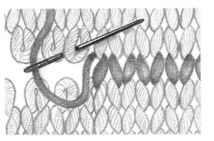

4 Insert the yarn needle purlwise into the first stitch on the back piece again. Draw the yarn through.

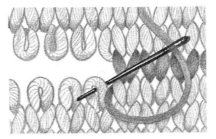

5 Insert the yarn needle knitwise into the next stitch on the back piece. Draw the yarn through. Repeat steps 2 through 5.

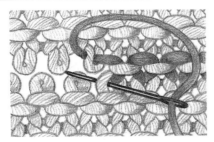

2 Insert the yarn needle knitwise into the first stitch on the front piece again. Draw the yarn through.

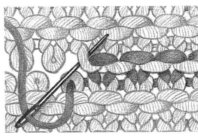

3 Insert the yarn needle purlwise into the next stitch on the front piece. Draw the yarn through.

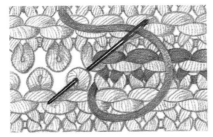

4 Insert the yarn needle knitwise into the first stitch on the back piece again. Draw the yarn through.

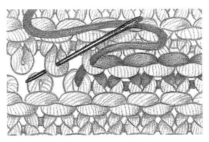

5 Insert the yarn needle purlwise into the next stitch on the back piece. Draw the yarn through. Repeat steps 2 through 5.

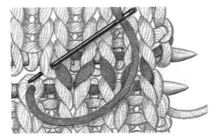

2 Graft all the knit stitches on one side of the piece as shown.

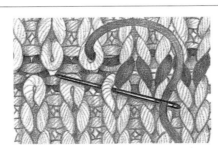

3 Turn the work. Graft all the knit stitches on the other side.

Vertical to horizontal

A finished seam showing open stitches grafted to rows on stockinette stitch.

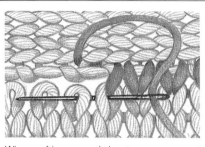

When grafting open stitches to rows, you must compensate for the difference in stitch and row gauge by occasionally picking up two horizontal bars for every stitch.

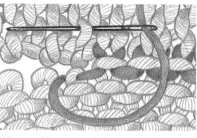

A finished seam showing open stitches grafted to rows on reverse stockinette stitch.

When grafting open stitches to rows in reverse stockinette stitch, pick up the loop of the purl stitch inside the edge, as shown.

Open stitches to bound-off stitches

A finished seam showing open stitches grafted to bound-off stitches on stockinette stitch.

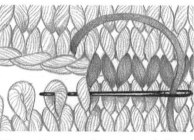

When grafting open stitches to bound-off stitches, insert the yarn needle under the stitch inside the bound-off edge and then into the corresponding stitch on the open edge.

A finished seam showing open stitches grafted to bound-off stitches on reverse stockinette stitch.

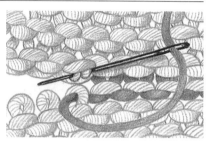

When grafting open stitches to bound-off stitches on reverse stockinette stitch, pick up two vertical strands just inside the bound-off edge, as shown.

Joining knit one, purl one ribbing

When joining ribbing with a purl stitch at each edge, insert the yarn needle under the horizontal bar in the center of a knit stitch on each side.

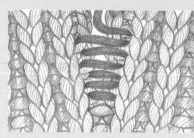

When joining ribbing with a knit stitch at each edge, use the bottom loop of the purl stitch on one side and the top loop of the corresponding purl stitch on the other side.

When joining purl and knit stitch edges, skip knit stitch and join two purl stitches as at left.

gauge **18-19, 57-59**

binding off **47-52**

Slip stitch crochet

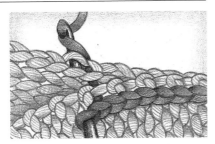

This seam can be worked any distance from the edge.

With the right sides together, insert the crochet hook through both thicknesses. Catch the yarn and draw a loop through. *Insert the hook again. Draw a loop through both thicknesses and the loop on the hook. Repeat from the *, keeping the stitches straight and even.

Single crochet

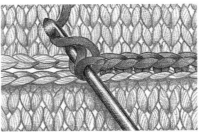

The single crochet seam is worked on the right side of the work, forming a decorative, raised seam.

Insert the hook into the inside loop of a bound-off stitch from each piece. Catch the yarn and pull a loop through. *Pull up a loop through the next two bound-off stitches, then catch the yarn and pull it through both loops on the hook. Repeat from the *.

Two-needle crochet

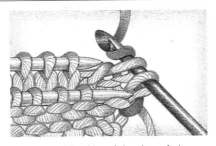

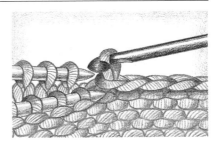

This seam is worked by using a crochet hook to join two pieces which are still on the knitting needles.

1 With the right sides of the pieces facing each other, insert the hook knitwise into the first stitch on both needles and slip them from the needles. Wrap the yarn around the hook as shown.

2 Pull the yarn through both loops on the hook. *With the hook, slip the next stitch from both needles. You now have three loops on the hook. Wrap the yarn around the hook as shown.

3 Pull the yarn through all three loops. You now have one loop on the hook. Repeat from the *.

Bind-off seam

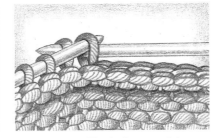

This is a finished bind-off seam on stockinette stitch. The seam is worked from the wrong side with the stitches still on the knitting needles.

1 *Insert a third needle knitwise into the first stitch on the front needle, then purlwise into the first stitch on the back needle and slip them off. Pull the first stitch over the second stitch. Repeat from the * to the end of the row.

2 Turn the work. Slip the first two stitches purlwise. *Pull the first stitch over the second. Slip the next stitch purlwise. Repeat from the * until all the stitches have been worked. Fasten off the last stitch.

crochet **210-11**   binding off **47-52**   knitwise/purlwise **66**

crochet hooks **18**   right/wrong sides **67-68**

Picking Up Stitches

When you add any type of border, such as a neckband, to finished pieces, you generally pick up stitches along the edge. It is important that you do so evenly to make a smooth join between the edge and the border.

The neatest way to pick up stitches is to do it from the right side of the work. It is also important to actually make knit stitches on a knitting needle with a separate strand of yarn rather than picking up a strand from the edge of the piece itself, which will stretch and distort the edge.

Begin picking up by attaching the yarn to the edge of the piece, or simply start picking up, pulling on the short end to make sure the stitches do not unravel.

You can use a knitting needle (straight or circular) or a crochet hook to pick up stitches. Be sure that it is one or two sizes smaller than the needles used for the main body. The smaller size is easier to insert into the fabric and will not stretch the picked-up stitches. After picking up, change to the needle size used for the edging.

If the instructions do not tell you how many stitches to pick up, measure the total area and multiply that figure by the stitch gauge of the edging to be added. To determine the gauge of the edging, pick up and add the edging to your gauge swatch or make a separate piece using the pattern stitch for the edging. If you have already used the edging in the main body of the sweater, measure your gauge from that.

Along a shaped edge, such as a neck, make sure you pick up inside the edge so as not to create any holes.

If you are making a band in a different color from the main piece, pick up stitches with the main color, then change the color on the first row.

If you change the size of the sweater from the instructions, make sure you adjust the number of stitches to be picked up accordingly.

When you pick up stitches on a long piece, such as the entire outside edge of a cardigan, there may be too many stitches to fit on a straight, single-pointed needle. Divide the edge in half, working first along the right front to the center back neck and then from the center back neck along the left front. Then seam your edging at the back neck. Alternately, all of your stitches may fit on a long circular needle.

When picking up for a neckband on a pullover with a single-pointed needle, sew one shoulder seam. Pick up the stitches required, work the edging, then sew the second shoulder seam and the side of the neckband. If using circular or double-pointed needles, sew both shoulder seams, pick up the required stitches, join and work the edging in rounds.

Marking edge for picking up stitches

Stitches must be picked up evenly so that the band will not flare or pull in. Place pins, markers or yarn, as shown, every two inches (5cm) and pick up the same number of stitches between each pair of markers. If you know the number of stitches to be picked up, divide this by the number of sections to determine how many stitches to pick up in each one.

Horizontal edge with knitting needle

Stitches picked up along a bound-off edge.

1 Insert the knitting needle into the center of the first stitch in the row below the bound-off edge. Wrap the yarn knitwise around the needle.

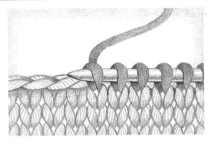

2 Draw the yarn through. You have picked up one stitch. Continue to pick up one stitch in each stitch along the bound-off edge.

Vertical edge with knitting needle

Stitches picked up along a side edge.

1 Insert the knitting needle into the corner stitch of the first row, one stitch in from the side edge. Wrap the yarn around the needle knitwise.

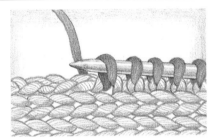

2 Draw the yarn through. You have picked up one stitch. Continue to pick up stitches along the edge. Occasionally skip one row to keep the edge from flaring.

Shaped edge with knitting needle

Stitches picked up along a curved edge.

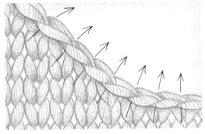

Pick up stitches neatly just inside the shaped edge, following the curve and hiding the jagged selvage.

Stitches picked up along a diagonal edge.

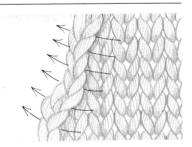

Pick up stitches one stitch in from the shaped edge, keeping them in a straight line.

binding off **47-52**   selvages **194-95**

knitwise **66**

Picking up along a neck edge

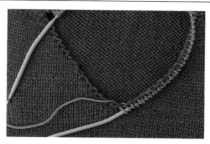

The stitches for this neckband are picked up around the V-neck using straight needles. Leave the right shoulder seam unsewn and begin picking up stitches at the right back neck. Work the neckband back and forth.

The stitches for this neckband are picked up around the V-neck using a circular needle. Sew both shoulders and begin picking up stitches at the right back neck. Place a marker and join the piece.

The stitches for this neckband are picked up around the V-neck using double-pointed needles. Sew both shoulders and begin picking up stitches at the right back neck. Use one needle for the back and one needle for each front. Place a marker and join the piece.

Picking up stitches with a crochet hook

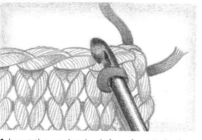

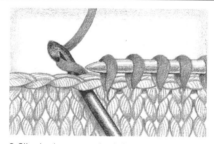

1 Insert the crochet hook from front to back into the center of the first stitch one row below the bound-off edge. Catch the yarn and pull a loop through.

2 Slip the loop onto the knitting needle, being sure it is not twisted. Continue to pick up one stitch in each stitch along the bound-off edge.

The number of stitches to pick up

If the correct number of stitches are picked up, the finished edge will be straight and even.

If too few stitches are picked up, the finished edge will pull in.

If too many stitches are picked up, the finished edge will flare out.

Sewing in a Sleeve

To make seaming easier, the sleeves are usually attached to your garment before you sew the side and sleeve seams. Block the body and sleeve pieces to the correct measurements before you start. Then, after working any neck edging and seaming the shoulders, you are ready to attach the sleeves.

Whatever type of sleeve you have, make sure that it will fit into the armhole. You may be able to ease in a slight difference, but if it is too pronounced, you should block your pieces again or, in some cases, you may have to rip out part of the sleeve and rework the shaping.

Work from the right side of your pieces. Fold the sleeve in half lengthwise and mark the center top. Pin this point to the shoulder seam, then pin the rest of the sleeve top evenly along the front and back armhole, easing in any fullness. Any shaping at the top of the sleeve should be matched to the shaping on the armhole. Once the sleeve is pinned securely, sew it in place.

When seaming the straight edge of a drop shoulder or angled sleeve to the armhole, it is essential to keep the seam straight. Weave a sewing thread or thin contrasting yarn along a row of stitches on the armhole edge. Attach the straight edge of the sleeve along this line and remove the thread once the seam is complete.

Since the top of a raglan sleeve is, in fact, part of the neck edge, you will have two separate seams on the front and back of the sweater instead of one continuous seam. Begin at the base of the sleeve cap by pinning any bound-off stitches of the sleeve to the corresponding bound-off stitches of the front and back armhole. Then pin the angled edge of the sleeve along the corresponding armhole edge of the sweater. The sleeve edge must fit the armhole edge exactly. Therefore, each matching edge must have the same number of rows.

Pin and sew a set-in sleeve cap into the armhole, as shown below.

Gathered and pleated sleeve caps have fullness along the top edge of the sleeve. This area should be sewn carefully in place to keep the top from bunching.

Pinning a set-in sleeve

If the sleeve cap is slightly larger than the armhole, you can ease in the extra fullness evenly around the armhole by pinning the center of the sleeve cap to the shoulder seam and then pinning from the center to the beginning of the armhole shaping on both sides. The sleeve can then be sewn in place.

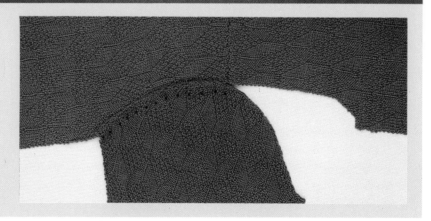

blocking **94-97**

right/wrong sides **67-68**

sleeves and cap shaping **110, 181-83**

binding off **47-52**

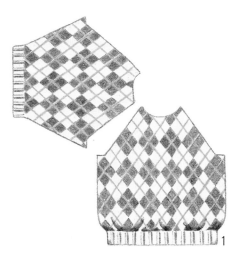

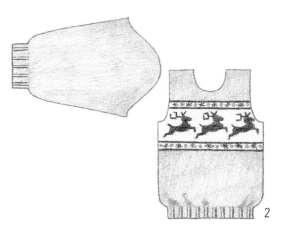

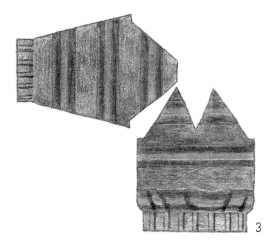

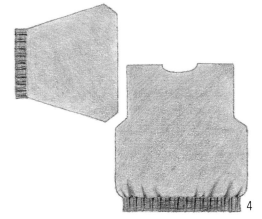

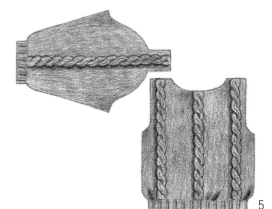

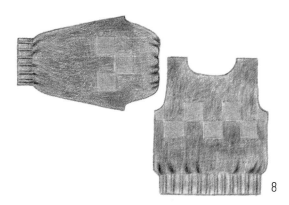

1
Raglan armhole/raglan sleeve with shaped neck
2
Shaped armhole/set-in sleeve
3
Raglan armhole/raglan sleeve
4
Angled armhole/angled sleeve
5
Shaped armhole/set-in sleeve with saddle shoulder
6
Straight armhole/straight sleeve
7
Shaped armhole/set-in sleeve with pleat
8
Shaped armhole/set-in, gathered sleeve

How to Attach and Hem

Attaching

You can make separate pieces, such as collars or elaborate edgings, and attach them later. Since these seams often follow a curve, it is important to keep the stitches even.

When you sew the open stitches of a border to the finished edge of a garment, place the open stitches on a contrasting yarn to keep them from unraveling. Remove the contrasting yarn a few stitches at a time while seaming.

Hemming

When securing a knitted-in hem, it is important that your stitching leaves no visible line on the right side of your garment.

Fold the hem to the wrong side (along the turning ridge if one has been worked), and carefully pin it in place.

Be sure that it is hemmed in a straight line. Do not pull the yarn tightly or the work will pucker.

You can hem with various types of stitches. The whip stitch is best used on medium or lightweight yarns. It creates a neat and firm seam. The stitch-by-stitch method is good for bulky yarns, as you eliminate a bulky cast-on edge by grafting open stitches to the back of the work.

Slip stitching a pocket

When attaching a separate piece, such as a patch pocket, to the knitted fabric, pick up the horizontal bar in the center of a stitch from the fabric, then the horizontal bar one stitch in from the pocket edge. Draw the yarn through.

Whip stitch on a hem

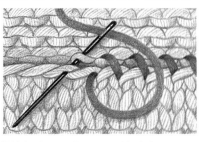

Fold the hem to the wrong side, being sure that the stitches are straight. Insert the needle into a stitch on the wrong side of the fabric and then into the cast-on edge of the hem. Draw the yarn through.

Herringbone stitch on a hem

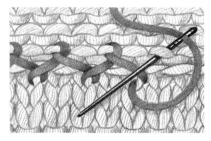

Working from left to right, attach the yarn to the upper left corner of the hem. Tack the cast-on edge of the hem to the fabric using the herringbone stitch as shown.

Backstitching and slip stitching a neckband

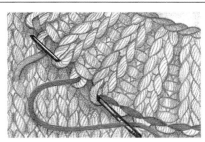

You can join open stitches of a neckband by backstitching them to the neck edge from the right side.

Backstitch instead of binding off the stitches of a band. Place the open stitches onto a contrasting yarn. Sew the stitches to the neck edge from the right side of the work using the backstitch as shown.

Slip stitch if working a doubled neckband. Pick up the stitches along the neck edge, then work the neckband to twice the desired depth. Do not bind off the stitches, but fold the band to the wrong side and slip stitch the open stitches to the fabric.

Stitch by stitch on a hem

A finished stockinette stitch hem worked stitch by stitch, shown on the right side.

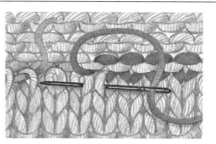

A finished stockinette stitch hem worked stitch by stitch, shown on the wrong side. Use an open cast-on for the hem.

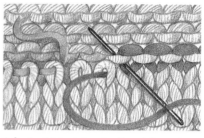

1 Graft the open cast-on stitches of the hem to the reverse stockinette side of the fabric, matching stitch for stitch.

2 On the fabric, follow the line of the purl stitches.

Knitted-in band on the right-hand side

A knit one, purl one band worked along the slip stitch selvage of a stockinette stitch piece.

1 Cast on and *rib one row of the band to the last stitch (a knit stitch) leaving it on the left needle. Insert the left needle under the first selvage stitch on the main piece and knit it together with the stitch on the left needle.

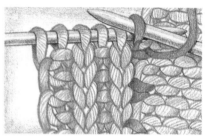

2 Turn the work and slip the first stitch purlwise with the yarn in the front, rib to the end. Repeat from the *

Knitted-in band on the left-hand side

A knit one, purl one band worked along the slip stitch selvage of a stockinette stitch piece.

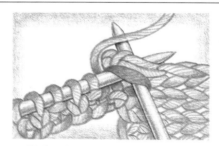

1 *Work to the last stitch of the band (a purl stitch). With the yarn in front, slip the last stitch purlwise. Turn the band. With the yarn in back, insert the left needle into the first selvage stitch on the main piece and knit it together with the slipped stitch.

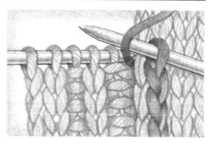

2 Leave the stitch on the right needle and rib to the end of the row. Repeat from the *.

cast on **24-29**
grafting **102-5**

selvages **194-5**
bands **207-9**

slip a stitch
purlwise **46**

ribbing **34-35, 172-73**
right/wrong sides **67-68**

IX. Care of Knitwear

Care of Knits

Cleaning and storing knits

Proper care is just as important to the life of your knit garments as the way you knit them in the first place. Take time to do it carefully. Since different fibers need different types of care, it is helpful to save information from the yarn's ball band or to sew a care label into your knit garments.

Preparing to clean

Prepare your garment for cleaning by removing any non-washable trims and making necessary repairs. To help cardigans keep their shape, baste the pockets and buttonholes closed. Check the garment for stains. You can highlight them by circling the stain with a contrasting yarn or thread.

To make sure that your sweater will have the same measurements once it is cleaned, draw a rough schematic with key measurements such as the body length and width, shoulder width and sleeve length and width.

Hand washing

You can hand wash many fibers if you do so properly, avoiding felting or shrinkage. The three causes of felting or shrinkage are friction, agitation (rubbing) and heat. The water temperature should be cool or lukewarm and be the same temperature both in the washing and rinsing stages. Wash one garment at a time in a large sink or tub and change the water after each piece.

Dissolve soap flakes or a mild detergent in the water before adding the knits. You can use hot water if the soap doesn't easily dissolve, but be sure to let the water cool down and don't use too much soap. Lay the knits flat and work the soap into the fabric by gently pressing it up and down. Do not twist, swirl or rub the knit. Let the garment soak a short time.

Machine washing

Take care before machine washing a knit. Begin by reading the yarn label. Yarns labeled "superwash" can be machine washed. Use a delicate synthetic or gentle wash cycle with cold water. Just as for hand washing, you can use warm water to dissolve the soap, allowing the water to cool before you add the garments.

Rinsing

You may need to rinse your garment several times to remove the soap residue. The water should be clear on the last rinse. You can rinse with a hand-held sprayer if your sink has one.

Squeeze out any excess water without wringing the garment. Press it against the tub or sink to remove water. Avoid stretching the garment as you lift it out by supporting it with both hands.

Tips for long-lasting sweaters

Experiment with the gauge swatch if you're in doubt about how to wash and care for a sweater. A ruined swatch can be reknit for further experimenting, but a ruined sweater will be gone forever.

Wool sweaters do not show soil readily. Spot clean with a mild solution of soap and water rather than washing the sweater frequently. This treatment also prevents wool

sweaters from becoming deeply soiled, which is when they are most difficult to clean.

Make your own care labels with the fiber content and a code, such as MW for machine washable. Use labeling tape and an indelible pen to make the labels, then sew labels into finished sweaters.

Prepare for repairs. Make a reeling from your sweater's yarn. Attach it to

a seam, or tack it on when washing your sweater to ensure that the color quality of the extra yarn is the same as your sweater.

Keep a notebook for finished knitting projects. File each project's yarn label and gauge swatch, and make notes for accurate care instructions. This becomes a reference when it's time to clean your sweaters.

care **113-16**   ball band **11**   gauge swatch **18-19, 57-59**

yarn label symbols **12**   schematic **55**

Drying and blocking

It is important to dry knits as quickly as possible. If they are left damp for any length of time, they may mildew. This is true with cotton fibers, especially heavy ones.

To further remove water, neatly roll the garment in a terry-cloth towel. You may want to repeat this process several times. You can also wrap the garment carefully in a towel and place it inside a washing machine. Use the spinning cycle to remove excess water.

All knits should be dried flat on an absorbent towel. After washing, prepare a surface for drying your garment. If you are using an area such as a bed, you may want to protect it with a piece of plastic. See Chapter VIII for ideas on blocking surfaces. You can also use a mesh drying screen (or clean window screen) placed over two chairs or a tub to allow air to circulate. As the garment dries, turn it over. You can speed the drying process by changing the damp towels, but don't ever dry pieces in direct sunlight or heat.

Using the measurements from your schematic drawing, reshape your gar-ment, pinning if necessary. Smooth the pieces out to prevent wrinkles. Careful blocking should eliminate the need for pressing, but if you need to, press sweaters carefully. Let the steam from your iron do most of the work. Lightly lift and lower the iron as you press. Don't move the iron back and forth—this could damage delicate fibers.

Machine dry your garment carefully. Dry it only at a low or delicate setting and remove it immediately from the machine. You can remove it before it is completely dry and lay it flat to air dry. To dry your garment more quickly and protect it at the same time, toss in a few absorbent towels. Check the progress of your garment as it dries. It's a good idea to test a knit swatch before you dry the whole garment.

Mohair and other hairy yarns tend to flatten and lose their loft when washed and dried. Renew the garment and fluff up the fibers by placing the sweater in a dryer for a minute or two. Use a cool air setting. Do this after the sweater has dried flat.

blocking **94-97**   swatch **57-59**

schematic **55**

Recycling yarn

To reuse yarn, first unravel it into balls. Discard any worn yarn. Always unravel from bound-off edges. Rewind balls into skeins. To remove kinks so that yarn can be used again, tie and wet the skeins. Hang and allow to dry, adding weight to take out crimps.

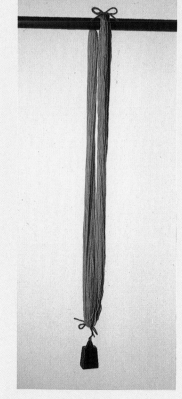

Folding and storing

Check for stains and needed repairs before you put your knits away. They should be stored folded and clean. In addition, you should always store knits flat and as loosely as possible.

If you are storing sweaters for the season, pack them loosely in tissue paper to allow the air to circulate. You may want to add tissue at the necks to keep them in shape. Divide your sweaters into two groups when storing—those that need moth prevention and those that don't. Moths are attracted to dirt, oils and animal proteins. Yarns such as cotton and synthetics will not be damaged by moths. Take special care of sweaters with lanolin and natural oils, since they are especially attractive to moths.

After dry cleaning a sweater, remove it from the plastic bag. Air it out before storage so the sweater harbors no chemical fumes.

Standard sweater

1 With the sweater face down, fold the front towards the back.

2 Fold the sleeve down, then fold the other side in the same way.

3 Fold the sweater in half.

Bulky sweater

1 With the sweater face down, fold back one sleeve.

2 Fold the other sleeve in the same way.

3 Fold the sweater in half.

X. Stitch Dictionary

Stitch Dictionary

With the use of pattern stitches, knitting can become more than a craft—it can become an art form. The wondrous versatility of knitted patterns produces every effect from delicate, webby lace to chunky winter jackets, from thick mats and rugs to soft baby clothes. Pattern stitches also make knitting fun. To knit the same fabric over and over, many times, would be boring. But with literally thousands of different fabric designs to choose from, the pattern knitter is never bored. Whether it is an allover design or a single panel of cabling or lace to set off an otherwise plain garment, patterning is the truly creative part of any handmade original.

Every knitter learns basic patterns traditionally used for borders and bands, such as ribbing, garter stitch, seed stitch and so on. But many knitters fail to realize that there are hundreds of other patterns, nearly as simple, which could add a note of true originality to their work. Practicing pattern stitches can stimulate the imagination and help even a relatively inexperienced knitter create conversation-piece garments. When you must invest so much of your time to produce any piece of handmade knitwear, why not invest it well? Why make just another dull average sweater, when with the same amount of time and little trouble you can make an original?

You can use patterns of your choice in almost any knitting project, even when commercial directions do not include them. For example, to add a patterned panel, you have only to decide how many stitches in width you want the panel to be, then place markers on the needle that many stitches apart, and work the pattern between markers as the knitting progresses.

Whether you follow commercial directions or design your own garments from scratch, it is important to check the gauge of every pattern stitch that you plan to use. With the same yarn and needles intended for the project, knit a good-sized test swatch of the pattern (about four inches/10 centimeters square), then measure the number of stitches and rows per inch/centimeter. Some patterns expand. Others contract. Some shorten in length and spread in width. Others do the opposite. Obviously, gauges of vertical pattern panels must match the general lengthwise gauge of the garment. Pattern panels that contract horizontally, like cables, may need more stitches in the panel or either side of the panel so the garment does not become too narrow. Pattern panels that expand horizontally, like eyelets and lace, may need fewer stitches so the garment does not become too wide.

To design your own borders, collars, cuffs, decorative items or entire garments from scratch with various pattern stitches, your first step is always to make test swatches. You must take the gauge of any pattern stitch(es) that you will use, so you can work to the measurements that you want. Multiply the number of stitches per inch/centimeter by the number of inches/centimeters desired, and you have the number of stitches you will need for any given portion of the work. Test swatches can be saved for future reference.

Another helpful hint: when reading directions for an unfamiliar or complicated pattern stitch, write down the number of each row as you work it, so you won't lose your place. Another method is to lay a card or a ruler over the page to cover up each row as you finish it.

Once you begin working extensively with patterns, you will probably never look back at plain stockinette stitch, because patterns are so much more interesting. Also, they offer you virtually infinite choices. The thousands of pattern stitches already invented have not exhausted all the possibilities, by any means. Almost any knitter can invent a new variation or two with a little thought—and sometimes, through a serendipitous mistake! Many delightful pattern stitches yet remain to be discovered: some of them, perhaps, by you.

Barbara G. Walker

Knit and Purl Stitches

Garter stitch on the bias

Cast on 3 sts.

Row 1 (RS): K1, yo, k1, yo, k1.

Row 2 and all WS rows: Knit.

Row 3: K1, yo, k3, yo, k1.

Cont to inc 1 st each side of every RS row as foll: RS rows: K1, yo, k to last st, yo, k1. Work to desired width.

Dec 1 st each side of every RS row as foll: RS rows: K1, SKP, k to last 3 sts, k2tog, k1.

Cont until 5 sts rem.

Next RS row: K1, sl 1, k2tog, psso.

Next WS row: Knit.

Bind off rem 3 sts.

Moss stitch

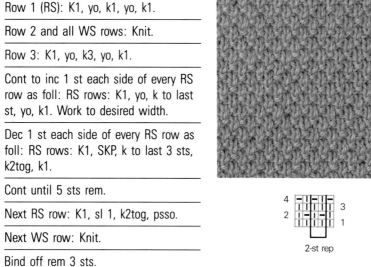

Multiple of 2 sts + 1 extra

Rows 1 and 3 (RS): Knit.

Row 2: P1, *k1, p1; rep from * to end.

Row 4: K1, *p1, k1, rep from * to end.

Rep rows 1-4.

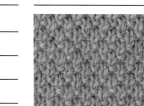

2-st rep

Simple texture stitch

Multiple of 4 sts

Row 1 (RS): *K3, p1; rep from * to end.

Rows 2 and 4: Purl.

Row 3: Knit.

Row 5: K1, *p1, k3; rep from *, end last rep k2.

Rows 6 and 8: Purl.

Row 7: Knit.

Rep rows 1-8.

4-st rep

Horizontal dash stitch

Multiple of 10 sts + 6 extra

Row 1 (RS): P6, *k4, p6; rep from * to end.

Row 2 and all WS rows: Purl.

Row 3: Knit.

Row 5: P1, *k4, p6; rep from *, end last rep p1.

Row 7: Knit.

Row 8: Purl.

Rep rows 1-8.

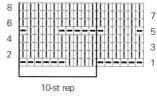

10-st rep

abbreviations explained **60-63**   knitting terminology **64-68**   symbolcraft charts **69-70**

Double alternate andalou stitch

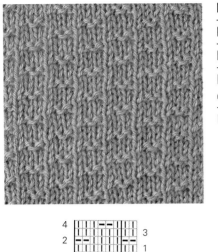

4
2
3
1

6-st rep

Multiple of 6 sts + 2 extra

Rows 1 and 3 (RS): Knit.

Row 2: K2, *p4, k2; rep from * to end.

Row 4: P2, *p1, k2, p3; rep from * to end.

Rep rows 1-4.

Vertical caterpillar stitch

12
10
8
6
4
2
11
9
7
5
3
1

6-st rep

Multiple of 6 sts

Rows 1, 3 and 5 (RS): *P2, k1 tbl, p3; rep from * to end.

Rows 2, 4 and 6: *K3, p1 tbl, k2; rep from * to end.

Rows 7, 9 and 11: *P5, k1 tbl; rep from * to end

Rows 8, 10 and 12: *P1 tbl, k5; rep from * to end.

Rep rows 1-12.

Reverse stockinette chevrons

6
4
2
5
3
1

6-st rep

Multiple of 6 sts + 5 extra

Row 1 (RS): K5, *p1, k5; rep from * to end.

Row 2: K1, *p3, k3; rep from *, end last rep k1.

Row 3: P2, *k1, p2; rep from * to end.

Row 4: P1, *k3, p3; rep from *, end last rep p1.

Row 5: K2, *p1, k5; rep from *, end last rep k2.

Row 6: Purl.

Rep rows 1-6.

Flying geese

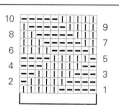

10-st rep

Multiple of 10 sts

Row 1 (RS): *P5, k5; rep from * to end.

Row 2: K1, *p5, k5; rep from *, end last rep k4.

Row 3: P3, *k5, p5; rep from *, end last rep p2.

Row 4: K3, *p5, k5; rep from *, end last rep k2.

Row 5: P1, *k5, p5; rep from *, end last rep p4.

Row 6: P4, *k5, p5; rep from *, end last rep p1.

Row 7: K2, *p5, k5; rep from *, end last rep k3.

Row 8: P2, *k5, p5; rep from *, end last rep p3.

Row 9: K4, *p5, k5; rep from *, end last rep k1.

Row 10: *K5, p5; rep from * to end.

Rep rows 1-10.

Parquet stitch

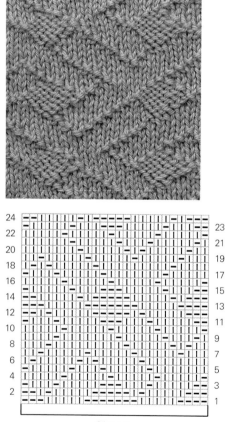

24-st rep

Multiple of 24 sts

Row 1 (RS): P4, *k5, p7; rep from *, end last rep p3.

Row 2: *K2, p1, k1, p5, k3; rep from * to end.

Row 3: *P2, k5, p1, k3, p1; rep from * to end.

Row 4: *P5, k1; rep from * to end.

Row 5: *K7, p1, k5, p1, k3, p1, k5, p1; rep from * to end.

Row 6: *P1, k1, p5, k1, p1, k1, p5, k1, p8; rep from * to end.

Row 7: *K3, p1, k2; rep from * to end.

Row 8: *P3, k1, p9, k1, p5, k1, p1, k1, p2; rep from * to end.

Row 9: *K1, p1, k3, p1, k5, p1, k7, p1, k4; rep from * to end.

Row 10: Rep row 4.

Row 11: *P2, k5, p1, k3, p1; rep from * to end.

Row 12: *K2, p1, k1, p5, k3; rep from * to end.

Row 13: *P4, k5, p3; rep from * to end.

Row 14: *K2, p5, k1, p1, k3; rep from * to end.

Row 15: *P2, k3, p1, k5, p1; rep from * to end.

Row 16: Rep row 4.

Row 17: *K5, p1, k7, p1, k5, p1, k3, p1; rep from * to end.

Row 18: *[P1, k1] twice, p5, k1, p9, k1, p4; rep from * to end.

Row 19: Rep row 7.

Row 20: *P7, k1, p5, k1, p1, k1, p5, k1, p2; rep from * to end.

Row 21: *K1, p1, k5, p1, k3, p1, k5, p1, k6; rep from * to end.

Row 22: Rep row 4.

Row 23: Rep row 15.

Row 24: Rep row 14.

Rep rows 1-24.

abbreviations explained **60-63**

knitting terminology **64-68**

symbolcraft charts **69-70**

Triangles

14-st rep

Multiple of 14 sts + 1 extra

Row 1 (RS): P1, *k13, p1; rep from * to end.

Row 2: K1, *k1, p11, k2; rep from * to end.

Row 3: *P3, k9, p2; rep from *, end p1.

Row 4: K1, *k3, p7, k4; rep from * to end.

Row 5: *P5, k5, p4; rep from *, end p1.

Row 6: K1, *k5, p3, k6; rep from * to end.

Row 7: *P7, k1, p6; rep from *, end p1.

Row 8: P1, *p6, k1, p7; rep from * to end.

Row 9: *K6, p3, k5; rep from *, end k1.

Row 10: P1, *p4, k5, p5; rep from * to end.

Row 11: *K4, p7, k3; rep from *, end k1.

Row 12: P1, *p2, k9, p3; rep from * to end.

Row 13: *K2, p11, k1; rep from *, end k1.

Row 14: P1, *k13, p1; rep from * to end.

Rep rows 1-14.

Basketweave

8-st rep

Multiple of 8 sts + 5 extra

Row 1 (RS): Knit.

Row 2: K5, *p3, k5; rep from * to end.

Row 3: P5, *k3, p5; rep from * to end.

Row 4: Rep row 2.

Row 5: Knit.

Row 6: K1, *p3, k5; rep from *, end last rep k1.

Row 7: P1, *k3, p5; rep from *, end last rep p1.

Row 8: Rep row 6.

Rep rows 1-8.

Basket stitch

6-st rep

Multiple of 6 sts + 2 extra

Row 1 and all RS rows: Knit.

Rows 2 and 8: Purl.

Rows 4 and 6: P2, *k4, p2; rep from * to end.

Rows 10 and 12: K2, *k1, p2, k3; rep from * to end.

Rep rows 1-12.

Five/five squares

Multiple of 10 sts + 5 extra

Row 1 (RS): K5, *p5, k5; rep from * to end.

Rows 2-7: K the knit sts and p the purl sts.

Row 8 (WS): Rep row 1.

Rows 9-14: K the knit sts and p the purl sts.

Rep rows 1-14.

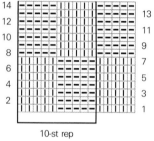

10-st rep

Brick stitch

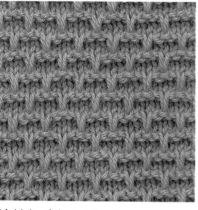

Multiple of 4 sts + 1 extra

Row 1 (RS): K4, *k1 wrapping yarn twice around needle, k3; rep from *, end k1.

Row 2: P4, *sl 1 purlwise dropping extra wrap, p3; rep from *, end p1.

Row 3: K4, *sl 1 purlwise, k3; rep from *, end k1.

Row 4: K4, *wyif, sl 1 purlwise, wyib, k3; rep from *, end k1.

Row 5: K2, *k1 wrapping yarn twice around needle, k3; rep from *, end last rep k2.

Row 6: P2, *sl 1 purlwise dropping extra wrap, p3; rep from *, end last rep p2.

Row 7: K2, *sl 1 purlwise, k3; rep from *, end last rep k2.

Row 8: K2, *wyif, sl 1 purlwise, wyib, k3; rep from *, end last rep k2.

Rep rows 1-8.

King Charles brocade

12-st rep

Multiple of 12 sts + 1 extra

Row 1 (RS): K1, *p1, k9, p1, k1; rep from * to end.

Row 2: K1, *p1, k1, p7, k1, p1, k1; rep from * to end.

Row 3: K1, *p1, k1, p1, k5, [p1, k1] twice; rep from * to end.

Row 4: P1, *[p1, k1] twice, p3, k1, p1, k1, p2; rep from * to end.

Row 5: K1, *k2, [p1, k1] 3 times, p1, k3; rep from * to end.

Row 6: P1, *p3, [k1, p1] twice, k1, p4; rep from * to end.

Row 7: K1, *k4, p1, k1, p1, k5; rep from * to end.

Row 8: Rep row 6.

Row 9: Rep row 5.

Row 10: Rep row 4.

Row 11: Rep row 3.

Row 12: Rep row 2.

Rep rows 1-12.

Embossed diamonds

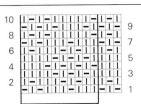

10-st rep

Multiple of 10 sts + 3 extra

Row 1 (RS): P1, k1, p1, *[k3, p1] twice, k1, p1; rep from * to end.

Row 2: P1, k1, *p3, k1, p1, k1, p3, k1; rep from *, end p1.

Row 3: K4, *[p1, k1] twice, p1, k5; rep from *, end last rep k4.

Row 4: P3, *[k1, p1] 3 times, k1, p3; rep from * to end.

Row 5: Rep row 3.

Row 6: Rep row 2.

Row 7: Rep row 1.

Row 8: P1, k1, p1, *k1, p5, [k1, p1] twice; rep from * to end.

Row 9: [P1, k1] twice, *p1, k3, [p1, k1] 3 times; rep from *, end last rep [p1, k1] twice, p1.

Row 10: Rep row 8.

Rep rows 1-10.

Diamond and lozenge pattern

12-st rep

Multiple of 12 sts

Rows 1 and 2: *K6, p6; rep from * to end.

Rows 3 and 4: *P1, k5, p5, k1; rep from * to end.

Rows 5 and 6: *K1, p1, k4, p4, k1, p1; rep from * to end.

Rows 7 and 8: *P1, k1, p1, k3, p3, k1, p1, k1; rep from * to end.

Rows 9 and 10: *[K1, p1] twice, k2, p2, [k1, p1] twice; rep from * to end.

Rows 11 and 12: *P1, k1; rep from * to end.

Rows 13 and 14: *K1, p1; rep from * to end.

Rows 15 and 16: *[P1, k1] twice, p2, k2, [p1, k1] twice; rep from * to end.

Rows 17 and 18: *K1, p1, k1, p3, k3, p1, k1, p1; rep from * to end.

Rows 19 and 20: *P1, k1, p4, k4, p1, k1; rep from * to end.

Rows 21 and 22: *K1, p5, k5, p1; rep from * to end.

Rows 23 and 24: *P6, k6; rep from * to end.

Rows 25 and 26: *P5, k1, p1, k5; rep from * to end.

Rows 27 and 28: *P4, [k1, p1] twice, k4; rep from * to end.

Rows 29 and 30: *P3, [k1, p1] 3 times, k3; rep from * to end.

Rows 31 and 32: *P2, [k1, p1] 4 times, k2; rep from * to end.

Rows 33 and 34: *P1, k1; rep from * to end.

Rows 35 and 36: *K1, p1; rep from * to end.

Rows 37 and 38: *K2, [p1, k1] 4 times, p2; rep from * to end.

Rows 39 and 40: *K3, [p1, k1] 3 times, p3; rep from * to end.

Rows 41 and 42: *K4, [p1, k1] twice, p4; rep from * to end.

Rows 43 and 44: *K5, p1, k1, p5; rep from * to end.

Rep rows 1-44.

abbreviations explained **60-63**   knitting terminology **64-68**   symbolcraft charts **69-70**

Ribs

Broken 2 X 2 rib

Multiple of 4 sts

Row 1 (RS): *K2, p2; rep from * to end.

Rows 2-6: Rep row 1.

Rows 7-12: *P2, k2; rep from * to end.

Rep rows 1-12.

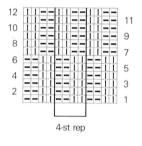

4-st rep

Beaded rib

Multiple of 5 sts + 2 extra

Row 1 (RS): K2, *p3, k2; rep from * to end.

Row 2: P2, *k1, p1, k1, p2; rep from * to end.

Rep rows 1 and 2.

5-st rep

Ribbed garter stitch

Multiple of 4 sts + 1 extra

Preparation row (RS): Knit.

Row 1: *K3, yo, sl 1 purlwise; rep from *, end k1. (Note: This row increases one st for every repeat.)

Row 2: K1, *k next st and yo tog tbl, k3; rep from * to end. (Note: This row decreases the sts that were increased in row 1.)

Rep rows 1 and 2.

Alternate fisherman's rib

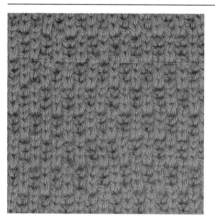

Multiple of 2 sts + 1 extra

Note: When alternating sts on row 7, and every 6th row after, make the st in row below under the extra yarn from the st from previous row.

Preparation row (RS): Knit.

Rows 1, 3 and 5: K1, *k1 in row below (k1-b), k1; rep from * to end.

Rows 2, 4 and 6: K1-b, *k1, k1-b; rep from * to end.

Rows 7, 9 and 11: K1-b, *k1, k1-b; rep from * to end.

Rows 8, 10 and 12: K1, *k1-b, k1; rep from * to end.

Rep rows 1-12.

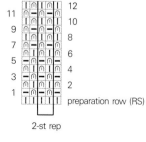

preparation row (RS)

2-st rep

abbreviations explained 60-63   knitting terminology 64-68   symbolcraft charts 69-70

Mistake-stitch ribbing

Multiple of 4 sts + 3 extra

Row 1: *K2, p2; rep from *, end k2, p1.

Rep this row.

4-st rep

Rickrack ribbing

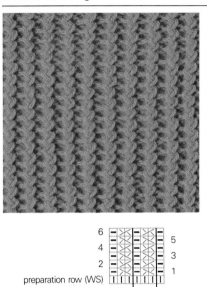

Multiple of 3 sts + 1 extra

2-st left twist (LT): Wyif and RH needle behind LH needle, skip next st and k the 2nd st tbl, then k skipped st, sl both sts from needle tog.

2-st right twist (RT): Wyif skip next st and purl the 2nd st, then purl skipped st, sl both sts from needle tog.

Preparation row (WS): Purl.

Row 1 (RS): P1, *LT, p1; rep from * to end.

Row 2: K1, *RT, k1; rep from * to end.

Rep rows 1 and 2.

preparation row (WS)

3-st rep

Twisted ribs

Multiple of 10 sts + 3 extra

3-st left twist: Slip 1 st to cn and hold to front of work, k2, k1 from cn.

3-st right twist: Sl 2 sts to cn and hold to back of work, k1, then k2 from cn.

Row 1 (RS): P3, *k3, p1, k3, p3; rep from * to end.

Row 2: K3, *p3, k1, p3, k3; rep from * to end.

Row 3: P3, *sl 1 purlwise wyib, k2, p1, k2, sl 1 purlwise wyib, p3; rep from * to end.

Row 4: K3, *sl 1 purlwise wyif, p2, k1, p2, sl 1 purlwise wyif, k3; rep from * to end.

Row 5: P3, *3-st left twist, p1, 3-st right twist, p3; rep from * to end.

Row 6: Rep row 2.

Rep rows 1-6.

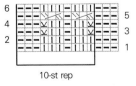

10-st rep

Diagonal cross rib

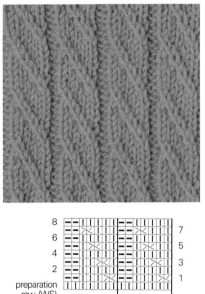

Multiple of 7 sts

Left twist (LT): K 2nd st on LH needle tbl, then k first 2 sts tog tbl.

Preparation row (WS): Purl.

Row 1 (RS): *LT, k3, p2; rep from * to end.

Row 2 and all WS rows: *K2, p5; rep from * to end.

Row 3: *K1, LT, k2, p2; rep from * to end.

Row 5: *K2, LT, k1, p2; rep from * to end.

Row 7: *K3, LT, p2; rep from * to end.

Row 8: Rep row 2.

Rep rows 1-8.

preparation row (WS)

7-st rep

abbreviations explained **60-63**

knitting terminology **64-68**

symbolcraft charts **69-70**

Embossed Stitches

Embossed stitch

9-st rep

Multiple of 9 sts

4-st right purl cable: Sl 1 st to cn and hold to back of work, p3, k1 from cn.

4-st left purl cable: Sl 3 sts to cn and hold to front of work, k1, p3 from cn.

Rows 1 and 7 (RS): Purl.

Rows 2, 6 and 8: Knit.

Row 3: *K5, 4-st right purl cable; rep from * to end.

Row 4: *P1, k3, p5; rep from * to end.

Row 5: *K4, 4-st right purl cable, k1; rep from * to end.

Row 9: *4-st left purl cable, k5; rep from * to end.

Row 10: *P5, k3, p1; rep from * to end.

Row 11: *K1, 4-st left purl cable, k4; rep from * to end.

Row 12: Knit.

Rep rows 1-12.

Mock cable

10 sts

Panel of 10 sts

Row 1 (RS): K4, p2, k4.

Row 2 and all WS rows: K the knit sts and p the purl sts.

Row 3: K3, p2, k4, p1.

Row 5: P1, k1, p2, k4, p2.

Row 7: P3, k4, p3.

Row 9: P2, k4, p2, k1, p1.

Row 11: P1, k4, p2, k3.

Rows 13, 15 and 17: Rep row 1.

Row 18: Rep row 2.

Rep rows 1-18.

abbreviations
explained **60-63**

knitting
terminology **64-68**

symbolcraft
charts **69-70**

Waved ribbing

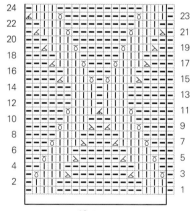

18-st rep

Multiple of 18 sts + 1 extra

Row 1 (RS): P1, *k3, p11, k3, p1; rep from * to end.

Row 2: K1, *p3, k11, p3, k1; rep from * to end.

Row 3: P1, *m1, k3, p2tog, p7, p2tog tbl, k3, m1, p1; rep from * to end.

Row 4: K2, *p3, k9, p3, k3; rep from *, end last rep k2.

Row 5: P2, *m1, k3, p2tog, p5, p2tog tbl, k3, m1, p3; rep from *, end last rep p2.

Row 6: K3, *p3, k7, p3, k5; rep from *, end last rep k3.

Row 7: P3, *m1, k3, p2tog, p3, p2tog tbl, k3, m1, p5; rep from *, end last rep p3.

Row 8: K4, *p3, k5, p3, k7; rep from *, end last rep k4.

Row 9: P4, *m1, k3, p2tog, p1, p2tog tbl, k3, m1, p7; rep from *, end last rep p4.

Row 10: K5, *p3, k3, p3, k9; rep from *, end last rep k5.

Row 11: P5, *m1, k3, p3tog, k3, m1, p9; rep from *, end last rep p5.

Row 12: K6, *p3, k1, p3, k11; rep from *, end last rep k6.

Row 13: P6, *k3, p1, k3, p11; rep from *, end last rep p6.

Row 14: Rep row 12.

Row 15: P4, *p2tog tbl, k3, m1, p1, m1, k3, p2tog, p7; rep from *, end last rep p4.

Row 16: K5, *p3, k3, p3, k9; rep from *, end last rep k5.

Row 17: P3, *p2tog tbl, k3, m1, p3, m1, k3, p2tog, p5; rep from *, end last rep p3.

Row 18: K4, *p3, k5, p3, k7; rep from *, end last rep k4.

Row 19: P2, *p2tog tbl, k3, m1, p5, m1, k3, p2tog, p3; rep from *, end last rep p2.

Row 20: K3, *p3, k7, p3, k5; rep from *, end last rep k3.

Row 21: P1, *p2tog tbl, k3, m1, p7, m1, k3, p2tog, p1; rep from * to end.

Row 22: K2, *p3, k9, p3, k3; rep from *, end last rep k2.

Row 23: P2tog tbl, *k3, m1, p9, m1, k3, p3tog; rep from *, end last rep p2tog.

Row 24: K1, *p3, k11, p3, k1; rep from * to end.

Rep rows 1-24.

Embossed twining vine leaf

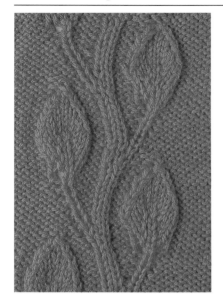

Panel of 26 sts

Knit inc: K into front and back of st.

Purl inc: P into front and back of st.

Row 1 (WS): K5, p5, k4, p3, k9.

Row 2: P7, p2tog, knit inc, k2, p4, k2, yo, k1, yo, k2, p5—28 sts.

Row 3: K5, p7, k4, p2, k1, p1, k8.

Row 4: P6, p2tog, k1, purl inc, k2, p4, k3, yo, k1, yo, k3, p5—30 sts.

Row 5: K5, p9, k4, p2, k2, p1, k7.

Row 6: P5, p2tog, k1, purl inc, p1, k2, p4, ssk, k5, k2tog, p5—28 sts.

Row 7: K5, p7, k4, p2, k3, p1, k6.

Row 8: P4, p2tog, k1, purl inc, p2, k2, p4, ssk, k3, k2tog, p5—26 sts.

Row 9: K5, p5, k4, p2, k4, p1, k5.

Row 10: P5, yo, k1, yo, p4, k2, p4, ssk, k1, k2tog, p5.

Row 11: K5, p3, k4, p2, k4, p3, k5.

Row 12: P5, [k1, yo] twice, k1, p4, k1, m1, k1, p2tog, p2, sl 2 knitwise, k1, p2sso, p5.

Row 13: K9, p3, k4, p5, k5.

Row 14: P5, k2, yo, k1, yo, k2, p4, k1, knit inc, k1, p2tog, p7—28 sts.

Row 15: K8, p1, k1, p2, k4, p7, k5.

Row 16: P5, k3, yo, k1, yo, k3, p4, k2, purl inc, k1, p2tog, p6—30 sts.

Row 17: K7, p1, k2, p2, k4, p9, k5.

Row 18: P5, ssk, k5, k2tog, p4, k2, p1, purl inc, k1, p2tog, p5—28 sts.

Row 19: K6, p1, k3, p2, k4, p7, k5.

Row 20: P5, ssk, k3, k2tog, p4, k2, p2, purl inc, k1, p2tog, p4—26 sts.

Row 21: K5, p1, k4, p2, k4, p5, k5.

Row 22: P5, ssk, k1, k2tog, p4, k2, p4, yo, k1, yo, p5.

Row 23: K5, p3, k4, p2, k4, p3, k5.

Row 24: P5, sl 2 knitwise, k1, p2sso, p2, p2tog, k1, m1, k1, p4, [k1, yo] twice, k1, p5.

Rep rows 1-24.

Embossed heart

Panel of 15 sts (inc to 21)

Purl inc: [P1 tbl, p1] into 1 st insert LH needle into horizontal strand between the 2 sts just made and p1 into this strand (3 sts made in one st.)

5 to 1 dec: Ssk, k3tog, pass ssk sts over k3tog sts.

Inc 1: K1 in row below, then k same st on needle.

Rows 1 and 3 (WS): Knit.

Row 2: Purl.

Row 4: P7, purl inc, p7—17 sts.

Row 5: K7, p3, k7.

Row 6: P5, p2tog, k1, purl inc, k1, p2tog, p5—17 sts.

Row 7: K6, p5, k6.

Row 8: P4, p2tog, k2, purl inc, k2, p2tog, p4—17 sts.

Row 9: K5, p7, k5.

Row 10: P3, p2tog, k3, purl inc, k3, p2tog, p3—17 sts.

Row 11: K4, p9, k4.

Row 12: P4, k4, purl inc, k4, p4—19 sts.

Row 13: K4, p5, k1, p5, k4.

Row 14: P4, k5, [p1, yo, p1] in next st, k5, p4—21 sts.

Row 15: K4, p5, k3, p5, k4.

Row 16: P4, 5 to 1 dec, inc 1, p1, inc 1, 5 to 1 dec, p4—15 sts.

Rep rows 1-16.

Chevron

8-st rep

Multiple of 8 sts + 1 extra

Row 1 (RS): K1, *p7, k1; rep from * to end.

Row 2: P1, *k7, p1; rep from * to end.

Row 3: K2, *p5, k3; rep from *, end last rep k2.

Row 4: P2, *k5, p3; rep from *, end last rep p2.

Row 5: K3, *p3, k5; rep from *, end last rep k3.

Row 6: P3, *k3, p5; rep from *, end last rep p3.

Row 7: K4, *p1, k7; rep from *, end last rep k4.

Row 8: P4, *k1, p7; rep from *, end last rep p4.

Row 9: Rep row 2.

Row 10: Rep row 1.

Row 11: Rep row 4.

Row 12: Rep row 3.

Row 13: Rep row 6.

Row 14: Rep row 5.

Row 15: Rep row 8.

Row 16: Rep row 7.

Rep rows 1-16.

Relief blocks

14-st rep

Multiple of 14 sts + 1 extra

Rows 1, 3, 11 and 13 (RS): Purl.

Rows 2 and 12: Knit.

Row 4: P1, *p5, sl next 3 sts purlwise wyif, p6; rep from * to end.

Row 5: *K6, sl next 3 sts purlwise wyib, p5; rep from *, end k1.

Rows 6, 8 and 10: Rep row 4.

Rows 7 and 9: Rep row 5.

Row 14: Sl 1 purlwise wyif, *sl 1 purlwise, p11, sl 2 purlwise; rep from * to end.

Row 15: *Sl 2 purlwise, k11, sl 1 purlwise; rep from *, end sl 1 purlwise.

Rows 16, 18 and 20: Rep row 14.

Rows 17 and 19: Rep row 15.

Rep rows 1-20.

Bobbles and Knots

Dot-knot stitch

6-st rep

Multiple of 6 sts + 1 extra

Dot-knot stitch: Insert RH needle from front to back under horizontal strand between first and 2nd sts on LH needle, wrap yarn and draw through a loop loosely; insert RH needle between same sts above horizontal strand, draw through another loop loosely; bring yarn to front between needles and purl the first st on LH needle; with point of LH needle, pass the first loop over the 2nd loop and the purled st and off needle; pass the 2nd loop over the purled st and off needle.

Row 1 (RS): Knit.

Row 2 and all WS rows: Purl.

Row 3: K3, *work dot-knot stitch, k5; rep from *, end last rep k3.

Rows 5: Knit.

Row 7: *Work dot-knot st, k5; rep from *, end k1.

Row 8: Purl.

Rep rows 1-8.

Peppercorn stitch

4-st rep

Multiple of 4 sts + 3 extra

Peppercorn st: K next st, [sl st just knit back to LH needle and knit it again tbl] 3 times.

Row 1 (RS): K3, *peppercorn st, k3; rep from * to end.

Rows 2: Purl.

Row 3: K1, *peppercorn st, k3; rep from *, end last rep k1.

Row 4: Purl.

Rep rows 1-4.

Trinity, cluster or bramble stitch

Multiple of 4 sts

Row 1 (RS): Purl.

Row 2: *[K1, p1, k1] in same st, p3tog; rep from * to end.

Row 3: Purl.

Row 4: *P3tog, [k1, p1, k1] in same st; rep from * to end.

Rep rows 1-4.

Berry stitch

Multiple of 4 sts

Row 1 (WS): *[K1, yo, k1] in same st, p3tog; rep from * to end.

Row 2: *K1, p3; rep from * to end.

Row 3: *K3, p1; rep from * to end.

Row 4: *P1, k3; rep from * to end.

Row 5: *P3tog, [k1, yo, k1] in same st; rep from * to end.

Row 6: *P3, k1; rep from * to end.

Row 7: *P1, k3; rep from * to end.

Row 8: *K3, p1; rep from * to end.

Rep rows 1-8.

Nosegay pattern

```
10 ===--==||||--=--=== 9
 8 ==-|--=||||--=-|--== 7
 6 --|-=--||||--=-|--
 4 ==-===|||--===== 5
 2 ==-==||||--===== 3
preparation ======||||-======= 1
row (WS)        16 sts
```

Panel of 16 sts

2-st left twist (LT): With RH needle behind LH needle, skip the first st and k 2nd st tbl, insert RH needle into backs of both sts, k2tog tbl.

2-st left purl twist (LPT): Sl 1 st to cn and hold to front of work, p1, k1 from cn.

2-st right twist (RT): K2tog leaving sts on LH needle, k first st again, sl both sts from needle.

2-st right purl twist (RPT): Sl 1 st to cn and hold to back of work, k1, p1 from cn.

Make bobble (MB): [K1, p1] twice into next st, turn, p4, turn, k4, turn [p2tog] twice, turn, k2tog.

Preparation row (WS): K7, p2, k7.

Row 1: P6, RT, LT, p6.

Row 2: K5, LPT, p2, RPT, k5.

Row 3: P4, RPT, RT, LT, LPT, p4.

Row 4: K3, LPT, k1, p4, k1, RPT, k3.

Row 5: P2, RPT, p1, RPT, k2, LPT, p1, LPT, p2.

Row 6: [K2, p1] twice, k1, p2, k1, [p1, k2] twice.

Row 7: P2, MB, p1, RPT, p1, k2, p1, LPT, p1, MB, p2.

Row 8: K4, p1, k2, p2, k2, p1, k4.

Row 9: P4, MB, p2, k2, p2, MB, p4.

Row 10 (WS): K7, p2, k7.

Rep rows 1-10.

Flower garden

Multiple of 12 sts + 13 extra

Rows 1, 3 and 5 (RS): P12, *k1 tbl, p11; rep from *, end p1.

Rows 2, 4, 6 and 8: K12, *p1 tbl, k11; rep from *, end k1.

Row 7: P8, *insert a crochet hook (or point of RH needle) from front through the fabric at right of the twisted knit st in first row, catch yarn and draw through a long, loose loop; sl this loop onto RH needle, knit next st and pass the loop over st; p3, k1 tbl, p3, draw through another loop from left of same st in first row, sl the loop onto RH needle, knit next st and pass loop over it; p3; rep from *, end p5.

Row 9: P12, *[k1, yo] 3 times and k1, all in the same st, making 7 sts from one, p11; rep from *, end p1.

Row 10: K12, *p7, k11; rep from *, end k1.

Row 11: P12, *k2tog tbl, k3tog, k2tog tbl, p11; rep from *, end p1.

Row 12: K12, *p3tog, k11; rep from *, end k1.

Rows 13, 15 and 17: P6, *k1 tbl, p11; rep from *, end last rep p6.

Rows 14, 16, 18 and 20: K6, *pl tbl, k11; rep from *, end last rep k6.

Row 19: P2, *draw through a long loop from right of twisted knit st in Row 13 and pass loop over next st as before; p3, k1 tbl, p3, draw through another loop from left of same st and pass loop over next st as before, p3; rep from *, end last rep p2.

Row 21: P6, *make 7 sts from one as before, p11; rep from *, end last rep p6.

Row 22: K6, *p7, k11; rep from *, end last rep k6.

Row 23: P6, *k2tog tbl, k3tog, k2tog tbl, p11; rep from *, end last rep p6.

Row 24: K6, *p3tog, k11; rep from *, end last rep k6.

Rep rows 1-24.

Berry-in-a-box

Multiple of 6 sts + l extra

5 to 1 dec: K2tog tbl, k3tog, pass k2tog over k3tog.

Row 1 (RS): P3, *k1, p5; rep from *, end k1, p3.

Row 2: K3tog, *yo, [k1, yo, k1] in next st, yo, 5 to 1 dec; rep from *, end yo, [k1, yo, k1] in next st, yo, k3tog tbl.

Rows 3 and 5: K1, *p5, k1; rep from * to end.

Row 4: P1, *k5, p1; rep from * to end.

Row 6: Inc in first st, *yo, 5 to 1 dec, yo, [k1, yo, k1] in next st; rep from *, end yo, 5 to 1 dec, yo, inc in last st.

Row 7: Rep row 1.

Row 8: K3, *p1, k5; rep from *, end p1, k3.

Rep rows 1-8.

abbreviations explained **60-63**

knitting terminology **64-68**

Diagonals and Chevrons

Elongated chevron

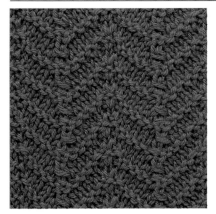

18-st rep

Multiple of 18 sts + 1 extra

Row 1 (RS): P1, *[k2, p2] twice, k1, [p2, k2] twice, p1; rep from * to end.

Row 2: K1, *[p2, k2] twice, p1, [k2, p2] twice, k1; rep from * to end.

Rows 3 and 4: Rep rows 1 and 2.

Row 5: [P2, k2] twice, *p3, k2, p2, k2; rep from *, end last rep p2.

Row 6: [K2, p2] twice, *k3, p2, k2, p2; rep from *, end last rep k2.

Rows 7 and 8: Rep rows 5 and 6.

Rows 9 and 11: Rep row 2.

Rows 10 and 12: Rep row 1.

Rows 13 and 15: Rep row 6.

Rows 14 and 16: Rep row 5.

Rep rows 1-16.

Chevron layette

Multiple of 13 sts

Rows 1 and 3 (RS): *Inc 1 (k into front and back of st), k4, sl 1, k2tog, psso, k4, inc 1; rep from * to end.

Row 2: Purl.

Row 4: Knit.

Rep rows 1-4.

Herringbone

Multiple of 7 sts + 1 extra

Rows 1 and 3 (WS): Purl.

Row 2: *K2tog, k2, inc in next st as foll: place point of RH needle behind LH needle, insert point of needle from the top down through the (purled) head of st below next st, and k this st; then k the st above, k2; rep from *, end k1.

Row 4: K1, *k2, inc in next st, k2, k2tog; rep from * to end.

Rep rows 1-4.

abbreviations explained **60-63**   knitting terminology **64-68**   symbolcraft charts **69-70**

Diagonal stitch

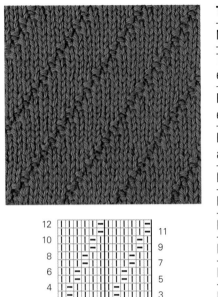

To the right

Multiple of 6 sts

The purl st is shifted to the right on every other row.

Row 1 (RS): *K5, p1; rep from * to end.

Row 2 and all WS rows: K the knit sts and p the purl sts.

Row 3: *K4, p1, k1; rep from * to end.

Row 5: *K3, p1, k2; rep from * to end.

Row 7: *K2, p1, k3; rep from * to end.

Row 9: *K1, p1, k4; rep from * to end.

Row 11: *P1, k5; rep from * to end.

Row 12: Rep row 2.

Rep rows 1-12.

6-st rep

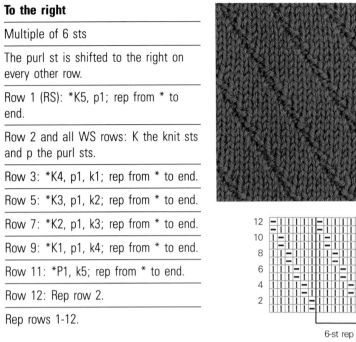

To the left

Multiple of 6 sts

The purl st is shifted to the left on every other row.

Row 1 (RS): *P1, k5; rep from * to end.

Row 2 and all WS rows: K the knit sts and p the purl sts.

Row 3: *K1, p1, k4; rep from * to end.

Row 5: *K2, p1, k3; rep from * to end.

Row 7: *K3, p1, k2; rep from * to end.

Row 9: *K4, p1, k1; rep from * to end.

Row 11: *K5, p1; rep from * to end.

Row 12: Rep row 2.

Rep rows 1-12.

6-st rep

German herringbone rib

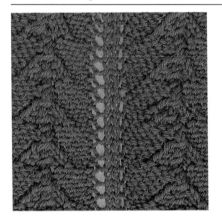

15-st rep

Multiple of 15 sts + 2 extra

Row 1 (RS): P2, *m1, k3, p2, p3tog, p2, k3, m1, p2; rep from * to end.

Row 2: K2, *p4, k5, p4, k2; rep from * to end.

Row 3: P2, *m1, k4, p1, p3 tog, p1, k4, m1, p2; rep from * to end.

Row 4: K2, *p5, k3, p5, k2; rep from * to end.

Row 5: P2, *m1, k5, p3 tog, k5, m1, p2; rep from * to end.

Row 6: K2, *p6, k1, p6, k2; rep from * to end.

Rep rows 1-6.

Embossed honeycomb

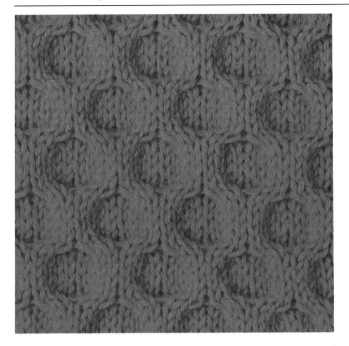

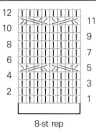

8-st rep

Multiple of 8 sts

4-st left cable: Sl 2 sts to cn and hold to front of work, k2, k2 from cn.

4-st right cable: Sl 2 sts to cn and hold to back of work k2, k2 from cn.

Rows 1, 3, 7 and 9 (RS): Knit.

Row 2 and all WS rows: Purl.

Row 5: *4-st left cable, 4-st right cable; rep from * to end.

Row 11: *4-st right cable, 4-st left cable; rep from * to end.

Row 12: Purl.

Rep rows 1-12.

Smocking stitch

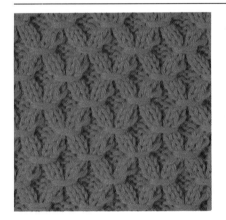

Multiple of 8 sts + 2 extra

Smocking st: Insert RH needle from front between 6th and 7th sts on LH needle and draw through a loop; sl this loop onto LH needle and k tog with the first st on LH needle.

Rows 1 and 3 (WS): K2, *p2, k2; rep from * to end.

Row 2: P2, *k2, p2; rep from * to end.

Row 4: P2, *smocking st, k1, p2, k2, p2; rep from * to end.

Rows 5 and 7: Rep rows 1 and 3.

Row 6: Rep row 2.

Row 8: P2, k2, p2, *smocking st, k1, p2, k2, p2; rep from *, end k2, p2.

Rep rows 1-8.

Smocked honeycomb

Multiple of 8 sts + 3 extra

Tie st: Sl 5 sts to cn and hold to back of work, wrap yarn around these 5 sts 3 times, return sts to LH needle, then work them as foll: K1, p3, k1.

Rows 1, 3 and 5 (RS): P3, *k1, p3; rep from * to end.

Rows 2, 4 and 6: K3, *p1, k3; rep from * to end.

Row 7: P3, *tie st, p3; rep from * to end.

Rows 8, 10, 12 and 14: Rep row 2.

Rows 9, 11 and 13: Rep row 1.

Row 15: P3, k1, p3, *tie st, p3; rep from *, end k1, p3.

Row 16: Rep row 2.

Rep rows 1-16.

8-st rep

abbreviations explained **60-63**   knitting terminology **64-68**   symbolcraft charts **69-70**

Woven stitch

Multiple of 2 sts + 1 extra

Row 1 (RS): K1, *sl 1 wyif, k1; rep from * to end.

Row 2: Purl.

Row 3: K2, *sl 1 wyif, k1; rep from *, end k1.

Row 4: Purl.

Rep rows 1-4.

Three-dimensional honeycomb

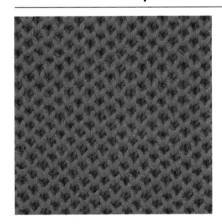

Note: Slip all sts with yarn in back. Bind off on a RS row, knitting yo tog with next k st while binding off.

Even number of sts

Preparation row (WS): *K1, yo, sl 1; rep from * to end.

Row 1: K1, *sl yo st, k2; rep from *, end last rep sl yo st, k1.

Row 2: *Yo, sl 1, k yo and next st tog; rep from * to end.

Row 3: *K2, sl yo st; rep from * to end.

Row 4: *K yo and next st tog, yo, sl 1; rep from * to end.

Rep rows 1-4.

Linen stitch

Multiple of 2 sts

Row 1 (RS): *K1, sl 1 purlwise wyif, bring yarn to back between needles; rep from *, end k2.

Row 2: *P1, sl 1 purlwise wyib, bring yarn to front between needles; rep from *, end p2.

Rep rows 1 and 2.

Crossed Stitches

Knit twist lattice

16-st rep

Multiple of 16 sts + 2 extra

2-st left twist (LT): With RH needle behind LH needle, skip next st on LH needle, k 2nd st tbl, then k skipped st in front lp, sl both sts from LH needle.

2-st right twist (RT): Skip next st on LH needle, k 2nd st in front of skipped st, then k skipped st, sl both sts from LH needle.

Row 1 (RS): K1, *LT, k4, RT; rep from *, end k1.

Row 2 and all WS rows: Purl.

Row 3: K2, *LT, k2, RT, k2; rep from * to end.

Row 5: K3, *LT, RT, k4; rep from *, end last rep k3.

Row 7: K4, *RT, k6; rep from *, end last rep k4.

Row 9: K3, *RT, LT, k4; rep from *, end last rep k3.

Row 11: K2, *RT, k2, LT, k2; rep from * to end.

Row 13: K1, *RT, k4, LT; rep from *, end k1.

Row 15: K8, *LT, k6; rep from *, end k2.

Row 16: Rep row 2.

Rep rows 1-16.

Tree of life

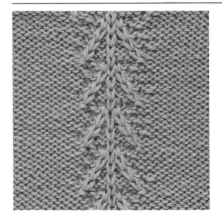

15 sts

preparation row (RS)

Panel of 15 sts

2-st left twist (LT): With RH needle behind LH needle, skip next st on LH needle, k 2nd st tbl, then k skipped st in front lp, sl both sts from LH needle.

2-st right twist (RT): Skip next st on LH needle, k 2nd st in front of skipped st, then k skipped st, sl both sts from LH needle.

Preparation row (RS): P2, k1, p4, sl 1 wyib, p4, k1, p2.

Row 1: K2, sl 1 wyif, k4, p1, k4, sl 1 wyif, k2.

Row 2: P2, LT, p3, sl 1 wyib, p3, RT, p2.

Row 3: K3, sl 1 wyif, k3, p1, k3, sl 1 wyif, k3.

Row 4: P3, LT, p2, sl 1 wyib, p2, RT, p3.

Row 5: K4, sl 1 wyif, k2, p1, k2, sl 1 wyif, k4.

Row 6: P4, LT, p1, sl 1 wyib, p1, RT, p4.

Row 7: K5, sl 1 wyif, k1, p1, k1, sl 1 wyif, k5.

Row 8: P2, k1, p2, LT, sl 1 wyib, RT, p2, k1, p2.

Rep rows 1-8.

abbreviations explained **60-63**   knitting terminology **64-68**   symbolcraft charts **69-70**

Double lattice

```
12 |||||||||||||||
10 |||||||||||||||  11
8  ××|||||||××  9
6  |||×|||×|||  7
4  ××|||||||××  5
2  |||×|||×|||  3
   ×××|||×××   1
```
6-st rep

Multiple of 6 sts + 4 extra

2-st left twist (LT): With RH needle behind LH needle, skip next st on LH needle, k 2nd st tbl, then k skipped st in front lp, sl both sts from LH needle.

2-st right twist (RT): Skip next st on LH needle, k 2nd st in front of skipped st, then k skipped st, sl both sts from LH needle.

Row 1 (RS): *LT, [RT] twice; rep from *, end LT, RT.

Row 2 and all WS rows: Purl.

Row 3: K1, LT, *RT, [LT] twice; rep from *, end k1.

Row 5: [LT] twice, *k2, [LT] twice; rep from * to end.

Row 7: K1, *[LT] twice, RT; rep from *, end LT, k1.

Row 9: RT, *LT, [RT] twice; rep from *, end LT.

Row 11: K3, *[RT] twice, k2; rep from *, end k1.

Row 12: Rep row 2.

Rep rows 1-12.

Herringbone rib

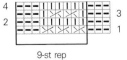

```
4 ==||||||||==  3
2 ==||×|||==    1
```
9-st rep

Multiple of 9 sts + 3 extra

2-st right twist (RT): Skip next st on LH needle, k 2nd st in front of skipped st, then k skipped st, sl both sts from LH needle.

Row 1 (RS): P3, *[RT] 3 times, p3; rep from * to end.

Row 2: K3, *p6, k3; rep from * to end.

Row 3: P3, *k1, [RT] twice, k1, p3; rep from * to end.

Row 4: Rep row 2.

Rep rows 1-4.

Tuck stitch

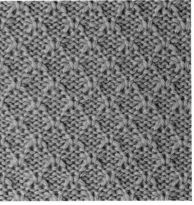

Multiple of 4 sts + 3 extra

Tuck st: Insert RH needle through the center of st two rows below and knit this stitch.

Row 1 (RS): Purl.

Row 2 and all WS rows: Knit.

Row 3: *P3, tuck st; rep from *, end p3.

Row 5: Purl.

Row 7: *P1, tuck st, p2; rep from *, end p1, tuck st, p1.

Row 8: Knit.

Rep rows 1-8.

Dropped Stitches

Indian cross stitch

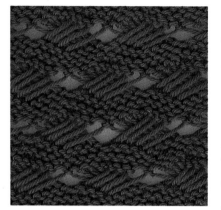

Multiple of 8 sts

Cross st: Insert needle into next st and wrap yarn 4 times around needle, then the st, withdrawing all the wraps along with the needle.

Rows 1-4: Knit.

Row 5: K1, *cross st; rep from *, end k1.

Row 6: *Sl 8 sts wyib, dropping all extra wraps, forming 8 long sts on RH needle. Then insert LH needle into first 4 of 8 long sts and pass them over the second 4. Return all sts to LH needle keeping them twisted and k 8; rep from * on each group of 8 sts.

Rows 7-10: Knit.

Row 11: Rep row 5.

Row 12: Sl 4 sts dropping extra wraps, then cross 2 over 2 as in row 6 and knit these 4; *sl 8, cross, and knit as in row 6; rep from * on each group of 8 sts across row to last 4 sts, end crossing 2 over 2.

Rep rows 1-12.

Simple drop stitch

Over any number of sts

Rows 1, 3, 5 and 7 (RS): Knit.

Rows 2, 4, 6 and 8: Purl.

Row 9: Knit, wrapping yarn 3 times around needle.

Row 10: Purl, letting extra 2 loops drop.

Rep rows 1-10.

Twisted drop stitch

Over any number of sts

Rows 1, 3, 5 and 7 (RS): Knit.

Rows 2, 4, 6 and 8: Purl.

Row 9: Knit, wrapping yarn around both needles once, then around RH needle once more.

Row 10: Purl.

Rep rows 1-10.

Double twisted drop stitch

Over any number of sts

Rows 1, 3, 5 and 7 (RS): Knit.

Rows 2, 4 and 6: Purl.

Row 8: Knit, wrapping yarn around both needles once, then around RH needle once more.

Row 9: Rep row 8.

Row 10: Knit.

Rep rows 1-10.

abbreviations explained **60-63**   knitting terminology **64-68**

Seafoam pattern

Multiple of 10 sts + 6 extra

Rows 1 and 2: Knit.

Row 3 (RS): K6, *yo twice, k1, yo 3 times, k1, yo 4 times, k1, yo 3 times, k1, yo twice, k6; rep from * to end.

Row 4: Knit, dropping all yo's off needle.

Rows 5 and 6: Knit.

Row 7: K1; rep from * of row 3, end last rep k1.

Row 8: Rep row 4.

Rep rows 1-8.

Vertical drop stitch

Multiple of 8 sts + 4 extra

Preparation row (RS): K1, *p2, k1, yo, k1, p2, k2; rep from *, end p2, k1.

Rows 1, 3 and 5 (WS): P1, *k2, p2, k2, p3; rep from *, end k2, p1.

Rows 2 and 4: K1, *p2, k3, p2, k2; rep from *, end p2, k1.

Row 6: K1, *p2, k1, drop next st off needle and unravel down to the yo 6 rows below; k1, p2, k1, yo, k1; rep from *, end p2, k1.

Rows 7, 9 and 11: P1, *k2, p3, k2, p2; rep from *, end k2, p1.

Rows 8 and 10: K1, *p2, k2, p2, k3; rep from *, end p2, k1.

Row 12: K1, *p2, k1, yo, k1, p2, k1 drop next st off needle and unravel 6 rows below, k1; rep from *, end p2, k1.

Rep rows 1-12.

Garter drop stitch

Over any number of stitches

Rows 1-4: Knit.

Row 5 (RS): *K1, yo twice; rep from * to end.

Row 6: Knit, dropping the extra loops.

Rep rows 1-6.

abbreviations
explained **60-63**

knitting
terminology **64-68**

Novelty Stitches

Bowknot stitch

Multiple of 18 sts + 9 extra

Row 1 (RS): K9, *p9, k9; rep from * to end.

Row 2: P9, *k9, p9; rep from * to end.

Rows 3 and 5: Knit.

Rows 4 and 6: Purl.

Rows 7 and 8: Rep rows 1 and 2.

Row 9: K13, *insert needle into front of next st 9 rows below, and draw up a loop, sl this loop to LH needle and k tog with next st tbl, k17; rep from *, end last rep k13.

Row 10: Purl.

Row 11: P9, *k9, p9; rep from * to end.

Row 12: K9, *p9, k9; rep from * to end.

Rows 13 and 15: Knit.

Rows 14 and 16: Purl.

Rows 17 and 18: Rep rows 11 and 12.

Row 19: K4, *draw up a loop from 9 rows below and k tog with next st tbl, k17; rep from *, end last rep k4.

Row 20: Purl.

Rep rows 1-20.

Jack-in-the-pulpit

Multiple of 4 sts + 3 extra

Row 1 (RS): K2, p1, *yo, p4; rep from *, end yo, p2, k2.

Row 2: K3, *yo, sl 1 wyif, drop yo of last row off needle, bring yarn to back over RH needle to make a yo, k3; rep from * to end.

Row 3: K2, p1, *sl both the yo and sl st of last row wyif, bring yarn to back over RH needle to make a yo, then to front again between the needles, p3; rep from *, end last rep p1, k2.

Row 4: K3, *sl 2 yo's and sl st of last rows wyif, bring yarn to back over RH needle to make a yo, k3; rep from * to end.

Row 5: K2, p1, *sl 3 yo's and sl st of last rows wyif, bring yarn to back over RH needle to make a yo, then to front again between the needles, p3; rep from *, end last rep p1, k2.

Row 6: K3, *wyif, insert RH needle from behind under the bundle of 4 yo strands (but not the sl st) and purl these strands tog, removing them from LH needle but leaving the sl st behind on LH needle; then knit the sl st; then insert LH needle from front under the 4 yo strands and purl them tog again; k3; rep from * to end.

Row 7: K2, *k2tog, p1, ssk, p1; rep from *, end last rep k2 instead of p1.

Row 8: Knit.

Rep rows 1-8.

Checkerboard bows

Multiple of 16 sts + 9 extra

Triple yo: Wrap yarn 3 times around needle.

Row 1 (RS): Knit.

Row 2: K4, *triple yo, k1, triple yo, k15; rep from *, end last rep k4.

Row 3: K4, *drop 3 yo's, k1, drop 3 yo's, k15; rep from *, end last rep k4.

Tie bows: Insert point of free needle into each pair of loops and pull up snugly to take out slack between and on either side of these 2 loops. Tie each pair of loops tog in a firm square knot.

Rows 4 and 6: Rep row 2.

Rows 5 and 7: Rep row 3.

Rows 8 and 9: Knit.

Row 10: K12, *triple yo, k1, triple yo, k15; rep from *, end last rep k12.

Row 11: K12, *drop 3 yo's, k1, drop 3 yo's, k15; rep from *, end last rep k12. Tie bows, as before.

Rows 12 and 14: Rep row 10.

Rows 13 and 15: Rep row 11.

Row 16: Knit.

Rep rows 1-16.

Butterfly stitch

Multiple of 10 sts + 9 extra

Bowknot st: On next st (which is at center of the slipped group) insert RH needle down through the 5 loose strands, bring needle up and transfer 5 strands to LH needle, p5 strands and next st tog to make one st.

Rows 1, 3, 5, 7 and 9 (RS): K2, *sl 5 wyif, k5; rep from *, end sl 5, k2.

Rows 2, 4, 6 and 8: Purl.

Row 10: P4, *bow knot st, p9; rep from *, end last rep p4.

Rows 11, 13, 15, 17 and 19: K7, *sl 5 wyif, k5; rep from *, end sl 5, k7.

Rows 12, 14, 16 and 18: Purl.

Row 20: P9, *bowknot st, p9; rep from * to end.

Rep rows 1-20.

Blind buttonhole stitch

Multiple of 10 sts + 2 extra

Rows 1, 3, 11 and 13 (RS): Purl.

Rows 2, 4, 10, 12 and 14: Knit.

Rows 5, 7 and 9: K1, *k5, [sl 1 wyib] 5 times; rep from *, end k1.

Rows 6 and 8: P1, *[sl 1 wyif] 5 times, p5; rep from *, end p1.

Rows 15, 17 and 19: K1, *[sl 1 wyib] 5 times, k5; rep from *, end k1.

Rows 16 and 18: P1, *p5, [sl 1 wyif] 5 times; rep from *, end p1.

Row 20: Knit.

Rep rows 1-20.

10-st rep

Quilted lattice

Multiple of 6 sts + 3 extra

Row 1 and all WS rows: Purl.

Row 2 (RS): K2, *sl 5 wyif, k1; rep from *, end k1.

Row 4: K4, *insert RH needle under loose strand and knit next st, bringing st out under strand; k5; rep from *, end last rep k4.

Row 6: K1, sl 3 wyif, *k1, sl 5 wyif; rep from *, end k1, sl 3 wyif, k1.

Row 8: K1, *k next st under loose strand, k5; rep from *, end last rep k1.

Rep rows 1-8.

Scallop stitch

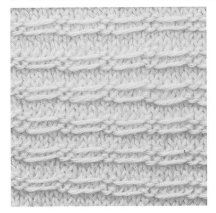

Multiple of 5 sts + 2 extra

Row 1 (RS): Knit.

Row 2 and all WS rows: Purl.

Rows 3 and 5: P2, *sl 3 wyif, p2; rep from * to end.

Row 6: Purl.

Rep rows 1-6.

5-st rep

Eyelets and Lace

Tiny tower stitch

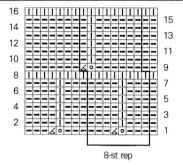

8-st rep

Multiple of 8 sts + 1 extra

Row 1 (RS): P4, *yo, p2tog, p6; rep from *, end yo, p2tog, p3.

Rows 2, 4 and 6: K4, *p1, k7; rep from *, end k4.

Rows 3, 5 and 7: P4, *k1, p7; rep from *, end p4.

Row 8: Purl.

Row 9: P8, *yo, p2tog, p6; rep from *, end p2tog, p7.

Rows 10, 12 and 14: K8, *p1, k7; rep from *, end p1, k8.

Rows 11, 13 and 15: P8, *k1, p7; rep from *, end k1, p8.

Row 16: Purl.

Rep rows 1-16.

Tulip lace

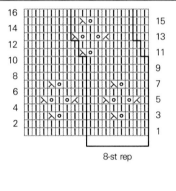

8-st rep

Multiple of 8 sts

Row 1: Knit.

Row 2 and all WS rows: Purl.

Row 3: K3, *yo, ssk, k6; rep from *, end last rep k3.

Row 5: K1, *k2tog, yo, k1, yo, ssk, k3; rep from *, end last rep k2.

Row 7: Rep row 3.

Row 9: Knit.

Row 11: K7, *yo, ssk, k6; rep from *, end k1.

Row 13: K5, *k2tog, yo, k1, yo, ssk, k3; rep from *, end k3.

Row 15: Rep row 11.

Row 16: Rep row 2.

Rep rows 1-16.

Flower eyelet

Multiple of 16 sts + 8 extra

Yo twice: wrap yarn around the needle twice.

Row 1 (RS): K10, *k2tog, yo twice, ssk, k12; rep from *, end last rep k10.

Row 2 and all WS rows: Purl, working [k1, p1] into each yo twice.

Row 3: K8, *[k2tog, yo twice, ssk] twice, k8; rep from * to end.

Rows 5 and 9: Rep row 1.

Row 7: Rep row 3.

Row 11: K2, *k2tog, yo twice, ssk, k12; rep from *, end last rep k2.

Row 13: *[K2tog, yo twice, ssk] twice, k8; rep from *, end [k2tog, yo twice, ssk] twice.

Rows 15 and 19: Rep row 11.

Row 17: Rep row 13.

Row 20: Rep row 2.

Rep rows 1-20.

Open triangles

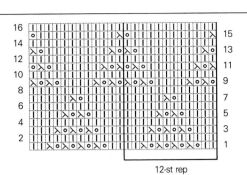

12-st rep

Multiple of 12 sts

Row 1 (RS): *K2, [yo, SKP] 4 times, k2; rep from * to end.

Row 2 and all WS rows: Purl, working each yo as a st.

Row 3: *K3, [yo, SKP] 3 times, k3; rep from * to end.

Row 5: *K4, [yo, SKP] twice, k4; rep from * to end.

Row 7: *K5, yo, SKP, k5; rep from * to end.

Row 9: *[Yo, SKP] twice, k4, [yo, SKP] twice; rep from * to end.

Row 11: *SKP, yo, SKP, k6, yo, SKP, yo; rep from * to end.

Row 13: *Yo, SKP, k8, yo, SKP; rep from * to end.

Row 15: *SKP, k10, yo; rep from * to end.

Row 16: Purl.

Rep rows 1-16.

Basic faggoting stitch

Even number of sts.

Row 1: K1, *yo, ssk; rep from *, end k1.

Rep this row.

2-st rep

Purse stitch

Multiple of 2 sts + 2 extra

Row 1: K1, *yo, p2tog; rep from *, end k1.

Rep this row.

2-st rep

Stitch Dictionary

Horizontal lace stitch

Multiple of 2 sts

Rows 1, 3, 5, 7 and 9 (RS): Knit.

Rows 2, 4, 6 and 8: Purl.

Row 10: Knit.

Row 11: *Yo, p2tog; rep from * to end.

Row 12: Knit.

Rep rows 1-12.

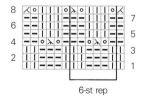

2-st rep

Eyelet rows

Multiple of 2 sts + 2 extra

Rows 1, 5, 7, 9, 13 and 15 (RS): Knit.

Row 2 and all WS rows: Purl.

Row 3: K1, *yo, SKP; rep from *, end k1.

Row 11: K1, *SKP, yo; rep from *, end k1.

Row 16: Knit.

Rep rows 1-16.

Dewdrop pattern

Multiple of 6 sts + 1 extra

Rows 1 and 3 (WS): K2, *p3, k3; rep from *, end p3, k2.

Row 2: P2, *k3, p3; rep from *, end k3, p2.

Row 4: K2, *yo, sl 1, k2tog, psso, yo, k3; rep from *, end yo, sl 1, k2tog, psso, yo, k2.

Rows 5 and 7: P2, *k3, p3; rep from *, end k3, p2.

Row 6: K2, *p3, k3; rep from *, end p3, k2.

Row 8: K2tog, *yo, k3, yo, sl 1, k2tog, psso; rep from *, end yo, k3, yo, ssk.

Rep rows 1-8.

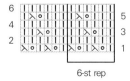

6-st rep

Diagonal openwork pattern

Multiple of 6 sts

Row 1 (RS): *[K1, yo, ssk] twice; rep from * to end.

Row 2 and all WS rows: Purl.

Row 3: *K2, yo, ssk, k2; rep from * to end.

Row 5: *K3, yo, ssk, k1; rep from * to end.

Row 6: Purl.

Rep rows 1-6.

6-st rep

abbreviations explained **60-63**　knitting terminology **64-68**　symbolcraft charts **69-70**

Mermaid's mesh

Multiple of 9 sts + 4 extra

Yo twice: wrap yarn around the needle twice.

Row 1 (RS): K1, yo, *[ssk, yo] 3 times, k3tog, yo twice; rep from *, end ssk, k1.

Row 2 and all WS rows: Purl, working [k1, p1] into yo twice.

Row 3: *K2tog, yo twice, [ssk, yo] twice, k3tog, yo; rep from *, end k2tog, yo, k2.

Row 5: K1, *k2tog, yo twice, ssk, yo, k3tog, yo, k2tog, yo; rep from *, end k2tog, yo, k1.

Row 7: K2tog, yo, *k2tog, yo twice, sl 1, k2tog, psso, [yo, k2tog] twice, yo; rep from *, end k2.

Row 9: K1, k2tog, yo, *k2tog, yo twice, sl 1, k2tog, psso, [yo, k2tog] twice, yo; rep from *, end k1.

Row 11: K2tog, yo, *k2tog, yo twice, ssk, yo, sl 1, k2tog, psso, yo, k2tog, yo; rep from *, end k2.

Row 13: K1, k2tog, *yo twice, [ssk, yo] twice, sl 1, k2tog, psso, yo, k2tog; rep from *, end yo, k1.

Row 15: K2tog, *yo twice, [ssk, yo] 3 times, k3tog; rep from *, end yo twice, ssk.

Row 16: Rep row 2.

Rep rows 1-16.

Lace entrelac

12 10 8 6 4 2 | 11 9 7 5 3 1

13-st rep

Multiple of 13 sts + 2 extra

Row 1 (RS): K1, *k2, SKP, k4, k2tog, k2, yo, k1, yo; rep from *, end k1.

Row 2 and all WS rows: K the knit sts and p the purl sts.

Row 3: K1, *yo, k2, SKP, k2, k2tog, k2, yo, k3; rep from *, end k1.

Row 5: K1, *k1, yo, k2, SKP, k2tog, k2, yo, k4; rep from *, end k1.

Row 7: K1, *yo, k1, yo, k2, SKP, k4, k2tog, k2; rep from *, end k1.

Row 9: K1, *k3, yo, k2, SKP, k2, k2tog, k2, yo; rep from *, end k1.

Row 11: K1, *k4, yo, k2, SKP, k2tog, k2, yo, k1; rep from *, end k1.

Row 12: Purl.

Rep rows 1-12.

Flemish block lace

12 10 8 6 4 2 | 11 9 7 5 3 1

14-st rep

Multiple of 14 sts + 3 extra

Row 1 (RS): K2, *k2tog, yo, k1, yo, ssk, k3, k2tog, yo, k4; rep from *, end k1.

Row 2 and all WS rows: Purl.

Row 3: K1, *k2tog, yo, k3, yo, ssk, k1, k2tog, yo, k4; rep from *, end k2.

Row 5: K2tog, yo, *k5, yo, sl 1, k2tog, psso, yo, k4, k2tog, yo; rep from *, end k1.

Row 7: K2, *yo, ssk, k4, yo, ssk, k3, k2tog, yo, k1; rep from *, end k1.

Row 9: K3, *yo, ssk, k4, yo, ssk, k1, k2tog, yo, k3; rep from * to end.

Row 11: K4, *yo, ssk, k4, yo, k3tog, yo, k5; rep from *, end last rep k4.

Row 12: Rep row 2.

Rep rows 1-12.

Lozenge stitch

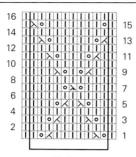

10-st rep

Multiple of 10 sts + 2 extra

Row 1 (RS): K1, *yo, SKP, k5, k2tog, yo, k1; rep from *, end k1.

Row 2 and all WS rows: Purl.

Row 3: K1, *k1, yo, SKP, k3, k2tog, yo, k2; rep from *, end k1.

Row 5: K1, *k2, yo, SKP, k1, k2tog, yo, k3; rep from *, end k1.

Row 7: K1, *k3, yo, sl 1, k2tog, psso, yo, k4; rep from *, end k1.

Row 9: K1, *k2, k2tog, yo, k1, yo, SKP, k3; rep from *, end k1.

Row 11: K1, *k1, k2tog, yo, k3, yo, SKP, k2; rep from *, end k1.

Row 13: K1, *k2tog, yo, k5, yo, SKP, k1; rep from *, end k1.

Row 15: K1, *yo, k7, yo, sl 1, k2tog, psso; rep from *, end k1.

Row 16: Purl.

Rep rows 1-16.

Traveling vine

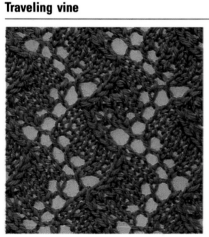

Multiple of 8 sts + 4 extra

Row 1 (RS): K2, *yo, k1 tbl, yo, ssk, k5; rep from *, end k2.

Row 2: P6, *p2tog tbl, p7; rep from *, end last rep p5.

Row 3: K2, *yo, k1 tbl, yo, k2, ssk, k3; rep from *, end k2.

Row 4: P4, *p2tog tbl, p7; rep from * to end.

Row 5: K2, *k1 tbl, yo, k4, ssk, k1, yo; rep from *, end k2.

Row 6: P3, *p2tog tbl, p7; rep from *, end p1.

Row 7: K2, *k5, k2tog, yo, k1 tbl, yo; rep from *, end k2.

Row 8: P5, *p2tog, p7; rep from *, end last rep p6.

Row 9: K2, *k3, k2tog, k2, yo, k1 tbl, yo; rep from *, end k2.

Row 10: *P7, p2tog; rep from *, end p4.

Row 11: K2, *yo, k1, k2tog, k4, yo, k1 tbl, rep from *, end k2.

Row 12: P1, *p7, p2tog; rep from *, end p3.

Rep rows 1-12.

Lily of the valley

Panel of 27 sts

Make bobble (MB): [K1, p1, k1, p1, k1] in the same st, making 5 sts from one; then pass the 4th, 3rd, 2nd and first over the last st made.

Row 1 (RS): P2, ssk, k6, [yo, k1] twice, sl 1, k2tog, psso, [k1, yo] twice, k6, k2tog, p2.

Row 2 and all WS rows: K2, p23, k2.

Row 3: P2, ssk, k5, yo, k1, yo, k2, sl 1, k2tog, psso, k2, yo, k1, yo, k5, k2tog, p2.

Row 5: P2, ssk, k4, yo, k1, yo, MB, k2, sl 1, k2tog, psso, k2, MB, yo, k1, yo, k4, k2tog, p2.

Row 7: P2, ssk, k3, yo, k1, yo, MB, k3, sl 1, k2tog, psso, k3, MB, yo, k1, yo, k3, k2tog, p2.

Row 9: P2, ssk, k2, yo, k1, yo, MB, k4, sl 1, k2tog, psso, k4, MB, yo, k1, yo, k2, k2tog, p2.

Row 11: P2, ssk, [k1, yo] twice, MB, k5, sl 1, k2tog, psso, k5, MB, [yo, k1] twice, k2tog, p2.

Row 13: P2, ssk, yo, k1, yo, MB, k6, sl 1, k2tog, psso, k6, MB, yo, k1, yo, k2tog, p2.

Row 14: Rep row 2.

Rep rows 1-14.

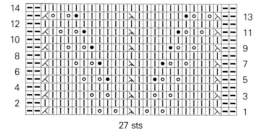

27 sts

abbreviations explained **60-63**

knitting terminology **64-68**

symbolcraft charts **69-70**

Simple Vine

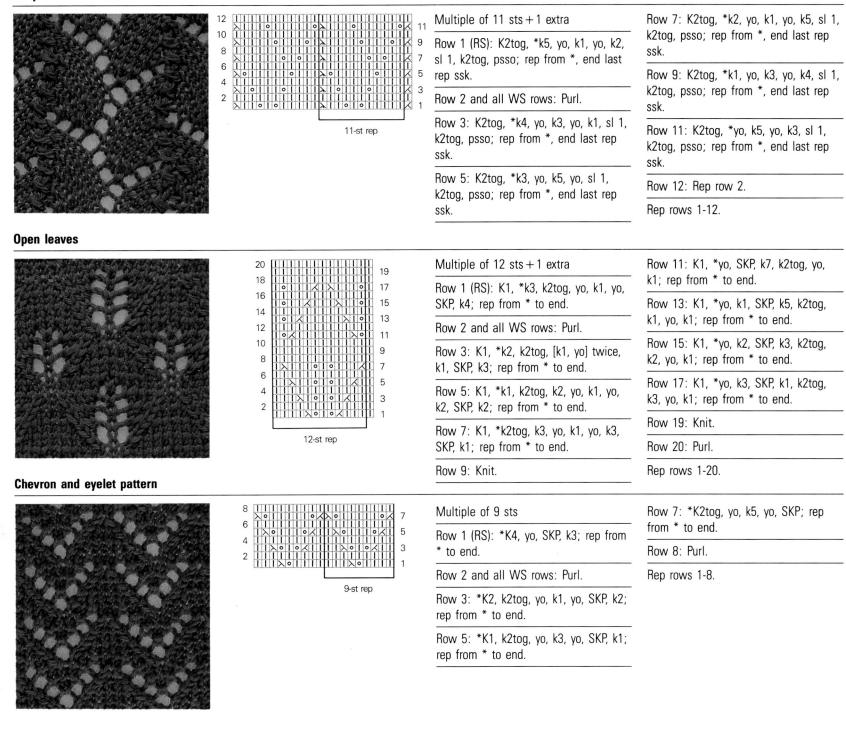

11-st rep

Multiple of 11 sts + 1 extra

Row 1 (RS): K2tog, *k5, yo, k1, yo, k2, sl 1, k2tog, psso; rep from *, end last rep ssk.

Row 2 and all WS rows: Purl.

Row 3: K2tog, *k4, yo, k3, yo, k1, sl 1, k2tog, psso; rep from *, end last rep ssk.

Row 5: K2tog, *k3, yo, k5, yo, sl 1, k2tog, psso; rep from *, end last rep ssk.

Row 7: K2tog, *k2, yo, k1, yo, k5, sl 1, k2tog, psso; rep from *, end last rep ssk.

Row 9: K2tog, *k1, yo, k3, yo, k4, sl 1, k2tog, psso; rep from *, end last rep ssk.

Row 11: K2tog, *yo, k5, yo, k3, sl 1, k2tog, psso; rep from *, end last rep ssk.

Row 12: Rep row 2.

Rep rows 1-12.

Open leaves

12-st rep

Multiple of 12 sts + 1 extra

Row 1 (RS): K1, *k3, k2tog, yo, k1, yo, SKP, k4; rep from * to end.

Row 2 and all WS rows: Purl.

Row 3: K1, *k2, k2tog, [k1, yo] twice, k1, SKP, k3; rep from * to end.

Row 5: K1, *k1, k2tog, k2, yo, k1, yo, k2, SKP, k2; rep from * to end.

Row 7: K1, *k2tog, k3, yo, k1, yo, k3, SKP, k1; rep from * to end.

Row 9: Knit.

Row 11: K1, *yo, SKP, k7, k2tog, yo, k1; rep from * to end.

Row 13: K1, *yo, k1, SKP, k5, k2tog, k1, yo, k1; rep from * to end.

Row 15: K1, *yo, k2, SKP, k3, k2tog, k2, yo, k1; rep from * to end.

Row 17: K1, *yo, k3, SKP, k1, k2tog, k3, yo, k1; rep from * to end.

Row 19: Knit.

Row 20: Purl.

Rep rows 1-20.

Chevron and eyelet pattern

9-st rep

Multiple of 9 sts

Row 1 (RS): *K4, yo, SKP, k3; rep from * to end.

Row 2 and all WS rows: Purl.

Row 3: *K2, k2tog, yo, k1, yo, SKP, k2; rep from * to end.

Row 5: *K1, k2tog, yo, k3, yo, SKP, k1; rep from * to end.

Row 7: *K2tog, yo, k5, yo, SKP; rep from * to end.

Row 8: Purl.

Rep rows 1-8.

abbreviations explained **60-63**   knitting terminology **64-68**   symbolcraft charts **69-70**

Lucina shell pattern

Multiple of 9 sts + 3 extra

Row 1 (RS): K2, *yo, k8, yo, k1; rep from *, end k1.

Row 2: K3, *p8, k3; rep from * to end.

Row 3: K3, *yo, k8, yo, k3; rep from * to end.

Row 4: K4, *p8, k5; rep from *, end last rep k4.

Row 5: K4, *yo, k8, yo, k5; rep from *, end last rep k4.

Row 6: K5, *p8, k7; rep from *, end last rep k5.

Row 7: K5, *k4tog tbl, k4tog, k7; rep from *, end last rep k5.

Row 8: Knit.

Rep rows 1-8.

Eye of the lynx pattern

Multiple of 8 sts + 6 extra

Rows 1 and 3 (RS): Purl.

Row 2: Knit.

Rows 4 and 6: P5, *p1, sl 2 wyif, p5; rep from *, end p1.

Row 5: K1, *k5, sl 2 wyib, k1; rep from *, end k5.

Row 7: K1, *SKP, yo, k2tog, k1, sl 2 wyib, k1; rep from *, end SKP, yo, k2tog, k1.

Row 8: P2, p into front and back of yo, p1, *p1, sl 2 wyif, p2, p into front and back of yo, p1; rep from *, end p1.

Row 9: K1, *k5, sl 2 wyib, k1; rep from *, end k5.

Rows 10 and 12: Knit.

Row 11: Purl.

Rows 13 and 15: K1, *k1, sl 2 wyib, k5; rep from *, end k1, sl 2 wyib, k2.

Row 14: P2, sl 2 wyif, p1, *p5, sl 2 wyif, p1; rep from *, end p1.

Row 16: P2, sl 2 wyif, p1, *p2tog, yo, p1 and return st to LH needle, pass next st over it and sl to RH needle, p1, sl 2 wyif, p1; rep from *, end p1.

Row 17: K1, *k1, sl 2 wyib, k2, k into front and back of yo, k1; rep from *, end k1, sl 2 wyib, k2.

Row 18: Rep row 14.

Rep rows 1-18.

Hearts

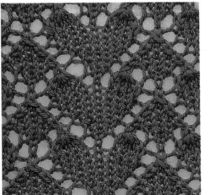

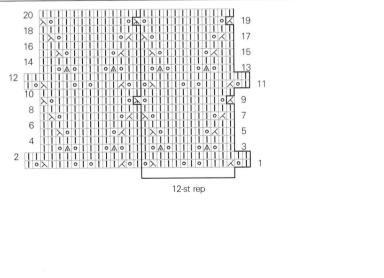

12-st rep

Multiple of 12 sts + 1 extra

Row 1 (RS): K1, *yo, k2tog, k3, yo, k1, yo, k3, SKP, yo, k1; rep from * to end.

Row 2 and all WS rows: Purl.

Row 3: K2, *yo, k4tog, yo, k3; rep from *, end last rep k2.

Row 5: K1, *k1, k2tog, yo, k5, yo, SKP, k2; rep from * to end.

Row 7: K1, *k2tog, yo, k7, yo, SKP, k1; rep from * to end.

Row 9: K2tog, yo, k9, yo, *sl 1, k2tog, psso, yo, k9, yo; rep from *, end SKP.

Row 10: Purl.

Rep rows 1-10.

abbreviations explained **60-63**   knitting terminology **64-68**   symbolcraft charts **69-70**

Cables

Oxox cable

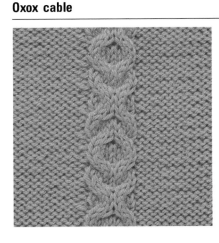

16
14
12
10
8
6
4
2

15
13
11
9
7
5
3
1

12 sts

Panel of 12 sts

4-st right cable: Sl 2 sts to cn and hold to back of work, k2, k2 from cn.

4-st left cable: Sl 2 sts to cn and hold to front of work, k2, k2 from cn.

Row 1 (RS): P2, k8, p2.

Row 2 and all WS rows: K the knit sts and p the purl sts.

Row 3: P2, 4-st right cable, 4-st left cable, p2.

Row 5: Rep row 1.

Row 7: P2, 4-st left cable, 4-st right cable, p2.

Row 9: Rep row 1.

Row 11: Rep row 7.

Row 13: Rep row 1.

Row 15: Rep row 3.

Row 16: Rep row 2.

Rep rows 1-16.

Alternate fancy cables

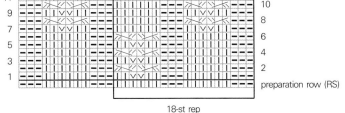

11
9
7
5
3
1

12
10
8
6
4
2

preparation row (RS)

18-st rep

Multiple of 18 sts + 12 extra

3-st right twist: Sl 2 sts to cn and hold to back of work, k1, k2 from cn.

3-st left twist: Sl 1 st to cn and hold to front of work, k2, k1 from cn.

Preparation Row (RS): *P3, k6, p3, k6; rep from *, end p3, k6, p3.

Rows 1, 3 and 5: K3, p6, k3, *p2, sl 2 purlwise wyif, p2, k3, p6, k3; rep from * to end.

Rows 2, 4 and 6: *P3, k6, p3, 3-st right twist, 3-st left twist; rep from *, end p3, k6, p3.

Rows 7, 9 and 11: K3, p2, sl 2 purl-wise, p2, k3, *p6, k3, p2, sl 2 purlwise, p2, k3; rep from * to end.

Rows 8, 10 and 12: *P3, 3-st right twist, 3-st left twist, p3, k6; rep 3 from *, end p3, 3-st right twist, 3-st left twist, p3.

Rep rows 1-12.

abbreviations explained **60-63**   knitting terminology **64-68**   symbolcraft charts **69-70**

Giant cable

Right cable

8 6 4 2 / 7 5 3 1
16 sts

Panel of 16 sts

12-st right cable: Sl 6 sts to cn and hold to back of work, k6, k6 from cn.

Rows 1 and 3 (RS): P2, k12, p2.

Row 2 and all WS rows: K the knit sts and p the purl sts.

Row 5: P2, 12-st right cable, p2.

Row 7: Rep row 1.

Row 8: Rep row 2.

Rep rows 1-8.

Left cable

8 6 4 2 / 7 5 3 1
16 sts

Panel of 16 sts

12-st left cable: Sl 6 sts to cn and hold to front of work, k6, k6 from cn.

Rows 1 and 3 (RS): P2, k12, p2.

Row 2 and all WS rows: K the knit sts and p the purl sts.

Row 5: P2, 12-st left cable, p2.

Row 7: Rep row 1.

Row 8: Rep row 2.

Rep rows 1-8.

Ribbed cable

Right cable

Panel of 11 sts

7-st right cable: Sl 4 sts to cn and hold to back of work, k1 tbl, p1, k1 tbl, then [p1, k1 tbl] twice from cn.

Rows 1, 3, 5, 7 and 9 (WS): K2, [p1 tbl, k1] 3 times, p1 tbl, k2.

Row 2: P2, 7-st right cable, p2.

Rows 4, 6, 8 and 10: P2, [k1 tbl, p1] 3 times, k1 tbl, p2.

Rep rows 1-10.

Left cable

Panel of 11 sts

7-st left cable: Sl 3 sts to cn and hold to front of work, [k1 tbl, p1] twice, then k1 tbl, p1, k1 tbl from cn.

Rows 1, 3, 5, 7 and 9 (WS): K2, [p1 tbl, k1] 3 times, p1 tbl, k2.

Row 2: P2, 7-st left cable, p2.

Rows 4, 6, 8 and 10: P2, [k1 tbl, p1] 3 times, k1 tbl, p2.

Rep rows 1-10.

abbreviations
explained **60-63**

knitting
terminology **64-68**

symbolcraft
charts **69-70**

Cabled chains

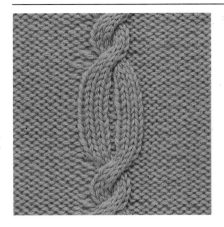

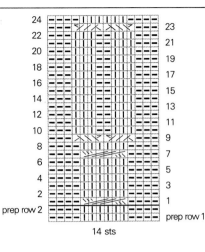

14 sts

Panel of 14 sts

4-st right purl cable: Sl 1 st to cn and hold to back, k3, p1, from cn.

4-st left purl cable: Sl 3 sts to cn and hold to front of work, p1, k3 from cn.

6-st right cable: Sl 3 sts to cn and hold to back of work, k3, k3 from cn.

Preparation Row 1 (RS): P4, k6, p4.

Preparation Row 2: K4, p6, k4.

Rows 1 and 7: P4, 6-st right cable, p4.

Row 2 and all WS rows: K the knit sts and p the purl sts.

Rows 3 and 5: Rep row 2.

Row 9: P3, 4-st right purl cable, 4-st left purl cable, p3.

Rows 11, 13, 15, 17, 19 and 21: Rep row 2.

Row 23: P3, 4-st left purl cable, 4-st right purl cable, p3.

Row 24: Rep row 2.

Rep rows 1-24.

Plait cable

Right cable

13 sts

Panel of 13 sts

6-st right cable: Sl 3 sts to cn and hold to back of work, k3, k3 from cn.

6-st left cable: Sl 3 sts to cn and hold to front of work, k3, k3 from cn.

Row 1 (RS): P2, k9, p2.

Row 2 and all WS rows: K the knit sts and p the purl sts.

Row 3: P2, 6-st left cable, k3, p2.

Row 5: Rep row 1.

Row 7: P2, k3, 6-st right cable, p2.

Row 8: Rep row 2.

Rep rows 1-8.

Left cable

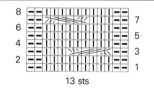

13 sts

Panel of 13 sts

Row 1 (RS): P2, k9, p2.

Row 2 and all WS rows: K the knit sts and p the purl sts.

Row 3: P2, 6-st right cable, k3, p2.

Row 5: Rep row 1.

Row 7: P2, k3, 6-st left cable, p2.

Row 8: Rep row 2.

Rep rows 1-8.

abbreviations explained **60-63**   knitting terminology **64-68**   symbolcraft charts **69-70**

Horseshoe cable

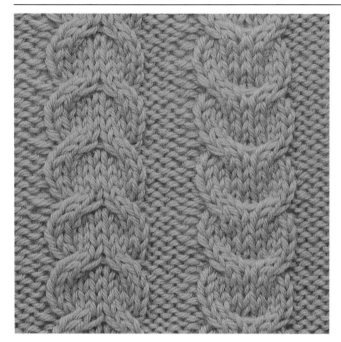

Right cable

6 — 4 — 2

5 — 3 — 1

12 sts

Panel of 12 sts

4-st right cable: Sl 2 sts to cn and hold to back of work, k2, k2 from cn.

4-st left cable: Sl 2 sts to cn and hold to front of work, k2, k2 from cn.

Rows 1 and 3 (RS): P2, k8, p2.

Row 2 and all WS rows: K the knit sts and p the purl sts.

Row 5: P2, 4-st right cable, 4-st left cable, p2, k4, p2.

Row 6: Rep row 2.

Rep rows 1-6.

Left cable

6 — 4 — 2

5 — 3 — 1

12 sts

Panel of 12 sts

Rows 1 and 3 (RS): P2, k8, p2.

Row 2 and all WS rows: K the knit sts and p the purl sts.

Row 5: P2, 4-st left cable, 4-st right cable.

Row 6: Rep row 2.

Rep rows 1-6.

Crossed cable

8 — 6 — 4 — 2

7 — 5 — 3 — 1

12 sts

Panel of 12 sts

4-st right cable: Sl 2 sts to cn and hold to back of work, k2, k2 from cn.

3-st right cable: Sl 1 st to cn and hold to back of work, k2, k1 from cn.

3-st left cable: Sl 2 sts to cn and hold to front of work, k1, k2 from cn.

Row 1 (RS): P4, 4-st right cable, p4.

Row 2: K4, p4, k4.

Row 3: P3, 3-st right cable, 3-st left cable, p3.

Row 4: K3, p6, k3.

Row 5: P2, 3-st right cable, k2, 3-st left cable, p2.

Row 6: K2, p8, k2.

Row 7: P1, 3-st right cable, k4, 3-st left cable, p1.

Row 8: K1, p10, k1.

Rep rows 1-8.

Aran braid

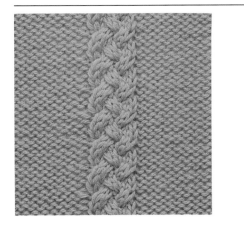

```
4  ══ | | | | | | | | | ══  3
2  ══ | | | | | | | | | ══  1
        12 sts
```

Panel of 12 sts

4-st right cable: Sl 2 sts to cn and hold to back of work, k2, k2 from cn.

4-st left cable: Sl 2 sts to cn and hold to front of work, k2, k2 from cn.

Row 1 (RS): P2, [4-st right cable] twice, p2.

Rows 2 and 4: K2, p8, k2.

Row 3: P2, k2, 4-st left cable, k2, p2.

Rep rows 1-4.

Shadow cable

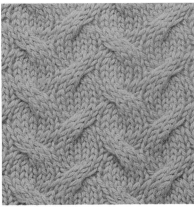

```
8  | | | | | | | | | | | | |  7
6  | | | | | | | | | | | | |  5
4  | | | | | | | | | | | | |  3
2  | | | | | | | | | | | | |  1
        12-st rep
```

Multiple of 12 sts + 2 extra

6-st right cable: Sl 3 sts to cn and hold to back of work, k3, k3 from cn.

6-st left cable: Sl 3 sts to cn and hold to front of work, k3, k3 from cn.

Rows 1 and 5 (RS): Knit.

Row 2 and all WS rows: Purl.

Row 3: K1 *6-st left cable, k6; rep from *, end k1.

Row 7: K1, *k6, 6-st right cable; rep from *, end k1.

Row 8: Purl.

Rep rows 1-8.

Sand pattern

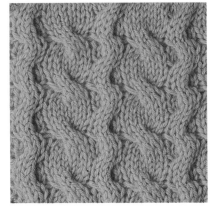

```
8  | | | | | | | | | | | | |  7
6  | | | | | | | | | | | | |  5
4  | | | | | | | | | | | | |  3
2  | | | | | | | | | | | | |  1
        12-st rep
```

Multiple of 12 sts

6-st left cable: Sl 3 sts to cn and hold to front of work, k3, k3 from cn.

6-st right cable: Sl 3 sts to cn and hold to back of work, k3, k3 from cn.

Rows 1 and 5 (RS): Knit.

Row 2 and all WS rows: Purl.

Row 3: *6-st left cable; rep from * to end.

Row 7: *K6, 6-st right cable; rep from * to end.

Row 8: Purl.

Rep rows 1-8.

abbreviations
explained **60-63**

knitting
terminology **64-68**

symbolcraft
charts **69-70**

Alternate broken ribs

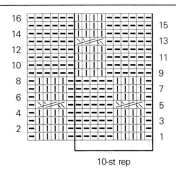

10-st rep

Multiple of 10 sts + 6 extra

4-st right cable: Sl 2 sts to cn and hold to back of work, k2, k2 from cn.

Row 1 (RS): *P1, k4, p5; rep from *, end p1.

Row 2 and all WS rows: K the knit sts and p the purl sts.

Rows 3, 7, 11 and 15: K the knit sts and p the purl sts.

Row 5: *P1, 4-st right cable, p5; rep from *, end p1.

Row 9: *P6, k4; rep from *, end p6.

Row 13: *P6, 4-st right cable; rep from *, end p6.

Row 16: Rep row 2.

Rep rows 1-16.

Double-knotted lattice

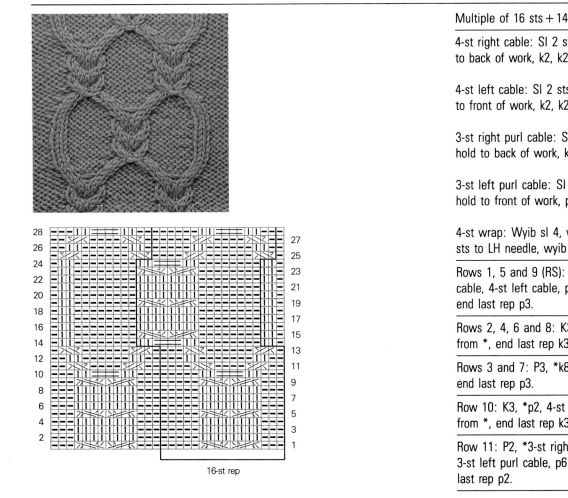

16-st rep

Multiple of 16 sts + 14 extra

4-st right cable: Sl 2 sts to cn and hold to back of work, k2, k2 from cn.

4-st left cable: Sl 2 sts to cn and hold to front of work, k2, k2 from cn.

3-st right purl cable: Sl 1 st to cn and hold to back of work, k2, p1 from cn.

3-st left purl cable: Sl 2 sts to cn and hold to front of work, p1, k2 from cn.

4-st wrap: Wyib sl 4, wyif sl same 4 sts to LH needle, wyib sl same 4 sts.

Rows 1, 5 and 9 (RS): P3, *4-st right cable, 4-st left cable, p8; rep from *, end last rep p3.

Rows 2, 4, 6 and 8: K3, *p8, k8; rep from *, end last rep k3.

Rows 3 and 7: P3, *k8, p8; rep from *, end last rep p3.

Row 10: K3, *p2, 4-st wrap, p2, k8; rep from *, end last rep k3.

Row 11: P2, *3-st right purl cable, p4, 3-st left purl cable, p6; rep from *, end last rep p2.

Row 12: K2, *p2, k6; rep from *, end last rep k2.

Row 13: P1, *3-st right purl cable, p6, 3-st left purl cable, p4; rep from *, end last rep p1.

Row 14: K1, p2, *k8, p2, 4-st wrap, p2; rep from *, end k8, p2, k1.

Rows 15, 19 and 23: P1, k2, *p8, 4-st right cable, 4-st left cable; rep from *, end p8, k2, p1.

Rows 16, 18, 20 and 22: K1, p2, *k8, p8; rep from *, end k8, p2, k1.

Rows 17 and 21: P1, k2, *p8, k8; rep from *, end p8, k2, p1.

Row 24: Rep row 14.

Row 25: P1, *3-st left purl cable, p6, 3-st right purl cable, p4; rep from *, end last rep p1.

Row 26: Rep row 12.

Row 27: P2, *3-st left purl cable, p4, 3-st right purl cable, p6; rep from *, end last rep p2.

Row 28: Rep row 10.

Rep rows 1-28.

abbreviations explained **60-63**

knitting terminology **64-68**

symbolcraft charts **69-70**

Lattice cable

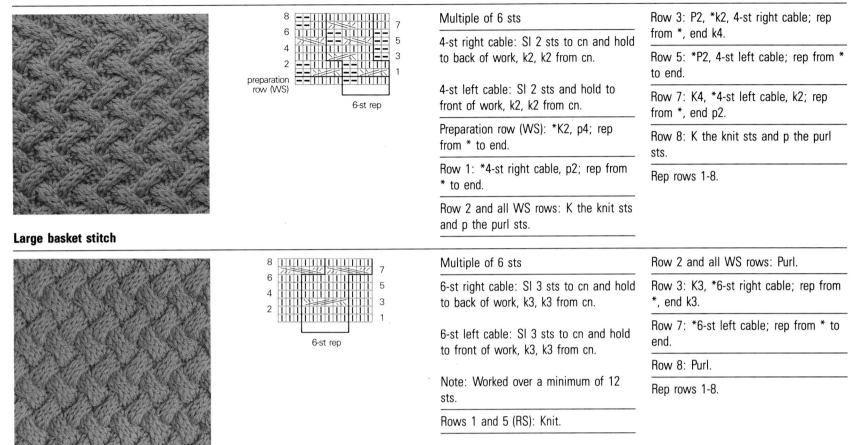

Multiple of 6 sts

4-st right cable: Sl 2 sts to cn and hold to back of work, k2, k2 from cn.

4-st left cable: Sl 2 sts and hold to front of work, k2, k2 from cn.

Preparation row (WS): *K2, p4; rep from * to end.

Row 1: *4-st right cable, p2; rep from * to end.

Row 2 and all WS rows: K the knit sts and p the purl sts.

Row 3: P2, *k2, 4-st right cable; rep from *, end k4.

Row 5: *P2, 4-st left cable; rep from * to end.

Row 7: K4, *4-st left cable, k2; rep from *, end p2.

Row 8: K the knit sts and p the purl sts.

Rep rows 1-8.

Large basket stitch

Multiple of 6 sts

6-st right cable: Sl 3 sts to cn and hold to back of work, k3, k3 from cn.

6-st left cable: Sl 3 sts to cn and hold to front of work, k3, k3 from cn.

Note: Worked over a minimum of 12 sts.

Rows 1 and 5 (RS): Knit.

Row 2 and all WS rows: Purl.

Row 3: K3, *6-st right cable; rep from *, end k3.

Row 7: *6-st left cable; rep from * to end.

Row 8: Purl.

Rep rows 1-8.

Crossed V stitch

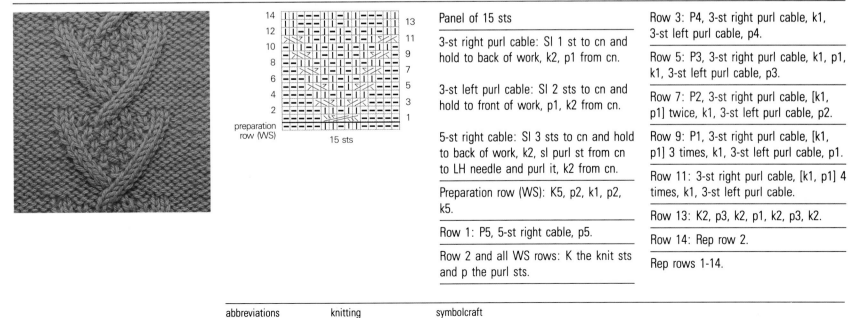

Panel of 15 sts

3-st right purl cable: Sl 1 st to cn and hold to back of work, k2, p1 from cn.

3-st left purl cable: Sl 2 sts to cn and hold to front of work, p1, k2 from cn.

5-st right cable: Sl 3 sts to cn and hold to back of work, k2, sl purl st from cn to LH needle and purl it, k2 from cn.

Preparation row (WS): K5, p2, k1, p2, k5.

Row 1: P5, 5-st right cable, p5.

Row 2 and all WS rows: K the knit sts and p the purl sts.

Row 3: P4, 3-st right purl cable, k1, 3-st left purl cable, p4.

Row 5: P3, 3-st right purl cable, k1, p1, k1, 3-st left purl cable, p3.

Row 7: P2, 3-st right purl cable, [k1, p1] twice, k1, 3-st left purl cable, p2.

Row 9: P1, 3-st right purl cable, [k1, p1] 3 times, k1, 3-st left purl cable, p1.

Row 11: 3-st right purl cable, [k1, p1] 4 times, k1, 3-st left purl cable.

Row 13: K2, p3, k2, p1, k2, p3, k2.

Row 14: Rep row 2.

Rep rows 1-14.

Hollow oak

20
18
16
14
12
10
8
6
4
2

19
17
15
13
11
9
7
5
3
1

15 sts

Panel of 15 sts

3-st right purl cable: Sl 1 st to cn and hold to back of work, k2, p1 from cn.

3-st left purl cable: Sl 2 sts to cn and hold to front of work, p1, k2 from cn.

Make bobble (MB): [K1, p1] 3 times, k1 in one st (7 sts made), then pass 2nd, 3rd, 4th, 5th, 6th and 7th st over last st made.

Row 1 (RS): P5, k2, MB, k2, p5.

Rows 2, 4 and 6: K5, p5, k5.

Row 3: P5, MB, k3, MB, p5.

Row 5: Rep row 1.

Row 7: P4, 3-st right purl cable, p1, 3-st left purl cable, p4.

Row 8: K4, p2, k1, p1, k1, p2, k4.

Row 9: P3, 3-st right purl cable, k1, p1, k1, 3-st left purl cable, p3.

Row 10: K3, p3, k1, p1, k1, p3, k3.

Row 11: P2, 3-st right purl cable, [p1, k1] twice, p1, 3-st left purl cable, p2.

Row 12: K2, p2, [k1, p1] 3 times, k1, p2, k2.

Row 13: P2, k3, [p1, k1] twice, p1, k3, p2.

Rows 14, 16 and 18: Rep rows 12, 10 and 8.

Row 15: P2, 3-st left purl cable, [p1, k1] twice, p1, 3-st right purl cable, p2.

Row 17: P3, 3-st left purl cable, k1, p1, k1, 3-st right purl cable, p3.

Row 19: P4, 3-st left purl cable, p1, 3-st right purl cable, p4.

Row 20: Rep row 2.

Rep rows 1-20.

Enclosed cable

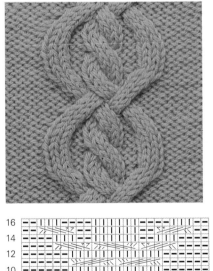

16
14
12
10
8
6
4
2

15
13
11
9
7
5
3
1

24 sts

Panel of 24 sts

6-st right cable: Sl 3 sts to cn and hold to back of work, k3, k3 from cn.

6-st left cable: Sl 3 sts to cn and hold to front of work, k3, k3 from cn.

5-st right purl cable: Sl 2 sts to cn and hold to back of work, k3, p2 from cn.

5-st left purl: Sl 3 sts to cn and hold to front of work, p2, k3 from cn.

Rows 1 and 5 (RS): P2, k3, p4, k6, p4, k3, p2.

Row 2 and all WS rows: K the knit sts and p the purl sts.

Row 3: P2, k3, p4, 6-st left cable, p4, k3, p2.

Row 7: P2, 5-st left purl cable, p2, k6, p2, 5-st right purl cable, p2.

Row 9: P4, 5-st left purl cable, 6-st left cable, 5-st right purl cable, p4.

Row 11: P6, [6-st right cable] twice, p6.

Row 13: P4, 5-st right purl cable, 6-st left cable, 5-st left purl cable, p4.

Row 15: P2, 5-st right purl cable, p2, k6, p2, 5-st left purl cable, p2.

Row 16: Rep row 2.

Rep rows 1-16.

Clustered braid

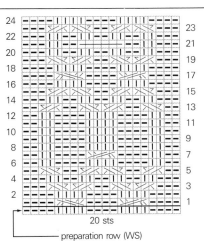

24 22 20 18 16 14 12 10 8 6 4 2

23 21 19 17 15 13 11 9 7 5 3 1

20 sts

preparation row (WS)

Panel of 20 sts

3-st right purl cable: Sl 1 st to cn and hold to back of work, k2, p1 from cn.

3-st left purl cable: Sl 2 sts to cn and hold to front of work, p1, k2 from cn.

4-st right cable: Sl 2 sts to cn and hold to back of work, k2, k2 from cn.

4-st left cable: Sl 2 sts to cn and hold to front of work, k2, k2 from cn.

Wrapped sts: K2, p2, k2, sl the last 6 sts worked onto cn and wrap yarn 4 times counterclockwise around these 6 sts; then sl the 6 sts back to RH needle.

Preparation row (WS): K4, [p4, k4] twice.

Row 1: P4, 4-st right cable, p4, 4-st left cable, p4.

Row 2 and all WS rows: K the knit sts and p the purl sts.

Row 3: P3, 3-st right purl cable, 3-st left purl cable, p2, 3-st right purl cable, 3-st left purl cable, p3.

Row 5: P2, [3-st right purl cable, p2, 3-st left purl cable] twice, p2.

Row 7: P2, k2, p4, 4-st right cable, p4, k2, p2.

Row 9: P2, k2, p4, k4, p4, k2, p2.

Row 11: Rep row 7.

Row 13: P2, [3-st left purl cable, p2, 3-st right purl cable] twice, p2.

Row 15: P3, 3-st left purl cable, 3-st right purl cable, p2, 3-st left purl cable, 3-st right purl cable, p3.

Rows 17 and 19: Rep rows 1 and 3.

Row 21: P3, k2, p2, work wrapped sts, p2, k2, p3.

Row 23: Rep row 15.

Row 24: Rep row 2.

Rep rows 1-24.

Simple mock cable

4 2

3 1

4-st rep

Multiple of 4 sts + 2 extra

2-st right twist (RT): K2tog leaving both sts on needle; insert RH needle between 2 sts, and k first st again; then sl both sts from needle.

Row 1: P2, *k2, p2; rep from * to end.

Rows 2 and 4: K2, *p2, k2; rep from * to end.

Row 3: P2, *RT, p2; rep from * to end.

Rep rows 1-4.

abbreviations explained **60-63**

knitting terminology **64-68**

symbolcraft charts **69-70**

Baby cross-cable ribbing

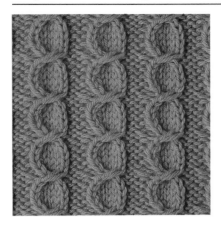

Multiple of 8 sts + 3 extra

5-st cross: Sl 4 sts to cn and hold to back of work, k1, sl 3 sts back to LH needle and place rem st on cn to front of work, k3 from LH needle, k1 from cn.

Rows 1 and 3 (RS): *P3, k5; rep from *, end p3.

Rows 2 and 4: *K3, p5; rep from *, end k3.

Row 5: *P3, 5-st cross; rep from *, end p3.

Row 6: Rep row 2.

Rep rows 1-6.

Knotted cable

Knot inc cable: Sl 1 st to cn and hold to front of work, sl 2 sts to cn and hold to back of work, p into front and back of next st, k2 from back cn, p into front and back of st on front cn.

Note: Use 2 cable needles.

Rows 1 and 3 (RS): P3, k2, p2, k2, p3.

Rows 2 and 4: K3, p2, k2, p2, k3.

Row 5: P3, knot dec cable, p3.

Row 6: K4, p2, k4.

Row 7: P4, k2, p4.

Row 8: K3, knot inc cable, k3.

Rows 9, 11, 13 and 15: Rep row 1.

Rows 10, 12, 14 and 16: Rep row 2.

Rep rows 1-16.

Panel of 12 sts

Knot dec cable: Sl 2 sts to cn and hold to back of work, sl 2 sts to 2nd cn and hold to front of work, p2tog, k2 from front cn, p2tog from back cn.

Wavy cables

Panel of 15 sts

9-st cable: Sl 3 sts to cn and hold to back of work, sl 3 sts to 2nd cn and hold to front of work, k3, k3 from front cn, k3 from back cn.

Note: Use 2 cable needles.

Row 1 (RS): P3, k9, p3.

Rows 2-8: K the knit sts and p the purl sts.

Row 9: P3, 9-st cable, p3.

Rows 10-16: K the knit sts and p the purl sts.

Rep rows 1-16.

Alternate broken ribs

Multiple of 10 sts + 6 extra

4-st right cable: Sl 2 sts to cn and hold to back of work, k2, k2 from cn.

Row 1 (RS): *P1, k4, p2, k2, p1; rep from *, end p1, k4, p1.

Row 2 and all WS rows: K the knit sts and p the purl sts.

Rows 3, 7, 11 and 15: K the knit sts and p the purl sts.

Row 5: *P1, 4-st right cable, p2, k2, p1; rep from *, end p1, 4-st right cable, p1.

Row 9: *P2, k2, p2, k4; rep from *, end p2, k2, p2.

Row 13; *P2, k2, p2, 4-st right cable; rep from *, end p2, k2, p2.

Rep rows 1-16.

abbreviations explained **60-63**   knitting terminology **64-68**

XI. Designing

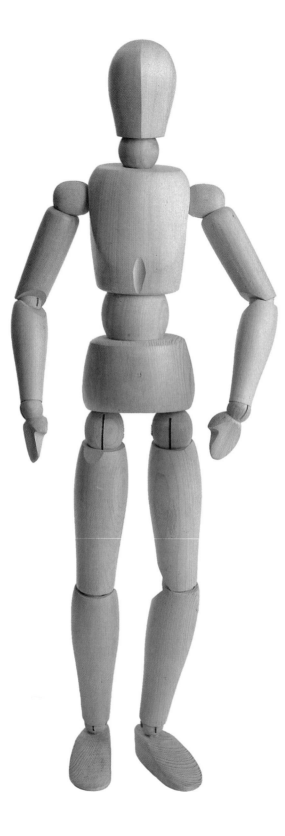

Introduction to Design

The dictionary defines the word "design" in more than one way. One meaning is "to conceive and plan out in the mind," and another, quite different, is "to create, fashion, execute or construct according to a plan." These two parts of designing—conception and execution—are not separate processes. Ultimately they must mesh to create the finished product.

This chapter discusses both phases of design, and even if you do not plan to create your own designs, you will find many sections useful. Learning about various knitting processes can help you more fully understand printed instructions. You can also learn how to alter existing sweater patterns and make garments that will fit better.

You may have already done some simple designing without even realizing it. If you have altered the neckline or sleeve on an existing pattern or made changes in the color or pattern stitch as you worked, you were moving toward designing a garment without a knitting pattern. This chapter will help you move further along in this process.

Planning is the most important step of designing. The more you have worked out on paper in advance, the easier it will be to complete your design. Just remember that your plans are not etched in stone—you can change your mind. What looks good on paper may not always work in your knitted piece. Make changes as you need to— it is, after all, your design. The best designers redo and adjust as they work. Don't be afraid to make an error. From each mistake you'll learn a new technique or a new way to solve a problem, and that can be the most interesting part of designing.

One of the most important elements in design, as in all knitting, is the relationship of the gauge to the size of the knitted pieces. Read the helpful suggestions on gauge in Chapter IV before you knit a gauge swatch. As you begin to shape pieces and add patterns to your designs, you must always begin with an accurate gauge to achieve the results you plan.

To make your own proportioned sketch, place a piece of tracing paper over the mannequin and draw your garment onto the paper. Attach the finished sketch to the worksheet page in the appropriate area.

Conceptual Process

The design process begins with an idea. To translate this idea into a workable plan, you must consider a number of elements, such as color, shaping, stitch patterns and fit, among others. It will help to write them down. Don't worry about the order, because the elements of design are interdependent, and their relationships will change with each new idea. For example, you may have a silhouette in mind before you search for an appropriate yarn and stitch pattern. Other times you may decide on a particular yarn before you begin to think about the shape of the garment. Just remember that designing is an evolutionary process. You may realize that the yarn you love doesn't create the texture you want in one stitch pattern, and you may have to change to another. Or you may decide that a cropped sweater, not a tunic, suits the yarn you have chosen.

Listed below are some important elements you should consider as you create a design.

Silhouette

The silhouette is the outside line and general shape of a garment. Sketching a simple silhouette of your design is a good place to begin. Your drawing can be fairly abstract, without any details or measurements.

Measurements and fit

Once you have an idea of the general silhouette of your design, you can begin to think about the fit you desire and the approximate finished measurements. To have a better understanding of the measurements and how they affect the fit of your knit garment, look at the fit chart in Chapter IV. This provides measurements in your particular size for garments that are close-fitting, loose-fitting, oversized and so on.

Begin with a simple design. You can get ideas for size, shape and silhouette from an existing sweater. Try it on and see how it fits. Lay the sweater flat and measure it. Use the worksheet page to note the measurements as well as any changes you would like to make.

Type of garment

Where will you wear it? In what season? Will it be worn strictly in the daytime, or the evening? Is it an outdoor garment? Do you want a pullover, cardigan or vest? Do you plan to make an "everyday" sweater or one for special occasions? These are just a few of the questions that will help you decide what type of garment you want to make.

Stitch patterns, yarn and color

It is important that you choose yarn and stitch or color patterns that work with the silhouette and type of garment you plan to make. For example, thick yarns are usually unsuitable for close-fitting, dressy sweaters. The combination of yarn and stitch or color patterns affects the final outcome of your design, and you should consider them together. An allover stitch pattern creates more weight and texture than a lacy pattern. On the other hand, a lacy pattern may not hold its shape as well and probably would not be a good choice for a less resilient yarn, such as silk, that may stretch.

Generally, thinner yarns drape well, while thicker yarns are firmer and less flexible. It is easier to work intricate stitch and color patterns in thinner yarns. Thicker yarns should be limited to less intricate patterns. They also create extra weight, especially when used for stranded colorwork.

Not only is the thickness of the yarn a factor, but the type of yarn also affects your design. Some yarns, such as silks, rayons and some cottons, lack resiliency and may not be suitable for patterns that require elasticity, such as ribbing or lace. Brushed or hairy yarns are best used with simple patterns, since the texture of the yarn can obliterate an intricate design. This is also

fit chart **54**   color stranding **82**

yarn types **10-15**   ribbing **34-35, 172-73**

true for many novelty yarns. Flat, smooth yarns are best for stitch patterns and color motifs.

You should also consider the color of the yarn when you choose stitch or color patterns. Dark-colored yarns make it hard to see many stitch patterns. Some dark colors, when teamed with light colors, show through when working stranded patterns. If you're working two yarns together, it's also a good idea to check their colorfastness.

Type of construction

How you ultimately construct your garment will depend on your yarn, your patterns, and the type of garment you plan to make. You can make a simple sweater in four sections (the back, front and two sleeves), starting from the lower edge of the back and working up through the neck and shoulders. You could also work the same garment on circular needles, omitting the side seams. Or you might want to work the garment in one piece, beginning at one sleeve edge and working horizontally across the piece to the other sleeve edge. For each of these constructions, you will have different concerns. If you are a novice, begin with the simplest method before you try other, more complex construction techniques.

Edgings/ribbings

Read the sections of this chapter that discuss ribbings, bands and hems before you decide how you will proceed with your garment. Subtle details can have a strong impact on the look of your design.

Sleeves/armholes

When planning sleeves and armholes, think about them in relationship to the other aspects of your design. If it is important to keep the visual continuity of intricate colorwork or stitch patterns, your armhole shaping may be limited. If you want to achieve a tailored, fitted silhouette, you might think of working a set-in sleeve. If you are using a thick yarn, you may want to have less bulk at the underarm by making a square or angled armhole. In this case, the sleeve top fits into the armhole, so the depth of the armhole must correspond to the width of the sleeve at the upper arm. If you are making a deep armhole, you need to make a wider, fuller sleeve. All these aspects will affect your overall design.

Neckline/collar

The neckline band or collar will be influenced by how you plan to wear your finished garment. The neckline must be compatible to the style of your sweater, its construction and the yarn and pattern you use. The depth of the neckline may be limited by stitch or color patterning, since you may not want to interrupt some motifs with the beginning of a neck shaping. If you are working with a lacy pattern stitch, your band may simply be a narrow edge or a plain crochet picot. Turtlenecks or highnecks are well suited to outdoor sweaters.

Trims

How will you complete your design? Do you want to add cording, braiding or ribbon? Do you want to work lavish embroidery? What size buttons do you want, what style and how many? Do you want several front pockets or side pockets? Although you can add some of these touches after the pieces are complete, many should be worked in as part of the design. For example, you may want to get a button or two and sew them to your gauge swatch before you even begin to knit. If you are planning a beaded evening sweater, you can add the beads as you knit.

Planning Yarn Amounts

When you design a sweater, you may either start with an idea and then purchase yarn, or you may already have the yarn and want to plan your design around it. In either case, you can estimate the amount of yarn you'll need by using your schematic drawing and the calculation method below.

Some yarn ball bands give you a rough estimate of the amount of yarn required for an "average sweater," but your design may not fit into this category. Also you may knit your sweater at a different gauge than that called for on the ball band, and that would affect the amount of yarn you use.

Ask your yarn shop about the yarn you plan to purchase. If it is a yarn they sell often, they will have a good idea of the average amount needed for a sweater. You should purchase a couple of extra balls just to make sure you have enough. Check to see if they have a return policy for unused balls.

There are ways to extend your yarn if you know you don't have enough for your design. Most ways involve some changes to your basic design. For example, depending on how much yarn you have, you might shorten the sleeves or the length of the sweater or make it less roomy. You could also add other colors or types of yarn by creating a yoke effect in a colorwork pattern. If you have almost the right amount, you can work the picked-up bands in a contrasting color.

Enter all the information about your yarn on the worksheet, such as how much you have purchased, the yarn name, color number, dye lot and even the date and name of the store where you purchased it. You may need this information to buy more yarn.

Measuring and weighing

Planning yarn amounts is not an exact science, but you can come up with a close estimate by using one of two methods: measuring the length of the yarn in the unraveled swatch or weighing the swatch. For both techniques, you use a 4 × 4 inch (10 × 10cm) knit swatch and your schematic drawing measurements to calculate the square inches/centimeters of your sweater pieces.

First, multiply the width of the back piece at the widest point by the total length. Then repeat the process for the front piece and each sleeve. Add the square inches/centimeters of all four pieces together to get the total number of square inches/centimeters in your garment. Find the square inches of your swatch as follows: 4 × 4 inches = 16 square inches (10 × 10cm = 100 square centimeters). Divide the total number of square inches/square centimeters in your sweater by the 16 square inches/100 square centimeters of your swatch. This final result is used in both methods below.

Length
Unravel your swatch and measure the length of the yarn in it. To find the total yards/meters needed, multiply the final result from the calculation by the yards/meters in your swatch.

Weight
Weigh the swatch. To find the total ounces/grams needed, multiply the final result from the calculation by the weight of the swatch. If your swatch is too light to get an accurate weight, knit a larger swatch and use it to recalculate the square inches/ square centimeters.

Measurements

Whether you are designing your very own garment or making one from an existing pattern, you must begin with an accurate set of body measurements. Below are the most important measurements and where they are taken on the body. If you are taking your own measurements, you will find it much easier and more accurate to have someone help you. Enter the measurements in the appropriate spot on the worksheet page.

Bust/chest

This is the most important measurement and often the focal point of most designs. Measure around the fullest part of the bust. Don't let the tape measure slip down on the back. The bust measurement is the beginning point in determining how much ease to allow in the sweater.

Waist and hips

To help you find your natural waistline, tie a piece of string or elastic around your waist and let it fall naturally. The waist should be measured loosely for a better fit. Wrap the tape measure around your waist and move it from side to side, allowing it to settle. Measure the hip at the widest point below the waist. Although these measurements are not always essential, they are helpful when looking at the overall body type and are necessary for some garment designs. The waist measurement is important for garments with fitted waistlines or for cropped sweaters. The hip measurement is essential for long sweaters and dresses.

Crossback

The crossback includes the two shoulders and the neck width. It should be measured across the back from the tip of one shoulder bone to the other. This measurement is important when you create garments that should fit well at the shoulders, such as those with set-in sleeves.

Width at upper arm

The upper arm is measured around the arm at its widest point. Although most sweaters are designed to be roomy at the upper arm, this may be an important measurement for close-fitting garments.

Wrist

The wrist is measured just above the hand. Most sweaters usually have a generous amount of ease above the cuff; other, more fitted sweaters may have a tight measurement above the cuff. The width of the sleeve at the lowest edge should be wide enough to go over the hand with a closed fist.

Back neck to waist

This is determined by measuring from the bone at the base of the back of your neck to the waist. If you want the lower edge of the sweater to fall below the hips, measure from waist to the lower edge and add this amount to the measurement.

One shoulder

This should be measured from the center back neck to the point where the arm joins the body. This measurement is used most often in conjunction with the crossback measurement.

Center back neck to wrist

Take this measurement from the bone in the center of the back of your neck to the wrist bone with your arm extended, or to the point you want your sleeve cuff to end. This measurement is used to determine the finished sleeve length. To determine the sleeve length to the shoulder, take the measurement from the center back neck to the shoulder and subtract it from the measurement of the center back neck to the wrist.

Front neck to waist

Measure from the shoulder over the fullest part of the bust to the waist. This measurement is particularly helpful if the bustline is full, otherwise the back neck to waist measurement, which is slightly easier to take, is adequate.

Waist to underarm

This is measured from the waistline to approximately one inch (2.5cm) before the actual underarm. This measurement will help you decide where to begin the armhole shaping of your sweater.

Neck width

Measure around the neck at its fullest point. The neck width of the finished garment is larger than this measurement to accommodate the size of your head.

Wrist to underarm

Measure from the wrist bone along the underside of your arm, with your elbow slightly bent, to approximately one inch (2.5cm) before your underarm. This measurement is used to determine the sleeve length for a set-in sleeve.

worksheet **168-71**   fit chart **54**

ease **55**   set in sleeve **109-10**

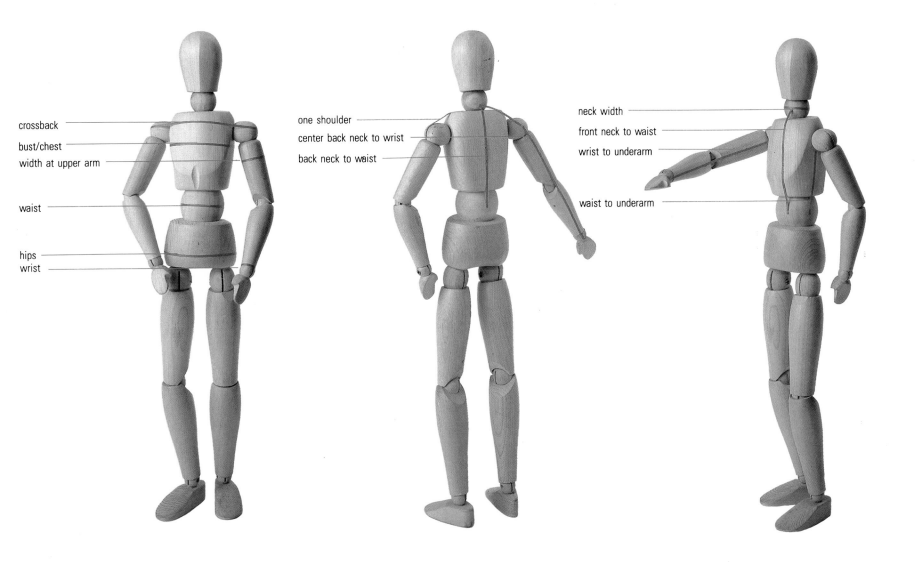

crossback

bust/chest

width at upper arm

waist

hips

wrist

one shoulder

center back neck to wrist

back neck to waist

neck width

front neck to waist

wrist to underarm

waist to underarm

Using the Vogue Knitting Worksheet

Once you have considered the conceptual elements of a design, you are ready to move on to its technical aspects. Use the worksheet to organize every element and essential detail, creating a step-by-step plan that will actually become your working pattern. The worksheet also serves as a record and you can refer to it for future projects. To help you fill out your own worksheet, study the sample below.

Checklist

square graph paper	colored pencils
knitter's graph paper	scissors
ruler	calculator
tape measure	tracing paper
notebook	knit gauge
yarn	knitting needles
stitch dictionary	

Project
This box is for general information. It is especially helpful if you put a project aside, because you will have the information at hand when you return to the work. Write down a brief description of the project, the beginning and ending dates, and information about yarn, needles and any other tools or accessories.

Sketch area
Use the sketching mannequin at the beginning of the chapter to draw your idea. This can be as simple or as elaborate as you wish, but it should give the general proportions you want without using exact measurements. Lay a piece of tracing paper over the photograph of the mannequin and draw the sweater onto it. Attach the tracing paper here.

Body and sweater measurements
Enter your measurements in the body measurement section, which is broken down into widths and lengths. Using these figures and the amount of ease you desire, plan your sweater measurements. Write them in pencil, since you may want to change the measurements as you work out further details.

Gauge and gauge swatch
Enter stitch and row gauge here for four inches (10cm). To help you calculate the measurements of your sweater, include the number of stitches and rows for one inch (or 1cm).

The gauge swatch box is four inches (10cm) square. Don't forget that in some cases more than one gauge swatch will be necessary. After measuring each swatch, attach it to a separate piece of paper to keep with the worksheet.

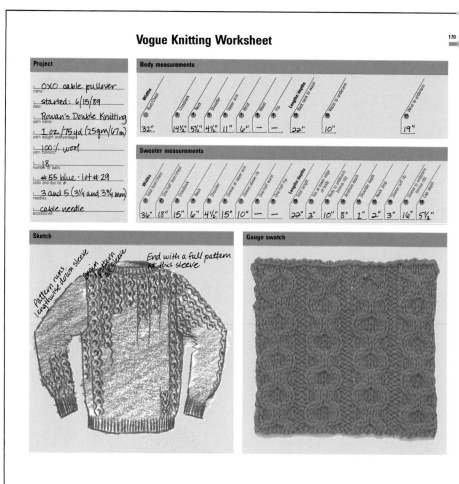

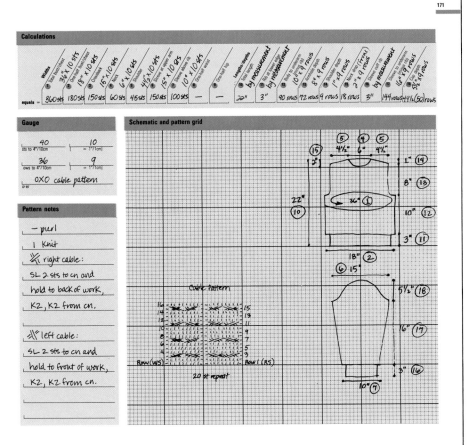

Calculations

Each sweater measurement must be multiplied by the stitch or row gauge (depending on whether it is a width or length measurement) to find the number of stitches and rows in your design. You may want to highlight the number of stitches and rows you will be using as you knit for easier working.

Pattern notes

Add any information here that you think will be helpful as you work. The sample worksheet shows an explanation of the symbolcraft used in the cable pattern. If you are using a written pattern, copy and attach it here. You may want to add a color key or notes regarding the placement or working of a stitch pattern. You can also add information about special cast-ons or other construction details.

Schematic and pattern grid

This area gives ample room for plotting a schematic drawing of your sweater. A schematic drawing is made to scale and shows flat pieces before finishing and without selvages. To draw the schematic, use the grid as if one square equaled one inch (2.5cm). Using your sweater measurements, mark points on the graph paper and connect them. If working with a fraction, use a partial square to note this measurement on the grid. Include details such as pockets and shoulder shaping. When lower edge ribbing pulls in, the schematic is drawn to show it.

You could also draw a small colorwork chart or stitch pattern on the grid.

Vogue Knitting Worksheet

Project

name:

date:

yarn name:

yarn weight and yardage:

yarn content:

number of balls:

color and dye lot #:

needles:

accessories:

Body measurements

Widths

1. Bust/Chest
3. Crossback
4. Neck
5. Shoulder
6. Upper arm
7. Wrist
8. Waist
9. Hip

Lengths/depths

10. Back neck to waist
12. Waist to underarm
17. Wrist to underarm

Sweater measurements

Widths

1. Total bust/chest
2. One-half bust/chest
3. Crossback
4. Neck
5. Shoulder
6. Sleeve at upper arm
7. Sleeve above rib
8. One-half waist
9. One-half hip

Lengths/depths

10. Total length
11. Rib at lower edge of body
12. Body to underarm (minus rib)
13. Armhole depth
14. Shoulder depth
15. Neck drop
16. Sleeve cuff rib
17. Sleeve to underarm (minus rib)
18. Cap depth

Sketch

Using the mannequin at the beginning of the chapter, make your sketch and attach it here.

Gauge swatch

Place your 4 × 4" (10 × 10 cm) swatch here.

Calculations

Widths

1. Total bust/chest
2. One-half bust/chest
3. Crossback
4. Neck
5. Shoulder
6. Sleeve at upper arm
7. Sleeve above rib
8. One-half waist
9. One-half hip

Lengths/depths

10. Total length
11. Rib at lower edge of body
12. Body to underarm (minus rib)
13. Armhole depth
14. Shoulder depth
15. Neck drop
16. Sleeve cuff rib
17. Sleeve to underarm (minus rib)
18. Cap depth

equals =

Gauge

sts to 4"/10cm   [= 1"/1cm]

rows to 4"/10cm   [= 1"/1cm]

over

Pattern notes

Schematic and pattern grid

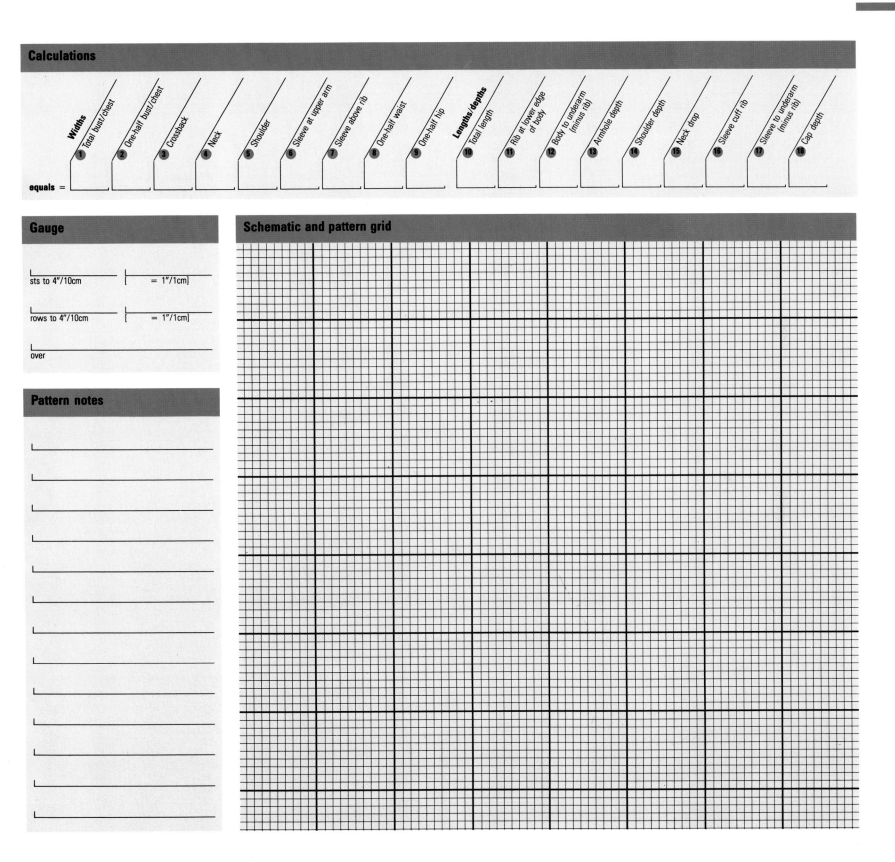

Ribbing

The elastic property of ribbing allows it to grip at key areas, such as the wrists and the waist. When designing, you must plan every aspect of the ribbing carefully, including how much it pulls in, how it is cast on, how it is seamed, and the type of pattern you are using.

To make ribbing more elastic, work it on a needle that is one or two sizes smaller than the needle you will use for the main part of the garment. It may be necessary to use an even smaller needle with less resilient yarns.

The number of stitches cast on for the ribbing is not always the same as for the body of the piece. Generally, if you want the piece to pull in, you cast on fewer rib stitches than you will use for the main body. If you want a re-laxed rib (one that doesn't pull in at all), cast on the same or nearly the same number of stitches. In some

cases, you might cast on more stitches for the ribbing than for the main body, such as when the stitch used above the ribbing has a very loose gauge. If you want to see the effect the ribbing will have on the main body stitch, work a large swatch of the ribbing and the pattern stitch together.

Many stitch patterns other than knit and purl stitches can be used for rib-bing. For example, you could use stitches such as mock cables alone or in combination with knit and purl stitches. Ribbing can also be worked in two or more colors in vertical stripes (called corrugated rib) or horizontal stripes.

You can use a basic cast-on for rib-bing or choose one that will enhance its look, such as the Guernsey or the tubular cast-on. As the cast-on edge looks different on each side, plan which will be the right side of the work. Use the same side for each piece so that

when you sew them together, their edges will match perfectly.

To make your ribbing match at the seams, you must begin and end with the correct stitch. In knit one, purl one ribbing, you can begin and end with a purl stitch and sew in one-half of a knit stitch from each side to make one full knit stitch (using the purl stitches as a selvage). On knit two, purl two rib-bing, you can begin and end with either two knits or two purls and sew in a whole stitch on each side. When working in the round, you must have an exact multiple of stitches to keep a continuous ribbing.

Measuring ribbing gauge

When you lay the ribbed piece flat without stretching it, it will look like the piece pictured above. When taking the gauge, don't forget to count the purl stitches, which tend to disap-pear between the knit stitches.

Unless otherwise stated, you should measure your ribbing slightly stretched. Just pull the ribbing apart slightly to measure the gauge.

When ribbing is measured stretched (some-times called relaxed ribbing), it must be pulled apart even more than the slightly stretched piece. If the ribbing is to remain in this state, it should be wet blocked or steamed.

seaming **98-101**

swatch **57-59**

corrugated ribbing **91**

horizontal stripes **90**

circular
knitting **75-78, 188-93**

selvages **194-95**

Measuring ribbing length

Measure the ribbing when you have knit half way through a row on the longer side and your work is on two needles. If the stitches are bunched together on one needle, the piece will measure longer than it actually is.

The ribbing above is approximately 1½ inches (4cm) long when measured with the stitches quite close together on one needle.

To get a more accurate measurement, work to the center of a row and lay the piece flat. Notice that the ribbing now measures 1¼ inches (3cm).

Increasing above the ribbing

When the ribbing pattern continues up to become part of the body pattern, each increase on the last row of the ribbing must be carefully placed. Work a swatch before beginning your piece to determine the best placement.

A knit two, purl two ribbing can be worked into a knit four, purl two pattern by increasing one stitch on either side of the two knit stitches on the last row of ribbing.

You can work a mock cable and a knit one, purl two ribbing pattern into a four-stitch cable with a knit three, purl two ribbing by adding one stitch on either side of the mock cable and the knit stitch.

Differences in ribbing

There is a visible difference in the way knit one, purl one ribbing pulls in compared to knit two, purl two ribbing.

The knit two, purl two ribbing shown above pulls in more than a knit one, purl one ribbing (above left) over the same number of stitches.

The depth of the ribbing also affects how much it pulls in. This is especially important to know when you work with fibers that are not resilient, such as cotton. Using a deeper ribbing with cotton yarns is a good idea.

The deeper ribbing (above) pulls in more than the shorter ribbing (above left) over the same number of stitches.

Body Shaping

You can change the form of a knit piece by increasing, decreasing, casting on or binding off stitches or by making partial rows called short rows.

Shaping can be done at side edges, several stitches in from the edge or well inside the edge, as with darts and neckline shaping. Shaping is usually done on the right side of the work. Shaping can be nearly invisible or decorative, as in full-fashioning.

Three factors affect the angle or curve of the shaped piece: the finished width (stitches) before and after shaping, the length (rows) over which the shaping has taken place, and the placement of the shaping. As you work through various types of shaping in this section, you will note that all of these factors are considered.

To attain precise shapes, you must work out the calculations carefully using the stitch and row gauge. You may need to round the numbers slightly, especially if you want to work with even numbers of rows. After you work out the shaping mathematically, a good way to double check the numbers is to chart the shaping on graph paper.

Once you have calculated the width and length measurements on the worksheet pages, you can begin to plan the shaping. Remember that many pieces of a sweater correspond to each other. For example, the armhole depth of the front and back pieces is almost always the same. On pullovers, the width of the crossback on the front and back is the same. Also the width of a sleeve at the upper arm usually corresponds to the armhole depth.

After you have calculated your shaping, you can check the fit using a knit fabric, such as cotton double knit. Draw your pattern measurements on the fabric (adding a seam allowance), cut the

pieces, baste them together and try on the shell. If you're not satisfied with the fit, re-figure your pieces and make a second shell.

Unless otherwise noted, the following discussion refers to the shaping of a pullover sweater. The gauge is a standard one for knitting worsted yarn in stockinette stitch of five stitches and seven rows to one inch, given in inches only. When shaping is done by increasing or decreasing, it occurs on right-side rows.

These guidelines are not hard and fast rules, but they will help you to plan and shape many types of garments. Experiment with shaping. Don't be afraid of failure—you will learn something new from each experiment.

Plotting on graph paper

For calculations, the most versatile size graph paper is 10 squares to one inch. One square equals one stitch and a horizontal line of squares equals one row. The first line of squares is your first row and represents the right side of your work. Mark it with an arrow pointing to the left. Mark an arrow pointing to the right on the next wrong-side row. The arrows indicate the direction in which

a row is knit. In the grid shown, shaping occurs only on the right-side rows. The shaping begins after four rows. Count up four rows, then draw a line out one square on either side to represent one increase stitch on each end of the next right-side row. The grid shows an increase of four stitches (two each side) and is bound off on the eleventh row.

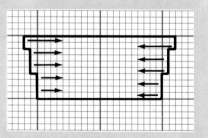

Shaping: lower edge to underarm

Usually several increases are worked across the first row after the ribbing, with additional increases at the side edges until the piece reaches the desired width at the underarm. This is the simplest form of shaping. Another method is to add darts, which is discussed later in this section.

Must know

Stitch gauge: 5 stitches = 1″
Row gauge: 7 rows = 1″
Width at lower edge (above rib): 12″
Width at underarm: 16″
Length to underarm (minus rib): 10″

What to do

Work 6 rows even, then increase 1 stitch on each side of the next row. Repeat the increase on every 6th row 9 times more. Work 9 rows even.

How to calculate

Widths (stitches):
12″ × 5 = 60 sts (lower edge)
16″ × 5 = 80 sts (underarm)

Length (rows):
10″ × 7 = 70 rows (to underarm)

Determine the increases:
80 sts − 60 sts = 20 sts (10 sts each side)

Calculate increases, leaving about 1½″ (10 rows) worked even:
70 rows − 10 rows = 60 rows for incs
60 rows ÷ 10 incs = 6 rows or work incs every 6th row

Total: 20 sts and 70 rows

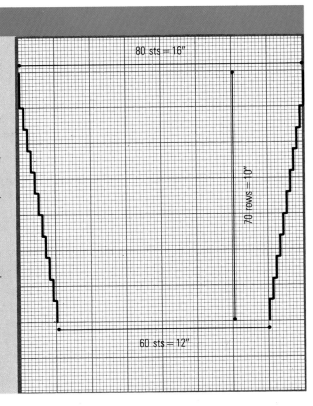

Shaping: lower edge to underarm with waist shaping

To shape a piece in to the waist by decreasing and then out to the underarm by increasing, you must plan two types of shaping. The dotted line across the center indicates the waistline.

Must know

Stitch gauge: 5 stitches = 1″
Row gauge: 7 rows = 1″
Width at lower edge (above rib): 16″
Width at waist: 12″
Width at underarm: 16″
Length to waist (minus rib): 6″
Length from waist to underarm: 6″

What to do

Work 4 rows even, then decrease 1 stitch on each side of the next row. Repeat the decrease on every 4th row 9 times more. Work 1 row even to the waist. Work another 4 rows even (above the waist), then increase 1 stitch each side of the next row. Repeat the increase on every 4th row 9 times more. Work 1 row even.

How to calculate

Widths (stitches):
16″ × 5 = 80 sts (lower edge)
12″ × 5 = 60 sts (waist)
16″ × 5 = 80 sts (underarm)

Lengths (rows):
6″ × 7 = 42 rows (to waist)
6″ × 7 = 42 rows (from waist to underarm)

Determine the decreases to waist:
80 sts − 60 sts = 20 sts (10 sts each side)

Calculate the decreases:
42 rows ÷ 10 incs = 4.2 (thus every 4th row)

Total: 20 sts and 42 rows

Determine the increases to underarm:
80 sts − 60 sts = 20 sts (10 sts each side)

Calculate the increases:
42 rows ÷ 10 incs = 4.2 (thus every 4th row)

Total: 20 sts and 42 rows

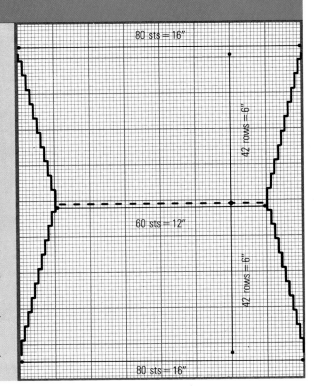

Armhole Shaping

Armholes can be square or angled or shaped for a set-in or raglan sleeve. Generally, the same shaping is used on the front and back pieces. The simplest shapes are the square and angled armholes. To make a square armhole, a number of stitches are bound off all at one time and the rest of the armhole is worked even. This type of shaping is ideal for an oversized sweater since it reduces bulk at the underarm. When you work an angled armhole, the stitches are decreased evenly over a small number of rows—usually one to two inches. This armhole also prevents bulk at the underarm.

Shaping an armhole for a set-in or raglan sleeve is more complicated. The following examples are for these two armhole types.

Shaping: armhole for a set-in sleeve

Set-in sleeves are used in fitted sweaters. The armhole shaping for this style is simple, but the corresponding sleeve-cap shaping is more complicated.

Once you have determined the number of stitches in your crossback, subtract this number from the stitches at the underarm. Half this number of stitches are decreased on each side. Bind off one-half the number to be decreased for each side on the first two rows, then decrease one stitch every other row for the remaining stitches. This creates a gradual curve at the underarm. An alternate method is to bind off approximately one inch of stitches and then gradually bind off the remaining stitches.

Must know
Stitch gauge: 5 stitches = 1″
Row gauge: 7 rows = 1″
Width at underarm: 16″
Width of crossback: 12″
Depth of armhole: 8½″

What to do
Bind off 5 stitches at the beginning of the next 2 rows. Decrease 1 stitch on each side of the next row, then every other row 4 times more. Work even for 49 rows.

How to calculate

Widths (stitches):
16″ × 5 = 80 sts (underarm)
12″ × 5 = 60 sts (crossback)

Length (rows):
8½″ × 7 = 59.5 (rounded 60) rows (armhole depth)

Determine the decreases:
80 sts − 60 sts = 20 sts (10 sts each side)
Half the number of sts = 5 sts each side

Total: 20 sts and 11 rows

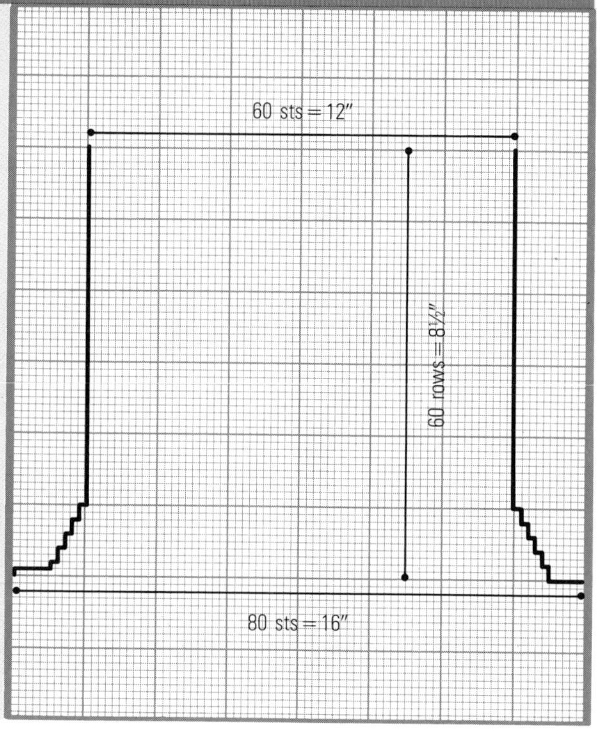

60 sts = 12″
60 rows = 8½″
80 sts = 16″

Raglan Armhole Shaping

A raglan garment should have the same number of rows in the slanting armhole as in the corresponding sleeve cap. To create an even slant, work the shaping gradually up to the neck. The decreases on a raglan go up to the very top of the piece, so it is essential that you determine the row gauge correctly.

The raglan armhole must be planned along with the raglan sleeve, since the tops of the front and back raglan pieces plus the two sleeve tops form the neck of the sweater. Once you establish the desired measurement for the circumference of the neck, subtract an amount for the top of each sleeve (usually two to four inches) and divide the remaining amount in half for the front and back necks. When planning the total sweater length, one-half of the top of the sleeve becomes part of the finished length. For example, if the top of the sleeve measures two inches, add one inch to the finished length of the garment.

Remember that since raglan armholes are usually slightly deeper than armholes in more fitted garments, the corresponding sleeve length to the underarm should be shorter.

You must calculate a raglan shape by trial and error on paper until you achieve the desired result. Various combinations of decreases produce different slants over the same depths.

Shaping: raglan armhole

You can shape a raglan armhole without an initial bind-off, but for a better fit, bind off several stitches (approximately one-half inch) at the underarm, then gradually shape the remaining rows.

The ideal shaping is worked at even intervals, such as every fourth row. However, if your calculations don't come out even, a diagonal shape can be worked by alternating decreases, such as every other row, then every fourth row.

Must know
Stitch gauge: 5 stitches = 1"
Row gauge: 7 rows = 1"
Width at underarm: 16"
Width of back neck: 6"
Depth of raglan: 10"

What to do
Bind off 3 stitches at the beginning of the next 2 rows. Work 2 rows even. Decrease 1 stitch on each side of the next row, then [every 2nd row once, every 4th row once] 10 times, then every 2nd row once. Work 3 rows even. Bind off the remaining 30 stitches or place the stitches on a holder to pick up for the neckband.

How to calculate

Widths (stitches):
16" × 5 = 80 sts (underarm)
6" × 5 = 30 sts (back neck)

Length (rows):
10" X 7 = 70 rows (raglan depth)

Determine the decreases:
80 sts − 30 sts = 50 sts (25 sts each side)
Initial bind-off = 3 sts (each side)
over 2 rows
70 rows − 2 rows = 68 rows for decs
25 sts − 3 sts = 22 sts each side in 68 rows

Placing the decreases:
work 2 rows even = 2 rows
then dec 1 time = 2 sts and 1 row
Alternately (i.e., 2nd, 4th, 2nd, 4th . . .)
every 2nd row 10 times = 20 sts and 20 rows
every 4th row 10 times = 20 sts and 40 rows
       40 sts and 60 rows
every 2nd once = 2 sts and 2 rows
work 3 rows even = 3 rows

Total: 25 decs = 50 sts and 70 rows

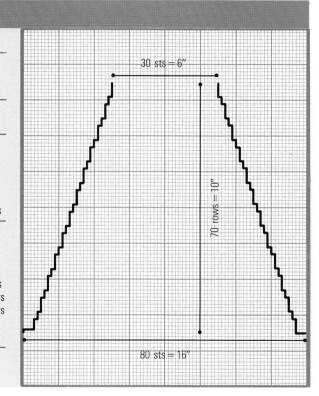

Shaping: shoulder

The outside of the shoulder should be lower than the inside (neck) edge to conform to the natural slope of the shoulder. Shoulders can be shaped by binding off a series of stitches (as evenly as possible) over a number of rows (three-fourths to 1¼ inches in depth). The more rows in the shoulder shaping, the greater the slope. You can also work short row shaping, which creates a sloped edge without making a stair-step line along the shoulder.

Must know
Stitch gauge: 5 stitches = 1″
Row gauge: 7 rows = 1″
Width of back neck: 6″
Width of shoulder: 4″
Width of crossback: 14″
Depth of shoulder shaping: 1″

What to do
Bind off 7 stitches at beginning of next 4 rows. Bind off 6 stitches at the beginning of the next 2 rows. Note that the left side of the shaping (worked on wrong-side rows) is 1 row longer than the other side. Bind off the remaining stitches for the neck or place them on a holder to work the neckband.

How to calculate

Widths (stitches):
6″ × 5 = 30 sts (back neck)
4″ × 5 = 20 sts (shoulder)
14″ × 5 = 70 sts (crossback)

Length (rows):
1″ × 7 = 7 (rounded 6) rows (shoulder)

Determine the decreases:
70 sts − 30 sts = 40 sts (20 sts each shoulder)
6 rows ÷ 2 = 3 rows each side for decs
20 sts ÷ 3 rows = 6.66 sts
The 20 stitches will be decreased in 3 bind-offs on each side

Calculating the decreases:
The decreases on each side must be a combination of 6 and 7 stitches:
7 + 7 + 6 = 20 sts
bind off 7 sts twice = 14 sts and 4 rows
bind off 6 sts once = 6 sts and 2 rows

Total: 20 sts and 6 rows

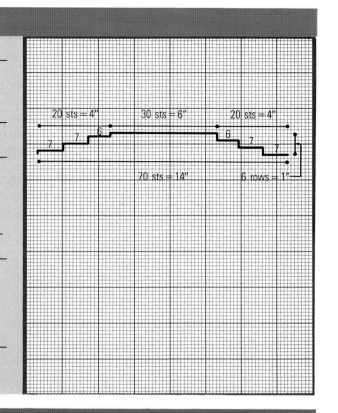

Shaping: shoulder with back neck shaping

Slight shaping at the back neck is sometimes desirable and can be worked at the same time as the shoulder shaping. Since the neck is generally shaped over a small number of rows, bind off approximately 80 percent of the total number of stitches in the first center bind-off and the rest of the stitches over the remaining rows.

Must know
Stitch gauge: 5 stitches = 1″
Row gauge: 7 rows = 1″
Width of back neck: 6″
Width of shoulder: 4″
Depth of shoulder shaping: 1″
Shoulder shaping (same as above table)

What to do
Using the same shoulder shaping as in the previous example, work the back neck shaping at the same time. Bind off the center 24 stitches first, then decrease 1 stitch from each neck edge 3 times on every other row.

How to calculate

Widths (stitches):
6″ × 5 = 30 sts (back neck)
4″ × 5 = 20 sts (shoulder)

Length (rows):
1″ × 7 = 7 (rounded 6) rows (shoulder)

Determine the back neck decreases:
80% of 30 = 24 sts (center bind-off)
30 sts − 24 sts = 6 sts (3 sts each side)

Calculating the decreases:
24 sts once = 24 sts and 2 rows
1 st 2 times = 4 sts and 4 rows
fasten off the last stitch = 2 sts

Total: 30 sts and 6 rows

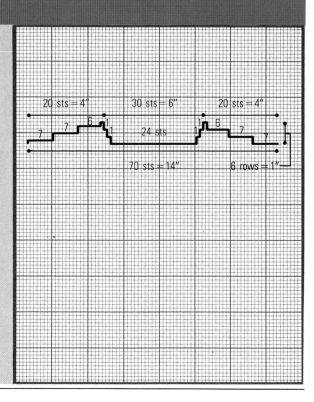

Front Neck Shaping

The shape of the front neck is an essential design element which should enhance the finished look and fit of your sweater. The most common types of neck shaping are crewneck, highneck, round neck with placket, V-neck, square neck, curved boatneck and U-neck. The examples given are a crewneck, round neck with placket and V-neck. Square neck shaping is simple to work, since all of the stitches are bound off at one time, and each side is worked straight to the shoulder. The

U-neck shape is similar to crewneck shaping but the neck is deeper (an average of six to seven inches).

The front neck is almost always the same width as the back neck. The finished neck is usually edged, so its measurement will be the width of the neck plus the edging.

The neck opening must be large enough to fit over your head. If you want a small neck opening, it is preferable to work the edging or neckband from stitches placed on a holder rather

than bound-off stitches, since stitches that have not been bound off are more elastic. A front or back button placket is often necessary for close-fitting necks.

You can work each side of the neck either separately, leaving the rest of the stitches on a holder; or, at the same time, using separate balls of yarn. The examples that follow assume that both sides are worked at one time. Doing so helps you keep track of the stitches decreased on either side of the neck.

Shaping: crewneck

The average woman's crewneck depth is between two and three inches. For children it should be shorter; for men it should be longer. The neck depth should be measured from the highest point of the shoulder shaping. If the neck shaping is not complete once you reach the shoulder shaping, work both of them simultaneously.

A shallower shaping is used for turtlenecks and highneck garments. With fewer rows over which to shape, you must bind off more stitches on the first (center) bind-off and in subsequent bind-off rows.

To make a rounded curve, bind off one-third of the stitches in the center bind-off, then a number of stitches over the next few rows, then decrease the remaining stitches.

Must know
Stitch gauge: 5 stitches = 1"
Row gauge: 7 rows = 1"
Width of back neck: 6"
Width of shoulder: 4"
Depth of armhole: 8½"
Depth of neck: 3"
Depth of shoulder shaping: 1"

What to do
Work 30 stitches from the side edge, join a second ball of yarn and bind off the center 10 stitches. Work to the end of the row. Working both sides at the same time, on the next (wrong-side) row, bind off 3 stitches from the first side of the neck. On next row, bind off 3 stitches from the other side of the neck. Bind off 2 stitches from each neck edge on the next 2 rows. Decrease 1 stitch from each neck edge every other row 5 times. Work even to the shoulder and work the shoulder shaping.

How to calculate

Widths (stitches):
6" × 5 = 30 sts (back neck)
4" × 5 = 20 sts (shoulder)

Length (rows):
8½" × 7 = 59.5 (rounded 60) rows (armhole depth)
1" × 7 = 7 rows (rounded 6) (shoulder)

Total: 66 rows

3" × 7 = 21 rows (neck depth)

Determine the decreases and center bind-off:
⅓ of 30 = 10 sts (center bind-off)
30 sts − 10 sts = 20 sts (10 sts each side)

Calculating the decreases:
10 sts once = 10 sts and 1 row
3 sts once = 6 sts and 2 rows
2 sts once = 4 sts and 2 rows
1 st 5 times = 10 sts and 10 rows
then 6 rows worked even to shoulder top

Total: 30 sts and 21 rows

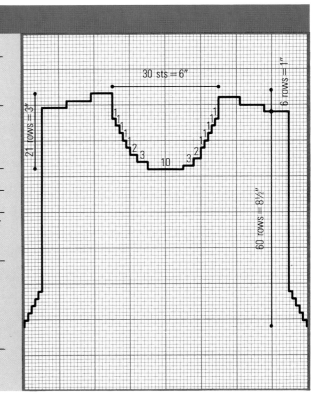

Shaping: crewneck with placket

When planning a crewneck with a placket, begin by planning the depth of the neck plus the placket. When you reach the beginning of the placket, bind off the desired number of placket stitches at the center of the piece and work even on each side with separate balls of yarn until the placket is complete. At this point, begin to shape the neck on either side of the placket opening.

Must know

Stitch gauge: 5 stitches = 1″
Row gauge: 7 rows = 1″
Width of back neck: 6″
Width of shoulder: 4″
Width of placket: 2″
Depth of armhole: 8½″
Depth of shoulder shaping: 1″
Depth of neck: 3″
Depth of placket: 3″

What to do

When you reach the lower edge of the placket, bind off the center 10 stitches and join a 2nd ball of yarn. Work even on each side separately for 3″ (22 rows). Complete as for the crewneck after the center bind-off was worked.

How to calculate

Worked same as crewneck except as follows:
Width (stitches): 2″ × 5 = 10 sts (placket width)

Length (rows):
3″ × 7 = 21 rows (placket depth)

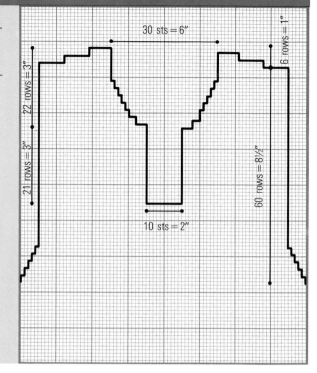

Shaping: V-neck

If you have an odd number of stitches, you can shape a V-neck by binding off a center stitch or, if you have an even number, you can separate the neck without a center stitch as in this example. V-neck shaping is worked much like raglan armhole shaping—gradually over a large number of rows.

V-necks can be many depths. Shorter V-necks are usually used for classic-style sweaters. Long V-necks should be made with a narrow back neck width, since a wide neck combined with the weight of the sleeves can stretch out a deep V-neck.

Must know

Stitch gauge: 5 stitches = 1″
Row gauge: 7 rows = 1″
Width of back neck: 6″
Width of shoulder: 4″
Depth of armhole: 8½″
Depth of shoulder shaping: 1″
Depth of neck: 5″

What to do

Find the center of the piece and place a marker. Work to 2 stitches before the marker, decrease 1 stitch (k2tog), join a 2nd ball of yarn, decrease 1 stitch (ssk) and work to the end. Work 1 row even. Then decrease 1 stitch on each side of the neck every right-side row 14 times more. Work even to the shoulder and work the shoulder shaping.

How to calculate

Length (rows):
5″ × 7 = 35 rows (neck depth)

Determine the decreases:
Neck decreases: 30 sts (15 sts each side)

Calculating the decreases:
1 st 15 times = 30 sts and 30 rows
then work 5 rows even

Total: 30 sts and 35 rows

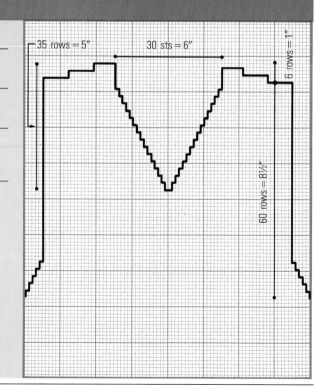

Sleeve Shaping

When designing a sleeve, you must decide on key points before you calculate the measurements. These points are the wrist measurement, the width at upper arm, the sleeve length to underarm, the sleeve shaping and the cap shaping (if any). Cap shaping is worked for set-in and raglan sleeves only and is discussed on the following two pages.

Wrist measurement

The ribbing of a sleeve is often worked with fewer stitches on smaller needles so that it fits snugly around the wrist. The number of stitches increased after the ribbing can vary greatly and depends on the fullness desired above the rib. A more fitted sleeve may have no stitches increased. Remember that the finished sleeve cuff must be large enough to fit over the hand.

Width at upper arm (no cap shaping)

Generally, if working a drop-shouldered (straight), square or angled armhole, the measurement at the top of the sleeve must be double the armhole depth. For example, if the front and back armhole depth is 10 inches, the width of the sleeve at its widest point must be 20 inches.

Width at upper arm (with cap shaping)

When working a sleeve that has a set-in or raglan sleeve cap, the width at the upper arm can vary from the armhole depth. The measurement you use depends on the type of garment and how much ease you are allowing for your design.

Sleeve length (no cap shaping)

The total sleeve length for a drop shouldered, angled armhole or square armhole garment includes the sweater shoulder (which extends past the shoulder point of the body). Therefore it should be shorter than a sleeve with cap shaping which is measured to the underarm. To calculate the sleeve length for this type of garment, measure from your center back neck to your wrist or the point at which you want the sleeve to end. Subtract an inch or two for stretch. The finished measurement of the sweater from the center of the neck to the bottom of the sleeve cuff will be the same as this measurement.

Sleeve length to underarm (with cap shaping)

This is measured from the wrist (or where you want the sleeve to end) to the underarm. This measurement is necessary when working a garment with sleeve caps, since the cap begins at the underarm.

Sleeve shaping (no sleeve cap)

The first step in calculating sleeve shaping is to subtract the number of stitches at the wrist from the number of stitches at the top of the sleeve. To find the number of stitches, multiply the stitch gauge by the width measurements. The number of rows in the shaping is determined by the sleeve length and row gauge. The process is the same as for shaping from the lower edge to the underarm on body pieces. The calculations should allow you to work the increases in an even slant up

to within the last inch (to avoid bulk at the underarm). For a square armhole, the amount of rows worked even to the top of the sleeve should correspond to the bound-off stitches at the underarm of the body pieces. For example, if you bind off two inches for the underarm, you should work two inches straight at the sleeve top.

Sleeve shaping (with sleeve cap)

Calculate sleeve shaping with a sleeve cap the same as sleeve shaping without a sleeve cap up to the width at the upper arm. Just work one inch even at the upper arm before the sleeve cap begins.

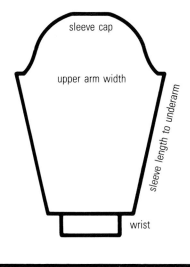

sleeve cap

upper arm width

sleeve length to underarm

wrist

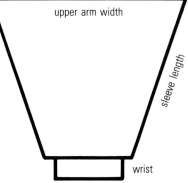

upper arm width

sleeve length

wrist

---

measurements **166**   ease **55**

ribbing **34-35, 172-73**   gauge **18-19, 57-59**

Set-in Cap Shaping

Designing a shaped armhole and set-in sleeve cap is one of the most complex types of shaping, since the measurement along the curved edge of the sleeve cap must be equal to the measurement along the armhole edge.

The general rules for working a shaped sleeve cap are as follows:

The first bind-off should be the same as the armhole bind-off at the underarm of the body. This allows the armhole to fit properly into the sleeve when the pieces are joined.

The final bind-off at the sleeve cap top is usually two to three inches wide for narrower caps and three to five inches for wider caps.

The shaping should begin with an even slant, then continuing with a sharper decreasing angle towards the top, ending with frequent bound-off stitches in the last few rows to curve the top of the sleeve cap.

After determining the final bind-off, plan the curved shaping at the top of the cap. A good rule of thumb is to

bind off one inch of stitches over one-half inch of rows just before the final bind-off.

To find the sleeve cap depth, you must think in terms of one-half the sleeve cap fitting into one side of the armhole (front or back). Take the armhole depth measurement and subtract one-half of the final bind-off of the sleeve cap, one inch for the stitches and one-half inch for the rows (curved shaping at the top of the cap). The resulting number is the sleeve cap depth.

Shaping: set-in sleeve cap

To help you achieve a better-fitting sleeve cap, draw your armhole and sleeve cap shaping on knitter's graph paper which has the same gauge as your knitting. Measure one-half of the curved edge of your cap with a tape measure (set the tape measure on its side and follow the curve exactly). Then measure the curve of the armhole edge. If the two measurements are approximately the same, the sleeve cap will fit into the armhole.

The previous example of a shaped armhole has an 8½ inch armhole depth. The following sleeve cap is designed to fit this armhole.

Must know
Stitch gauge: 5 stitches = 1"
Row gauge: 7 rows = 1"
Width of sleeve at upper arm: 15½"
Depth of armhole: 8½"
Final bind-off of sleeve cap: 2½"
First armhole bind-off: 1" (each side)

What to do
Bind off 5 stitches at the beginning of the next 2 rows, then decrease 1 stitch each side of the next row, then every other row 12 times more, then every row 9 times, then bind off 3 stitches at the beginning of the next 4 rows. Bind off the remaining 12 stitches.

How to calculate

Widths (stitches):
15½" × 5 = 77.5 (rounded 78) sts (upper arm)
2½" × 5 = 12.5 (rounded 12) sts (cap top)
2½" ÷ 2 = 1¼" (½ of final bind-off)

A. Rounded shaping at top:
1" of sts: 1" × 5 = 5 (rounded 6) sts
½" of rows: ½" × 7 = 3.5 (rounded 4) rows
B. Cap depth (total number of rows):
armhole depth − 1" (sts) − ½" (rows) − ½ of the final bind-off = cap depth
8½" − 1" − ½" − 1¼" = 5¾" × 7 = 40.25 (rounded 40) rows
C. Rows for the remaining cap shaping:
total cap rows − first bind-off rows − ½" of rows = rows for cap shaping
40 rows − 2 rows − 4 rows = 34 rows
D. Stitches for the remaining cap shaping:
upper arm − first bind-offs − final bind-off − 1" of stitches (each side) = stitches for cap shaping
78 sts − 10 sts − 12 sts − 12 sts = 44 sts

Thus: 22 sts decreased each side in 34 rows.

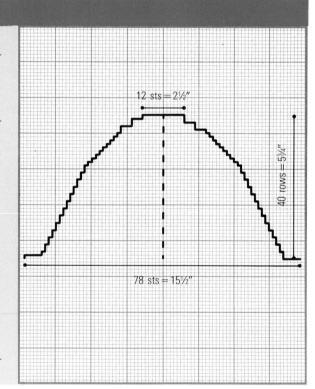

12 sts = 2½"

40 rows = 5¾"

78 sts = 15½"

Raglan Cap Shaping

When shaping a raglan sleeve cap, the sides of the cap must have exactly the same number of rows as the back and front pieces of the raglan armhole. Raglan garments actually have no shoulder seam, and the sleeve cap becomes the shoulder. For more definition at the shoulder, you can work a dart up the center of the sleeve cap.

In the simplest raglan shaping, the front and back pieces are exactly the same depth. For this shaping, the sleeve cap top is straight. In an alternate method of shaping, the front piece is shorter than the back piece to accommodate the neck curve. The two sides of the sleeve cap are then shaped differently to match the corresponding front and back pieces with the side that will be joined to the front piece shorter than the side that will be joined to the longer back piece. Plan a curve or angle connecting the two uneven points of the sleeve cap. The shaping on the cap of the right and left sleeves must be reversed for proper fit around the neck.

Shaping: raglan sleeve cap

This is a simple method of raglan cap shaping with the stitches at the top of the sleeve cap bound off at one time. The decreases continue up the full length of the cap, with no rows worked even. Alternating decreases have been used at certain points to keep the slant even.

Must know
Stitch gauge: 5 stitches = 1″
Row gauge: 7 rows = 1″
Width of sleeve at upper arm: 16″
Width of sleeve top: 3¼″
Depth of raglan: 10″

What to do
Bind off 3 stitches at the beginning of the next 2 rows. Then decrease 1 stitch on each side [every 2nd row once, every 4th row once] 5 times, then decrease 1 stitch every other row 19 times. Bind off the remaining 16 stitches.

How to calculate

Widths (stitches):
16″ × 5 = 80 sts (sleeve upper arm)
3¼″ × 5 = 16.25 (rounded 16) sts (sleeve top)

Length (rows):
10″ × 7 = 70 rows (raglan depth)

Determine the sleeve decreases:
80 sts − 16 sts = 64 sts (32 sts each side)
Initial bind-off = 3 sts (each side) over 2 rows
32 sts − 3 sts = 29 sts each side
70 rows − 2 rows = 68 rows

Placing the decreases:
Alternately (i.e., 2nd, 4th, 2nd, 4th . . .)
every 2nd row 5 times = 10 sts and 10 rows
every 4th row 5 times = 10 sts and 20 rows
                        20 sts and 30 rows
every 2nd row 19 times = 38 sts and 38 rows

Total: 64 sts and 70 rows

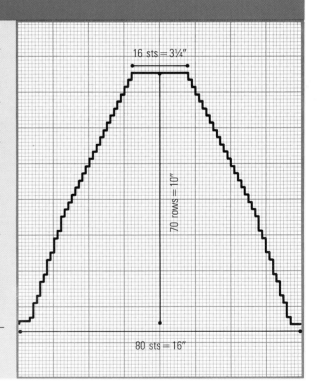

16 sts = 3¼″

70 rows = 10″

80 sts = 16″

Cardigan Shaping

Cardigans have many of the same shaping as pullovers, with the same variety of armhole and shoulder shapes. The major difference is that a cardigan has two front pieces. Generally these are the same width, and each piece mirrors the shape of the other.

Since cardigans are often worn over other clothing, they should be slightly roomier than pullovers. The front pieces are frequently designed somewhat larger (when together) than the back to accommodate the bustline and to allow for the roomier style. The addition of a front band adds width to the front—the width of one of the bands when they are overlapped. The shoulder shaping is the same on the front and back pieces. The difference is in the neck stitches.

Any armhole or side shaping for cardigan fronts is worked at the outside edges to correspond to the back. Each front is worked separately with the shaping of each the reverse of the other. You can work both cardigan fronts at the same time with separate balls of yarn to ensure that the pieces will be uniform in length and shaping.

Shaping: cardigan

When planning the size of your front pieces, you must also consider how any pattern repeat will match at the center. You may have to alter the number of stitches slightly to make it work.

Once you've planned the total width, armholes, neck shaping and length, you must think about how you will finish the front edge of the cardigan. You may want to include one or more selvage stitches at this edge as you knit. You can finish the front edges by adding a band later (with or without buttons and buttonholes) or you can knit in a band at the same time you are knitting the fronts.

Must know
Stitch gauge: 5 stitches = 1″
Row gauge: 7 rows = 1″
Width of back at underarm: 18″
 (not shown)

Width of a front at underarm: 9½″
Width of shoulder: 4″
Width of back neck: 6″ (not shown)
Length to underarm (minus rib): 10″
Depth of neck: 1½″
Depth of armhole: 8½″
Depth of shoulder shaping: 1″

What to do
To work one front, cast on 48 stitches and work 70 rows above the ribbing. Work armhole shaping as for crewneck. Work even until 55 rows have been worked from beginning of the armhole shaping. From the neck edge, bind off 6 stitches once, then 3 stitches 4 times. At the same time, when 60 rows have been worked from the beginning of the armhole, work the shoulder shaping as for crewneck.

How to calculate

Widths (stitches):
9½″ × 5 = 47.5 (rounded 48) sts (one front)
4″ × 5 = 20 sts (shoulder)

Length (rows):
10″ × 7 = 70 rows (to underarm)
8½″ × 7 = 59.5 (rounded 60) rows (armhole depth)
1½″ × 7 = 10.5 (rounded 10) rows (neck depth)
8½″ + 1″ = 9½″ (armhole and shoulder)
9½″ − 1½″ = 8″ (armhole to neck)
8″ × 7 = 56 (rounded 55) rows (armhole to neck)

Determine front neck decreases:
48 sts (front) − 10 sts (armhole shaping) −
20 sts (shoulder) = 18 sts (½ front neck)

Calculating the neck shaping:
bind off 6 sts (about 1″) = 6 sts and 2 rows
10 rows − 2 rows (first bind-off) = 8 rows for remaining shaping
18 sts − 6 sts = 12 sts in 8 rows
every other row 4 times: 12 ÷ 4 = 3 sts

Total: 18 sts and 10 rows

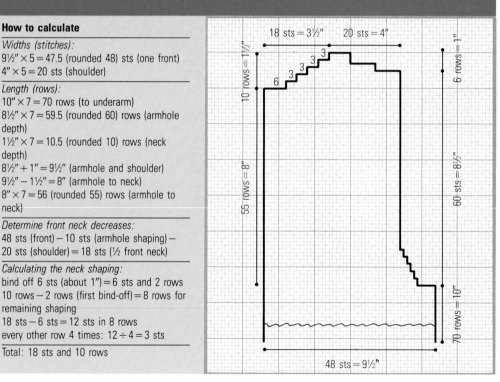

Dart Shaping

Darts are not often used in hand-knitting since knit fabric usually has enough give. However, darts can be used to solve special fit problems, such as shaping the front piece of a sweater to accommodate a larger bust without increasing the shoulder width. They can also be used for fitted or tailored pieces such as jackets, skirts or dresses.

Darts make the knitting curve. How much depends on the width and depth of the dart. As with sewn darts in woven fabrics, you can shape knit garments with both vertical and horizontal darts. Unlike sewn darts, which leave some fabric on the wrong side of the garment, knit darts are made by simply decreasing, eliminating that bulk. The concept behind knit and sewn darts is the same—you are taking in a wedge of fabric. With knit darts you don't actually create a wedge, but to make planning easier, think in terms of removing a wedge from your knit piece.

You may wish to actually cut a front from a piece of knit fabric and pin the darts to determine the best width, length and placement.

Place darts carefully not only for fit, but also to keep the stitch or colorwork pattern consistent.

Vertical darts

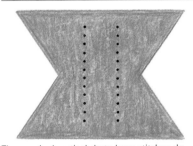

These paired vertical darts have stitches decreased to the waist and increased above it.

Vertical darts are used to shape the front of a fitted garment or to define the center of a raglan sleeve cap. One or two stitches are increased or decreased on either side of a marked stitch. They are often worked in pairs. Darts are usually used instead of side shaping when fullness is desired at points other than the side seams. For garments with fitted waists, you can work darts by decreasing to the waist and then increasing to the desired bustline width.

To work a vertical dart, use the following steps:

First find the placement of the darts. An easy formula for placing two vertical darts is to think of the whole piece (X) and divide it into fourths vertically. Place the darts one-fourth of X in from each side edge.

Multiply the dart width (the amount of fabric you want to take in) by the stitch gauge to find the total number of stitches to decrease. Divide this by two

since you will place a decrease on either side of a center stitch. (For a dart with two decreases on either side, divide by four.)

Find the number of rows in the dart by multiplying the dart depth by the row gauge.

Divide the number of rows in the length of the dart by one-half the decreased stitches to determine how many rows to work between each dart.

Horizontal darts

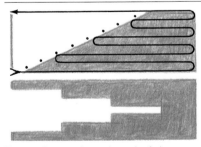

The top diagram shows the path of short row shaping on a horizontal dart. The lower diagram shows a horizontal dart which has bound-off and then cast-on stitches.

Horizontal darts, used for side bust darts, are made by working short rows or by binding off stitches and casting them on again. Short row darts are the most invisible, since bound-off darts require seaming. Matching darts can be worked on either side of a front piece directly across from each other. When working short row shaping, one side is shaped as a left slant and the opposite side is made as a right slant.

Measure the length of pieces with horizontal darts at the side seam, not over the area of the dart shaping. To work a horizontal dart, use the following steps:

Determine the placement of the dart at the side seam.

Multiply the dart depth (usually one or two inches) by the row gauge to find the number of rows in the dart.

Dart shaping is worked on every other row (a right dart is worked at the end of right-side rows and a left dart at the end of wrong-side rows). Divide the number of rows by two to find the number of decreases on each side.

Find the number of stitches in the dart by multiplying the dart width by the stitch gauge.

Divide the stitches by half the number of rows to find the number of stitches to leave unworked or to bind off on each side of the row.

Once all the stitches are left unworked or bound off, work across the whole piece, hiding the short row wraps, or casting on the same number of stitches as you bound off.

measurements **166**   gauge **18-19, 57-59**   wraps and
                                                      hiding wraps **186**
raglan sleeve cap **183**   short rows **186-87**

Short Row Shaping

Short rows are partial rows of knitting that are used to shape or curve sections or to compensate for patterns with different row gauges. The result is that one side or section has more rows than the other, but no stitches are decreased. This technique is sometimes called turning because the work is turned within the row. Short rows can be worked on one or both sides of a piece at the same time.

Shaping with short rows eliminates the jagged edges that occur when you bind off a series of stitches such as at shoulders or on collars. After working short rows at a shoulder, bind off all the stitches at one time or join them to another piece directly from the needles.

When working with patterns of varying row gauges, short rows can be used to add rows to the shorter sections, allowing the finished piece to lie flat.

Short row shaping can also be used for darts, back necks on circular yokes, hats and medallions with circular pieces and sock heels.

When you add an extra row into the knit piece, you must make a smooth transition between the edge where one row is worked and the edge that has the extra row. Do this by wrapping a slipped stitch, using one technique for wrapping knit stitches and another for wrapping purl stitches.

Wrapping stitches (knit side)

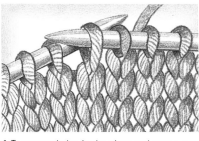 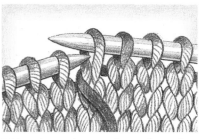 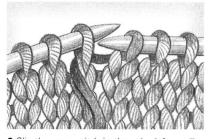 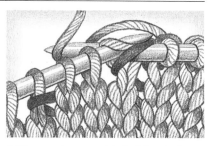

1 To prevent holes in the piece and create a smooth transition, wrap a knit stitch as follows: With the yarn in back, slip the next stitch purlwise.

2 Move the yarn between the needles to the front of the work.

3 Slip the same stitch back to the left needle. Turn the work, bringing the yarn to the purl side between the needles. One stitch is wrapped.

4 When you have completed all the short rows, you must hide the wraps. Work to just before the wrapped stitch. Insert the right needle under the wrap and knitwise into the wrapped stitch. Knit them together.

Wrapping stitches (purl side)

  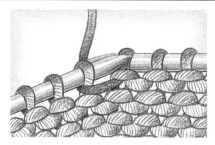 

1 To prevent holes in the piece and create a smooth transition, wrap a purl stitch as follows: With the yarn at the front, slip the next stitch purlwise.

2 Move the yarn between the needles to the back of the work.

3 Slip the same stitch back to the left needle. Turn the work, bringing the yarn back to the purl side between the needles. One stitch is wrapped.

4 After working the short rows, you must hide the wraps. Work to just before the wrapped stitch. Insert the right needle from behind into the back loop of the wrap and place it on the left needle, as shown. Purl it together with the stitch on the left needle.

Differing row gauges

When you use two stitch patterns with different row gauges in the same piece, you can add rows to the pattern with the shorter row gauge to make both patterns the same length. The gauges used in this example are: 34 rows in stockinette stitch = four inches/10cm (8.5 rows = one inch/3.4 rows = 1cm) and 42 rows in garter stitch = four inches/10cm (10.5 rows = one inch/4.2 rows = 1cm).

Two different row gauges Shown are 17 rows of stockinette stitch and the same number in garter stitch. Two more rows in each inch (2.5cm) must be added to the garter stitch pattern to compensate for the longer stockinette stitch row gauge.

Garter stitch at an edge To make a garter stitch band, begin on the right side and work the last garter stitch. Wrap the next stitch, turn the work to add an extra garter stitch row. Hide the wrap on the next row.

Garter stitch center panel Work to the last stitch of the garter stitch panel. Wrap the next knit stitch, turn the work. Work the panel, wrap the next purl stitch, turn the work. Work to the end of the row, hiding the knit wrap. On the next row, hide the purl wrap.

Right slant

This short row technique creates a right slant and is used to shape shoulders, darts or collars.

This example in stockinette stitch is given over 20 stitches, divided into four sections of five stitches each, and begins on a right-side row. On the first row, knit 15 stitches, wrap the next stitch, turn the work (five unworked stitches are on the right needle). Purl the 15 stitches on the left needle. Knit 10 stitches on the next row and wrap one stitch, turn the work (10 stitches are unworked on the right needle). Purl 10 stitches on the left needle. Knit five stitches on the next row and wrap one stitch, turn the work (15 stitches are unworked on the right needle). Purl five stitches on the left needle. On the next row, you will have three wrapped stitches. Knit across all the stitches, hiding the three wraps as you come to them.

Left slant

This short row technique creates a left slant and is used to shape shoulders, darts or collars.

This example in stockinette stitch is given over 20 stitches, divided into four sections of five stitches each, and begins on a wrong-side row. On the first row, purl 15 stitches, wrap the next stitch, turn the work (five unworked stitches are on the right needle). Knit the 15 stitches on the left needle. Purl 10 stitches on the next row and wrap one stitch, turn the work (10 stitches are unworked on the right needle). Knit 10 stitches on the left needle. Purl five stitches on the next row and wrap one stitch, turn the work (15 stitches are unworked on the right needle). Knit five stitches on the left needle. On the next row, you will have three wrapped stitches. Purl across all the stitches, hiding the three wraps as you come to them.

measurements **166**
gauge **18-19, 57-59**

wraps and
hiding wraps **186**

darts **185**
collars **198-201**

Circular Design

Circular garments are generally worked as a whole rather than in pieces, but most of the basic principles that apply to straight knitting also apply to circular knitting. The first two pullovers discussed in this section are worked from the bottom up and separated at the underarm. The second has a circular yoke which joins the sleeves to the body. The final pullover is worked from the top down. It is possible to work any of these pullovers as cardigans. You can work a cardigan as one piece and then cut it down the center or make it with a center opening by working back and forth as with straight needles.

When knitting a garment in the round, you're always working on the right side of the work. Most stitch patterns are planned for flat knitting with definite right-side and wrong-side rows,

so you may need to adapt the patterns for circular knitting. For example, stockinette stitch is made by knitting every round, and garter stitch by knitting one round and purling the next. Plan stitch or colorwork patterns with full repeats since the pattern must continue in an unbroken circle. Supposedly, all patterns can be worked in the round, but some are not worth the trouble. Stitches such as brioche and fisherman ribs are very difficult to work on circular needles.

Your gauge on circular needles may differ from that on straight needles. Read the information on gauge in Chapter IV.

Not only can you make body pieces on circular needles, you can also work sleeves in the round. You can start at the cuff with double-pointed needles or an 11½ inch (29cm) circular needle and then change to a longer circular needle once you have enough stitches. Or you can work back and forth on a circular

needle until you have increased enough stitches to fit around the needle and then join the piece and work circularly. Place a marker at the beginning of the round. Increase the stitches at each side of the marker.

Take care when measuring a circular piece. Lay it as flat as possible. You can slip one-half the stitches to a thread before measuring or slip one-half the stitches to a second circular needle. You can also remove the stitches completely from the needle, but only if you have no difficulty in picking stitches back up. Take care not to drop any stitches.

Measuring a circular piece

To keep a circular piece flat when measuring, slip half the stitches onto a thread.

Mock seams

A mock seam adds fold lines to the sides of a circular garment. Try a swatch first, since mock seams may not be appropriate for all patterns.

Before binding off stitches, begin at the point where the seam is desired (most likely the underarm), drop one stitch and unravel it to the ribbing or hem, forming a ladder. Pick up the dropped stitch with a crochet hook. For stockinette stitch, pull

through two threads of the ladder to hook up a stitch, then hook up one thread of the ladder. Alternate up the ladder by working first two threads, then one, until the seam is complete. For garter stitch, just work two threads into one stitch each time, which will form a stockinette stitch seam.

Pull through two threads.

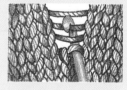

Pull through one thread.

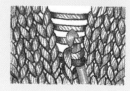

Circular Design Without Yoke

All circular garments that are worked from the bottom up are worked essentially the same way to the underarm— as a circular tube. At this division point you can use any one of several methods to complete the piece.

You can make a yoke by joining all the pieces and working circularly to the neck, or you can work the front and back sections separately with any kind of armhole and add the sleeves later.

To work a circular garment without a yoke, begin at the lower edge by placing a marker at the beginning of the round. This becomes an imaginary side seam. (Unless you will be increasing at the side seams, a second marker need not be placed until the underarm.)

When dividing the garment at the underarm for the back and front pieces, you can work the armhole shaping on the dividing row or on the next row. It is slightly easier to divide the stitches first and then go on to shape the armholes. To divide without shaping, begin at the left side seam marker and work across the front. Place a second marker at the half-way point for the right side seam, if you haven't already done so. Slip the stitches onto a holder. The remaining stitches are for the back piece.

To shape your armhole on the dividing row, bind off the armhole stitches at the first marker, work to the second marker and slip the stitches to a holder as before. Bind off the back armhole stitches on the next two rows. Continue working back and forth as with straight needles across the back, using the attached yarn.

When you work the front, you must slip the stitches back to the needle; begin at the right-side seam and work the first row on the wrong side. This is very important, especially with a pattern stitch or special shaping. If you have shaped the armhole on the dividing row, don't forget to bind off the armhole stitches at the right-side seam on the first wrong-side row.

Dividing work

To divide the back and front sections, begin at the first marker, work across the front to the second marker. Slip the front stitches to a holder. Continue across the back stitches.

Cutting in sleeves

Knitting a circular tube up to the shoulders, then cutting in armholes works well with Fair Isle patterns. Or use this technique to create the center front of a cardigan.

Measure armhole depth and baste down center of one stitch. Machine sew down length of the armhole (one or two stitches over), across underarm and up the other side. Snip down center of basted stitch. After seaming, neaten the inside by working a herringbone stitch along armhole. The stitches will not unravel.

Or use the traditional Scottish knitted steek method by adding stitches inside the armhole (number will vary depending on yarn). After you cut down the center, as in the previous method, the steek creates a small facing that folds back and is slip stitched down.

measurements **166**   herringbone stitch   stitch holders **18-19**
markers **18**   **111** (embroidery, **232**)

Circular Design With Yoke

A circular sweater with a yoke is one that joins the front, back and sleeves at the underarm and then continues in a circular piece to the neckband. The yoke becomes the sleeve cap, shoulders, front and back. A circular yoke must include the armhole as well as the shoulder, so the yoke should be slightly deeper than the depth of a standard armhole.

Traditional yokes are generally worked in colorwork pattern bands with plain decrease rows in the main color between them. The example given on the next page is a circular yoke with decreases spaced evenly around four decrease rounds. You can also work raglan armholes by shaping the yoke at specific points over a number of rounds.

As you decrease closer to the neck and have fewer stitches to spread around the needle, you may need to change to a shorter circular needle.

The most important step to making a circular sweater with a yoke is joining the body and the sleeves. It is shown below in several steps.

Placing stitches on a holder for underarm

Work the body piece and both sleeves to the underarm. At this point, leave a number of stitches unworked for the underarm on both the body and the sleeves. The unworked stitches usually equal two to three inches (5 to 7.5cm), depending on the weight of the yarn and the size of the sweater, and are centered on the marker. These stitches are left on a holder and are grafted together when the yoke is complete to join the side and sleeve at the underarm.

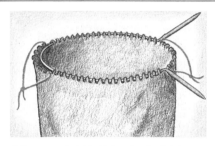

1 If you need eight stitches for the total underarm at each side seam, place four stitches to the left of the seam marker and four to the right onto a holder. Be sure to end at the left underarm on the back piece.

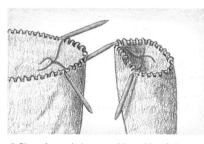

2 Place four stitches on either side of the sleeve seam marker on a holder. Place each sleeve so the stitches on the holder face the underarm stitches on the body piece. You are ready to join the yoke.

Joining the yoke

Before you join the yoke, mark the front or back of the piece at the lower edge with a safety pin or marker. Beginning at the left front underarm, work across the front, ending at the right underarm. Join one sleeve by working across all stitches except those on the holder. Beginning at the right back underarm, join the back by working across to the left underarm. Join the other sleeve by working across all stitches, omitting those on the holder. Place a new marker to denote the beginning of the round.

Joining all the pieces is the first crucial step to making a circular yoke. The underarm stitches should be left on holders until the yoke is complete.

Making a yoke

When planning the yoke depth, remember that it will include the armhole plus the shoulder, so should be slightly deeper than usual.

Stitches are decreased over several decrease rounds, usually three to five, depending on the number of stitches to be decreased, the size of the sweater and the gauge and weight of yarn you are using. You can work with percentages of the total yoke to establish the number of stitches to be decreased (with fewer stitches decreased on each round). For simplicity, the example given has the same number of stitches decreased for each round. To plan the number of stitches to be decreased, subtract the total (finished) neck stitches from the total yoke stitches (body plus two sleeves, less the number of stitches on holders for underarm).

Must know
Stitch gauge: 5 sts = 1"
Row gauge: 7 rows = 1"
Body circumference: 40"
Sleeve circ. at upper arm: 20"
Neck circumference: 16"
Depth of yoke: 10"
Width of underarm sts: 2½"

What to do
After picking up the 352 stitches, work 16 rounds. Decrease round 1: *[k4, k2tog] 3 times, [k3, k2tog] 14 times; rep from * around the yoke for the first decrease round—284 sts. Work 16 rounds. Decrease round 2: *[k3, k2tog] 3 times, [k2, k2tog] 14 times; rep from * around the yoke for the second decrease round—216 sts. Work 16 rounds. Decrease round 3: *[k2, k2tog] 3 times, [k1, k2tog] 14 times; rep from * around the yoke for the third decrease round—148 sts. Work 16 rounds. Decrease round 4: *[k1, k2tog] 3 times, k2tog 14 times; rep from * around the yoke for the

fourth decrease round—80 sts. Work 2 rounds even. You are now ready to work the neckband.

How to calculate

Widths (stitches):
40" × 5 = 200 sts (body)
20" × 5 = 100 sts (sleeve)
16" × 5 = 80 sts (neck)
2½" × 5 = 12.5 (rounded 12) sts (underarm)

Length (rounds):
10" × 7 = 70 rounds (yoke depth)

Determine the number of decreases:
200 body + 100 sleeve + 100 sleeve =
400 sts − 48 underarm sts = 352 − 80
neck = 272 sts to be decreased in 70 rounds

Calculating the 4 decrease rounds:
272 ÷ 4 = 68 sts each dec round
70 − 4 dec rounds = 66 rounds without decs

Placing the rounds between decreases:
66 ÷ 4 = 16.5 or about 16 rounds

Total number of rounds:
16 × 4 = 64 rounds + 4 decrease rounds
+ 2 rounds worked even = 70 rounds

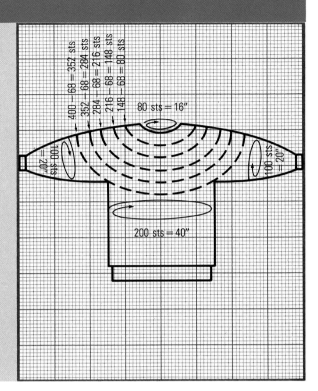

Neckbands for yoked sweaters

To work a neckband on your yoked sweater, you can simply change to smaller needles and begin the ribbing. This creates a neckband that will be the same height in the front and the back. For a shaped neck with the front lower than the back, first use decrease stitches or short row shaping to shape the neck before you

work the neckband. Begin by marking the center of each shoulder on either side of the neck opening.

To shape the front neck by decreasing, determine the number of stitches in the center neck and slip them to a holder. Working back and forth as with straight needles, shape the neck on either side of the stitches on the holder until you reach the shoulder. Bind off the back neck

stitches. To work the neckband, pick up stitches all around the neck (those on the holder, on the needle and along the shaped edges). Work the neckband as desired.

measurements **166**

gauge **18-19, 57-59**

stitch holders **18-19**

k2tog **42, 61**

ribbing **34-35, 172-73**

short rows **186-87**

abbreviations explained **60-63**

knitting terminology **64-68**

Circular Design From the Top Down

As with regular circular knitting from the bottom up, circular knitting from the top down avoids seaming. One advantage to this type of construction is that you can try on the piece periodically as you work. You can check the length of the garment from the neck to the underarm as well as from the underarm down. Another advantage is that the lengths of the body and sleeves can be changed at a later date, which is ideal for growing children.

For comfort, allow a roomy raglan armhole depth on garments knit from the top down—at least an inch or two (2.5 or 5cm) longer than a standard armhole.

If you use a stitch or colorwork pattern, remember that you must work the pattern upside down or it will be inverted. Some stitch patterns are not suitable for this type of construction.

The most common type of garment constructed from the top down is a raglan pullover or cardigan. The pullover

is discussed below, but you can easily make a cardigan by not joining it at the front neck and working back and forth as with straight needles.

Begin with a short circular needle and change to a longer one as you increase the stitches.

To begin, it is best to separate sections with different colored markers. For example, use one color for the front increases, another for the front and sleeve edges and a third for back edges.

The basic formula is that stitches for the four sections (one back, two sleeves and one front) are worked and increased at eight points to the underarm. You also increase at the front neck edges (two points) until the neck is joined. Increases on either side of the seam stitches can be worked by knitting into the front and back of the stitch or more decoratively by making yarn overs.

Plan your measurements on paper. Before you begin you must know the back neck width and raglan depth. The

back neck measurement is the beginning point on this design. Use this measurement to determine the sleeve top width which is one-third of the back neck stitches for each sleeve.

So that the back neck is higher than the front neck, cast on for the back neck and two sleeves with only one stitch on either side of the sleeves for the front neck. After casting on, work back and forth as with straight needles, increasing until the front neck is the desired depth. Then cast on stitches for the center front neck edge and join the piece.

After you cast on the stitches (56 stitches in the example), it is important that you place the markers properly. This is instrumental in the process that follows.

Casting on and placing markers

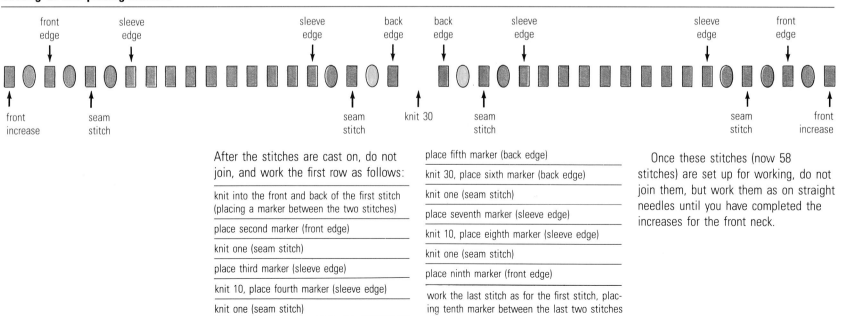

After the stitches are cast on, do not join, and work the first row as follows:

knit into the front and back of the first stitch (placing a marker between the two stitches)

place second marker (front edge)

knit one (seam stitch)

place third marker (sleeve edge)

knit 10, place fourth marker (sleeve edge)

knit one (seam stitch)

place fifth marker (back edge)

knit 30, place sixth marker (back edge)

knit one (seam stitch)

place seventh marker (sleeve edge)

knit 10, place eighth marker (sleeve edge)

knit one (seam stitch)

place ninth marker (front edge)

work the last stitch as for the first stitch, placing tenth marker between the last two stitches

Once these stitches (now 58 stitches) are set up for working, do not join them, but work them as on straight needles until you have completed the increases for the front neck.

Planning the front neck

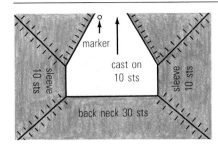

After working the first row and placing markers, you are ready to increase for the front neck. Purl the next row and all wrong-side rows. The first two rows have been worked and one stitch has been increased at each front edge. Continue to increase eight times more, increasing 10 stitches on each right-side row as follows: an increase on either side of the seam stitches (eight stitches) and an increase at the front edges (two stitches).

Each row is worked as follows: Increase one, work to the marker, slip the marker, *work to one stitch before the next marker, increase one, slip the marker, knit one, slip the marker, increase one; repeat from the *, end by working to last marker, slip the marker, work to last stitch, increase one stitch in last stitch.

To determine the number of cast-on stitches for the center front neck, take the total number of stitches on the front neck after increasing and subtract

them from the number of stitches on the back neck. Cast on the difference or 10 stitches at the end of the nineteenth row. Place a marker for the beginning of the twentieth round to join the work. Remove the first and last front markers as you come to them. Work one round even.

Continue the raglan shaping until you reach the raglan depth (70 rounds) by increasing on either side of the seam stitches on every other round.

Working the body

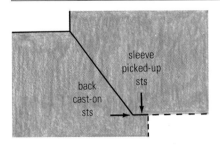

The stitches can be placed on a thread, and you can try on the piece before you work the body and the sleeves. You may decide to make the raglan slightly deeper or rip out a few rows. At the desired raglan depth, place the sleeve stitches on holders, removing the markers (leave two seam stitches with each sleeve). Join the front and the back to work the body as a circular piece. You can cast on stitches on either side of the front and back piece

for the underarm. The amount of stitches can be an inch (2.5cm) or more. Use this variable to your advantage—within reason—to achieve the desired body and sleeve width. Work down to the ribbing. Decrease stitches for a tighter rib and rib on a smaller needle, taking care to use a loose bind-off.

You can work the sleeves on a circular needle or on straight needles. Cast on the same number of stitches at each

sleeve edge as on the front and back pieces (for underarm) or pick up these stitches along the underarm of the front and back pieces to avoid seaming. Just remember that since you are working from the top down, you'll be reversing the process—making decreases instead of increases.

Once you've worked the body and sleeve, all you have to do is add a neckband—no seaming is necessary except at the underarm.

Circular yoke from the top down

Must know
Stitch gauge: 5 sts = 1″
Row (round) gauge: 7 rows = 1″
Stitch pattern: stockinette stitch
Back neck width: 6″
Depth of neck: 2½″
Length of raglan: 10″

What to do
Cast on and set up the markers on the first row as shown on the previous page and work the neck shaping, as shown above.

How to calculate

Widths (stitches):
6″ × 5 = 30 sts (back neck)

Length (rows or rounds):
2½″ × 7 = 17.5 (rounded 18) rows (neck depth)
10″ × 7 = 70 rounds (raglan)

Planning the placement of neck sts:
30 ÷ 3 = 10 sts (⅓ of back neck) (sleeves)

Cast on:
30 (back neck) + 10 (sleeve) + 10 (sleeve) + 2 (front sts) + 4 (seam sts) = 56 sts

Calculating the front neck cast-on:
Total neck incs after 18 rows:
9 (front increase) + 9 (front edge) = 18 sts (for each front) = 36 sts

Front neck cast-on:
46 stitches (back neck) − 36 stitches (front neck) = 10 sts.

Selvages

The selvage (or selvedge) of knit fabric is an edge formed by changing the stitch pattern at the beginning and end of every row. This stabilizes the fabric and prepares it for seaming or creates a finished edge on pieces which will have no further finishing.

You can add selvage stitches to an existing pattern or when designing your own garments. Be sure to add them to the total stitch count. Usually a selvage is one stitch, but it can be two or more. Multiple-stitch selvages are most often used to prevent curling on non-seamed pieces, such as scarves.

Selvage stitches form a firm edge which is helpful when working open-work patterns that tend to widen, or with slippery yarns, such as silk or rayon, which have a tendency to slide out of shape.

Selvage stitches can be used to avoid interrupting colorwork or stitch patterns with a seam. The selvage stitches serve as the seam allowance and disappear when the pieces are sewn.

Some selvages, such as garter or slip-stitch selvages, can help you keep track of rows. The knots or chains created on every other row make it easy to count the rows.

You should work all increases and decreases inside selvage edges, but when you shape a piece by binding off stitches, the selvage stitch will also disappear. Establish it again on the first row that is worked even. Always measure inside selvage edges.

One-stitch selvages

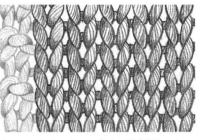

Garter stitch selvage (left side) This selvage is best worked on stockinette stitch fabrics and is the easiest selvage for beginners.

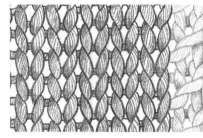

Garter stitch selvage (right side) The selvage looks slightly different on the right edge as shown here. Work left and right edges as follows: *Row 1:* Knit one, work to the last stitch, knit one. Repeat this row.

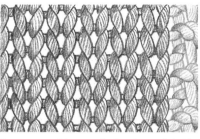

Reverse stockinette stitch selvage Suitable for stockinette stitch, this is easy for beginners. Work both sides as follows: *Row 1 (right side):* Purl one, work to the last stitch, purl one. *Row 2:* Knit one, work to the last stitch, knit one. Repeat these two rows.

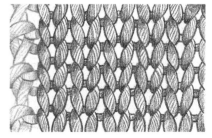

Slip garter stitch selvage (left side) This selvage is similar to the garter stitch selvage, only firmer. It is ideal for patterns that tend to spread laterally. The left side shown above is slightly different than the right side.

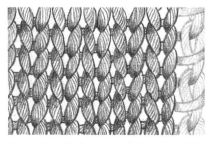

Slip garter stitch selvage (right side) Work both sides of the slip garter stitch selvage as follows: *Row 1:* Slip the first stitch knitwise, work to the last stitch, knit one. Repeat this row.

Chain stitch selvage This selvage is for garter stitch and is worked as follows: *Row 1:* With the yarn in front, slip the first stitch purlwise, with the yarn in back, knit to the end. Repeat this row.

slip a stitch
knitwise/purlwise **46**   measurements **166**

Slip-stitch selvages

This method has three variations. All of them make a chain stitch edge, with each chain loop representing two rows. It is perfect to use when you must later pick up stitches.

English method *Row 1 (right side):* Slip the first stitch knitwise, work to the last stitch, slip the last stitch knitwise. *Row 2:* Purl one, work to the last stitch, purl one. Repeat these two rows.

French method *Row 1 (right side):* Slip the first stitch knitwise, work to the last stitch, knit one. *Row 2:* Slip the first stitch purlwise, work to the last stitch, purl one. Repeat these two rows.

German method: *Row 1 (right side):* Knit the first stitch, work to the last stitch. With the yarn in back, slip the last stitch purlwise. *Row 2:* Purl the first stitch, work to the last stitch. With the yarn in front, slip the last stitch purlwise. Repeat these two rows.

Two-stitch selvages

Double garter stitch selvage This is ideal for free-standing edges, such as scarves, and is worked as follows: *Row 1:* Slip the first stitch knitwise through the back loop, knit the second stitch, work to the last two stitches, knit two. Repeat this row.

Chain garter stitch selvage This selvage is good for patterns with more depth, such as double knits.

Work the chain garter stitch selvage as follows: *Row 1 (right side):* With the yarn in back, slip the first stitch knitwise. With the yarn in front, purl the next stitch. Work to last two stitches, purl the next stitch, slip the last stitch knitwise with the yarn in back. *Row 2:* Purl two, work to the last two stitches, purl two. Repeat these two rows.

Decorative selvages

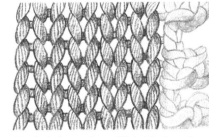

Beaded picot selvage Work this decorative alternative to a simple selvage as follows: *Row 1:* Cast on two or three stitches (as desired). Bind off these stitches, work to the end. On the next row, repeat row 1. Repeat these two rows as desired.

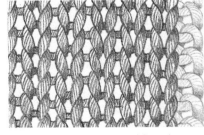

Picot selvage This makes a dainty trim on baby garments and shawls. It can also be used as a buttonloop for small buttons.

The picot selvage is worked as follows: *Row 1 (right side):* Bring the yarn over the right needle to the back and knit the first two stitches together. Work to the last two stitches, slip these two stitches knitwise with the left needle and pass the first stitch over the second stitch. *Row 2:* Bring the yarn over the right needle from front to back and to the front again and purl two, work to the last two stitches, purl two. Repeat these two rows.

measurements **166**

picking up **106-8**

slip a stitch knitwise/purlwise **46**

with yarn in front/back **35**

front/back loops **37**

Neckbands

Neckbands are edges of various sizes applied to blocked pieces to neaten raw edges. They are generally worked on needles one or two sizes smaller than those used for the body. Ribbing is often used for neckbands because it pulls in and is elastic.

Neckbands differ from collars in that neckbands are joined edges that are usually narrower than collars.

There are three common methods for working a neckband. You can work it on straight needles after you sew one shoulder seam and pick up stitches around the neck edge. Sew the neckband along the side edges with the second shoulder seam. The second method is worked on circular or double-pointed needles after you sew both shoulder seams and pick up the stitches. You can also work a separate neckband and sew it on; however, this involves the most planning and the neckband must be carefully sewn in place.

The size of the neck opening must be large enough and the neckband bind-off must be elastic enough to fit over the head. To make the neckband more elastic, bind off in the ribbing pattern. An invisible bind-off gives an especially nice and elastic finish.

When planning your stitch pattern, you may want to add an edge stitch for seaming. Omit an edge stitch when you work the neckband in the round for a continuous pattern.

Basic crewneck

A crewneck is a curved front neck opening which is usually about two to three inches (5 to 7.5cm) deep. It can either have a shaped or straight back neck.

The average neckband for a crewneck is three-quarters to 1½ inches (2 to 4cm) deep. The neckband can be bound off or worked doubled and sewn to the inside.

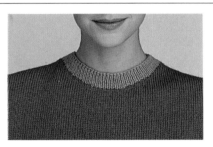

Single crewneck This type of neckband is worked to the desired depth and bound off loosely in pattern. Both the single and double crewneck can be worked by picking up stitches around the entire neck or as a combination of stitches from holders and picked up stitches. Working from stitches on holders is ideal for close-fitting crewnecks since it creates a more elastic neckband.

Doubled crewneck To make a doubled crewneck, pick up the stitches and work to double the desired depth. Then sew the bound-off edge to the inside. You can work a turning ridge at the halfway mark to create a folding line by purling one row on the right side. Continue in pattern until the second half is complete. To retain elasticity, thread the stitches on a contrasting yarn and sew them to the inside.

Crewneck cardigan The neckband for a crewneck cardigan is worked much like that of a pullover. The neckband is usually worked after the front bands are complete. Pick up an odd number of stitches around the neck, beginning at the right front band edge. This allows you to begin and end with a knit stitch for a neater edge. You may wish to work a buttonhole in the center of the neckband, matching the buttonholes on the front band.

V-neckband

You can work V-neckbands back and forth on straight needles or in rounds on a circular needle. The V-neckbands shown are worked on a circular needle in knit one, purl one ribbing as follows: Sew both shoulders, then beginning at the right shoulder, pick up an odd number of stitches along the back neck, an even number of stitches along the left front neck and place a marker (if working with a center stitch, pick up an extra stitch and mark this stitch), and an even number along the right front neck edge. Join the band at the right shoulder. Begin the round with a knit one and work to the marker, including the decrease (if working a center stitch, knit this stitch). Work the decrease, then knit the next stitch and work to the end of the round.

No center stitch: version A Place a marker at the center point of the V. *Every round:* Work to two stitches before the marker, slip, slip, knit (ssk), slip the marker, knit two together, work to the end of the round. Repeat this round.

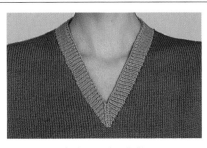

No center stitch: version B Place a marker as for version A. *Every round:* Work to two stitches before the marker, knit two together, slip the marker, slip, slip, knit (ssk), work to the end of the round. Repeat this round.

Crossover Pick up an odd number of stitches around the neck, beginning and ending at the center. Work back and forth without joining. With the left side overlapping the right, sew the band in place.

A center stitch: version A Mark the center stitch. *Every round:* Work to two stitches before marked stitch, ssk, knit center stitch, knit two together, work to end of round. Repeat this round.

A center stitch: version B Mark center stitch. *Every round:* Work to one stitch before center stitch, slip next stitch and center stitch knitwise at the same time, knit one, pass slip stitches over knit stitch, work to end of round. Repeat this round.

V-neck cardigan The V-neckband and front bands on a cardigan can be worked at the same time. Work the band by picking up stitches around the entire piece or split the piece at the center back neck and sew the band together once it is complete.

Square neckband

Square-neck shaping is simple to do but the neckband is more complicated, since the corners must conform to the square shape. Essentially, you use the same decrease method at the two corners as for a V-neckband.

To work a square neck with a center stitch, pick up an odd number of stitches along each edge with an additional marked stitch at each corner on the front edge.

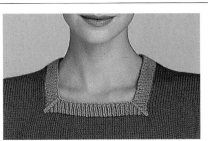

Mark corner stitches. *Every round:* Work to one stitch before marked stitch, *slip the next stitch and marked stitch knitwise at the same time, knit one, pass slip stitches over knit stitch, work to one stitch before next marked stitch; repeat from the *, then work to the end of the round. Repeat this round.

measurements **166**

markers **18**

slip a stitch
knitwise/purlwise **46**

ssk **63, 43**

Collars

Whether a collar is functional or purely decorative, it should suit the design, yarn and style of your garment. Some collars are simple to make; others require involved planning.

A collar may simply be an extension of a neckband such as a turtleneck, or it may be worked separately and then applied. Some collars, such as those on coats and cardigans, are extensions of the front bands.

To keep a collar from curling, it can be made with non-curling stitches, such as garter or seed stitch, but if you want to use stockinette stitch, apply a crocheted or non-rolling border or frame the edges with a non-curling stitch to keep the collar flat.

When making a separate collar, keep in mind that the base has to fit the neckline. For an exact fit, measure the neckline and work a gauge swatch with the needles, yarn and stitch pattern you'll use for the collar. Make calculations or graph the collar based on the stitch and row gauge.

To shape the collar, you can use short row shaping, increasing, decreasing, casting on or binding off.

Plan collars for close-fitting necklines with front or back neck plackets for ease in wearing.

Once complete, block the collar and sew it onto blocked pieces. Pin or baste it in place, centering it at the back neck, before the final sewing.

Picked up collars

Turtleneck A turtleneck can be made as an extension of a crewneck. Turtlenecks are usually ribbed and can be worked on the same number of stitches, changing to larger needle sizes as you progress to prevent the folded over portion from pulling up.

Cowl A cowl is somewhat like a turtleneck, but is usually wider and longer and may not be worked in ribbing. To widen the collar, work increases or change the needle size or do both. This cowl is worked in the round from the wrong (purl) side and folded over.

Side split collar This collar is made in knit two, purl two ribbing. Increase stitches at one shoulder seam by casting on or pick up a few stitches at each end to overlap the split. Work back and forth without joining. Begin and end with a knit stitch for a neater edge.

Picked up polo collars

Front split polo Pick up stitches, beginning at the center front neck. Join and work as for a turtleneck for one-half to one inch (1.5 to 2.5cm), ending at the center. Work back and forth without joining, adding one or two stitches to balance the pattern on both sides.

Simple polo This collar is often worked with a placket. Begin picking up stitches in the center of one side of the placket and end in the center of the other. Make the collar deep enough to lie flat when worn. It may be easier to work back and forth on a circular needle.

Shaped polo Pick up stitches as for simple polo, work each row as follows: *Row 1:* Work three stitches in pattern, work a make-one increase, work to end. Repeat this row on every row. Continue to desired depth. Bind off in pattern.

Wrapped collar for round neck

  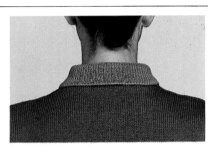 

The wrapped collar is a modified shawl collar made by casting on stitches equal to the entire neck measurement plus the amount of the overlap and working short row shaping on both ends of the collar.

This semi-circular collar is sewn along the cast-on edge, overlapping the pieces at least an inch (2.5cm) at the center front. You will need to know the collar depth (number of rows) and the front and back neck widths plus the overlap (number of stitches).

When the cast-on edge is sewn in place, the collar is folded over and the upper or bind-off edge is on the outside. The back view above shows the folded collar.

Cast on all the collar stitches. The stitches equalling the back neck width are not worked in short rows. For front-neck shaping, divide the collar rows by the stitches on the front neck plus overlap to find the stitches to be left unworked at each short row interval.

Square neck shawl collar

This collar is a knit one, purl one rectangular piece which is sewn so that the ribbing runs vertically. Both collars can be worked in other types of ribbing or in garter stitch.

This simple collar is a knit one, purl one rectangular piece sewn into a square neck so that the ribbing runs horizontally.

On the horizontal collar shown, the cast-on edge is sewn along the neck opening; the side edges are overlapped. On the vertical collar, one side edge is sewn along the neck opening and the cast-on and bound-off edges are overlapped in the front.

In the horizontal rib piece, the cast-on edge fits along two sides and back neck. The rows are sewn to square opening. In the vertical rib piece, the cast-on and bound-off edges are sewn along square opening and the rows fit along two side edges and back neck.

V-neck shawl collar

The shawl collar for a V-neck is worked by casting on stitches equal to the back neck and then gradually casting on stitches to the length of the front V-neck on both sides, then decreasing at the V-points to the desired collar depth.

When the collar is complete, the cast-on edge is sewn in place, and the collar is worn folded over. The first step to working this collar is to calculate the total measurement around the collar and multiply it by the stitch gauge.

The cast-on edge of the collar is sewn along the front edge to the V-point and the overlapped, decreased sides are sewn to opposite sides of the V.

Subtract the back neck stitches from the total number of collar stitches. Calculate the front neck cast-ons based on the collar depth less one to 1½ inches (2.5 to 4cm) for the overlapped side edges. Work the cast-ons and then decrease one stitch at each end on every right-side row for the overlap.

measurements **166**   ribbing **34-35, 172-73**   bands,
short rows **186-87**   gauge **18-19, 57-59**   borders, edges **207-11**

Shawl collar for V-neck cardigan

A doubled shawl collar for a V-neck shaped cardigan is worked once the double-width front bands are complete. It fits along the neck opening from one front band to the other.

Once the collar is complete, with right sides facing, sew the bound-off edge along the neck opening. Sew short edges invisibly to the top of the bands.

Turn the cardigan to the inside and carefully stitch the cast-on edge to the neck opening, enclosing the seam.

This collar is made casting on stitches the width of the back neck, then casting on at each side edge to desired length around neck-line. Work even until you complete doubled width of front band. Bind off at same intervals back to the original number of stitches.

Midi collar for a cardigan

A midi or sailor collar is made to fit along a V-neck shaping. It should be wide enough to fit over the shoulders and can be made with an attached front band.

This collar is worked from the back square to the back neck, and then the front is worked to fit along the V-neck. The collar, when made in stockinette stitch, has a knit-in ribbing or seed stitch edge, which frames the outside edges and prevents the collar from curling.

Place the right side of the collar next to the wrong side of the cardigan and sew the collar invisibly along the V-shaping and back neck, until the front band begins and the collar ends. Then turn the piece over and stitch the band to the right side of the cardigan.

Work this collar even to back neck, then bind off center stitches equalling back neck measurement. Shaping (at outside edge inside seed stitch border) is worked until all stockinette stitches are decreased. Continue front bands by working even in seed stitch.

Notched collar with lapels

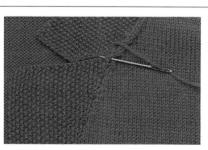

This traditional jacket collar is worked in two steps, with the lapel shaped as part of the front edge and the upper collar applied later. The lapels are worked in seed stitch, which is reversible and will need no further finishing.

To work the lapel, an increase/decrease row is worked at intervals on right-side rows as follows: Work to within three stitches of the seed stitch, decrease one stitch, purl one, increase one stitch. On every wrong-side row, slip the stitch between the shaped stitches.

After careful blocking, the upper collar is sewn around the neck edge to the top of the lapel, as shown.

Begin the collar piece by casting on stitches equalling the opening of the entire neck. Work in seed stitch, casting on or increasing stitches until the notch begins where the collar and lapel are joined. Work even until you achieve the desired collar length.

measurements **166**   blocking **94-97**

bands **207-9**   seed stitch **34**

Collar Shaping

Short rows

When making a collar for a round neck, such as the wrapped collar, cast on a total number of stitches equalling the circumference of the neck. The back stitches are ribbed on every row with no short row shaping, so that you can measure the total depth of the collar at the back neck. The stitches on either side of the back neck are curved using short rows until reaching the desired back neck depth.

In this example, 25 stitches are cast on for the back neck width and 18 stitches for each side of the front neck (61 stitches in all). The depth of the collar will be 18 rows or nine short row intervals on each side (half the total number of rows). Divide 18 by nine to find that you will leave two more stitches unworked on each side of the collar edge nine times.

1 Rib to the last two stitches, *wrap next stitch on the needle and slip it back to the left needle, turn the work. Repeat this row on every row, leaving two more stitches unworked on every row. At the end of the tenth row 10 stitches are left unworked, as shown.

2 When 18 stitches are unworked on either end, turn the work. As above, you will have 18 stitches on the right needle. Work across the row (hiding the wraps on the short rowed stitches). Work across the next row, hiding the wraps on the last 18 stitches.

Casting on

When making a collar such as the V-neck shawl collar, first cast on the number of stitches that equals the width of the back neck. The back stitches are ribbed on every row, but on each end you cast on a series of stitches until you have the total number of stitches for each side of the front neck. You can measure the total depth of the collar at the back neck.

In this example, 25 stitches are cast on for the back neck width and 24 stitches for each side of the front neck (73 stitches in total). The depth of the collar will be 16 rows or eight cast-ons on each side (half the total number of rows). Divide 24 by eight to find that you will cast on three stitches on each side of the collar edge.

1 *Rib to the end of the row, turn the work. Cast on three stitches (cable cast-on method), rib these three stitches, keeping to the pattern. Repeat from the * until all the stitches have been cast on. The collar above shows six stitches cast on at either end.

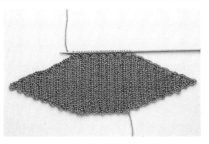

2 The collar above has all 24 stitches cast on at either end. The collar can now be worked to the desired total depth. Sew the most uneven edge, the cast-on edge, to the neckline.

Binding off

When making a collar for a V-neck cardigan, such as the doubled shawl collar, you must cast on stitches to the desired width of the collar, then bind off the same number of stitches. The cast-on edge of the collar is sewn along the outside edge, and the bound-off edge is sewn to the inside. As in the example above, begin by casting on stitches that will equal the width of the back neck and then cast on the planned series of stitches. Bind off until you return to the original number of cast-on stitches. The deepest collar point is measured from the cast-on edge to the bound-off edge at the back neck.

In this example, 26 stitches are cast on for the back neck width and 32 stitches are added for each side of the front neck (90 stitches in total). Half the depth of the collar will be 16 rows or eight cast-ons (half the total number of rows). Divide 32 by eight to give you the series of four stitches to be cast on and then bound off on every row.

1 After casting on the initial 26 stitches, increase 32 stitches on either side, working in knit two, purl two ribbing. The above collar has four stitches bound off.

2 At the beginning of the next 16 rows, bind off four stitches. This will bring you back to your original 26 stitches, as shown. The bind-offs will mirror the cast-on stitches. Both the cast-on and bind-off edges are uneven and sewn to the neck.

measurements **166**
short rows **186-87**

wraps and
hiding wraps **186**

cast ons **24-29**
binding off **47-52**

Plackets

Plackets are used to create an opening for the neck at the front, back or on a shoulder edge. Usually the placket border is worked and then the collar or neckband is added. Collars can be worked to the edges of the placket or to the center so that the collar meets when the buttons are closed.

Plan the depth and width of a placket to fit into the overall design. With a center cable pattern, the placket can be the width of that center cable.

A long placket can create the illusion of a mock cardigan. A wide placket can be made with two rows of buttonholes for a double-breasted effect. A narrow, short placket is ideal for children's or baby garments.

As with other types of ribbed bands, plackets are usually worked on smaller needles, and care should be taken to pick up the correct number of stitches and to work to the correct length. Too many or too few stitches or rows will result in a placket that doesn't lie flat.

The button-band side of the placket is usually worked first. Mark the placement of the buttons on the button band and then work the buttonhole side. Overlap the plackets with the button band under the buttonhole band. The lower edge should be sewn neatly so that the placket doesn't bunch or buckle.

Vertical plackets

Ribbed placket: horizontal A placket can be worked as shown by picking up stitches along the side edges and working to the depth of the placket width. Bind off evenly for a neat edge.

Ribbed placket: vertical This is worked by picking up stitches along the lower edge of the placket. Sew the side edges once the band is complete.

Making a vertical placket To work a vertical ribbed placket, leave the stitches on a holder until the piece is complete. Work the button band by picking up stitches behind the stitches on the holder. Work the buttonhole band directly from the holder stitches.

Horizontal plackets

When working a horizontal placket along the shoulder, make the left armhole depth shorter to accommodate the depth of the picked-up placket on the front and back pieces. You can work the ribbing along with the piece. Work the neckband once the placket is complete.

To sew the sleeve onto the horizontal placket, overlap the placket, pin the sleeve and sew it in place through both layers of the overlapped placket.

---

measurements **166**   picking up **106-8**   stitch holders **18-19**
neckbands **196**   binding off **47-52**

Buttonholes

Many different types of buttonholes include horizontal, vertical, eyelet, button loops and those made from contrasting thread. You can also use the yarn overs of lace stitch patterns as buttonholes. Such a yarn over buttonhole will need to be reinforced by overcasting after it is completed. You can also make buttonholes on loose knits by simply slipping the button through the stitch. (This type of buttonhole must also be reinforced.)

Which buttonhole you use will depend on the type of garment, how it will be worn, the position of the buttonhole, the size and type of button and your yarn. For example, a coat with large buttons that is frequently buttoned will need large, durable buttonholes, and heavier yarn will make a larger buttonhole than finer yarn over the same number of stitches.

If possible, buy your buttons before making the buttonholes. Make a sample swatch with buttonholes to determine whether your buttons are the correct size. The buttonhole should be just large enough to slip the button through it. Since knitted fabric stretches, a buttonhole that is too large will eventually cause buttons to unfasten. The buttonhole for a flat button must be smaller than that for a raised button of the same diameter.

Mark button placement on the appropriate band with contrasting yarn or safety pins before you work the buttonholes. On the opposite band, work the buttonholes to correspond to the button markers. Buttons are usually placed on the left side for women and the right side for men. Make sure that you use enough buttons to prevent the band from gapping.

Horizontal buttonholes should always be centered on bands. On vertical bands, try to have at least two stitches on either side of the buttonhole to prevent the buttonhole from stretching out. On horizontal bands, work the buttonholes when you have completed one-half the band.

You must work two identical buttonholes on foldover bands so that they will align when the band is folded.

To stabilize the buttonhole area when you use silk or rayon yarns, add a matching sewing thread when you work the buttonhole.

When making buttonholes, remember that when you bind off stitches, you must offset them by casting on (usually on the next row). Yarn overs must be offset by decreases. You usually work the first row of a buttonhole on the right side of the piece unless otherwise stated.

Perfect buttonholes take practice, so try a few before actually making them on your garment.

Spacing buttonholes

Buttonholes should be spaced so that the band will not gap when it is buttoned. It is better to have one or two buttons too many than to have too few.

Place markers on the button band for the first and last buttonholes no more than one-half inch (1.5cm) from the upper and lower edges. Measure the distance between them, and place markers evenly for the remaining buttonholes.

You can position them more accurately by counting the number of rows between each buttonhole. To determine the correct number of rows, take the gauge from the button band. If you are working the button and buttonhole bands at the same time, you may have to work a gauge swatch for the band to calculate the number of rows. Remember that for the horizontal two-row buttonhole, you must allow two rows for each buttonhole.

When you work buttonholes opposite the markers, vertical buttonholes should begin slightly below the marker and end slightly above it (depending on the length of buttonhole). Horizontal buttonholes should be made directly opposite the marker on vertical bands and centered on horizontal bands.

Two-row horizontal buttonholes

The two-row buttonhole is made by binding off a number of stitches on one row and casting them on again on the next. The last stitch bound off is part of the left side of the buttonhole. The single cast-on makes the neatest edge for the upper part of the buttonhole. Some versions have techniques to strengthen the corners. All the horizontal buttonholes given below are worked over four stitches.

Simple two-row buttonhole This buttonhole is frequently used in knitting instructions.

1 On the first row, work to the placement of the buttonhole. Knit two, with the left needle, pull one stitch over the other stitch, *knit one, pull the second stitch over the knit one; repeat from the * twice more. Four stitches have been bound off.

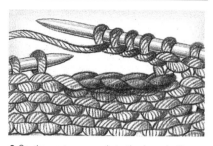

2 On the next row, work to the bound-off stitches, cast on four stitches using the single cast-on method. On the next row, work these stitches through the back loops to tighten them.

Version A *Row 1:* Work as for simple two-row. *Row 2:* Work to within one stitch of the bound-off stitches, increase one stitch (work into front and back of stitch), then cast on three stitches (the bound-off stitches less one) with the single cast-on method.

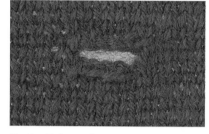

Version B *Row 1:* Bind off three stitches. Slip the last one to left needle, knit it together with the next stitch. *Row 2:* At the bound-off stitches, cast on five stitches. *Row 3:* Work to one stitch before the extra cast-on stitch, knit two together.

Version C *Row 1:* Work as for simple two-row. *Row 2:* At bound-off stitches, cast on four stitches, insert right needle from back to front under both loops of first bound-off stitch leaving loops on needle, work to end. *Row 3:* Knit bound-off loops with last cast-on stitch.

One-row horizontal buttonhole

The horizontal one-row buttonhole is the neatest buttonhole and requires no further reinforcing. It is shown above worked from the right side (lower buttonhole) and from the wrong side (upper buttonhole).

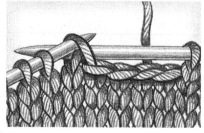

1 Work to the buttonhole, bring yarn to front and slip a stitch purlwise. Place yarn at back and leave it there. *Slip next stitch from left needle. Pass the first slipped stitch over it; repeat from the * three times more (not moving yarn). Slip the last bound-off stitch to left needle and turn work.

2 Using the cable cast-on with the yarn at the back, cast on five stitches as follows: *Insert the right needle between the first and second stitches on the left needle, draw up a loop, place the loop on the left needle; repeat from the * four times more, turn the work.

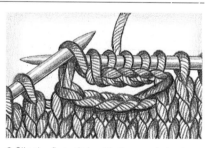

3 Slip the first stitch with the yarn in back from the left needle and pass the extra cast-on stitch over it to close the buttonhole. Work to the end of the row.

---

measurements **166**

front/back loops **37**

(bring) with yarn in front/back **35**

slip a stitch purlwise/knitwise **46**

Vertical buttonholes.

Vertical buttonhole slits are made by working two sections with separate balls of yarn at the same time or individually. If the latter, work the first side to desired depth (end at buttonhole edge). Work second side with one row less ending on wrong side. Turn work, cut second ball of yarn. Then with yarn from first side, rejoin by working across all stitches.

Finish and strengthen by making a horizontal stitch at upper and lower joining points (use yarn from joining).

Seed stitch Vertical buttonholes can be worked on narrow bands. This type of buttonhole is not suited for large buttons or stress, and is best used for decorative purposes, such as on pocket flaps. Seed stitch is ideal for vertical buttonholes since it lies flat.

Double buttonholes Since stockinette stitch rolls inward, vertical buttonholes should only be used on stockinette stitch for double bands as shown above. To make a neater edge, add a selvage stitch on either side of the slit.

Closed double buttonholes When the band is complete, fold it, match the buttonholes and reinforce them by embroidering with the buttonhole stitch. Note that the band is worked with a slip stitch at the center to make a neater folding edge.

Contrasting yarn buttonhole

Another buttonhole method is to work the buttonhole stitches with a short piece of contrasting yarn. Then slip the stitches back to left needle and reknit them with main-color yarn. Leave contrasting yarn in the buttonhole.

1 From the back of the work, using main color and a crochet hook, pull through a loop in each stitch on the lower edge of the buttonhole, and pick up one stitch from the side edge. Slip these five loops from the hook to a cable needle.

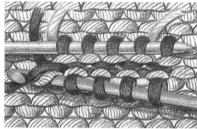

2 Working along the top edge, pick up four loops and one from the side. Transfer the five loops to a cable or double-pointed needle. Cut the yarn, leaving a strand about eight inches (20cm) long.

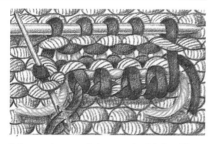

3 Fasten down each loop to the fabric with a yarn needle. Remove the contrasting yarn. Use this method when you add a ribbon band for reinforcement. Cut the space for the buttonhole on the ribbon before you pick up the loops and anchor them over the ribbon.

Eyelet buttonholes

One-stitch eyelet: version A Eyelet buttonholes are small and are ideal for small buttons and children's garments. Work as follows: *Row 1:* Work to the buttonhole, knit two together, yarn over. *Row 2:* Work the yarn over as a stitch on next row.

One-stitch eyelet: version B *Row 1:* Work to the buttonhole, yarn over. *Row 2:* Slip yarn over, then yarn over again. *Row 3:* Slip one stitch knitwise before yarn overs, knit them together, leaving them on left needle. Pass slip stitch over the stitch just made. Knit yarn overs together with the next stitch on needle.

Two-stitch eyelet: version A *Row 1:* Work to the buttonhole, knit two together, yarn over twice, slip, slip, knit (ssk). *Row 2:* Work the yarn overs as follows: purl into the first yarn over and then purl into the back of the second yarn over.

Two-stitch eyelet: version B *Row 1:* Work to the buttonhole, yarn over twice, knit two together through back loops. *Row 2:* Work to the yarn overs, purl the first yarn over and drop the second yarn over from the needle.

Overcast button loop

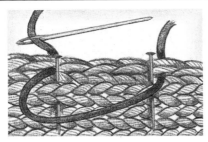

Button loops are worked after the piece is complete and are generally used where only one or two buttons are needed. Loops are ideal for plackets in fine yarns, baby garments or closures on jackets or coats.

1 Mark placement for beginning and ending point of loop on the side edge. To form the core of the loop, using a yarn needle and yarn, bring needle up at the lower edge. Insert needle at upper marker. Pull yarn through, leaving a loop the desired size.

2 Make a double strand by bringing the needle up at the lower marker once more. Depending on the size of the loop, this can be done once more to make a three-strand core.

3 Work the buttonhole stitch over all the loops by bringing the yarn to the left of the needle. Then insert the needle under the loops and over the yarn, pull the yarn through and tighten.

Crocheted button loop

You can easily adjust the size of this loop to the size of the button. The button loop should be just large enough to allow the button to pass through. If the loop is too large, the button will not stay securely.

1 Mark the placement as for the overcast button loop. With a crochet hook, pull up a loop at the upper marker and work a crochet chain to the desired length.

2 Remove the hook from the loop and insert it through the fabric at the lower marker, then through the last loop of the chain. Draw the loop through the fabric. Catch the yarn and pull it through the loop on the hook.

3 To work a row of single crochet over the chain, insert the hook under the chain and pull up a loop. Catch a strand of yarn with the hook and pull it through both loops on the hook. Fasten off the last loop and weave in ends.

Finishing buttonholes

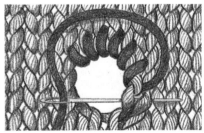

Sometimes even the best buttonholes need a bit of reinforcing. How you do so will depend on the yarn and the size of the buttonhole. The buttonhole stitch shown is good for both single and double buttonholes.

Buttonhole stitch Use either a whole or split strand of yarn with this reinforcing technique. Work from right to left around the buttonhole, with the needle pointing towards the center. Don't work the stitches too closely or you may distort the buttonhole.

The overcasting method is good for simple eyelets used to make small buttonholes.

Overcasting This reinforcing technique is worked by overcasting evenly around the buttonhole.

measurements **166**   markers **18**   crochet   crochet chain **210**

placket **202**   overcasting **101**   hooks and sizes **18**

Bands, Borders and Edges

Bands, borders and edges are used to complete garments and to cover and flatten raw edges on knit pieces that have a tendency to curl. Bands and borders are usually wider than edges; they are used to give stability to pieces. Edges, such as those in lace patterns, are often used to add a decorative touch.

The classic ribbing stitch is often used for bands, but you can use a number of other stitch patterns. Choose those that don't curl, such as garter or seed stitch, except when curling is desired or for folded bands.

You can work a band at the same time as the piece, but for a firmer edge, work it separately on smaller needles. You can either pick up stitches to work a separate band or apply the band once the piece is complete. Prepare pieces for picked-up bands by adding selvage stitches on the edges. For picked-up bands, be sure to have the correct number of stitches. Too few stitches will make the band pull in; too many will cause it to wobble or ruffle. Check the band gauge on your knit swatch.

You can make bands and borders of single or double thickness. They are usually not more than an inch or two (2.5 or 5cm) wide, so that they remain stable. Bands can also be reinforced with ribbon or tape to keep them firm.

Ribbed bands

Ribbed bands are flexible and elastic, which makes them perfect for areas that are intended to grip. They can be simple knit one, purl one or knit two, purl two ribbing or some of the other variations shown below.

Horizontal This band, more elastic than a vertical one, is often used on cardigan or jacket fronts. It is the easiest type of band to work, but requires careful attention to make sure that you pick up the correct number of stitches for an even, flat edge.

Vertical For an unbroken line, you can work vertical bands from ribbing stitches left on a holder after the lower edge is complete. Once beginning the band, add a selvage stitch for seaming.

To attach the vertical band, pin it along the edge as you work, without stretching it. Then either bind off the stitches or leave them on a holder to work the neckband. Sew the band in place.

Purl three, knit one ribbing (a multiple of four stitches plus three extra) *Row 1 (right side):* *Purl three, knit one; repeat from the *, end purl three. *Row 2:* *Knit three, purl one; repeat from the *, end knit three. Repeat these two rows.

Stockinette/garter stitch ribbing (a multiple of four stitches plus two extra) *Row 1 (right side):* Knit. *Row 2:* *Purl two, knit two; repeat from the *, end purl two. Repeat these two rows.

Stockinette/seed stitch ribbing (a multiple of four stitches plus two extra) *Row 1 (right side):* *Knit two, purl one, knit one; repeat from the *, end knit two. *Row 2:* *Purl two, knit one, purl one; repeat from the *, end purl two. Repeat these two rows.

Stockinette stitch bands

Doubled on a curve This band is picked up and worked with a turning ridge. It works best with lighter-weight yarns. To keep the curved edges flat, decrease stitches on every knit row up to the turning ridge, then increase to correspond on the second half.

Picot band An odd number of stitches is picked up for this doubled band. Work the picot row on the right side as follows: *Knit two together, yarn over; repeat from the *, end knit one. Work the inside band to the same depth as the outside.

Bias band This band is worked separately and then sewn onto the piece. Increase one stitch at the beginning of each right-side row and decrease one stitch at the end of the same row.

Outside rolled band Pick up the stitches from the right side along the edge. Beginning with a purl row, work in stockinette stitch for about four or five rows or as desired. Bind off with a larger needle. The purl side rolls to the outside (right side).

Inside rolled band Pick up the stitches from the right side along the edge. Beginning with a knit row, work in stockinette stitch for about four or five rows or as desired. Bind off with a larger needle. The purl side rolls to the inside (wrong side).

Knit-in borders

The advantage of knit-in borders is that your piece is complete once you have finished the knitting. The best stitches are those that lie flat, such as ribbing, seed stitch or the bias edge shown here. Avoid working stitches which may differ in row gauge from your piece, such as stockinette with garter stitch. When working bands in contrasting colors, twist yarns on the wrong side to prevent holes.

Ribbing on a curve To shape an armhole and make the band at the same time, rib two stitches, then decrease one stitch. On right-side rows, keep increasing one stitch at the edge (in rib) and decreasing inside the ribbing edge until the armhole is shaped and the desired stitches are in the rib pattern.

Seed stitch This is a good choice for a border on a stockinette stitch body, since it has the same row gauge as stockinette stitch. Also, a seed stitch pattern makes a nice flat edge.

Bias Leave this stockinette stitch band flat or fold it in half to the inside and sew it in place. On right-side rows, slip the first stitch knitwise, work a make-one increase, work to the last two stitches of the band, knit two together. On wrong-side rows, purl all border stitches.

---

measurements **166**	turning ridge **212**	gauge **18-19, 57-59**
picking up **106-8**	yarn overs **63**	make one increase **39**

Garter stitch borders with corners

These borders, ideal for jackets, shawls or blankets, are worked separately. Since corners are wider at the outer edge, you make decreases on either side of a central stitch at each corner. To determine number of stitches to cast on, measure all side edges and multiply this number by stitch gauge. Then find required number of decreases by multiplying band width by row gauge. Add the number of decreases (for each corner) to find the number of stitches to be cast on.

Knit corner Cast on and mark each corner. Knit to two stitches before the corner, knit two together, knit the corner stitch, knit two together through the back loops. On wrong-side rows, purl the corner stitches and knit the remaining stitches.

Eyelet corner Cast on and mark each corner. Work to three stitches before the corner, knit three together, yarn over, knit the corner stitch, yarn over, knit three together through the back loops. On wrong-side rows, purl the corner stitch and knit all the others.

Miscellaneous bands

Garter stitch band Work this band by picking up two stitches for every three rows along a straight edge. Knit every row. To bind off, use the decrease bind-off.

Pick up and knit border This border makes a good firm narrow edge and is sometimes called "mock crochet." Pick up the stitches and then bind them off on the next row. Or knit one row and then bind off.

Held miter band Cast on stitches to desired width, plus width of band. Work one stitch less on each row, placing it on a holder. When reaching the desired band depth, work the piece, leaving the stitches on a holder for the mitered edge.

Pick up stitches along the side edge. On right-side rows, knit a band stitch with a holder stitch, then work a make-one increase. On wrong-side rows, work to the last stitch, make one, work the last stitch together with the next holder stitch.

Open chain cast-on

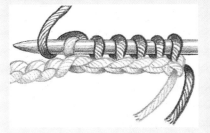

1 Use this cast-on to later add a band. Chain the number of stitches above the rib in contrasting yarn. With main-color yarn, pick up one stitch in the back loop of each chain.

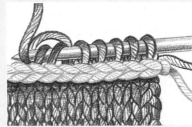

2 After the piece is complete, to work band with a smaller needle, pick up the main-color loops under the chain, working two loops together as shown, if decreasing is desired.

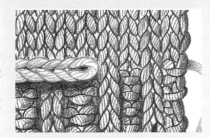

3 When the band is complete, remove the chain from the piece.

| picking up **106-8** | make one increase **39** | gauge **18-19, 57-59** | front/back loops **37** | crochet chain **210** |
| binding off **47-52** | measurements **166** | yarn overs **63** | main color/MC **62** | |

Crochet Edges

Crochet edges are another option for finishing knit garments. These edges are easy to make and can easily be re-done until you achieve the desired effect. Crochet edges add stability and flatten curling pieces. You can make a firm edge by working into each stitch or you can make a lacy, decorative edge by chaining one or two loops be-tween stithes.

To work a crochet edge, always in-sert your hook from front to back under both loops of the previous crochet stitches or bound-off stitches. Use a crochet hook a size or two smaller than your knitting needles.

As with knitting, you should space crochet stitches evenly along an edge. Too many stitches will cause the piece to ripple; too few will cause it to pull in. To go around a corner, you must work more than one crochet stitch into the corner stitch.

Crochet edges are usually worked from the right side of the piece and from right to left along the edge. If you crochet with your left hand, reverse the direction. You can easily crochet edges of finished garments in rounds, elim-inating the need for further seaming.

Practice on a swatch to make sure that you have the correct size crochet hook and to become familiar with the stitch pattern.

Slip-stitch edge

You can use slip stitch alone as a narrow edge but it is best used as a base for other crochet stitches since it falls to the side of the piece. It can be also used decoratively on top of the knit fabric to create a line, such as with a plaid.

1 Insert the crochet hook into the fabric, catch the yarn and pull up a loop.

2 Go into the next stitch of the fabric and draw a new loop through the fabric and the loop on the hook, leaving one loop on the hook. Make each loop a little loose so the edge won't be tight. Repeat this step to the end.

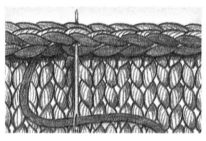

3 To join a round of slip stitches, insert the hook into the center of the first slip stitch and draw through a loop. Cut the yarn, pull it to the right side. With a yarn needle, trace the path of the first stitch, then take it back into the last stitch to the wrong side.

Making a slip knot and chain

Leaving an end to weave in, make a slip knot on the crochet hook. Keep-ing the working yarn taut with your left index finger, pass the hook under, then over the yarn and catch with the hook. Draw the yarn through the loop on the hook. This makes one chain stitch.

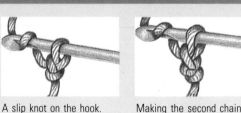

A slip knot on the hook.   Making the second chain.   A finished chain showing the front and back.

Single crochet

  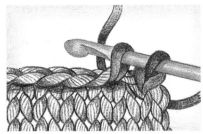 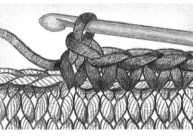

One row of single crochet, shown above, makes a neat, narrow edge; several rows form a firm edge. You can also use it as a base for other crochet edges.

Single crochet can be worked on a slip stitch base as shown here.

1 Draw through a loop as for a slip stitch, bring the yarn over the hook and pull it through the first loop. *Insert the hook into the next stitch and draw through a second loop.

2 Yarn over and pull through both loops on the hook. Repeat from the* to the end.

Backwards single crochet

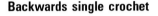
  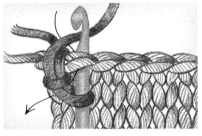 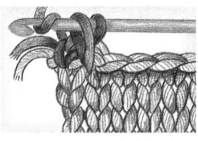

Work a backwards single crochet edge the same as a single crochet, but from left to right rather than right to left.

This edge, a variation of the simple backwards single crochet, is worked by making a backwards single crochet in one space, making a chain one and skipping a stitch.

1 Pull through a loop on the left edge. Chain one. *Go into the next stitch to the right. Catch the yarn as shown, and pull it through the fabric, then underneath (not through) the loop on the hook.

2 Bring yarn over top of crochet hook and around as shown, and draw the yarn through both loops. Repeat from the *.

Picot edge

   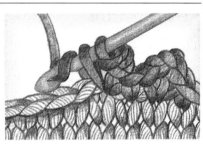

A slip stitch picot edge is worked with two slip stitches between each three-chain picot.

A single crochet picot edge is made with two single crochets between each three-chain picot.

Slip stitch picot Work one slip stitch, *chain three, insert the hook into the same stitch and pull the yarn through both the stitch and the loop on the hook, slip stitch in the next two stitches; repeat from the * to end.

Single crochet picot Work a single crochet, *chain three, insert the hook in the same stitch and pull up a loop, pull yarn through both loops as shown, single crochet in the next two stitches; repeat from the * to end.

Hems

A hem or facing is an edge that folds under to keep the knitting from curling or stretching. It is usually made to replace ribbing and can be made horizontally or vertically. It allows pieces to hang properly and is ideal for edges that do not hug the body. Hems can be used for lower edges of knit garments or necklines and front edges of cardigans and coats.

A hem can also be used to form a casing for elastic such as at the top of a skirt. It can be worked at the same time as the piece or picked up after it is complete.

The edge of the hem can be distinct (turning ridge) or rounded (without turning ridge). The folded part of the hem should be made in a smooth stitch such as stockinette, regardless of the stitch pattern used for the piece, and should be worked on a needle at least one size smaller—possibly even two or three sizes smaller—than the needles used for the main body. You may have to increase or decrease stitches once

the hem is complete, depending on the gauge of the stitch pattern above the hem. Try a small sample before you begin. Hems are not ideal to use with openwork patterns, since the folded area will show through.

The folded edge should be sewn to the garment as invisibly as possible with whip stitch or blind stitch, or sewn stitch by stitch from the knitting needle.

Turning ridges

A turning ridge is used to create a clean line that makes a neat edge when the hem is sewn in place. All ridges are made after the hem is the desired depth, whether they are at the lower or the upper edge. The piece worked before (at the lower edge) or after (at the upper edge) is the hem.

Purl A ridge is formed by knitting the stitches through the back loops on the wrong side, thus forming a purl ridge on the right side of the work. On the following (right-side) row, begin the body pattern.

Picot This ridge is worked over an even number of stitches. Work the picot row on the right side as follows: Knit one stitch, *knit two stitches together, yarn over; repeat from the *, ending with a knit one.

Slip stitch This turning ridge is worked over an odd number of stitches. Work the slip stitch row on the right side as follows: *Knit one. With the yarn at the front, slip one stitch, knit one; repeat from the * to the end.

Knit-in hem

To reduce bulk, the cast-on edge is worked together with stitches on the needle so that sewing is not necessary. This hem can be worked with a regular cast-on or with an open cast-on as described in Chapter III.

This knit-in hem was worked using a regular cast-on. Stitches were picked up along the cast-on row and placed on a spare needle. It should be noted that a knit-in hem is not easy to unravel if corrections must be made.

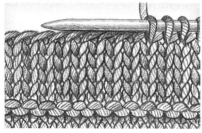

1 Work the hem to the desired depth and then make a turning ridge. Work the main piece until it is the same depth as the hem, end with a wrong-side row. Using a spare needle and separate yarn, pick up one loop from the cast-on edge for each stitch on the main needle.

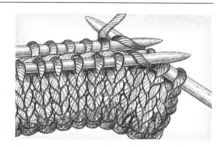

2 Cut the extra yarn. Then fold up the hem and knit one stitch from the spare needle together with one stitch from the main piece, as shown. Continue in pattern, beginning with a wrong-side row.

measurements **166**

gauge **18-19, 57-59**

whip stitching to attach **111**

front/back loops **37**

picking up **106-8**

slip a stitch **46**

yarn overs **63**

Vertical facings

Vertical facings can be worked at the same time the garment is made or picked up and worked later. These facings are ideal for tailored jacket and cardigan fronts. When the facing is to be picked up later, make a selvage stitch at the edge to aid in the pick-up. Steam or wet block the pieces carefully before stitching the facing in place.

Garter stitch A simple facing can be made by using garter stitch as a turning ridge. On every row, knit the turning ridge stitch.

Slip stitch For a cardigan front, a band can be worked with double buttonholes. Work the slip stitch turning ridge by slipping the stitch purlwise on right-side rows and purling it on wrong-side rows. Fold the band and reinforce the buttonholes through both thicknesses.

Picked-up After the piece is worked, pick up three stitches for every four along the edge and work the desired depth. Stitches can be bound off as shown or sewn down stitch by stitch.

Mitered facing and hem

When making a garment with a horizontal hem and vertical facing, you can reduce bulk and create a smooth edge by making edges that meet but don't overlap. To do this, calculate the number of rows in the hem depth. Divide this in half and reduce the number of stitches you cast on by the result (about one inch/2.5cm).

After casting on, work the hem by increasing one stitch every other row until all the stitches are added back. Make a turning ridge. For the front facing, increase one stitch every other row, adding one stitch for the front turning ridge.

On this mitered edge, increase one every other row four times before making the purl turning ridge, then make the facing by increasing one stitch every other row plus one stitch for the garter stitch turning ridge. Sew the hem and facing, carefully matching the corners.

Curved facings

Inside curve A picked-up hem that curves to the inside, such as the neck edge shown, must be increased as it is worked to make the curve larger.

After the stitches are picked up along the neck edge, knit one row on the wrong side as a turning ridge. As you make the facing, work increases at the points where the curving takes place. You may wish to place a marker at these points.

Outside curve A picked-up hem, such as the lower edge of a cardigan, has an outside curve and needs decreases to make the curve smaller.

After the stitches are picked up along the curve, knit one row on the wrong side as a turning ridge. Make decreases evenly along the most curved part of the edge as you work the facing.

| measurements **166** | selvages **194-95** | turning ridge **212** |
| picking up **106-8** | blocking **94-97** | markers **18** |

Pockets

Generally, pockets are worked in un-shaped areas of a garment so as not to interrupt its design. The most common types are patch, horizontal inset and vertical inset. Pockets should be in proportion to your garment. For example, don't make a tiny pocket opening on a bulky jacket.

The average size of a woman's pocket is five to 6½ inches (12.5 to 16.5cm) wide by 5½ to seven inches (14 to 17.5cm) deep. For a man's pocket, add an inch (2.5cm) and for a child's pocket, subtract an inch (2.5cm) or more.

Place the pocket at a level that is comfortable for your hands. The easiest way is to check an existing sweater.

On a woman's sweater, the lower edge of a horizontal or patch pocket should be no further than 21 or 22 inches (53 or 56cm) from the shoulder and approximately 2½ to four inches (6.5 to 10cm) from the center front edge. Vertical or side seam pockets are easier to wear in cropped sweaters.

If you want to add pockets to a garment, you will need to decide what type of pocket and edging, where to place the pocket and whether it should contrast or match your sweater's yarn and pattern. Work with the stitch and row gauge of your design to calculate the number of stitches and rows needed for the pocket. Don't forget to add a little extra yarn to the amount required for the garment.

Patch pockets

Simple square or rectangular patch pockets are easiest to make. You can also work patch pockets in contrasting stitch patterns, colors or other shapes such as circles or triangles.

It is essential to work neatly. Apply pocket subtly with a nearly invisible stitch or boldly using a contrasting color in blanket stitch. Pockets in non-curling stitches, such as garter or seed stitch are easiest to apply. For a neater edge, add a slip stitch selvage to side edges.

Simple pocket Patch pockets should be applied to firmly knit pieces in stable yarns that can support the extra weight of the pocket. For easier application, place the pocket directly above the rib or hem. This gives you a straight line along the lower edge.

Simple with a cable A patch pocket can be made with a center cable which goes over the body cable. Line up the pocket cable over the body cable and sew in place.

Curved lower edge For this pocket, cast on the desired number of stitches, less four to six depending on the pocket size and yarn. *Work one row even. Cast on one stitch at each end of the next row. Repeat from the * to add back the four to six stitches.

Applying a patch pocket

Block or press the pocket. Measure it and outline an area the same size on the garment, using a contrasting yarn in the basting stitch. Pin the pocket over the area before applying. Then overcast the pocket in place.

An alternate method of applying a patch pocket is to run a needle in and out of one-half of every other row along both vertical edges of the pocket and one-half of every stitch along the lower edge of the pocket.

Pin the pocket in place in the center of the needles and, using the overcast stitch, sew one stitch from the needle and one stitch from the pocket.

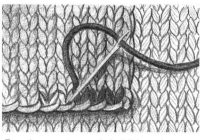

To make a neater, nearly invisible pocket seam, use duplicate stitch along the edges through the pocket and the body piece as shown.

---

measurements **166**   blanket stitch **232**   blocking **94-97**   duplicate stitch **233**

gauge **18-19, 57-59**   selvages **194-95**   overcast **206**

Patch pockets with hemmed edges

The hemmed patch pocket has folded lower and side edges. Cast on the desired number of stitches and work tightly in stockinette stitch for approximately one-half inch (1.5cm), depending on the weight of the yarn (heavier yarn may need more depth).

1 Work a turning ridge by knitting one row through the back loops on the purl (wrong) side. Work the same depth above the turning ridge. Cast on two to four stitches at the beginning and end for side hems.

2 Continue to work pocket, slipping the first stitch inside of the side hems on right-side rows and purling this stitch on wrong-side rows. Work to the desired length.

3 Add a ribbed edge (about one-half to one inch/1.5 to 2.5cm) or work another turning ridge at the top of the pocket and fold edge under. Bind off all stitches. Backstitch the lower edge as shown, then flip the pocket up and whip stitch the two side edges.

Picked-up patch pockets

This patch pocket looks like a set-in pocket. You can knit the pocket as a flap and then sew it in place, or you can pick up the side edges and apply it as you knit.

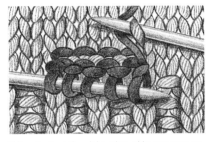

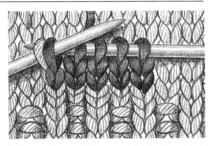

1 If desired, baste a line along the desired placement line of the pocket. With a crochet hook, pick up and knit one stitch for each stitch of the pocket, placing the stitches on a knitting needle. Work one row even on the wrong side.

2 To attach at the right edge, skip one row on the piece. With the right needle, pick up one-half of the stitch in the next row (directly over first stitch of pocket), slip it to the left needle, and knit it together with the first stitch of the pocket.

3 To attach at the left edge, slip the last stitch knitwise to the right needle and with the left needle, pick up one-half of the stitch on the piece, slip the stitch back to the left needle and knit it together with the picked-up stitch through the back loops as shown.

Pocket flaps

Pocket flaps can be picked up and knit or made separately and sewn on. The flap should be the width of the pocket. Apply the flap slightly above the pocket opening.

You can attach flaps as you knit by working the flap first and leaving the stitches on a holder. Then knit together a stitch of the flap and one of the piece.

Rectangle This pocket flap can be made with or without a border. It can also be used without a pocket to create the look of a mock pocket.

Triangle This pocket flap is made with a buttonhole. The buttonhole can be vertical or horizontal and can be decorative or functional.

Outside flap When the pocket is the desired depth, you can make a flap on the outside of the pocket. First make a turning ridge and then work the flap by reversing the stitch pattern so that wrong-side rows become right-side rows.

| measurements **166** | front/back loops **37** | backstitch **101** | ˙crochet hooks **18** | slip a stitch | picking up **106-8** |
| turning ridge **212** | ribbing **34-35, 172-73** | whip stitching **111** | stitch holders **18-19** | knitwise/purlwise **46** | |

Inset Pockets

Inset pockets, the most common type, are inconspicuous. They can be made with a horizontal, vertical or slanted opening. Although the ways to make this pocket vary, they all have the same basic elements.

The lining of the inset pocket is usually made before the piece is begun. (Information on making linings appears later in this section.)

Inset pockets can be made with a knit-in border or with one added later, which is usually three-fourths to 1½ inches (2 to 4cm). A disadvantage of the knit-in border is that it may be too loose if the needle is the same size as the body. To make an added border, you can bind off the stitches or place them on a holder until you are ready to work the edge. To create a firmer edge on a ribbing border, bind off all the stitches knitwise.

Horizontal inset pockets: version A

The horizontal inset pocket is one of the most frequently used methods for adding a pocket. You must first make a pocket lining, which is usually attached from the wrong side of the work.

1 On the right side, work to the pocket placement and bind off to prepare for adding the pocket lining. The pocket edge is worked after the piece is complete.

2 On the next row, work the lining over the place where the stitches were bound off. For a neater join, add two extra stitches to the lining and work them together with the first and last stitches of the piece.

1 An alternate method of joining the lining in one row is to place the stitches on a holder. With the right side of the lining facing the wrong side of the piece, work the stitches of the lining, then work to the end of the row.

Horizontal inset pockets: version B

This inset pocket has an attached double lining that is worked in a strip and rejoined to the piece. The sides of the pocket are sewn later and the pocket lining hangs free.

1 To begin this horizontal pocket on the right side, work to the pocket opening, place these stitches on a holder. Purl across stitches for the opening to make a turning ridge and place the remaining stitches on a holder.

2 Continue in stockinette stitch on the pocket lining for about eight inches (20cm), ending with a knit row. Fold the pocket lining in half and work the stitches from the second holder to the end of the row.

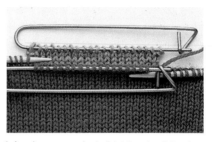

3 To rejoin the lining to the body, work to the pocket lining on the next row. Work across the stitches of the pocket lining. Slip the remaining stitches to a knitting needle and work to the end of the row. Sew sides of pocket lining and work the edging.

measurements **166**   turning ridge **212**

stitch holders **18-19**

Vertical inset pockets: version A

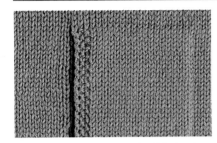   

This vertical inset pocket on the right-hand side of the piece is made with a knit-in seed stitch border and an attached lining, or a lining flap for attaching a fabric or knit lining. Reverse the process for a left-side pocket.

1 On the right side of the piece, work to the pocket opening and place the remaining stitches on a holder. Continue to the desired depth, working a seed-stitch border at the pocket edge, ending with a wrong-side row. Place these stitches on a holder.

2 At the first holder, work the lining (or lining flap) by joining a second ball of yarn and casting on the additional stitches. It is shown here after a few rows have been worked. Work these stitches to the same depth as the first half of pocket.

3 To rejoin the pocket, work to the pocket lining, then knit the lining stitches together with the stitches on the holder. Work to the end of the row. Continue in pattern.

Vertical inset pockets: version B

This vertical inset pocket is made by working a few rows of the pocket lining on separate needles, ending with a right-side row. Shown above is a pocket on the right-hand side of the piece. Reverse the process to make a pocket on the left-hand side.

1 Work to the edge of the pocket and place these stitches on a holder. Work to the end of the row. On the next row, work to the pocket edge, then work across the lining stitches. Work to the desired depth. Place these stitches on a holder.

2 Return to the stitches on the first holder and work to the depth of the lining stitches, ending with a wrong-side row. On the next row, work across all stitches (working the lining stitches together with the pocket stitches).

3 To work an edge along the vertical opening, pick up stitches along the pocket opening. After working the edging, sew down the side edges. Sew the lining to the wrong side.

Slanted/diagonal inset pockets

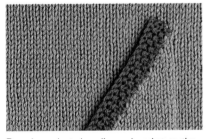 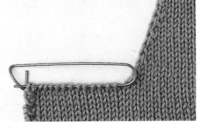  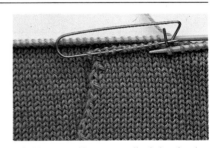

To make a slanted or diagonal pocket on the right-hand side of the piece, as shown above, you must know the desired depth, width and angle of the pocket. A slanted pouch pocket can be made with two openings slanting in opposite directions on either side.

1 Work to the pocket opening and place the remaining stitches on a holder. Work the stitches, making decreases at the pocket opening edge as planned. Work to desired depth and place these stitches on a second holder, ending with a wrong-side row.

2 Slip the stitches from first holder to a needle. With a second ball of yarn, cast on stitches for the lining equal to the total number of stitches in the pocket width. Work to depth of stitches on the second holder, ending with a wrong-side row.

3 Rejoin by working across all stitches (working lining stitches together with pocket stitches). An edge is added once piece is complete. For a slanting edge, increase one stitch at top of opening and decrease one stitch at the lower edge on every other row.

measurements **166**
stitch holders **18-19**
joining a second
ball of yarn **36**

Side-seam pockets

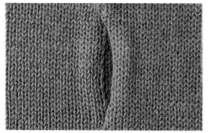

You can add a side-seam pocket on either side as an afterthought since it is worked once the pieces are complete.

Single A side-seam pocket can have a single pocket lining that is sewn to the wrong side of the front piece as shown. The lining can be a rectangle or curve to fit the hand.

Double A side-seam pocket can also have a pocket lining that is worked double. It is sewn together and allowed to hang free after the top and bottom edges are sewn to the front and back of the piece.

Attached You can also work the lining at the same time as the piece, making identical linings on the front and the back, which are sewn together to create a double lining.

Pouch pockets

A pouch pocket can be made by making two vertical openings on either side of the front with one lining joining the two openings.

1 Work to the first pocket opening. Place the pocket stitches on a holder and leave at the front of the work. Cast onto the right needle the same number of stitches that you placed on the holder. Work to the end.

2 Work the desired pocket depth on all stitches. Place the stitches just worked on a holder. Work the stitches from the first holder to the same depth as the main piece, ending with a wrong-side row.

3 Join the pocket stitches to the lining by working one stitch from the pocket with one stitch from the lining. When the entire piece is complete, sew the lower edge of the lining to the front. Work an edging on either side of the pouch.

Cut-in pockets

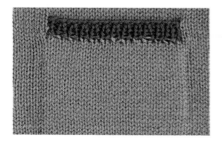

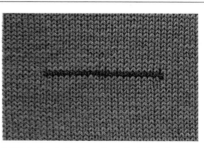

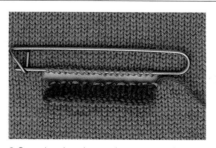

You can add a pocket by snipping one thread and pulling out the desired number of stitches. Make this easier by working the desired number of stitches in a contrasting yarn while you are knitting the piece.

1 Work the desired number of stitches in a contrasting yarn. Slip these stitches back to the left needle and knit them once more with the main color.

2 Once the piece is complete, remove the contrasting strand. Place the stitches on the upper edge on a holder. Apply a border to the stitches on the lower edge.

3 Work the lining down from the upper edge stitches as shown. Then sew down the lining stitches and attach the sides of the border to the front of the piece.

measurements **166**   pockets **214-19**

stitch holders **18-19**

Making a pocket lining

Linings are most often knit from the same yarn as the piece. Although it is called a lining, this piece is really a backing for the pocket.

You can make the lining with the exact number of stitches of the pocket or you can add a stitch to either side. Then work them together with the sweater piece or bind them off before you join the lining to the piece.

After you work the lining, block it, keep the stitches on a holder until you are ready to join it to the piece.

Stockinette stitch is the flattest stitch for a lining. When your body pattern is not stockinette, work a few rows of the stockinette lining in the same stitch as the body to keep continuity of pattern.

When you use a bulky yarn, you can make the lining with a lighter yarn or of fabric which is attached to a knit flap approximately 1½ to two inches (4 to 5cm) wide or deep. This keeps the lining from showing. When using lightweight yarn, use the heavier yarn for the last few rows that will show.

Double-strand garments should have a single-strand lining.

The lining should not go below the ribbing, as it may stretch and hang below the sweater edge. The lining should be tightly knit.

When attaching the lining, pin it first to make sure that it lies completely flat. Carefully slip stitch the lining in place, being sure that the stitching doesn't show through on the front of the piece.

Pocket edges/borders

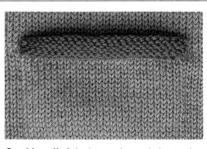

Outside rolled An interesting variation to the usual ribbed border is this stockinette stitch border that rolls to the outside of the pocket.

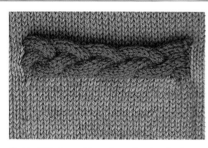

Cable This is another alternative to simple bands. This cable strip was made separately and then sewn onto the pocket.

Picot hem A stockinette stitch hem can be used to edge a pocket. The one shown above has a picot edge with a bobble pattern below the picot turning ridge.

Tips for making pocket edges

Pocket edges are often worked in the same stitch and with the same size needles as the sweater edges or ribbing.

Other than ribbing, good stitches for edges or borders are garter stitch, seed stitch or reverse stockinette stitch. Crocheted edges also make good pocket openings.

Take care to pick up the correct number of stitches. Too few stitches will cause the pocket to pull in and too many will cause it to gap.

The proper bind-off is essential. You can bind off stitches in ribbing or knitwise—depending on the border and how loose or tight you need the edge to be.

The edging pattern should be centered so that the first and last stitches match on either end.

Fasten corners of pockets securely, as these edges receive the most stress. Use a double strand of yarn to reinforce edges.

To eliminate further seaming as you work the border, attach the first and last stitches of the piece in the same way as you work a picked-up patch pocket.

Pleats and Tucks

Pleats and tucks look best in fine weight yarns, such as lightweight wool that retains its shape in stockinette or another flat stitch. However, knit pleats are not quite as sharp as fabric pleats. Pleats are most often used for skirts, but they can be used on sweaters to form special details or draping effects.

A mock pleat is simply a pattern stitch with a pleated effect. True pleats consist of three layers with the same number of stitches—the face, the fold-under and the underside. Each underside joins with the face of the next pleat. Slip stitches and purl stitches are used to define the folded areas. Knife, box, inverted and accordian pleats are all forms of true pleats and are made in somewhat the same manner. To find the number of stitches to cast on for a true pleated garment, multiply the stitches for one pleat (face, fold-under, underside plus a slip stitch and a purl stitch) by the number of inches in the piece.

You can sew true pleats together at the top or bind them off, working three folds of fabric into one bind-off to reduce the bulk at the top of the piece. You can pick up stitches for a waistband along this edge.

A horizontal pleat (really a tuck) is worked as you knit, much like a hem.

Horizontal tuck

One or more tucks can be used as decorative detail. They are best made in flat yarns in flat stitches such as stockinette. As with hems, several types of turning ridges can be used, such as purl or picot. The tucks can also be worked in contrasting colors.

1 The two tucks above are worked eight rows apart with 14 rows worked in the tuck, including one row for the turning ridge. Work to the placement of the first tuck, ending with a wrong-side row. Mark both sides of the last row. Work seven rows in stockinette stitch.

2 A purl turning ridge is made by knitting the stitches through the back loops of the eighth (wrong-side) row. After making the turning ridge, work six more rows.

3 With a smaller needle, working from right to left on the wrong side at the marked row, pick up one stitch for each stitch. With the needles together, work one stitch from each needle together across the next row.

Mock pleats

You can create a pleated effect simply with knit and purl stitches. To reduce the bulk of the fabric at the waistline, decrease two stitches on either side of the center purl stitch several times as you get closer to the waist.

Version A This pleat is made with a multiple of eight stitches. After casting on, work as follows: *Row 1 (right side):* *Knit seven, purl one; repeat from the * to end. *Row 2:* Knit four, *purl one, knit seven; repeat from the *, ending purl one, knit three.

Version B This pleat is made with a multiple of four stitches plus three extra. Work as follows: *Row 1 (right side):* Knit three, *slip one with yarn at front, knit three; repeat from the * to the end. *Row 2:* Knit one, *slip one with yarn at front, knit three; repeat from the *, end slip one, knit one.

True pleats

Pleats are based on a formula of the desired finished pleat width (when folded) multiplied by the stitch gauge and then multiplied by three (the three layers). To get the total number of stitches in each pleat, add a slip stitch and a purl stitch. Depending on which side you place the purl stitch, the pleats fold to the left or to the right.

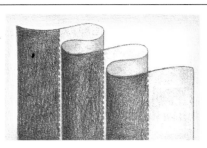

The illustration above shows a pleat that folds to the left. The face (blue), fold-under (dark grey) and underside (grey) are the same number of stitches. The underside of the last pleat joins with the face of the next pleat.

The face (right) of a left-folding pleat is edged with a slip stitch that is purled on wrong-side rows. The fold-under portion (center) joins the underside (left) with a purl stitch. For a right-folding pleat, reverse the slip stitches and purl stitches.

Knife and box pleats

Large knife This pleat folds to the left and is based on 21 stitches (seven for the face or outside of one pleat, seven for the fold-under and seven for the underside portion). Add one slip stitch and one purl stitch for each pleat.

Small knife This pleat, which folds to the right, has 15 stitches for the pleat.

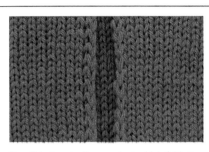

Box This is actually one pleat which folds to the left and a second facing pleat which folds to the right. Box pleats are frequently used for skirts and are less bulky than knife pleats.

Inverted This inverted pleat, sometimes used alone for a coat pleat, is decreased on the fold-under side and the underside to come to a point at the top. To plan this pleat, you must know its length and the number of decrease stitches.

Binding off a pleat

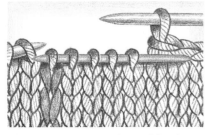

1 This method, which can be used for pleats folding right or left, is given for a left-folding pleat. Bind off until you reach the first pleat, leaving the last bound-off stitch on the right needle. **Slip the face stitches and the slip stitch purlwise to a double-pointed needle.

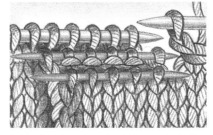

2 Slip the stitches for the fold-under, including the purl stitch, to another needle. Turn these stitches so that the wrong sides of the face and the fold-under are together. Handle the stitches carefully to keep them from slipping off the needles.

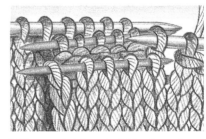

3 Slip one stitch from the fold-under to the right needle, knit the first stitch from the underside and pass the two stitches over it one at a time.

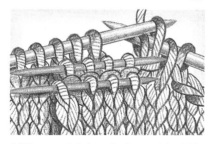

4 *Slip one stitch from the face and the fold-under to the right needle. Knit the first stitch from the underside and pass the three stitches over it one at a time. One stitch remains. Repeat from the * until the pleat is bound off. Repeat from the **.

measurements **166**
gauge **18-19, 57-59**

slip a stitch
purlwise/knitwise **46**

Gathers, Ruching and Flares

Gathers on knits are used to make ruffled areas on lower edges, collars, front edges, and on sleeve cuffs or caps. They can also be used to shape waistlines. They are worked by decreasing stitches at a certain point or by changing needle sizes. Gathers can eliminate fabric without creating a bulky area. The degree of gathering will vary depending on the number of stitches that are reduced or the difference in needle sizes. When decreasing many stitches, you may want to do it over more than one row.

To make a gather by decreasing, you will need to know the width of the piece before and at the gather. Multiply these widths by the stitch gauge to determine the number of stitches to decrease. Choose invisible decreases for this technique.

Gathering by changing needle size isn't quite as exact. To decide on the needle size to use, make a swatch with the needles and pattern you plan to use.

Ruching, similar to gathering, creates an intentional puckering of the fabric.

Flares also create an intentional fullness in knit fabrics, but unlike gathers, flares are worked over a longer area and are smoother. They are most often used to make A-line type skirts.

Gathers

Gathers can be worked within a piece such as for waist shaping. When a gather is worked close to the edge it can form a decorative ruffle. Gathers can also be used at the very edge of a piece to change the size of the finished edge.

Cuff The cuff above has been gathered both by changing needle size and by decreasing stitches.

Waist The gathered area is ribbed and worked on needles two sizes smaller than the needles used for the main body piece. It is worked over 1½ inches (4cm) to increase the gathering effect.

Sleeve cap To make a puffed sleeve, the sleeve cap is gathered on the last row or two to fit into the armhole. This sleeve cap was worked by knitting three stitches together across the row and binding off at the same time.

Ruching

This ruching pattern creates bands of gathering. It is done by changing the number of stitches and the needle size. The pattern, a 14-row repeat, is worked over any number of stitches.

Row 1 and all wrong-side rows: Purl. *Rows 2, 4, 6, 10 and 12:* Knit. *Row 8:* To double the stitches, knit into the front and back of each stitch. Change to one size smaller needles. *Row 14:* To return to the original number of stitches, knit two together across the row. Change back to the original needles.

Flares

A skirt made with flares is worked from the top down and has less fabric than a pleated skirt. Subtract the number of stitches at the waist from the number at the lower edge (using the stitch gauge to calculate the stitches) to find the number of stitches that must be increased.

Beginning at the upper edge, the flare begins with a knit four, purl two pattern. At the specified interval, increase one stitch on either side of the four knit stitches. As you work toward the lower edge, the knit sections will increase and the purl sections will remain constant.

Finishing Touches

The most important part of finishing is all the little details that don't show when the sweater is worn. Careful attention to these details can improve the look and fit of your knit garments.

Remember that knit fabric is not stable and must be treated somewhat differently than woven fabric. To help stabilize your knits, you can add seam binding to shoulder seams, ribbon facings to the front of cardigans and linings to jackets and skirts.

To make the garment hang better, you can knit matching shoulder pads. As with woven pieces, you can add zippers to skirts and jackets and elastic waistbands to skirts. You can make matching buttons or attach purchased buttons in special ways to prevent the fabric from stretching.

Your finishing materials and the yarn for your garment should be compatible in their cleaning. If not, dry clean, or attach any notions so that you can remove them easily before cleaning.

Ribbon facings

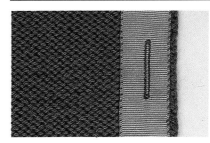

A ribbon facing is sewn in place and finished with machine-sewn buttonholes.

Ribbon facings, usually grosgrain ribbon, are generally sewn to the inside of the band, but decorative ribbon can also be used on the outside at the edges. On the button band, the ribbon helps support the button. On the buttonhole band, the ribbon adds stability to the buttonhole openings. You can knit in buttonholes and then cut matching openings in the ribbon and join the two edges with the buttonhole stitch. Or once the ribbon is in place, you can machine sew the buttonholes through the knitting and the ribbon and cut through both layers.

Wash and dry the ribbon before attaching to pre-shrink it. The ribbon should be applied to blocked pieces. Cut two pieces to fit along the front edges with a one-fourth inch (1cm) seam allowance on each end. Fold the seam allowance under and pin or baste the ribbon to the band. Pin the center and work out to either side to make an even edge. With a matching sewing thread, sew the band in place, easing in the knitting. Work the buttonhole band first. After machine- or hand-sewing the buttonholes, check the length with the button-band side. Making buttonholes can shorten the buttonhole side slightly.

Taping a seam

A narrow twill tape or seam binding can be used along seams to prevent them from stretching. This can be done after seaming and is especially good for areas such as shoulders that may need to be stabilized. The tape can also be used to ease in a shoulder that is too wide.

Cut a piece of tape the length of the desired shoulder width and whip stitch the tape on either side along the shoulder seam, easing in the fullness as desired.

Shoulder Pads

Lightweight

The number of strands of yarn you use and the size of the knitting needle will change the finished size of the shoulder pad. Cast on three stitches. Work in garter stitch, increasing one stitch at each end of the next row (mark for right side of pad) and on every right-side row until there are 21 stitches, end with a right-side row. Mark the center stitch. *Decrease row (wrong side):* Knit to one stitch before the center stitch, slip this stitch and the center stitch together knitwise, knit one, pass the two slip stitches over the knit stitch, knit to end. Continue to increase at each end of every other row until there are 25 stitches. Repeat the decrease row—23 stitches. Increase each end of every other row until there are 29 stitches. Repeat the decrease row—27 stitches. Bind off all stitches loosely on the next row and, at the same time, increase one stitch at each end, binding off after the increase is made. You can also make larger pads by stitching two smaller ones together and stuffing the center with extra yarn or fiberfill.

Medium weight

The number of strands of yarn you use and the size of the knitting needle will change the finished size of the shoulder pad. Cast on three stitches. Working in garter stitch, increase one stitch at each end of every other row seven times—17 stitches. Work five rows even. Knit, decreasing one stitch at each end of the row, then every other row until seven stitches remain. Bind off. Fold the seven-stitch piece to the inside where the decreases began and tack the bound-off edge to the inside of the pad.

Heavyweight

The number of strands of yarn you use (you must have at least three) and the size of the knitting needle will change the finished size of the shoulder pad. Cast on five stitches. *Rows 1, 3, 5 and 7 (wrong side):* Purl. *Row 2:* Knit two, knit into each of three strands in next stitch (called inc-3), knit two — seven stitches. *Row 4:* [Knit one, inc-3] three times, knit one—13 stitches. *Row 6:* Knit two, [inc-3, knit three] twice, inc-3, knit two—19 stitches. *Row 8:* Knit four, add another strand of yarn, knit 11, drop extra strand, knit four. *Row 9:* Purl four, pick up added strand, knit 11, drop strand, purl four. Repeat the last two rows until the pad measures five inches (12cm), ending with a right-side row. Bind off five stitches at the beginning of the next two rows—nine stitches. Work even with the original number of strands in garter stitch for 1½ inches (4cm). Fold the nine-stitch piece to the inside where the decreases began and tack bound-off edge to the inside of the the pad.

Using Elastic

Elastic waistbands are often used for knit skirts. The width of the elastic depends on the type of yarn and skirt you are making. In general, the most comfortable elastic for waistbands is at least one inch (2.5cm) wide. Some elastic made especially for waistbands is thicker and stronger than regular elastic. Cut the elastic to fit the waist plus an inch (2.5cm) for overlapping.

For a hem casing, the raw edges of the elastic should be overlapped and sewn together after the elastic is inserted into the casing. For the herringbone method, overlap and sew the elastic edges before working the herringbone stitching.

The simplest waistband is a hem casing worked in a flat stitch with a turning ridge. When sewn, the casing must be deep enough to allow the elastic to move easily. Sew the casing with a slip stitch, leaving two inches (5cm) open to insert the elastic. Attach a safety pin to one end of the elastic

and draw it through the casing, taking care not to twist it. You might wish to pin the other end of the elastic to the piece so it doesn't get drawn into the casing. Join the elastic and finish sewing the hem.

An alternate casing method is to use a long crochet chain and slip stitch it in a zig-zag over the elastic. This is slightly bulkier than the herringbone method, but less bulky than the hem casing method.

Herringbone method

The herringbone method makes a single thickness which adds no bulk to the waist. When you are finished, the elastic should move freely and not be caught in the stitching. Use a strong thread that won't fray as the elastic moves.

The first step is to place four pins an equal distance apart around the joined elastic. Then place four pins an equal distance apart around the skirt. Pin the elastic to the waist of the skirt, matching the pins and stretching the elastic to fit.

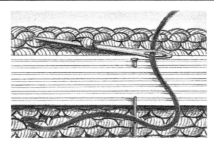

1 Use strong thread and a yarn needle. Working from left to right, secure the thread below the elastic. Insert the needle through one loop of the stitch which is three stitches to the right above the elastic.

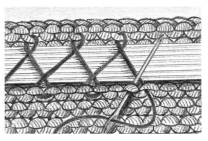

2 Insert the needle down into the loop of a stitch which is three stitches to the right and below the elastic, and then up into the loop of the next stitch to the left, as shown.

Adding elastic to ribbing

When working with a non-resilient yarn such as cotton, you can knit in a matching elastic thread. But you can also add or replace elastic on completed knit pieces. Working from the wrong side of the ribbing, thread the elastic through the back of each knit

stitch as shown and pull slightly to draw it in. Attach each elastic row to the side seams, keeping the same tension on all rows of elastic.

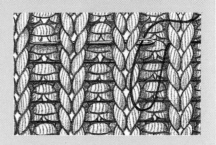

Adding Waistband Elastic

This method of adding elastic with a crochet hook produces an even, flat waistband. Use round cord elastic that is about four times your waist size and a crochet hook that is one size smaller than the knitting needle you used to make the skirt. Make a loop on one end of the elastic by folding back one inch (2.5cm) and wrapping it with sewing thread. Beginning at the tip of the loop, mark the elastic in four equal segments with a pencil, but do not cut the elastic.

In this method, you work single crochet over and under the elastic. Work loosely so that the hook will go under the chains on the following rounds.

When you have about two inches (5cm) left on the last round, try on the skirt and adjust the elastic. Mark the elastic at the point where you want it to end, and fold it over to make a loop. Wrap the loop with thread. Continue as before, working the last few stitches through the elastic loop. Work three or four stitches beyond the elastic, fasten off and weave in the yarn.

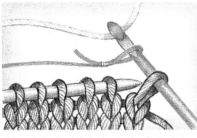

1 Insert the hook knitwise in the first stitch on the needle and slip the stitch off. Insert the hook through the elastic loop and under the yarn.

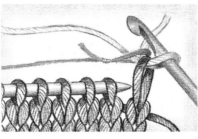

2 Pull the yarn through both the elastic loop and the stitch.

3 Insert the hook knitwise in the next stitch on the needle and through the elastic loop to catch the yarn.

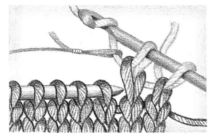

4 Pull the yarn through as before. (This leaves two loops on the hook.) With the hook over the elastic loop, catch the yarn.

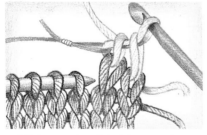

5 Pull the yarn through both loops on the hook, leaving one loop. The finished edge looks like a bound-off edge, but it encases the elastic cord. Repeat steps 3, 4 and 5 until the elastic loop contains as many stitches as it can hold (about two to four).

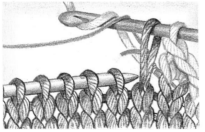

6 Insert the hook in the next stitch on the needle and under the elastic to catch the yarn. Pull the yarn through the stitch. (This leaves two loops on the hook.)

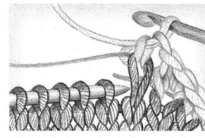

7 Put the hook over the elastic to catch the yarn. Pull the yarn through both loops to form a chain. Repeat steps 6 and 7 until you have worked all the stitches on the needle. Adjust the elastic until the first pencil mark is above the loop.

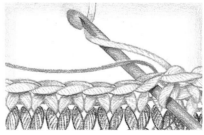

8 Continue another round of steps 6 and 7, but in step 6, insert the hook knitwise under both loops of the chain and under the elastic to catch the yarn as shown above.

measurements **166**   crochet   crochet **210-11**

crochet chain **210**   hooks and sizes **18**

Buttons

Buttons can add a striking contrast to your garment or they can blend in subtly with the knit fabric. You can also make perfectly matching crochet buttons, which are shown below.

The button should be appropriate to the yarn. For example, leather or stone buttons work best on tweedy, rugged yarns for outdoor garments, and fancy glass buttons are best suited to tailored or dressy styles.

Take along a yarn sample when you buy buttons to find a good match. If possible, purchase an extra button or two to replace any you may lose.

Match the size of your button carefully to the size of your buttonhole so that the button will fit properly.

Buttons that cannot be washed should always be removed before cleaning. When you purchase buttons, look for any special care instructions on the package.

Crochet button with ring

This type of button is made with a small plastic ring about one-half inch (1.5cm) wide. Leaving a six inch (15cm) tail, make a slip knot and work single crochets tightly around the ring. Join the last single crochet to the first. Cut the yarn, leaving an eight inch (20cm) strand and pull through the last loop. Thread the eight inch (20cm) strand through a yarn needle and pick up the outside loop from every other single crochet. Gather them together and pull the strand to the back. Tie this strand tightly to the other one and use it to sew on the button.

Stuffed crochet button

Make a slip knot and chain three. Slip stitch into the first chain to join. Work two single crochets in the three chains. Continue to increase until there are 12 single crochets. To decrease on the next round, work two single crochets together six times. Cut the yarn, leaving an eight inch (20cm) strand. Stuff the button with matching yarn. Work the second step as for the crochet button with ring.

Sewing on buttons

To sew on buttons, you can use yarn (if it goes through the button), matching thread or pearl cotton. When sewing on metal buttons, which tend to cut the thread, you may wish to use waxed dental floss. Double the thread and tie a knot on the end. Then slip your button onto the needle and thread. You can further secure the button, which is especially desirable on garments that receive heavy wear, such as jackets. After going

into the button and the fabric several times, wrap the thread around the button a few times and go back to the wrong side.

Add a small button or square of knitting or felt on the wrong side to keep the button in place.

Knotted thread has a tendency to pull through knit fabric. Lock it in place, by inserting thread into fabric on the right side and through the doubled thread. Clip knotted end.

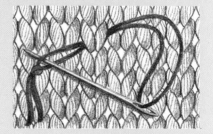

---

measurements **166**   yarn label symbols **12**

care **113-116**   crochet **210-11**

Zippers

Several types of zippers can be added to knit garments. Heavier zippers that separate are used for jackets and cardigans. Regular dressmaking zippers are used for skirt waists or on the back of close-fitting necks.

Zippers should be sewn in by hand rather than by machine. The opening should be the same length as the zipper so that the seam doesn't stretch or pucker.

To prepare the edges of a garment for the zipper, work a selvage such as the two-stitch garter selvage. If the edge is not smooth enough, a crocheted slip stitch edge will be helpful.

Place the zipper in a stitch or two from the edge to prevent the teeth from showing, and sew it down with a backstitch.

Adding a zipper

Whip stitch the zipper in place on the wrong side, then backstitch it on the right side close to the edge of the knit fabric.

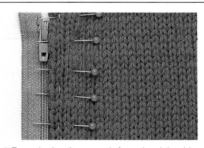

1 To apply the zipper, work from the right side of the piece or pieces with the zipper closed. Pin the zipper in place so that the edges of the knit fabric will cover the teeth of the zipper and meet in the center.

2 After pinning, baste the zipper and remove the pins. Turn the zipper to the wrong side and whip stitch in place. Turn the zipper to the right side, and backstitch in place.

| measurements **166** | selvages **194-95** | backstitch **101** |
| seaming **98-101** | crochet edges **210-11** | whip stitch **111** |

Linings

Lining knit garments is a matter of personal preference, although linings are desirable for tailored garments. Linings provide stability and shape, keep the yarn from directly touching the skin, and add body to sheer knits. Linings used with knit fabrics should be much less structured than linings for woven fabrics. Even the most structured knit blazer does not have the heavy interfacing and lining that a similar woven blazer would have.

When deciding whether to line a knit garment, remember that once it is lined, it should be dry cleaned or washed with the lining removed. Also keep in mind that lining material generally does not stretch and will restrict the stretchy quality of the knit. You can create some stretch in the lining, however, by cutting the fabric on the bias.

The lining material will depend on the garment. It can be in a matching color or, if you desire, a contrasting color or pattern. It should be a nonstretchy material.

You can use blocked knit pieces to make a pattern for the lining fabric with about a five-eighths inch (1.5cm) seam allowance. Since lining fabric can be slippery, it might be easier to make a pattern by tracing the knit piece onto brown paper or interfacing. Cut out the lining pieces and seam them before attaching the lining to the seamed knit garment. You are in effect almost making a duplicate of the knit piece in lining fabric.

Coat and jacket linings

Lining coats and jackets helps to keep them in shape, makes them easier to slip on and off and warmer to wear. You can use medium to heavyweight lining materials for coats and jackets.

The lining for a coat or jacket should have a two-inch (5cm) pleat in the center back for ease in wearing. The pleat should be folded at the neck edge and allowed to flair open at the lower edge. You can tack it down in one or two places several inches from the neck edge.

After basting the lining together, turn the coat or jacket inside out and slip the wrong side of the lining over the jacket. Adjust and baste the lining in place. Turn the garment right side out

and try it on. If you are satisfied with the results, sew the lining and then stitch it in place.

You can sew the lining onto the shoulder seams and slip stitch it around the neck and front edges. Turn the seam allowance under on these edges and attach them so that they will not show on the outside. The lower edge should be hemmed at least one inch (2.5cm) shorter than the finished knit piece and left to hang free. Shoulder pads can be added before you join the lining.

When lining a coat or jacket, add a folded center pleat plus seam allowance. The seam allowance is shown with a broken line.

When making a coat lining, you can add a back pleat by folding the back knit piece in half and placing it onto the folded lining piece one inch (2.5cm) from the lining fold line. When you unfold the lining, you will have added the additional two inches (5cm) for the pleat.

Linings on jackets, coats and skirts should be hemmed and allowed to hang free inside the garment. When the pieces are cut, leave a seam allowance at the lower edge to make the hem. The hemmed edge should be shorter than the finished knit garment to prevent it from showing.

Skirt lining

Skirts are generally lined to keep them in shape and to prevent them from sagging when worn. Lightweight taffetas and silks make the best linings for skirts.

Skirt linings should be large enough to allow you to put the skirt on, but fitted enough to avoid extra bulk under the knit fabric.

If the skirt has an elastic waistband, apply the lining so that it will not be too tight when you pull it on.

Cut the lining material with the same ease as the skirt, adding a seam allowance. Once the pieces are seamed, attach the lining to the skirt.

Since the hip measurement is larger than the waist, the lining needs to draw in at the waist without restricting movement. For a skirt with an elastic waist, attach the lining to the top edge before you make the casing, so that it becomes part of the casing. For a fitted skirt with a side zipper, add darts on the front and back lining sections to create a better fit. An alternative way to keep the waist area flexible is to attach a half slip to the waistband, using the elastic in the slip as the waistband elastic for the skirt, or inserting the elastic into a casing.

Instead of sewing the side seams of the skirt to the lower edge, measure side slits and finish them by whip stitching the raw edges.

Hem the lower edge last. Pin the hem and try on the skirt to make sure that the lining doesn't hang below the lower edge of the skirt.

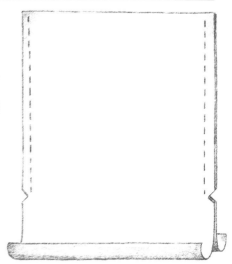

The skirt lining is shown with side slits. The lower edge shows the portion of the lining that is folded up to become the hem. The seam allowance is shown with a broken line.

XII. Embellishments

Embroidery

Embroidery is used to add another dimension to your work once the knitting and blocking is complete. Embroidery is most effective on simple stitch patterns—stockinette stitch is the best.

Many types of yarn can be used for embroidery, but you should select one that is smooth enough to go through the knitted fabric. Make sure that the weight and content of the yarn is appropriate for the knit piece. Yarns that are too thin will sink into the fabric, and a too-thick yarn will stretch out the piece. The embroidery yarn should have the same care properties as the yarn used for your sweater and should be colorfast.

Complex patterns can be drawn on lightweight non-fusible interfacing and basted in place. Embroider over the interfacing and through the knit fabric. Cut away the interfacing once the pieces are complete. If the knitted fabric is lightweight, back the embroidery with a non-fusible interfacing on the wrong side of the work.

Work evenly and not too tightly, using a blunt needle with an eye large enough to accommodate the yarn but not so large that it will split the stitches. Thread the yarn by folding it around the needle and inserting the folded end into the eye. It is best not to make a knot at the end of your yarn, but to weave it through to the place where you will begin your embroidery.

Back stitch is used for outlining and lines. Draw the needle up. In one motion, insert the needle a little behind where the yarn emerged and draw it up the same distance in front. Continue from right to left, by inserting the needle where the yarn first emerged.

Stem stitch is used for stems or outlining. Bring the needle up, then insert it a short distance to the right at an angle and pull it through. For stems, keep the thread below the needle. For outlines, keep the thread above the needle.

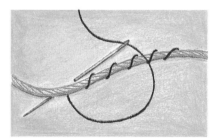

Couching is used to catch yarn laid on top of a knit piece. Place the yarn as desired, leaving a short strand at either end. Make stitches over the yarn as shown. To finish, thread the short strands and pull them through to the underside of the piece.

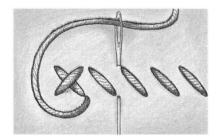

Cross stitch is a filling stitch. Pull the yarn through and make a diagonal stitch to the upper left corner. Working from right to left, make a parallel row of half cross stitches. Work back across the first set of diagonal stitches in the opposite direction, as shown.

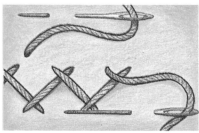

Herringbone stitch is used to hem, to fasten down facings or as a filling stitch. Working from left to right, bring the needle up, then across diagonally and take a short stitch. Go down diagonally and take a short stitch.

Blanket or buttonhole stitch can be used to apply pieces such as pockets, to reinforce buttonholes or for hemming. Bring the needle up. Keeping the needle above the yarn, insert it and bring it up again a short distance to the right, as shown. Pull the needle through to finish the stitch.

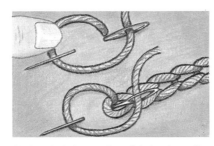

Chain stitch forms a line of chains for outlining or filling. Draw the needle up and *insert it back where it just came out, taking a short stitch. With the needle above the yarn, hold the yarn with your thumb and draw it through. Repeat from the *.

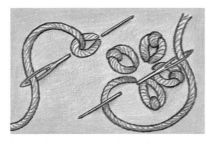

Lazy daisy stitch is used to make flowers. Work a chain stitch, but instead of going back into the stitch, insert the needle below and then above the stitch in one motion, as shown. Pull the needle through. Form new petals in the same way.

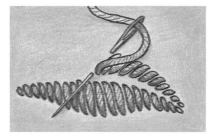

Satin stitch is ideal as a filling stitch. Be careful not to pull the stitches too tightly to avoid puckering. Bring the needle up at one side and insert it at an angle, covering the desired space in one motion. Repeat this step.

French knots can be used for flower centers, or they can be worked in a bulky yarn to form rosettes. Bring the needle up, wrap the thread once or twice around it, holding the thread taut. Reinsert the needle at the closest point to where the thread emerged.

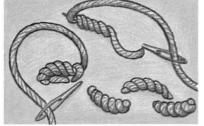

Bullion stitch is similar to French knots. Bring the needle up. Reinsert it as shown and wrap the yarn four to six times around it. Holding the yarn taut, pull the needle through. Reinsert the needle a short distance from where it emerged and pull it through.

Duplicate stitch covers a knit stitch. Bring the needle up below the stitch to be worked. Insert the needle under both loops one row above and pull it through. Insert it back into the stitch below and through the center of the next stitch in one motion, as shown.

Smocking

Smocking or the honeycomb stitch uses a ratio of three or four reverse stockinette stitches to one knit stitch, depending on the weight of yarn used. The fabric reduces approximately one-third when the smocking is complete. Run a contrasting yarn under the knit stitches to be smocked.

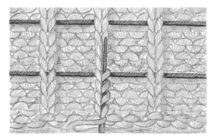

1 Beginning with the second knit rib at the lower right edge, bring the needle up the right side of that rib to the fourth stitch.

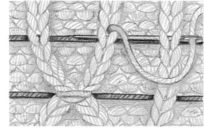

2 *Insert the needle from right to left into the fourth stitch (shown here after a few stitches have been smocked) of the first and second ribs. Bring the needle through and pull to join the ribs; repeat from the * once to complete a smocking stitch.

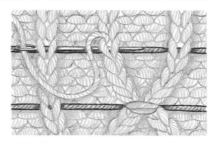

3 Bring the needle up the next four stitches on the left side of the second knit rib and work the smocking stitch, joining the second and third ribs by inserting the needle from left to right. Repeat steps 2 and 3 to the top of the piece.

Knitting with Beads

Knitting with beads is an age-old art that you can do in two ways. The first and easiest method, "beaded knitting," has beads spaced at planned or random intervals. The beads are added by threading them directly onto the working yarn. These beads usually fall over the stitches rather than between them. Beaded knitting is worked most often with one type or color of bead, but with advance planning as you thread, you can work out a sequence with several types or colors of beads. The techniques on the following page are for beaded knitting.

The second method, a traditional one first developed in the 18th and 19th centuries, was used for purses and other elaborately decorated items. It is called "bead knitting" (sometimes known as purse knitting). This method, also worked by threading the beads onto the working yarn, is done by placing one bead between each stitch, so

that the knitting stitches are completely hidden by beads. You can work intricate patterns in bead knitting by threading beads in reverse of the design (which must be completely accurate) and then working the beads into the knitting.

Most beads are made from glass, wood, plastic, clay and papier-mâché, but they can also be made from pearls, gems, buttons and some stones. Match your beads to the yarn by using luxurious beads on silks and other shiny yarns for evening wear and rougher beads and stones on tweeds and wools for day wear. When considering whether your beads and yarn are an appropriate match, just remember that beads will add weight to your sweater. Heavy yarns with vast numbers of beads will not be comfortable to wear and are likely to stretch out. Fragile yarns should be beaded with care, because some are not strong enough to withstand the beading process without fraying or becoming worn. If your yarn is too thick to thread and bead, you

can sew beads onto the finished pieces. When choosing suitable yarns and beads, make sure you can wash the beads if you are using a washable yarn. If you plan to dry clean the sweater, make sure the beads can be dry cleaned too.

Work stitches firmly on either side of the beads to keep them in place and from falling to the back of the work. To avoid edges that curl or that are difficult to seam, don't work beads close to the edge of your pieces.

You can be creative when you add beads to stitch patterns. Add beads in pattern indentations, at the sides or centers of cables or in the openings created by eyelet stitches.

Threading beads

For either beading method, thread beads onto balls of yarn before you knit. The threading needle must be large enough to accommodate the yarn, but small enough to go through the beads. Since this combination is not always possible, you can use an auxiliary thread to thread the beads. Using a sturdy thread, loop it through a folded piece of yarn and then pull both ends of the thread through the eye of the needle. Pass the bead over

the needle and thread it onto the yarn. (It may help to pass a bead back and forth over the folded yarn a few times to crease it.)

Beads are available pre-strung or loose. Individual beads take longer to thread. To thread pre-strung beads, carefully open the strand and insert the needle into the beads through the strand. Store threaded beads in a plastic bag or jar to keep them from tangling as you knit.

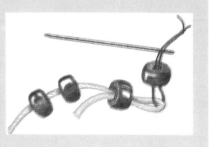

Stockinette stitch

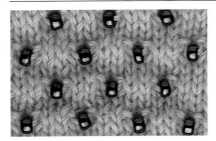

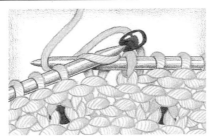

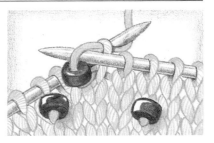

You can add beads in stockinette stitch on wrong-side rows by making a knit stitch (a purl on the right side of the work) on either side of the bead to help anchor it.

From the wrong side On a purl (wrong-side) row, work to one stitch before the point you wish to place a bead. Knit this stitch. With the yarn still at back of the work, slip the bead up to the work and knit the next stitch.

On right-side rows, beads are placed without the purl stitches on either side. The bead will lie directly in front of the stitch. Work the stitch firmly so that the bead won't fall to the back of the work.

From the right side Work to the stitch you wish to bead, then slip the bead up in back of the work. Insert the needle as if to knit and wrap the yarn around it. Push the bead to the front through the stitch on the left needle and complete the stitch.

Garter and reverse stockinette stitch

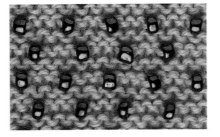

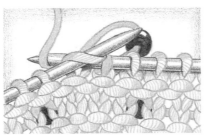

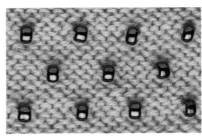

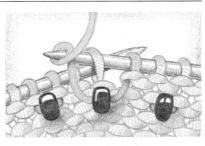

Add beads to garter stitch by working the wrong-side rows, so that the beads fall to the right side of the work. Work right-side rows with no beads.

Garter stitch With the yarn at the back, slip a bead close to the work, and then knit the next stitch from the left needle. The bead will sit between the two stitches.

Beads can be added in reverse stockinette stitch on right-side (purl) rows.

Reverse stockinette stitch Work to the stitch where the bead will be placed, insert the needle into the next stitch as if to purl. Push the bead up to the front of the work and purl the stitch.

Slip stitch

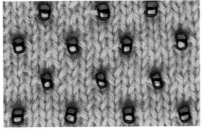

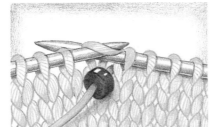

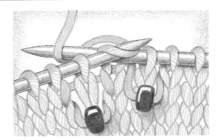

Adding beads with a slip stitch is done on stockinette stitch from the right side of the work. The bead falls directly in front of the slip stitch.

1 Work to where the bead is to be placed. Bring the yarn and the bead to the front of the work and slip the next stitch knitwise.

2 Bring the yarn to the back, keeping the bead to the front, and knit the next stitch firmly.

Knitting with Sequins

Adding sequins is a glamourous way to embellish simple sweaters. Sequins come in various shapes, colors and sizes and can be added all over to make a sequined fabric, placed at planned intervals or set into specific motifs in certain areas. They can be added to stockinette stitch, garter stitch and a variety of other stitch patterns. Sequins are a bit more difficult to work with than beads, because they are usually larger, more awkwardly shaped and sometimes difficult to separate. As with beads, always work sequins a stitch or two in from the edges for easier seaming. Accuracy is important when you work with sequins, because they are difficult to rip out once knit.

Sequins come with holes at the top or in the center. The hole placement determines how the sequin will lie, which will affect the finished look of your sweater.

Special care may be needed for sequined garments. Some sequins can be hand washed but not dry cleaned. Sequins shouldn't be steamed or pressed. It's also a good idea to check them for colorfastness.

Thread sequins onto a ball of yarn before you begin, using an auxiliary thread. String shaped sequins onto the yarn with the cup side facing the ball, so that the cup, which has more facets, will face out once it is knit. Add enough sequins to knit a full ball of yarn.

Stockinette stitch

A purl stitch worked on one side of a sequin on stockinette stitch helps the sequin to lie flat. This is done on the right side (knit rows).

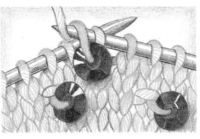

From the right side with a purl stitch Knit to the stitch where the sequin will be placed. Bring the yarn to the front and slide the sequin to the work. Purl the stitch.

Adding sequins without a purl stitch on stockinette is more time consuming, but may be desirable for certain garments where the sequins must be anchored.

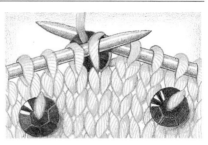

Without a purl stitch Work to where the sequin will be placed and insert the right needle into the back loop of the next stitch. Push the sequin close to the back of the work and then through the stitch with your finger while you finish the stitch.

Garter and reverse stockinette stitch

When you work sequins into garter stitch on wrong-side rows, the sequin will fall between the two stitches on the right side of the work.

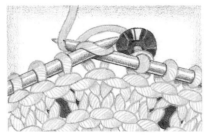

Garter stitch On the wrong-side row, work to where the sequin is to be placed and, with the yarn at the back, slip the sequin close to the work. Knit the next stitch, leaving the sequin between the two stitches.

Sequins can be worked on purl rows (the right side of reverse stockinette stitch).

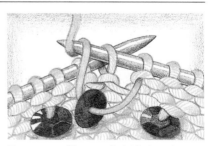

Reverse stockinette stitch Work to the placement of the sequin. Twist the next stitch on the needle by slipping it through the back loop and placing it back on the left needle. Push the sequin close to the work. Purl the twisted stitch, pushing the sequin through the stitch.

Additions

Your sweater can be a base for adding a wide variety of creative extras. You can apply pieces of knit fabric, leather or felt. You can also add ribbon, petals, purchased appliqués, cords, pompoms, tassels, beads, stones or knit bobbles. Look in craft or millinery supply stores to find creative additions or make your own from the instructions that follow.

Additions such as ribbon, leather strips and cords can be woven or laced into eyelets, lace stitches, loosely knit areas or dropped-stitch spaces. You can create a plaid effect by weaving in strands of contrasting yarn.

Apply additions securely. They should not bind, pull or pucker the knit fabric. If you plan to appliqué large areas, make sure that they will still have the

same flexibility as the rest of the piece. Baste trims or additions to the sweater to check their placement before you attach them. Additions that need to be cleaned differently than your garment should be detachable.

Cords

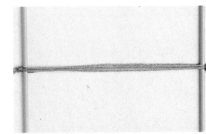

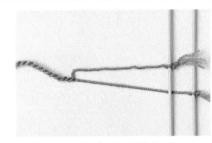

Twisted cord is made by twisting strands of yarn together. The thickness of the cord will depend on the number and weight of the strands. Cut strands three times the desired finished length and knot them about one inch (2.5cm) from each end.

1 If you have someone to help you, insert a pencil or knitting needle through each end of the strands. If not, place one end over a doorknob and put a pencil through the other end. Turn the strands clockwise until they are tightly twisted.

2 Keeping the strands taut, fold the piece in half. Remove the pencils and allow the cords to twist onto themselves.

I-cord is made on double-pointed needles. Cast on about three to five stitches. *Knit one row. Without turning the work, slip the stitches back to the beginning of the row. Pull the yarn tightly from the end of the row. Repeat from the * as desired. Bind off.

Spool knitting

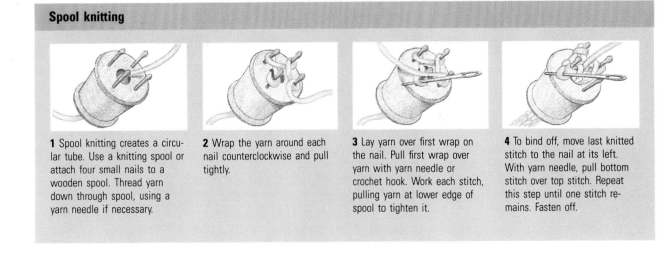

1 Spool knitting creates a circular tube. Use a knitting spool or attach four small nails to a wooden spool. Thread yarn down through spool, using a yarn needle if necessary.

2 Wrap the yarn around each nail counterclockwise and pull tightly.

3 Lay yarn over first wrap on the nail. Pull first wrap over yarn with yarn needle or crochet hook. Work each stitch, pulling yarn at lower edge of spool to tighten it.

4 To bind off, move last knitted stitch to the nail at its left. With yarn needle, pull bottom stitch over top stitch. Repeat this step until one stitch remains. Fasten off.

tools **16-20**
bobbles **62**

care **113-116**
yarn label symbols **12**

double-pointed
needles **16-17, 78**

knitting spool **19-20**

Fringe

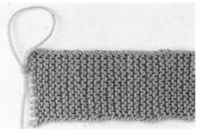

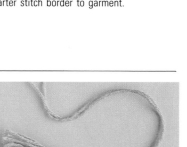

Simple fringe Cut yarn twice desired length plus extra for knotting. On wrong side, insert hook from front to back through piece and over folded yarn. Pull yarn through. Draw ends through and tighten. Trim yarn.

Knotted fringe After working a simple fringe (it should be longer to account for extra knotting), take one half of the strands from each fringe and knot them with half the strands from the neighboring fringe.

Knitted fringe This applied fringe is worked side to side. Cast on stitches to approximately one-fifth the desired length of fringe. Work garter stitch to desired width of fringe band. Bind off four to five stitches.

Unravel remaining stitches to create fringe, which may be left looped or cut. Apply fringe at garter stitch border to garment.

Tassels

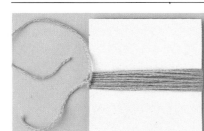

Tassel with shank Wrap yarn around a piece of cardboard that is the desired length of the tassel. Thread a strand of yarn, insert it through the cardboard and tie it at the top, leaving a long end to wrap around the tassel.

Cut the lower edge to free the wrapped strands. Wrap the long end of the yarn around the upper edge and insert the yarn into the top, as shown. Trim the strands.

Tassel without shank Wrap yarn around cardboard the length of the tassel, leaving a 12 inch (30cm) strand loose at either end. With a yarn needle, knot both sides to the first loop and run the loose strand under the wrapped strands. Pull tightly and tie at top.

Cut the lower edge of the tassel and, holding the tassel about three-fourths inch (2cm) from the top, wind the top strands (one clockwise and one counterclockwise) around the tassel. Thread the two strands and insert them through to the top of the tassel.

Pompom

You can use pompoms as a decorative trim, at the ends of cords, on hats or hoods and for children's garments. They are easy to make.

1 With two circular pieces of cardboard the width of the desired pompom, cut a center hole. Then cut a pie-shaped wedge out of the circle.

2 Hold the two circles together and wrap the yarn tightly around the cardboard. Carefully cut around the cardboard.

3 Tie a piece of yarn tightly between the two circles. Remove the cardboard and trim the pompom.

XIII. Modular Knitting Patterns

This modular system of sweater patterns for children, women and men offers a wide variety of design possibilities through different combinations of body, sleeve and neck-shaping.

Keep a few things in mind before starting to work with the modular system. First—read through all of the instructions for your chosen style. Make a copy of the instructions as they apply to your work. Fill in, in the spaces provided, all of the figures that apply to your size. This will give you a pattern that is clear and easy to follow. A ruler or straight edge may help you read across rows accurately.

Our model is wearing Women's size 36. Sizing is given for 15 sizes, from children's size 4 (23 inch chest) to men's size 48. The turtleneck with pleated sleeves (style 4) and the darted raglan (style 7) are sized for women and children only. All of the sweaters are designed with 2 inches of ease added to all chest/bust measurements for a standard fit. For a looser fit, you may want to go up one or two sizes. You may also adjust the length measurements, but be sure to adjust your yarn amounts correspondingly.

The system is designed in stockinette stitch, using medium or DK weight yarn, with a gauge of 22 stitches and 28 rows to 4 inches/10cm. If you want to substitute yarns or use a different stitch pattern it is important to match the gauge exactly or your overall measurements will be affected.

Ten examples of the modular system are shown on the following pages, but numerous variations can be based on the styles and calculations that are provided. Once familiar with the system, the experienced knitter may try interchanging certain elements (for example: the simple armhole shapings and sleeves of styles 5, 6 and 8, or the plain and pleated versions of the raglan sleeves in styles 3, 7 and 9). Be sure to work out the instructions on paper first, and make any necessary adjustments to the calculations.

The modular system is a challenging bridge between working established patterns and the beginnings of personal design.

1 Crewneck with set-in sleeves

2 Round neck with saddle shoulder

3 V-neck with raglan sleeves

6 Boatneck with drop shoulder

7 Shawl collar with darted raglan sleeves

7a detail

4 Turtleneck with set-in, pleated sleeves

4a detail

5 Polo with placket and angled armhole

8 Midi collar with square armhole

9 Crewneck cardigan with raglan sleeves

10 V-neck cardigan with set-in sleeves

Sizes (chest/bust)

		Children						Women						Men					
To fit	in.	23	25	27	29	30		30	32	34	36	38	40		38	40	42	44	46	48
or child's size	in.	4	6	8	10	12														

Finished Measurements

The foll measurements are the basic fit points for each size and style.
A few measurements will vary depending on the style, such as the upper arm for
square and angled armholes and the length for children's raglan styles.

		Children						Women						Men					
Finished chest/bust measurement at underarm	in.	25	27	29	31	32		32	34	36	38	40	42		40	42	44	46	48	50
Length	in.	15	16½	17½	19	20½		23½	24	24½	25	25½	26		26	26½	27	27½	28	28½
Sleeve width at upper arm (for shaped and angled armhole)	in.	11½	12	12½	13	13¼		13¾	14¼	14½	15	15½	16¼		16¾	17¼	17¾	18¼	18¾	19¼
Sleeve width at upper arm (for straight armhole)	in.	13	14	14	15	16		19	19	20	20	21	21		22	22	23	23	24	25

Materials

Medium or DK weight yarn:

		Children						Women						Men					
For styles #1 and #2	oz.	7	8¾	10½	10½	12¼		14	15¾	15¾	17½	17½	19¼		19¼	21	22¾	22¾	24½	24½
For styles #3,#6,#7,#8,#9,#10	oz.	8¾	10½	10½	12¼	14		17½	17½	19¼	19¼	21	21		21	22¾	24½	24½	26½	28
For styles #4,#5,#8	oz.	8¾	10½	12¼	12¼	14		17½	17½	19¼	21	22¾	22¾		22¾	24½	26¼	26¼	28	29¾

Knitting needles sizes 4 and 6 or size to obtain gauge.
Circular needle size 4: 24 in. for styles #7 and #9; 29 in. for style #10.

Buttons

	Children						Women						Men					
Style #5 (placket)	3	3	3	3	3		3	3	3	3	3	3		3	3	3	3	3	3
Style #9 (round-neck cardigan)	5	6	6	7	7		8	8	8	8	8	8		8	8	8	8	9	9
Style #10 (V-neck cardigan)	4	4	5	5	5		6	6	6	6	6	6		6	6	6	6	6	6

Gauge

22 sts and 28 rows = 4"/10 cm over St st using size 6 needles.
To save time, take time to check gauge.

Back (all styles)

		Children						Women						Men					
With smaller needles cast on	sts.	70	76	80	86	90		90	94	100	106	110	116		110	116	122	128	132	138

Work in k1, p1 rib for 2½". Change to larger needles. Work in St st (k on RS, p on WS)

		Children						Women						Men					
until piece measures, from beg	in.	8½	9½	10½	11½	12½		14	14½	14½	15	15	15½		15	15½	15½	16	16	16

abbreviations
explained **60-63**

knitting
terminology **64-68**

Armhole shaping

	Children					Women						Men					

Styles #1, #2 and #10 (shaped armhole)

	Children					Women						Men					
Bind off ___ sts	3	3	3	3	3	3	3	3	3	4	5	3	3	4	5	6	6
at beg of next 2 rows. Bind off ___ sts	0	0	0	0	2	0	0	0	2	2	2	0	0	2	2	2	3
at beg of next 2 rows. Dec 1 st each side every other row ___ times,	2	2	2	3	2	2	1	2	2	2	2	2	3	2	2	2	3
then every 4th row ___ times.	1	1	2	2	2	1	1	2	2	2	2	2	2	2	2	2	2

Styles #3, #7 and #9 (raglan)

Bind off ___ sts at beg of next 2 rows. *Raglan Dec Row 1* K2, k2tog, k to last 4 sts, ssk, k2. *Row 2* Purl. *Row 3* Knit. *Row 4* Purl. *Row 5* Rep raglan dec row 1. *Row 6* Purl. Rep last 6 rows ___ times more, then rep rows 1-4 ___ times, rep rows 5 and 6 ___ times.

	Children					Women						Men					
Bind off ___ sts	5	5	5	5	5	6	6	6	6	6	6	6	6	6	6	6	6
Rep last 6 rows ___ times	6	6	5	5	5	10	9	7	5	5	4	10	7	6	4	5	4
more, then rep rows 1-4 ___ times,	1	0	0	0	0	0	0	0	0	0	0	0	0	0	0	0	0
rep rows 5 and 6 ___ times.	0	4	7	9	11	0	3	10	16	18	21	5	14	18	24	23	28

Style #4 (shaped armhole for pleated sleeve)

Note: This armhole curves in deeper to accommodate the weight of a pleated sleeve which creates more volume at the shoulders. It is sized for women and children only.

	Children					Women						Men					
Bind off 3 sts at beg of next 2 rows, ___ sts	2	2	2	2	3	2	2	2	3	3	3						
at beg of next 2 rows, ___ sts	0	2	2	2	2	0	0	2	2	2	2						
at beg of next 2 rows, dec 1 st each side every other row ___ times,	2	1	1	2	2	2	2	1	2	2	3						

every 4th row once.

Style #5 (angled armhole)

	Children					Women						Men					
Dec 1 st each side every other row ___ times.	6	6	7	8	9	6	5	7	9	10	11	7	8	10	11	12	14

Style #6 (straight armhole)

Mark each end of last row for beg of armhole.

Style #8 (square armhole)

	Children					Women						Men					
Bind off at beg of next 2 rows ___ sts.	6	6	7	8	9	6	5	7	9	10	11	7	8	10	11	12	14

Neck and/or shoulder shaping

Styles #1, #8 and #10 (neck and shoulders)

	Children					Women						Men					
Work on ___ sts	58	64	66	70	72	78	84	86	88	90	94	96	100	102	106	108	110
until armhole measures ___ in.	6	6½	6½	7	7½	8½	8½	9	9	9½	9½	10	10	10½	10½	11	11½
Bind off from each armhole edge ___ sts	7	8	8	9	9	8	8	9	9	8	8	8	10	10	9	9	10
once and ___ sts	7	9	9	9	10	7	8	8	8	9	9	9	9	9	10	10	10
from each armhole edge ___ times,	1	1	1	1	1	2	2	2	2	2	2	2	2	2	2	2	2
AT SAME TIME, with first bind-off, bind off center ___ sts	10	10	12	10	10	10	12	12	14	14	18	20	20	22	24	26	26
for neck and working both sides at once, bind off from each neck edge ___ sts	5	5	5	6	6	6	6	6	6	6	6	6	6	6	6	6	6

twice.

	Children					Women						Men					

Style #2 (neck and saddle shoulders)

	Children					Women						Men					
Work even on ... sts	58	64	66	70	72	78	84	86	88	90	94	96	100	102	106	108	110
until armhole measures ... in.	4½	5	5	5½	6	7	7	7½	7½	8	8	8½	8½	9	9	9½	10

Shape shoulders and neck as for style #1.

Styles #3, #7 and #9 (straight neck)

	Children					Women						Men					
For back neck, bind off rem ... sts.	30	30	32	34	34	34	36	36	38	38	42	44	44	46	48	50	50

Style #4 (straight neck and shaped shoulders)

	Children					Women					
Work even on ... sts	54	58	62	66	68	74	78	82	84	88	92
until armhole measures ... in.	6	6½	6½	7	7½	8½	8½	9	9	9½	9½
Bind off from each armhole edge ... sts	6	7	7	8	8	6	7	7	7	9	9
once and ... sts	6	7	8	8	9	7	7	8	8	8	8
... times.	1	1	1	1	1	2	2	2	2	2	2
For back neck, bind off rem ... sts.	30	30	32	34	34	32	36	36	38	38	42

Style #5 (straight neck and shaped shoulders)

	Children					Women						Men					
Work even until armhole measures ... in.	6	6½	6½	7	7½	8½	8½	9	9	9½	9½	10	10	10½	10½	11	11½
Shape shoulders as for style #1. For back neck, bind off rem ... sts.	30	30	32	34	34	34	36	36	38	38	42	44	44	46	48	50	50

Style #6 (straight neck and shoulders)

	Children					Women						Men					
Work even until armhole measures ... in.,	4	4½	4½	5	5½	6½	6½	7	7	7½	7½	8	8	8½	8½	9	9½
end with a WS row. Change to smaller needles and k 1 row. Work ... in.	2½	2½	2½	2½	2½	3	3	3	3	3	3	3	3	3	3	3	3

in k1, p1 rib. Bind off loosely in rib.

Front(s)

Styles #1 and #2

	Children					Women						Men					
Work as for back until armhole measures ... in.	4½	5	5	5½	6	7	7	7½	7½	8	8	8½	8½	9	9	9½	10

Styles #3 and #7

	Children					Women						Men					
Work as for back, including raglan shaping, AT SAME TIME, when ... sts	70	64	68	72	74	72	76	80	86	88	94	84	90	96	102	102	106

rem, place marker at center of row, and beg V-neck shaping on next RS row.

Style #4

	Children					Women					
Work as for back until armhole measures ... in.	5	5½	5½	6	6½	7½	7½	8	8	8½	8½

Style #5

	Children					Women						Men					
Work as for back, including armhole shaping, until armhole measures ... in.	0	½	0	½	1	1	1	1½	1½	2	2	2½	2½	3	3	3½	4

Style #6

Work as for back.

Style #8

	Children					Women						Men					
Work as for back until armhole measures ... in.	½	1	1	1½	2	1½	1½	2	2	2½	2½	3	3	3½	3½	4	4½

Styles #9 and #10

	Children					Women						Men					
Left Front: With smaller needles, cast on ... sts.	36	38	40	44	46	46	48	50	54	56	58	56	58	62	64	66	70

	Children					Women						Men					
Work in k1, p1 rib for 2½". Change to larger needles and work in St st until piece measures _____ in. from beg, end with a WS row.	4	4	4	4	4	4½	4½	4½	4½	4½	4½	4½	4½	4½	4½	4½	4½
Pocket linings (make 2): With larger needles, cast on _____ sts.	20	20	22	22	22	25	25	25	25	25	25	25	25	25	25	25	25
Work in St st for _____ in.	4	4	4	4	4	4½	4½	4½	4½	4½	4½	4½	4½	4½	4½	4½	4½
Sl sts to a holder to work next row from WS.																	
Pocket opening: Next row (RS) Knit _____ sts,	6	8	8	12	14	9	11	13	17	19	21	17	19	21	23	25	29
bind off next _____ sts,	20	20	22	22	22	25	25	25	25	25	25	25	25	25	25	25	25

work to end. P next row, working across pocket sts to replace bound-off sts of previous row. Cont in St st until piece measures same as back to armhole.

Style #9
Work raglan shaping at armhole edge only (beg of RS rows) as for back until there are _____ sts on needle, end with a RS row.

	Children					Women						Men					
sts	20	21	23	25	25	23	25	25	27	27	28	29	29	31	31	32	33

Style #10
Work armhole shaping at underarm edge only (beg of RS rows) as for back until armhole measures _____ in.

	Children					Women						Men					
in.	1	1	1	1	1	2	2	2	2	2	2	2	2	2	2	2	2

Neck shaping

Style #1

	Children					Women						Men					
Bind off center _____ sts	8	8	10	12	12	8	10	10	12	12	16	12	12	14	16	18	18
and working both sides at once, bind off from each neck edge _____ sts	3	3	3	3	3	3	3	3	3	3	3	4	4	4	4	4	4
twice, _____ sts	3	3	3	3	3	2	2	2	2	2	2	2	2	2	2	2	2
_____ times,	1	1	1	1	1	2	2	2	2	2	2	3	3	3	3	3	3
and dec 1 st every other row _____ times,	2	2	2	2	2	3	3	3	3	3	3	2	2	2	2	2	2

AT SAME TIME, when same length as back to shoulder, shape shoulder same as back.

Style #2
Working shoulder shaping as for back, AT SAME TIME,

	Children					Women						Men					
bind off center _____ sts	16	16	16	18	18	18	20	20	22	22	22	26	26	28	28	30	30
and working both sides at once, bind off from each neck edge _____ sts	7	7	8	8	8	5	5	5	5	5	6	5	5	5	6	6	6
once and _____ sts once.	0	0	0	0	0	3	3	3	3	3	4	4	4	4	4	4	4

Styles #3 and #7
Cont to work raglan armhole shaping as for back, work to 4 sts before center marker, ssk, k2, join 2nd ball of yarn, k2, k2 tog, k to end. Working both sides at once, cont to dec 1 st at each neck edge every _____ row

	Children					Women						Men					
row	4th	4th	4th	0	0	4th	4th	4th	0	0	2nd	2nd	2nd	2nd	2nd	2nd	2nd
_____ times	4	4	1	0	0	6	5	5	0	0	4	8	8	10	15	18	18
more, then [every 2nd row once, every 4th row once] _____ times,	4	4	6	7	7	4	5	5	8	8	7	6	6	5	3	2	2
then every 2nd row _____ times.	1	1	1	1	1	1	1	1	1	1	1	0	0	1	1	1	1

When all shaping is complete, fasten off last st each side.

Style #4

	Children					Women					
Bind off center _____ sts	8	8	10	12	12	12	14	14	16	16	20
and working both sides at once, bind off from each neck edge 3 sts _____ times,	3	3	3	3	3	1	1	1	1	1	1
2 sts _____ times,	1	1	1	1	1	3	3	3	3	3	3

	Children					Women						Men					
1 st .... times,	0	0	0	0	0	2	2	2	2	2	2						

AT SAME TIME, when same length as back to shoulder, shape shoulder same as back.

Style #5

Placket shaping: Mark center 6 sts. Cont armhole shaping, if necessary, work to center 6 sts, join 2nd ball of yarn and bind off 6 sts for placket, work to end. Work both sides

	Children					Women						Men					
at once until placket opening measures .... in.	4½	4½	5	5	5	6	6	6	6	6	6	6	6	6	6	6	6
Neck shaping: Bind off from each neck edge ...... sts	3	3	4	4	4	3	3	3	3	3	4	4	4	4	5	5	5
.... times,	3	3	1	2	2	1	2	2	3	3	2	3	3	4	1	2	2
.... sts	0	0	3	3	3	2	2	2	2	2	3	3	3	0	4	4	4
.... times,	0	0	2	1	1	4	3	3	2	2	2	1	1	0	3	2	2
and dec 1 st every other row .... times,	3	3	3	3	3	3	3	3	3	3	4	4	4	4	4	4	4

AT SAME TIME, when same length as back to shoulder, shape shoulder same as back.

Style #8

	Children					Women						Men					
Row 1 (RS) Knit .... sts,	25	28	29	31	32	35	38	39	40	41	43	44	46	47	49	50	51

ssk, k2, join 2nd ball of yarn, k2, k2tog, k to end. Working both sides at once, cont to

	Children					Women						Men					
dec 1 st at each neck edge every .... row	2nd	2nd	2nd	2nd	2nd	4th	0	0	2nd	2nd	2nd	2nd	2nd	2nd	2nd	2nd	2nd
.... times	4	4	7	10	10	2	0	0	2	2	8	11	11	14	17	20	20
more, then [every 2nd row once, every 4th row once] .... times,	10	10	8	6	6	14	18	18	16	16	12	10	10	8	6	4	4

AT SAME TIME, when same length as back to shoulder, shape shoulder same as back.

Style #9

	Children					Women						Men					
Next row (WS) Bind off .... sts,	4	4	4	4	4	4	5	4	5	5	5	6	6	6	6	6	6
(neck edge), work to end. Cont raglan shaping, bind off .... sts	3	3	3	4	4	4	4	4	4	4	4	5	5	5	5	5	5
from neck edge once, then .... sts	3	3	3	3	3	3	3	3	3	3	3	3	3	4	4	4	4
.... times,	2	1	2	2	2	2	2	2	2	2	2	2	2	2	2	2	3
then 2 sts .... times,	0	1	0	1	1	1	1	1	2	2	3	3	2	2	2	3	1
and then 1 st .... times.	3	3	3	2	2	2	2	2	1	1	0	0	1	1	1	0	1

Right Front: Work to correspond to left front reversing shaping and pocket placement.

Style #10

Next row (RS) K to last 4 sts, ssk, k2. Cont armhole shaping, if necessary, and rep this

	Children					Women						Men					
row for neck dec every 2nd row .... times	13	6	9	11	9	5	8	1	7	3	6	8	5	9	9	8	7
more, then [every 2nd row once, every 4th row once] .... times,	1	4	3	3	4	6	5	8	6	8	7	7	8	7	7	8	9

AT SAME TIME, when same length as back to shoulder, shape shoulder same as back.
Right Front: Work to correspond to left front reversing shaping and pocket placement and working V-neck shaping at beg of RS rows as foll: k2, k2 tog, work to end.

Sleeves (all styles)

	Children					Women						Men					
With smaller needles, cast on .... sts.	36	36	38	40	40	42	44	44	46	46	46	48	50	50	52	52	54
Work in k1, p1 rib for .... in.	2½	2½	2½	2½	2½	3	3	3	3	3	3	3	3	3	3	3	3

Change to larger needles and cont in St st for chosen style as foll:

Styles #1, #2, #3, #4, #7, #9 and #10

	Children					Women						Men					
Inc 1 st each side of every .... row	2	0	0	6	6	6	6	6	6	6	6	6	6	6	6	6	6
.... times,	2	0	0	4	8	12	11	11	12	11	8	9	8	8	7	5	7

abbreviations explained **60-63**   knitting terminology **64-68**

	Children					Women						Men					
then every 4th row .... times.	12	15	16	12	9	5	7	8	7	9	14	13	15	16	18	21	19
Work even on .... sts	64	66	70	72	74	76	80	82	84	86	90	92	96	98	102	104	106
until piece measures, from beg .... in.	10½	11½	12½	13½	15	16¾	17	17½	17¾	18	18¼	18½	19	19½	20	20	20½

Style #5

	Children					Women						Men					
Inc 1 st each side of [every .... row	4th	0	4th	4th	4th	4th	4th	0	4th	0	4th	4th	4th	4th	4th	4th	4th
once, every .... row once]	6th	0	6th	6th	6th	6th	6th	0	6th	0	6th	2nd	6th	2nd	6th	2nd	2nd
.... times,	4	0	7	6	7	2	5	0	3	0	2	2	2	2	2	5	5
then every 4th row .... times.	7	18	3	7	7	22	15	28	21	29	25	27	26	29	28	25	26
Work even on .... sts	66	72	72	78	82	94	94	100	100	104	104	110	110	116	116	122	126
for .... in. more.	1	1	1¼	1½	1½	1	¾	1¼	1½	1¾	2	1¼	1½	1¾	2	2¼	2½

Style #6

	Children					Women						Men					
Inc 1 st each side [every 4th row once, every 2nd row once] .... times,	2	5	0	0	0	8	5	10	7	12	11	14	10	12	9	15	17
then every 4th row .... times.	14	11	20	22	24	15	20	13	18	11	13	9	16	14	19	10	8
Work even on .... sts	72	78	78	84	88	104	101	110	110	116	116	122	122	126	126	132	138
until piece measures .... in.	12¾	13¾	14¾	15¾	17¼	19	19¼	19¾	20	20¼	20½	20¾	21¼	21¾	22¼	22¼	22¾

from beg. Bind off.

Style #8

Work as for style #5. Bind off all sts.

Cap shaping

Styles #1 and #10

	Children					Women						Men					
Bind off .... sts	3	3	3	3	3	3	3	3	3	4	5	3	3	4	5	6	6
at beg of next 2 rows, dec 1 st each side every other row .... times,	2	5	3	6	9	1	0	0	0	4	4	4	2	7	7	11	15
bind off 2 sts at beg of next .... rows,	14	12	16	14	12	20	22	24	24	20	20	24	28	24	24	20	16
then bind off .... sts	2	2	2	2	2	3	4	3	4	4	4	4	4	3	4	4	4
at beg of next 2 rows. Bind off rem .... sts.	22	22	22	22	22	22	22	22	22	22	24	22	22	22	22	22	24

Style #2

	Children					Women						Men					
Work cap shaping as for style #1. Bind off .... sts	2	2	2	2	2	2	2	2	2	2	3	2	2	2	2	2	3
at beg of next 2 rows. Work even on rem 18 sts for .... in.	2½	3	3	3¼	3½	4	4¼	4½	4½	4¾	4¾	4¾	5	5	5¼	5¼	5½

Bind off all sts.

Styles #3 and #9

	Children					Women						Men					
Bind off .... sts	5	5	5	5	5	6	6	6	6	6	6	6	6	6	6	6	6

at beg of next 2 rows. *Note:* The foll decs are to be worked as for raglan dec row 1 on back raglan armhole shaping. However, when decs are worked every row, the raglan dec row on the purl side should be worked as foll: *Dec row (WS)* P2, p2tog the p to last 4 sts, p2tog, p2. Dec 1 st each side every 4th row ....

	Children					Women						Men					
.... times,	0	0	0	0	0	3	1	1	0	1	0	0	0	0	0	0	0
then every 2nd row .... times,	22	25	23	26	29	27	31	32	34	34	35	38	36	37	35	38	41
then every row .... times.	2	0	4	2	0	0	0	0	0	0	2	0	4	4	8	6	4
Bind off rem .... sts.	6	6	6	6	6	4	4	4	4	4	4	4	4	4	4	4	4

Style #4

	Children					Women					
Bind off .... sts	3	3	3	3	3	3	3	3	3	4	5

abbreviations explained **60-63**   knitting terminology **64-68**

	Children					Women						Men					
at beg of next 2 rows, ... ⌐___ sts	2	2	2	2	2	2	2	2	3	3	3						
at beg of next 2 rows, ... ⌐___ sts	0	0	0	0	0	2	2	2	2	2	2						
at beg of next 2 rows, then dec 1 st each side every 2nd row ...... ⌐___ times,	3	3	3	3	3	0	2	2	2	0	2						
then every 4th row .... ⌐___ times,	4	5	3	4	5	9	7	7	8	10	9						
then every 2nd row .... ⌐___ times,	2	2	6	6	6	1	3	3	3	3	3						

then bind off 2 sts at beg of next 4 rows, 3 sts at beg of next 2 rows.

| Bind off rem .... ⌐___ sts | 22 | 22 | 22 | 22 | 22 | 28 | 28 | 28 | 28 | 28 | 28 | | | | | | |

Style #5

| Work decs as for back armhole. Bind off rem .... ⌐___ sts. | 54 | 60 | 58 | 62 | 64 | 82 | 84 | 86 | 82 | 84 | 82 | 96 | 94 | 96 | 94 | 98 | 98 |

Style #7

This style is sized for women and children only. Work raglan cap shaping as for back

| until there are .... ⌐___ sts. | 28 | 26 | 30 | 28 | 26 | 34 | 34 | 34 | 34 | 34 | 36 | | | | | | |

Place marker at center of piece. *Dart dec row (RS)* Work to within 3 sts of center, ssk, k2, k2tog, k to end. *Dart dec row (WS)* Work to within 3 sts of center, p2tog, p2, p2tog through back lps, p to end. Cont dec in this way at same frequency as raglan

| armhole sleeve cap. Bind off rem .... ⌐___ sts. | 6 | 6 | 6 | 6 | 6 | 4 | 4 | 4 | 4 | 4 | 4 | | | | | | |

Finishing (all styles)

Block all pieces.

Neckband or collar

Style #1

| Sew one shoulder seam. With smaller needles, pick up and k .... ⌐___ sts | 94 | 94 | 98 | 102 | 102 | 102 | 106 | 106 | 110 | 110 | 118 | 122 | 122 | 126 | 130 | 134 | 134 |

evenly around neck edge. Work in k1, p1 rib for 9 rows. Bind off loosely in rib. Sew other shoulder seam, including neckband. Set in sleeves. Sew side and sleeve seams.

Style #2

Sew straight tops of sleeve caps to front and back shoulders, leaving one seam open.

| With smaller needles, pick up and k .... ⌐___ sts | 102 | 102 | 106 | 110 | 110 | 110 | 114 | 114 | 118 | 118 | 126 | 130 | 130 | 134 | 138 | 142 | 142 |

evenly around neck edge. Complete as for style #1.

Style #3

Sew raglan sleeve caps to raglan armholes, leaving one seam open.

| Pick up and k .... ⌐___ sts | 30 | 30 | 32 | 34 | 34 | 34 | 36 | 36 | 38 | 38 | 42 | 44 | 44 | 46 | 48 | 50 | 50 |
| along back neck, ... ⌐___ sts | 42 | 42 | 42 | 44 | 44 | 52 | 52 | 52 | 52 | 52 | 52 | 54 | 54 | 54 | 54 | 54 | 54 |

along left front neck, 1 st at center and mark this st. Pick up same number of sts

| along right front neck as left front for a total of .... ⌐___ sts. | 115 | 115 | 117 | 123 | 123 | 139 | 141 | 141 | 143 | 143 | 147 | 153 | 153 | 155 | 157 | 159 | 159 |

Row 1 (WS) *P1, k1; rep from * to end (center st is k1). *Row 2* Rib to 1 st before center marked st, sl 2 tog knitwise, work 1, psso, rib to end. Rep these 2 rows until 9 rows are completed. Bind off loosely in rib. Sew other shoulder seam. Sew side and sleeve seams.

	Children					Women						Men					

Style #4

Sew one shoulder seam. Pick up and k sts as for style #1. Work in k1, p1 rib for 7". Bind off loosely in rib. Sew other shoulder and turtleneck seam, sewing top half of neck from RS for foldback of collar. Make an inverted pleat at sleeve top and baste in place. Then baste sleeve into armhole and set in sleeves. Sew side and sleeve seams.

Style #5

Sew shoulder seams. Sew angled top of sleeve caps to angled armholes, then straight edge to armhole. Sew side and sleeve seams.

Placket band: With smaller needles, pick up and k _____ sts

Children					Women						Men					
31	31	35	35	35	41	41	41	41	41	41	41	41	41	41	41	41

along left (women's) or right (men's) placket opening. Work in k1, p1 rib for 9 rows. Bind off in rib. Place markers for 3 buttons, the first and last at ½" from outer edges and the other evenly spaced between. Work other placket edge to correspond, working buttonholes on 4th row opposite markers by binding off _____ sts

Children					Women						Men					
1	1	1	1	1	2	2	2	2	2	2	2	2	2	2	2	2

for buttonhole on first row and casting on same number over bound-off sts on 2nd row.

Polo collar: With smaller needles, beg and end at outside edge of placket band, pick up and k _____ sts

Children					Women						Men					
104	104	108	112	112	112	116	116	120	120	128	132	132	136	140	144	144

around neck edge. Work in k1, p1 rib for 3 rows. *Inc row* Rib 3 sts, m1, rib to last 3 sts, m1, rib 3 sts. Rep inc row every 4th row _____ times

Children					Women						Men					
4	4	4	4	4	5	5	5	5	5	5	5	5	5	5	5	5

more. When collar measures _____ in.,

Children					Women						Men					
3	3	3	3	3	3½	3½	3½	3½	3½	3½	3½	3½	3½	3½	3½	3½

bind off loosely in rib. Sew ends of placket in place, overlapping buttonhole band on top. Sew on buttons opposite buttonholes.

Style #6

Sew shoulder seams tog for _____ in.

Children					Women						Men					
2	2½	2¾	3¼	3½	3½	3¾	4¼	4½	5	5¼	5	5¼	5¾	6¼	6½	7

Sew top of sleeves to armholes between markers. Sew side and sleeve seams.

Style #7

Sew raglan sleeve caps to raglan armholes.

With circular needle, pick up and k _____ sts

Children					Women						Men					
52	52	54	56	56	56	60	60	62	62	68	70	70	72	74	78	78

along top of right sleeve, back neck and top of left sleeve. *Turn work, sl 1, work in k1, p1 rib to end. Working from left to right, pick up 4 sts along front neck edge, sl 1, rib to end. Pick up 4 sts along front edge, sl 1, rib to end *.

Rep between *'s _____ times

Children					Women						Men					
4	4	4	4	4	5	5	5	5	5	5	5	5	5	5	5	5

more, then rep between *'s, picking up 2 sts instead of 4 _____ times,

Children					Women						Men					
12	12	12	13	13	14	14	14	14	14	14	14	14	14	14	14	14

end at center front V-neck. Cont in rib on all _____ sts,

Children					Women						Men					
132	132	134	140	140	152	156	156	158	158	164	166	166	168	170	174	174

dec 1 st at beg of every row _____ times.

Children					Women						Men					
6	6	6	8	8	8	8	8	8	8	8	8	8	8	8	8	8

With larger needle, bind off all sts loosely in rib. Sew dec edge of collar to V-neck, overlapping right over left sides. Sew side and sleeve seams.

Style #8

Sew shoulder seams. Sew last _____ in.

Children					Women						Men					
1	1	1¼	1½	1½	1	¾	1¼	1½	1¾	2	1¼	1½	1¾	2	2¼	2½

of sleeve to bound-off sts of square armholes. Sew sleeves into armholes. Sew side and sleeve seams.

Midi collar: This collar is sized for women's and children's styles only.

With larger needles cast on _____ sts.

Children					Women					
58	64	66	70	72	78	84	86	88	90	94

	Children					Women						Men					

Row 1 *K1, p1; rep from * to end. *Row 2* K the purl and p the knit sts. Rep row 2 for seed st pat until 10 rows are worked from beg. *Next row* Work first 6 sts in seed st, then work in St st to last 6 sts, work last 6 sts in seed st. Cont in this way until piece measures, from beg, ... in.

Children					Women					
6	6½	6½	7	7½	8½	8½	9	9	9½	9½

Neck shaping: Bind off center .... sts

10	10	12	10	10	10	12	12	14	14	18

for neck and working both sides at once, bind off from each neck edge .. sts

5	5	5	6	6	6	6	6	6	6	6

twice. On next RS row, beg shaping at outside edge of collar as foll: *Next row (RS)* Work first 5 sts in seed st, p2tog, work to last 7 sts of 2nd half, p2tog, work 5 sts in seed st. Cont to dec in this way [every 2nd row once, every 4th row once] .... times,

5	2	2	1	0	4	2	1	1	0	0

then every 2nd row .... times.

12	11	11	14	17	12	18	21	21	24	24

Fasten off last st each side. Pin midi collar to V-neck. Sew collar in place from underside of collar.

Style #9

Sew raglan sleeve caps to raglan armholes. With RS facing and smaller needles, pick up and k .... sts

Children					Women						Men					
73	73	77	83	83	83	85	85	89	89	95	99	99	103	105	109	109

evenly around neck edge. Work in k1, p1 rib for 7 rows. Bind off loosely in rib. With smaller needles, pick up and k .... sts

87	95	103	111	121	137	141	143	147	151	153	153	157	159	163	167	168

along left front (right front for men's) edge, including neckband. Work in k1, p1 rib for 9 rows. Bind off loosely in rib. Place markers for required number of buttons, the first and last at ½" from outside edges, the others evenly spaced between. Work other band to correspond, working buttonholes on 4th row by binding off ..... sts

1	1	1	1	1	2	2	2	2	2	2	2	2	2	2	2	2

for each buttonhole, then casting on same number on next row. Sew side and sleeve seams. Sew on buttons.

Pocket Trims: With smaller needles, pick up and k .... sts

32	32	32	32	32	35	35	35	35	35	35	35	35	35	35	35	35

along pocket opening. Work in k1, p1 rib for 7 rows. Bind off loosely in rib. Sew edges of trims to fronts. Sew pocket linings to WS of pieces. Sew side and sleeve seams. Sew on buttons.

Style #10

Sew shoulder seams. With circular needle, pick up and k .... sts

Children					Women						Men					
31	31	33	35	35	35	37	37	39	37	43	45	45	47	49	51	51

along back neck, along each front edge pick up and k .... sts.

94	103	110	119	129	147	151	154	157	160	163	163	166	169	173	176	179

Work in k1, p1 rib on .... sts

219	237	253	273	293	329	339	345	353	359	369	371	377	385	395	403	403

as foll: Place markers on right side for women's, left side for men's, for required number of buttonholes; the first one at ½" from lower edge, the last one at beg of V-neck shaping and the others evenly spaced between. Rib for 9 rows, working buttonholes at markers on 4th row by binding off .... sts

1	1	1	1	1	2	2	2	2	2	2	2	2	2	2	2	2

for each buttonhole, then casting on same number on next row. When 9 rows are worked in rib, bind off loosely in rib. Work pocket trims as for style #9. Set in sleeves. Sew side and sleeve seams. Sew on buttons.

XIV. Traditional Knitting Patterns

Very Easy Very Vogue

Man's or woman's oversized Guernsey pullover with modified drop shoulder and ribbed highneck. Shown in size 36"/91cm.

Sizes

To fit 34 (36, 38, 40, 42)"/86 (91, 96, 101, 106)cm bust/chest. Directions are for smallest size with larger sizes in parentheses. If there is one figure it applies to all sizes.

Knitted measurements

Finished bust/chest at underarm

in	48	50½	52	54½	57
cm	120	126	130	136	142

Length

in	23½	24	24½	25	25½
cm	60	61	62	63.5	65

Sleeve width at upper arm

in	19½	20	20½	21	21½
cm	49.5	50	51	52	54

Materials

28 (32, 32, 36, 36)oz/840 (960, 960, 1080, 1080)g (each approx 172yd/156m per 4oz/120g ball) of a worsted weight wool in green

One pair each size 3 and 5 (3¼ and 3¾mm) needles or size to obtain gauge

Size 3 (3¼mm) circular needle 16"/40cm

Stitch markers

Gauge

20 sts and 28 rows to 4"/10cm over St st using size 5 (3¾mm) needles.

20 sts and 33 rows to 4"/10cm over double seed st using size 5 (3¾mm) needles.

To save time, take time to check gauges.

Horizontal stripe pat

(over any number of sts)
Row 1 (RS): Knit.
Rows 2 and 3: Purl.
Row 4: Knit.
Rep rows 1–4 for horizontal stripe pat.

Double seed st

(multiple of 4 sts + 2 extra) *Row 1 (RS):* K2, *p2, k2; rep from * to end. *Row 2:* K the knit sts and p the purl sts. *Row 3:* P2, *k2, p2; rep from * to end. *Row 4:* K the knit sts and p the purl sts. Rep rows 1–4 for double seed st.

Back

With smaller straight needles, cast on 102 (108, 112, 118, 124) sts. Work in k1, p1 rib for 3"/7.5cm. Change to larger needles. Keep first and last 2 sts at each end of every row in garter st (k every row) for border sts, work rem 98 (104, 108, 114, 120) sts in St st (k on RS, p on WS) until piece measures 6½ (6½, 6¾, 6¾, 7)"/16.5 (16.5, 17, 17, 18)cm from beg, end with a RS row. *Next row (WS)* Keeping first and last 2 sts in garter st border, k rem sts. Work in horizontal stripe pat with garter st border as foll: work rows 1–4 once, then rows 1–3 once more. *Inc row (WS)* K2 (border sts), inc 1 st in next st, k1 (2, 2, 3, 4), place marker, k94 (98, 102, 106, 110), place marker, k1 (2, 2, 3, 4), inc 1 st in next st, k2 (border sts). *Next row* K2, inc 1, work row 1 of horizontal stripe pat to marker, row 1 of double seed st to next marker, row 1 horizontal stripe pat to last 3 sts, inc 1, k2. *Next row* K2, row 2 of horizontal stripe pat to marker, row 2 of double seed st to next marker, row 2 of horizontal stripe pat to last 2 sts, k2. *Next row* K2, inc 1, row 3 of horizontal stripe pat to marker, row 3 of double seed st to next marker, row 3 of horizontal stripe pat to last 3 sts, inc 1, k2. Cont in pats, AT SAME TIME, inc 1 st each side (working inc sts inside of border sts) every 6th row 6 times more—120 (126, 130, 136, 142) sts.

Work even in pats until piece measures 12¾ (13, 13¼, 13½, 13¾)"/ 33 (33.5, 34, 35, 35.5)cm from beg.

Armhole shaping

Bind off 2 border sts at beg of next 2 rows—116 (122, 126, 132, 138) sts. Cont in pats until armhole measures 9¾ (10, 10¼, 10½, 10¾)"/24.5 (25, 25.5, 26, 27)cm.

Shoulder shaping

Bind off 11 (12, 12, 13, 14) sts at beg of next 2 (4, 2, 2, 4) rows, 12 (13, 13, 14, 15) sts at beg of next 4 (2, 4, 4, 2) rows. Bind off rem 46 (48, 50, 50, 52) sts for back neck.

Front

Work as for back until armholes measure 9¼ (9½, 9¾, 10, 10¼)"/23 (23.5, 24, 24.5, 25.5)cm.

Neck shaping

Next row (RS) Work across 44 (46, 47, 50, 53) sts, join 2nd ball of yarn, bind off 28 (30, 32, 32, 32) sts for neck, work to end. Working both sides at once, dec 1 st at each neck edge every row 9 (9, 9, 9, 10) times, AT SAME TIME, when same length as back to shoulder, shape shoulders as for back.

Sleeves

With smaller straight needles, cast on 42 (42, 44, 44, 46) sts. Work in k1, p1 rib for 3"/7.5cm. Change to larger needles. Work in St st, inc 1 st each side every other row 10 (10, 10, 8, 10) times, every 4th row 18 (19, 19, 22, 21) times—98 (100, 102, 104, 108) sts. Work even until piece measures 17¾ (18, 18¼, 19, 19¼)"/45 (45.5, 46.5, 48.5, 49)cm from beg. Bind off.

Finishing

Block pieces. Sew shoulder seams.

Highneck

With RS facing and circular needle, beg at right shoulder seam, pick up and k46 (48, 50, 50, 52) sts along back neck, 14 sts along curved left front neck edge, 28 (30, 32, 32, 32) sts along straight front neck edge and 14 sts along curved right front neck edge—102 (106, 110, 110, 112) sts. Place marker and join. Work in k1, p1 rib for 3"/7.5cm. Bind off in rib. Sew top of sleeves to straight edge of armholes. Sew last 3 rows of sleeve to bound-off armhole sts. Sew side and sleeve seams.

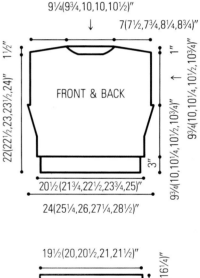

abbreviations
explained **60-63**

knitting
terminology **64-68**

understanding knitting
instructions **54-59**

Experienced

Man's or woman's oversized, reindeer pattern pullover with drop shoulders, round neck and corrugated ribs. Shown in size 38"/96cm.

Sizes

To fit 34 (36, 38, 40, 42)"/86 (91, 96, 101, 106)cm bust/chest. Directions are for smallest size with larger sizes in parentheses. If there is one figure it applies to all sizes.

Knitted measurements

Finished bust/chest at underarm

in	42	44	46	48	50
cm	105	110	115	121	125

Length

in	26¾	27¼	27¾	28¼	28¾
cm	68	69.5	70.5	71.5	73

Sleeve width at upper arm

in	20	21	21	22	22½
cm	50	53	53	55	56

Materials

15¾ (15¾, 17½, 17½, 19¼)oz/450 (450, 500, 500, 550)g (each approx 116 yd/106m per 1¾oz/50g ball) of a knitting worsted weight yarn in navy (A).

8¾ (10½, 10½, 10½, 12¼)oz/250 (300, 300, 300, 350)g off white (B)

One pair size 8 (5mm) needles or size to obtain gauge

Size 8 (5mm) circular needle 16"/40cm

Bobbins and stitch markers

Gauge

22 sts and 25 rows to 4"/10cm over chart #3 using size 8 (5mm) needles.

To save time, take time to check gauge.

Note 1: See color charts p. 268. *Note 2:* When changing colors, twist yarns on WS to prevent holes and carry yarn not in use loosely across back of work.

Note 3: Due to both stranding and intarsia colorwork techniques it may be necessary to use 1 size smaller than the needles on which you have obtained the gauge when working reindeer motif and St st section. *Note 4:* Use bobbins for working reindeer and for first 6 rows of tree design.

Back

With A, cast on 101 (107, 113, 119, 123) sts. Join B. *Beg rib: Row 1 (RS)* *K1 B, p1 A; rep from *, end k1 B. *Row 2* *P1 B, k1 A; rep from *, end p1 B. Rep rows 1 and 2 three times more. Work in St st with B for 2 rows. Beg and end as indicated, work chart #1 through row 4. Inc 1 st each side on next row and every 8th row 5 times more (as shown on chart). After all 45 rows of chart have been worked, and working 1 more inc on foll 8th row, work in St st with B for 5 (5, 7, 7, 9) rows. Beg and end as indicated, work chart #2 through row 48. *Note:* Final inc row for sizes 34 & 36"/86 & 91cm are worked on row 3 of chart #2, and for sizes 38 & 40"/96 & 101cm on row 1 of chart #2—115 (121, 127, 133, 137) sts. Work chart #3 through row 4. *Next Row (RS)* Work row 5 of chart #3 over 70 (73, 76, 79, 81) sts, place marker, work row 1 of chart #4 over next 22 sts, place marker, work chart #3 to end. Work rem rows of chart #4 over 22 sts between markers and cont chart #3 over rem sts. Cont chart #3 over all sts until piece measures 24¾ (25¼, 25¾, 26¼, 26¾)"/63 (64.5, 65.5, 66.5, 68)cm from beg.

Shoulder shaping

Bind off 6 sts at beg of next 6 (2, 0, 0, 0) rows, 7 sts at beg of next 6 (10, 10, 6, 4) rows, 8 sts at beg of next 0 (0, 2, 6, 8) rows. Bind off rem 37 (39, 41, 43, 45) sts for back neck.

Front

Work as for back until piece measures 23¼ (23¾, 24¼, 24¾, 25¼)"/59 (60.5, 61.5, 62.5, 64)cm from beg.

Neck shaping

Next row (RS) Work 52 (54, 56, 58, 59) sts, join 2nd strand of yarn and bind off 11 (13, 15, 17, 19) sts, work to end. Working both sides at once, bind off from each neck edge 3 sts twice, 2 sts twice. Dec 1 st every other row 3 times, AT SAME TIME, when same length as back to shoulders, work shoulder shaping as for back.

Sleeves

With A, cast on 57 (59, 59, 61, 63) sts. Join B and work 8 rows of rib as for back. Work in St st with B for 2 rows, and inc 1 st at each end of first row—59 (61, 61, 63, 65) sts. *Beg chart #1: Row 1 (RS)* Beg with the 14th (13th, 13th, 12th, 11th) st of chart, work to rep line, then work 19-st rep 3 times, work next 1 (2, 2, 3, 4) sts outside rep. Cont in chart pat, inc 1 st each side (working inc sts into pat) every other row 11 (11, 11, 13, 12) times, every 4th row 15 (16, 16, 16, 17) times, AT SAME TIME, when 17 rows of chart #1 have been worked, cont working incs and work in St st with B for 5 (5, 7, 7, 9) rows—79 (81, 83, 85, 89) sts. *Beg chart #2: Row 1 (RS)* Cont inc, beg with the 9th (8th, 7th, 6th, 4th) st of chart, work to rep line, then work 19-st rep 3 times, work next 11 (12, 13, 14, 16) sts outside rep. Cont to work chart #2 through row 48, then rep rows 1–16 of chart #3, being sure to line up pats, until all incs have been worked—111 (115, 115, 121, 123) sts. Work even in chart #3 until piece measures 16 (16½, 16½, 17, 17½)"/40.5 (42, 42, 43, 44.5)cm from beg. Bind off.

Finishing

Block pieces. Do not press rib. Sew shoulder seams.

Neckband

With RS facing, circular needle and A, pick up and k100 (104, 108, 112, 116) sts evenly around entire neck edge. Join, attach B. *Rnd 1* *K1 B, p1 A; rep from * around. Rep rnd 1 six times more. With A work 1 rnd k1, p1 rib. Bind off with A. Place markers 10 (10½, 10½, 11, 11¼")/25 (26.5, 26.5, 27.5, 28)cm down from shoulders in front and back. Sew top of sleeve between markers. Sew side and sleeve seams.

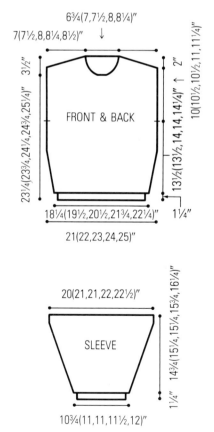

abbreviations explained **60-63**   knitting terminology **64-68**   understanding knitting instructions **54-59**

Experienced

Man's or woman's oversized, Aran pattern pullover with drop shoulders and doubled crewneck. Shown in size 38"/96cm.

Sizes

To fit 34 (36, 38, 40, 42)"/86 (91, 96, 101, 106)cm bust/chest. Directions are for smallest size with larger sizes in parentheses. If there is one figure it applies to all sizes.

Knitted measurements

Finished bust/chest at underarm

in	40	42	44	47	49
cm	103	107	111	119	123

Length

in	24½	25	25½	26	26½
cm	62	63.5	65	66	67.5

Sleeve width at upper arm

in	21	22	22	22½	24
cm	53	56	56	57	61

Materials

33¼ (35, 35, 36¾, 36¾)oz/950 (1000, 1000, 1050, 1050)g (each approx 92yd/85m per 1¾oz/50g ball) of a worsted weight wool in ecru

One pair each sizes 6 and 9 (4 and 5½mm) needles or size to obtain gauge

Size 6 (4mm) circular needle 16"/40cm

Cable needle and stitch markers

Gauge

All using size 9 (5½mm) needles:

20 sts and 26 rows to 4"/10cm over chart #1.

34 sts to 4½"/11.5cm over chart #6.

11 sts to 1¼"/3cm over chart #2.

6 sts to ¾"/2cm over charts #3 and #5.

16 sts to 2½"/6.5cm and 20 sts to 3"/7.5cm over chart #4.

To save time, take time to check gauges.

Note 1: See symbolcraft charts p. 269.

Stitch glossary

Right twist (over 2 sts): K 2nd st in front of first st, then k first st, sl both sts off needle.
Left twist (over 2 sts): K 2nd st behind first st tbl, k first st, sl both sts off needle.
6-st left cable: Sl 3 sts to cn and hold to front of work, k3, k3 from cn.
6-st right cable: Sl 3 sts to cn and hold to back of work, k3, k3 from cn.
4-st left purl cross: Sl 3 sts to cn and hold to front of work, p1, k3 from cn.
4-st right purl cross: Sl 1 st to cn and hold to back of work, k3, p1 from cn.

Back

With smaller needles, cast on 115 (119, 125, 133, 137) sts. Work in k1, p1 rib for 3"/7.5cm, inc 23 (23, 25, 25, 25) sts evenly across last row—138 (142, 150, 158, 162) sts. Change to larger needles. *Beg chart pats: Row 1 (RS)* Work row 1 of chart #1 over 13 (15, 15, 19, 21) sts, chart #2 over 11 sts, chart #3 over 6 sts, chart #4 over 16 (16, 20, 20, 20) sts, chart #5 over 6 sts, chart #6 over 34 sts, chart #3 over 6 sts, chart #4 over 16 (16, 20, 20, 20) sts, chart #5 over 6 sts, chart #2 over 11 sts, chart #1 over 13 (15, 15, 19, 21) sts. Cont in pats as established until piece measures 24½ (25, 25½, 26, 26½)"/62 (63.5, 65, 66, 67.5)cm from beg. Bind off.

Front

Work as for back until piece measures 21½ (22, 22½, 23, 23½)"/54.5 (56, 57.5, 58.5, 60)cm from beg, end with a WS row.

Neck shaping

Next row (RS) Work 57 (58, 61, 64, 66) sts, join 2nd ball of yarn, bind off 24 (26, 28, 30, 30) sts, work to end. Working both sides at once, dec 1 st at each neck edge every row 10 (10, 10, 10, 11) times. When same length as back to shoulder, bind off rem 47 (48, 51, 54, 55) sts each side for shoulders.

Sleeves

With smaller needles, cast on 60 (60, 64, 66, 66) sts. Work in k1, p1 rib for 3"/7.5cm, inc 18 (18, 22, 20, 20) sts evenly across last row—78 (78, 86, 86, 86) sts. Change to larger needles. *Beg chart pats: Row 1 (RS)* Work row 1 of chart #4 over 16 (16, 20, 20, 20) sts, chart #5 over 6 sts, chart #6 over 34 sts, chart #3 over 6 sts, chart #4 over 16 (16, 20, 20, 20) sts. Cont in pats, inc 1 st each side (working inc sts into pats in order of charts as for back) every other row 17 (20, 11, 13, 20) times, every 4th row 15 (14, 21, 20, 17) times—142 (146, 150, 152, 160) sts. Work even until piece measures 19½ (20, 20½, 21, 21½)"/49.5 (51, 52, 53.5, 54.5)cm from beg. Bind off.

Finishing

Block pieces. Sew shoulder seams.

Neckband

With RS facing and circular needle, beg at right shoulder seam, pick up and k44 (46, 48, 50, 52) sts along back neck, 66 (68, 70, 72, 72) sts along front neck—110 (114, 118, 122, 124) sts. Join and work in k1, p1 rib for 3"/7.5cm. Bind off in rib. Fold band to WS and sew in place. Place markers 10½ (11, 11, 11¼, 12)"/26.5 (28, 28, 28.5, 30.5)cm down from shoulders on front and back for armholes. Sew top of sleeves between markers. Sew side and sleeve seams.

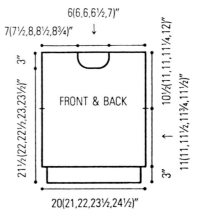

6(6,6,6½,7)"
7(7½,8,8½,8¾)"
3"
21½(22,22½,23,23½)"
10½(11,11,11¼,12)"
11(11,11½,11¾,11½)"
FRONT & BACK
3"
20(21,22,23½,24½)"

21(22,22,22½,24)"
16½(17,17½,18,18½)"
SLEEVE
3"
11(11,12,12,12)"

Experienced

Man's or woman's oversized, Fair Isle
vest with V-neck. Shown in size 34–
36"/86–91cm.

Sizes

To fit 32 (34–36, 38–40, 42–44)"/81 (86–91, 96–101, 106–112)cm bust/ chest. Directions are for smallest size with larger sizes in parentheses. If there is one figure it applies to all sizes.

Knitted measurements

Finished bust/chest at underarm

in	36	40	44	48
cm	90	100	110	120

Length				
in	23	23½	24	24½
cm	58.5	59.5	61	62

Materials

3½ (5¼, 5¼, 5¼)oz/100 (150, 150, 150)g (each approx 138yd/125m per 1¾oz/50g ball) of a double knitting yarn in grey (MC)

3½oz/100g each dark turquoise (A), light turquoise (B), orange (D), light yellow (E)

1¾oz/50g each light purple (C), light grey/brown (F) and beige (G)

Size 3 and 5 (3¼ and 3¾mm) circular needles 29"/80 cm, or size to obtain gauge

Size 4 (3½mm) circular needle 16"/40cm

Stitch markers and stitch holder

Gauge

24 sts and 28 rows to 4"/10cm over chart pat using size 5 (3¾mm) needles.

To save time, take time to check gauge.

Note 1: See color charts p. 269. *Note 2:* When changing colors, twist yarns on WS to prevent holes and carry yarn not in use loosely across back of work. To avoid excessively long strands at back of work, weave or twist yarns not in use around working yarn every 3 or 4 sts. *Note 3:* Vest is worked circularly to the underarm, then back and forth as with straight needles. *Note 4:* When working in the round, read all chart rows from right to left. When working back and forth, read RS rows from right to left and WS rows from left to right.

Body

With smaller 29"/80cm needle and MC, cast on 196 (220, 244, 268) sts. Place marker for left side and join, taking care not to twist sts. *Beg chart #1: Rnds 1 and 2* With MC, *p2, k2; rep from * around. *Rnds 3 and 4* *P2 MC, k2 A; rep from * around. Cont to work chart #1 through rnd 16, end at marker. *Inc rnd* With MC, k and inc 20 sts evenly around—216 (240, 264, 288) sts. Change to larger 29"/80cm needle. Working in St st (k every rnd), beg as indicated, work rnds 1–50 of chart #2 until piece measures 13"/33cm from beg, end last rnd at 7 sts before marker.

Divide for front and back

Bind off next 14 sts for left underarm, work next 95 (107, 119, 131) sts for front and sl those sts to a holder, bind off next 14 sts for right underarm, work rem 93 (105, 117, 129) sts for back, turn work.

Back

Working back and forth as with straight needles, work 1 row even. Bind off 3 sts at beg of next 2 rows, 2 sts at beg of next 2 rows. Dec 1 st each side every other row 4 times—75 (87, 99, 111) sts. Work even until armhole measures 9 (9½, 10, 10½)"/23 (24, 25.5, 26.5)cm.

Shoulder shaping

Bind off 6 (7, 8, 9) sts at beg of next 6 rows, 5 (6, 8, 9) sts at beg of next 2 rows. Bind off rem 29 (33, 35, 39) sts.

Front and V-neck shaping

Sl sts on holder to larger needle—95 (107, 119, 131) sts. Join yarn at right underarm and p 1 row. Complete armhole shaping same as back, AT SAME TIME, when 8 rows have been worked in armhole shaping, place center st on a holder and working both sides at once, dec 1 st at each neck edge every other row 2 (4, 5, 7) times, every 4th row 13 times—23 (27, 32, 36) sts each side. When same length as back to shoulders, work shoulder shaping as for back.

Finishing

Block piece. Sew shoulder seams.

Armhole bands

With RS facing, 16"/40cm circular needle and MC, beg at center of underarm bind-off, pick up and k136 (144, 152, 160) sts around entire armhole edge. Join and place marker. Work rib foll even rows only of chart #1 in reverse (that is, beg with row 16, then 14, 12, 10, etc.). With MC, bind off in rib.

V-neckband

With RS facing, 16"/40cm circular needle and MC, beg at right shoulder seam, pick up and k30 (32, 34, 36) sts along back neck, 54 (57, 58, 59) sts along left front neck, k st from holder and mark this st, pick up and k54 (57, 58, 59) sts along right front neck—139 (147, 151, 155) sts. Place marker between first and last picked up st. *Rnd 1* Work rib same as armhole bands to 2 sts before center st, SKP, with MC, k center st, k2tog, work rib to end of rnd. Cont in rib pat as for armhole bands, dec 1 st each side of center V st every rnd (always work center st in MC). With MC, bind off in rib.

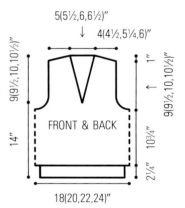

5(5½,6,6½)"
↓ 4(4½,5¼,6)"
9(9½,10,10½)"
1"
9(9½,10,10½)"
14"
FRONT & BACK
10¾"
2¼"
18(20,22,24)"

Intermediate

Man's or woman's oversized, Fair Isle pullover with circular yoke and doubled crewneck. Shown in size 36"/91cm.

Sizes

To fit 34 (36, 38, 40, 42)"/86 (91, 96, 101, 106)cm bust/chest. Directions are for smallest size with larger sizes in parentheses. If there is one figure it applies to all sizes.

Knitted measurements

Finished bust/chest measurement at underarm

in	42	44	47	49	52
cm	105	111	117	123	129

Length

in	25½	26½	27¼	28	28½
cm	63	67	69	70.5	72

Sleeve width at upper arm

in	19¾	21	22	23½	24
cm	49	52.5	55.5	58.5	60

Materials

21 (21, 21, 24½, 24½)oz/600 (600, 600, 700, 700)g (each approx 100yd/110m per 3½oz/100g ball) of a bulky weight wool in oatmeal (MC)

7oz/200g purple (A)

3½oz/100g pink (B)

Size 7 and 10½ (4½ and 6½mm) circular needles 29"/80cm or size to obtain gauge

Size 7 and 10½ (4½ and 6½mm) circular needle 16"/40cm

One set (4) each double pointed needles (dpn) size 7 and 10½ (4½ and 6½mm)

Stitch holders and stitch markers

Gauge

13 sts and 16 rows to 4"/10cm over St st using size 10½ (6½mm) needles.

To save time, take time to check gauge.

Note 1: See color charts p. 270.
Note 2: When changing colors, twist yarns on WS to prevent holes. Carry yarn not in use loosely across back of work. *Note 3:* Body of sweater is worked in one piece to the underarm.

Body

With longer size 7 (4½mm) needle and MC, cast on 136 (144, 152, 160, 168) sts. Place marker and join, taking care not to twist sts. Work in k1, p1 rib for 3"/7.5cm. Change to longer size 10½ (6½mm) needle. With MC, knit 1 rnd. Cont in St st (k every rnd) and work rnds 1–6 of chart #1. With MC, work in St st until piece measures 14½ (15, 15½, 16, 16½)"/35.5 (38, 39.5, 40.5, 42)cm from beg, ending last rnd 5 sts before marker.

Armhole shaping

Bind off next 10 (10, 10, 10, 9) sts, k until there are 58 (62, 66, 70, 75) sts from bind-off, sl sts to holder for front, bind off 10 (10, 10, 10, 9) sts, k rem 58 (62, 66, 70, 75) sts and sl to 2nd holder for back.

Sleeves

Note: Sleeves are started on dpns. Change to circular needle as sts are increased.

With size 7 (4½mm) double pointed needles and MC, cast on 36 (36, 38, 42, 42) sts. Place marker and join, taking care not to twist sts. Work in k1, p1 rib for 2½"/6cm, inc 4 (4, 2, 6, 6) sts evenly across last rnd—40 (40, 40, 48, 48) sts. Change to size 10½ (6½mm) dpn. With MC, work 1 rnd in St st. Work rnds 1–6 of chart #1. With MC, work in St st, inc 1 st before and after marker every other rnd 4 (6, 9, 5, 5) times, every 4th rnd 8 (8, 7, 9, 10) times—64 (68, 72, 76, 78) sts. Work even until piece measures 16 (16½, 17, 17½, 18)"/40.5 (42, 43, 44.5, 45.5)cm from beg, ending last rnd 5 (5, 5, 5, 4) sts before marker. Bind off next 10 (10, 10, 10, 8) sts. Place rem 54 (58, 62, 66, 70) sts on holder.

Yoke

With longer size 10½ (6½mm) needle, k sts from holders as foll: 54 (58, 62, 66, 70) sts of one sleeve, 58 (62, 66, 70, 75) sts of front, 54 (58, 62, 66, 70) sts of 2nd sleeve, 58 (62, 66, 70, 75) sts of back—224 (240, 256, 272, 290) sts. Join. With MC, work 2 (4, 5, 5, 4) rnds. *For size 42 only:* Work 1 rnd and dec 2 sts evenly around—288 sts. *For all sizes:* Work rnds 1–16 of chart #1. With MC, work 2 rnds. *First dec rnd —For size 34 only:* *[K4, k2tog, k3, k2tog] twice, k4, k2tog; rep from * around. *For all other sizes:* *[K3, k2tog] (3, 2, 1, 6) times, [k4, k2tog] (0, 1, 2, 1) times; rep from * around—184 (192, 208, 224, 232) sts. Work rnds 1–5 of chart #2. With MC, work 2 rnds. *2nd dec rnd:*

*[K1, k2tog] 5 (4, 2, 4, 3) times, [k2, k2tog] 2 (3, 5, 4, 5) times; rep from * around—128 (136, 152, 160, 168) sts. Work rnds 1–5 of chart #3. With MC, work 2 rnds. *3rd dec rnd:* *[K1, k2tog] twice, k2tog; rep from * around—80 (85, 95, 100, 105) sts. Work rnds 1–5 of chart #4. With MC, work 1 (1, 1, 2, 2) rnds. *4th dec rnd:* *[K1, k2tog] 2 (3, 29, 7, 1) times, [k2, k2tog] 1 (2, 2, 1, 0) times; rep from * around—56 (60, 64, 68, 70) sts. Change to shorter size 7½ (4½mm) needle (or dpn). Work in k1, p1 rib for 3"/7.5cm. Bind off loosely in rib. Fold band to WS and sew in place.

Finishing

Block sweater. Sew bound-off edges of underarms tog.

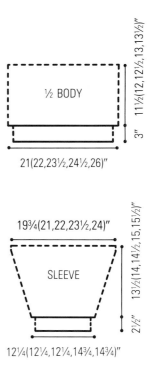

½ BODY

3" · 11½(12,12½,13,13½)"

21(22,23½,24½,26)"

19¾(21,22,23½,24)"

SLEEVE

13½(14,14½,15,15½)"

2½"

12¼(12¼,12¼,14¾,14¾)"

Experienced

Man's or woman's oversized, argyle pattern pullover with drop shoulders and V-neck. Shown in size 38"/96cm.

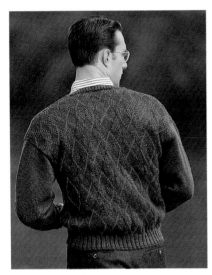

Sizes

To fit 34 (36, 38, 40, 42)"/86 (91, 96, 101, 106)cm bust/chest. Directions are for smallest size with larger sizes in parentheses. If there is one figure it applies to all sizes.

Knitted measurements

Finished bust/chest at underarm

in	40	42	43½	45½	48
cm	100	106	109	114	119

Length

in	24¼	24¾	25¼	25½	25¾
cm	61.5	62.5	64	64.5	65.5

Sleeve width at upper arm

in	18	19	20	20½	21
cm	45	47	50	51	53

Materials

15¾ (15¾, 17½, 17½, 19¼)oz/450 (450, 500, 500, 550)g (approx 125yd/115m per 1¾oz/50g) of a double knitting yarn in grey (MC)

7 (7, 8¾, 8¾, 8¾)oz/200 (200, 250, 250, 250)g steel blue (A)

1¾ (1¾, 3½, 3½, 3½)oz/50 (50, 100, 100, 100)g cranberry (B)

One pair each sizes 3 and 5 (3¼ and 3¾mm) needles or size to obtain gauge

Size 3 (3¼mm) circular needle 16"/40cm

Bobbins, stitch holder and stitch markers

Gauge

22 sts and 28 rows to 4"/10cm over St st using size 5 (3¾mm) needles.

23 sts and 26 rows to 4"/10cm over chart pat using size 5 (3¾mm) needles.

To save time, take time to check gauges.

Note 1: See color chart p. 270. *Note 2:* Use separate bobbins for each block of color. *Note 3:* When changing colors, twist yarns on WS to prevent holes. *Note 4:* Diamonds and crosses can be duplicate stitched after pieces are complete. *Note 5:* To knit in diamonds, cut a length 78"/198cm. Beg in middle of length to divide it in half and use for each side of diamond. *Note 6:* To knit in crosses, cut a 30"/76cm length for each diagonal cross.

Back

With smaller needles and A, cast on 104 (112, 116, 120, 128) sts. Work in k2, p2 rib for 2 rows. Change to MC and cont rib for 2"/5cm from beg, inc 11 (9, 9, 11, 9) sts evenly across last WS row—115 (121, 125, 131, 137) sts. Change to larger needles. *Beg chart pat: Row 1 (RS)* Working in St st, beg as indicated, work to rep line, work 32-st rep 3 times, end as indicated. Cont in chart pat until piece measures 23 (23½, 24, 24¼, 24½)"/58.5 (59.5, 61, 61.5, 62.5)cm from beg.

Shoulder shaping

Bind off 10 (11, 11, 11, 12) sts at beg of next 6 (8, 6, 2, 6) rows, 11 (0, 12, 12, 13) sts at beg of next 2 (0, 2, 6, 2) rows. Bind off rem 33 (33, 35, 37, 39) sts for back neck.

Front

Work as for back until piece measures approx 17¼"/44cm from beg, end with row 32 of chart.

V-neck shaping

Next row (RS) Work 57 (60, 62, 65, 68) sts, k center st and sl to holder, join 2nd strand of matching yarn, work to end. Working both sides at once, dec 1 st at each neck edge [every other row once, every 4th row once] 4 (5, 6, 6, 6) times, every other row 8 (6, 5, 6, 7) times—41 (44, 45, 47, 49) sts, AT SAME TIME, when same length as back to shoulder, work shoulder shaping as for back.

Sleeves

With smaller needles and A, cast on 60 (64, 68, 68, 72) sts. Work 2 rows in k2, p2 rib. Change to MC and cont rib for 2"/5cm from beg, inc 10 (8, 10, 10, 10) sts evenly across last WS row—70 (72, 78, 78, 82) sts. Change to larger needles. Work in St st, inc 1 st each side [every 6th row once, every 8th row once] 7 (6, 6, 5, 5) times, every 6th row 1 (4, 4, 7, 7) times—100 (104, 110, 112, 116) sts. Work even until piece measures 18 (18½, 18½, 19, 19)"/45.5 (47, 47, 48.5, 48.5)cm from beg. Bind off.

Finishing

Block pieces. Sew shoulder seams.

V-neckband

With RS facing, circular needle and MC, beg at right shoulder edge, pick up and k33 (33, 35, 37, 39) sts across back neck, 37 (38, 39, 40, 42) sts along left front neck, place marker, k center st from holder, pick up and k37 (38, 39, 40, 42) sts along right front neck—108 (110, 114, 118, 124) sts. Join and work in k1, p1 rib to 2 sts before marker, ssk, sl marker, k1, k2tog, rib to end. Rep last rnd 3 times more. Change to A, rep last rnd. Bind off in rib. Place markers 9 (9½, 10, 10¼, 10½)"/22.5 (23.5, 25, 25.5, 26.5)cm down from shoulders for armholes. Sew top of sleeves between markers. Sew side and sleeve seams.

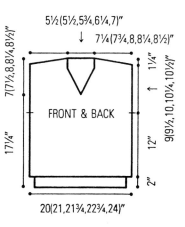

5½(5½,5¾,6¼,7)"
7¼(7¾,8,8¼,8½)"
7(7½,8,8¼,8½)"
1¼"
17¼"
9(9½,10,10¼,10½)"
FRONT & BACK
12"
2"
20(21,21¾,22¾,24)"

18(19,20,20½,21)"
16(16½,16½,17,17)"
SLEEVE
2"
12¾(13,14,14,15)"

abbreviations
explained **60-63**

understanding knitting
instructions **54-59**

knitting
terminology **64-68**

Experienced

Oversized, garter stitch fulled jacket with shawl collar, turned up cuffs and pocket flaps. Shown in size 36"/91cm.

Sizes

To fit 32 (34, 36, 38–40)"/81 (86, 91, 96–101)cm bust. Directions are for smallest size with larger sizes in parentheses. If there is one figure it applies to all sizes.

Knitted measurements

Before fulling:

Finished bust at underarm (buttoned)

in	45	47	49	51
cm	116	122	127	132

Length

in	26¾	26¾	28	28
cm	68.5	68.5	71.5	71.5

Sleeve width at upper arm

in	25½	25½	28	28
cm	66	66	72	72

After fulling:

Note: These measurements may vary as much as 1"/2.5cm up or down, but ease has been built into the jacket to accommodate this factor.

Finished bust at underarm (buttoned)

in	41	43	45	47
cm	104	111	113	121

Length

in	24	24	25	25
cm	61	61	63.5	63.5

Sleeve width at upper arm

in	23	23	25	25
cm	58.5	58.5	63.5	63.5

Materials

22¾ (24½, 26¼, 28)oz/650 (700, 750, 800)g (each approx 140yd/127m per 1¾ oz/50g ball) of a double knitting yarn in light grey (MC)

8¾ (10½, 10½, 12¼)oz/250 (300, 300, 350)g in medium grey (A)

1¾oz/50g in dark grey (B)

One each size 8 (5mm) circular needles 36"/90cm and 24"/60cm or size to obtain gauge

Three 1¼"/30mm buttons

Four ¾"/20mm buttons

Stitch holders

Small amount of lining fabric for pockets

Gauge

Before fulling:
34 sts and 64 rows to 8½"/22cm over garter st using size 8 (5mm) needles and 2 strands of yarn.

After fulling:
34 sts and 64 rows to 8"/20cm over fulled fabric. *Note:* It is essential to work a gauge swatch at least 8½"/22cm square to understand process and assure a close estimate of gauge and texture for final fulling of jacket. (See fulling instructions for working gauge.)

To save time, take time to check gauge.

Note 1: Use 2 strands of yarn held tog throughout. *Note 2:* When changing colors, twist yarns on WS to prevent holes. *Note 3:* Sl first st of every row purlwise with yarn in back to aid in finishing. *Note 4:* For ease in counting rows, remember 1 garter st ridge equals 2 rows.

Body

With longer circular needle and B, cast on 184 (192, 200, 208) sts. *Row 1 (RS)* With 2 strands of A, k18 (19, 19, 20); with 2 strands MC, k148 (154, 162, 168); with 2 strands A, k18 (19, 19, 20). Work even in garter st (k every row), sl first st of every row purlwise wyib matching colors for a total of 24 rows (approx 3¼"/8cm), end with a WS row. *Buttonhole row (RS)* Sl 1 wyib, k1, bind off 3 sts, k to end. *Next row* K, casting on 3 sts over bound-off sts. Work even, making 2 more buttonholes 48 rows (approx 6½"/16.5cm) apart, AT SAME TIME, after 103 rows (approx 14"/35.5cm) from beg, end with a RS row.

Divide for armholes

Row 104 (WS) Cont in pat, k46 (48, 49, 51) sts and sl sts to holder for left front, bind off 2 (2, 4, 4) sts, work until there are 88 (92, 94, 98) sts from bind-off, sl sts to holder for back, bind off 2 (2, 4, 4) sts, work rem 46 (48, 49, 51) sts for right front.

Right front section
Armhole shaping

Work 1 row even. *Next row (WS)* Bind off 2 sts, k to end. Cont to bind off 2 sts from armhole edge (WS rows) 3 times more—38 (40, 41, 43) sts. Work even until there are 128 rows (approx 17"/44cm) from beg, end with a WS row.

Collar shaping and pocket opening

Cont in pat, inc 1 st at beg of next row (collar edge), then at same edge (working inc sts in A) every 4th row 15 (16, 16, 17) times more, AT SAME TIME, work pocket opening as foll: *Row 1 (RS)*

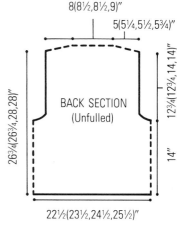

8(8½,8½,9)"
5(5¼,5½,5¾)"
26¾(26¾,28,28)"
12¾(12¾,14,14)"
14"
BACK SECTION (Unfulled)
22½(23½,24½,25½)"

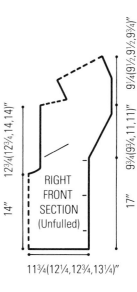

9¼(9½,9½,9¾)"
9¾(9¾,11,11)"
12¾(12¾,14,14)"
14"
17"
RIGHT FRONT SECTION (Unfulled)
11¾(12¼,12¾,13¼)"

12(12,12½,12½)"
3"
RIGHT SLEEVE (Unfulled)
16½(16½,17½,17½)"
25½(25½,28,28)"

Work to last 4 sts, k2tog, join 2 more strands MC (to form slit), k into front and back of next st (inc 1), k1. *Row 2* Working both sides at once, k2, inc 1, ssk, k to end. *Row 3* Work to 2 sts before slit, k2tog, inc 1, k to end. *Row 4* K to 1 st before slit, inc 1, ssk, k to end. Rep rows 3 and 4 for 7 times more. *Next row (RS)* K across all sts to close slit. Work even on 54 (57, 58, 61) sts after all incs have been made until 200 (200, 208, 208) rows have been worked (approx 26¾ (26¾, 28, 28)"/ 68.5 (68.5, 71.5, 71.5)cm from beg, end with a WS row.

Shoulder shaping
Next row (RS) K to last 5 (5, 6, 6) sts, turn. *Next row* Sl 1 purlwise, k to end. *Next row* K to last 5 (5, 6, 6) sts before last unworked sts, turn. *Next row* Sl 1 purlwise, k to end. Rep last 2 rows once more. *Next row* K until there are 5 (6, 4, 5) sts from last unworked sts, sl there 20 (21, 22, 23) sts to holder, turn. With A only, k3 rows on rem 34 (36, 36, 38) sts, end with a WS row.

Collar back shaping
Next row (RS) K to last 2 sts, inc 1 st in next st (back edge) k1. Cont to inc at back edge every 4th row 6 (7, 7, 7) times more—41 (44, 44, 46) sts. Work even until 30 (32, 32, 34) rows (½ back neck)—approx 4 (4¼, 4½, 4½)"/ 10.5 (11, 11, 11.5)cm from beg of collar back, end with a WS row. *Beg short rows: Row 1 (RS)* Sl 1, ssk (front edge), work to last 3 (6, 6, 8) sts, leave these sts unworked, turn. *Row 2 (WS)* Sl 1, k to end. Working short rows, dec 1 st at

front edge every 4th row 7 times more and leave 2 more sts unworked at back neck every RS row until all sts rem unworked. Sl 33 (36, 36, 38) sts on holder.

Back section
With RS facing and 2 strands MC, sl 88 (92, 94, 98) sts to needle.

Armhole and shoulder shaping
Bind off 2 sts at beg of next 8 rows—72 (76, 78, 82) sts. Work even until back section measures same as right front to shoulder, end with a WS row. *Beg short rows: Row 1 (RS)* Work to last 5 (5, 6, 6) sts, leave unworked, turn. *Row 2* Sl 1, work to last 5 (5, 6, 6) sts, turn. Rep rows 1 and 2 twice more. *Next short row* *Work until there are 20 (21, 22, 23) sts on LH needle, sl these sts to holder,* turn. *Next row* Sl 1; rep between *'s of last row, turn and k across center 32 (34, 34, 36) sts and place sts on holder for back neck.

Left front section
With RS facing and 2 strands of MC, beg with sts on holder at left armhole edge and work as for right front reversing all shaping and pocket opening.

Finishing (collar and pocket)
Weave fronts to back at shoulders. Weave left and right back collar tog along short rowed edge. Weave sl sts at inner edge of collar to sts on back neck holder.

Pocket flaps
With RS facing, shorter circular needle and 2 strands of MC, pick up and k22 sts evenly along top edge of pocket opening. Work in garter st, sl first st of every row for 8 rows—approx 1"/2.5cm. *Buttonhole row (RS)* K10, bind off 2 sts, k to end. K next row, casting on 2 sts over bound off sts. Work even until there are 16 rows—approx 2"/5cm from beg. Bind off.

Pocket flap trim
With RS facing, shorter circular needle and 2 strands of B, pick up and k1 st along side of flap for each sl st, 1 st in corner (mark this st), 20 sts along lower edge of flap, 1 st in corner (mark st), 1 st in each sl st along 2nd side of flap. K 1 row. Bind off, inc 1 st before and after marked sts.

Collar trim
Place marker in left front at same place as buttonhole on right front. With RS of left front collar facing (WS of front, RS of collar), longer circular needle and 2 strands of B, beg at marker, pick up and k1 st in every sl st around collar to opposite buttonhole on right front. K 1 row. Bind off.

Front and lower edge trim
With RS facing, longer circular needle and 2 strands of B, beg at left front collar trim, pick up and k1 st in each sl st to lower corner, 1 st in corner (mark st), 1 st in each cast-on st along lower edge, 1 st in corner (mark st), 1 st in each sl st to other collar trim. K 1 row. Bind off, inc 1 st before and after corner marked sts. Join front and collar trims.

Right sleeve
Mark center shoulder seam. With RS facing, shorter circular needle and 2 strands of MC, count down on back 12 (12, 13, 13) sl sts below marker and pick up 1 st in each sl st to marker, then pick up 1 st in each of next 12 (12, 13, 13) sl sts on right front armhole edge—24 (24, 26, 26) sts, turn. *Next row* Sl 1, k to end, pick up 1 st in next 4 sl sts, turn. Rep last row 15 (15, 17, 17) times more—88 (88, 98, 98) sts. Do not turn last row. Beg at armhole shaping, pick up 4 sts in bound-off sts at beg of next 2 rows, then 3 sts at beg of next 2 rows reaching center of lower underarm—102 (102, 112, 112) sts. Work in garter st, sl first st of every row and working back and forth on circular needle for 20 (20, 12, 12) rows—approx 2½ (2½, 1½, 1½)"/7 (7, 4, 4)cm, end with a WS row. Dec 1 st each end of next row, then every 4th row 26 (26, 30, 30) times more—48 (48, 50, 50) sts, end with a RS row—length from underarm approx 16½ (16½, 17½, 17½)"/42.5 (42.5, 45.5, 45.5)cm.

Cuff
Next row (WS of sleeve, RS of cuff) With 2 strands of A, k34 (34, 35, 35), join 2 more strands of A, k rem 14 (14, 15, 15). Cont working both sections at once, inc 1 st at outside edge every 4th row 5 times—39 (39, 40, 40) sts in larger section and 19 (19, 20, 20) sts in smaller section. Work even until 24 rows have been worked—approx 3"/8.5cm from beg of cuff. Bind off.

Cuff trim

Work trim as on other edges, picking up sts separately for each cuff section. Do not pick up sts for trim along sleeve seam edge. Overlap trims slightly at center separation and join. Place sleeve and cuff sides tog, sewing through sl sts so there is no seam. Join trim edges.

Left sleeve

Work as for right sleeve, reversing direction of picked up sts at armhole and placement of cuff section.

Fulling

For gauge swatch only:
Fill washing machine to low water setting at a warm temperature (approx 100–110°F/40–45°C. Add ⅛ cup of baking soda and ⅓ to ½ cup pure soap flakes (Ivory Snow or Borax) to make a sudsy solution. Add small towel to provide abrasion and balanced agitation. Use 10–12 minute wash cycle, including cold rinse and spin. Check if approx gauge has been achieved. If not, repeat process with progressively shorter cycles. Check every few minutes until getting approx gauge. Record details of water amount and temperatures and cycle lengths.
For knitted jacket:
Rep above process using high water setting, large towel, proportionate amount of soda and soap flakes (at least ¼ cup soda and 1 cup soap flakes). Run through 1 normal cycle.

Check garment frequently for signs of fulling. Proceed as for swatch, but due to difference in size and weight, jacket may full much quicker than swatch. Check jacket frequently using swatch as a guide. Remove when getting proper texture and size. Spin jacket to remove excess water. Lie jacket flat to dry on towels, changing when necessary. Some blocking may be done by patting and stretching. If outer edges have stretched in process, thread tapestry and run it in and out along these edges, between trim and body fabric, drawing in edge to desired length. Allow to dry thoroughly before removing holding yarn.

Finishing

Brush jacket if desired for soft surface. Make fabric pockets to fit openings and sew in place. Sew on buttons. Turn up cuffs and sew in place. Sew buttons on cuffs.

Guernsey pullover

Reindeer pattern pullover

Reindeer pattern pullover color charts

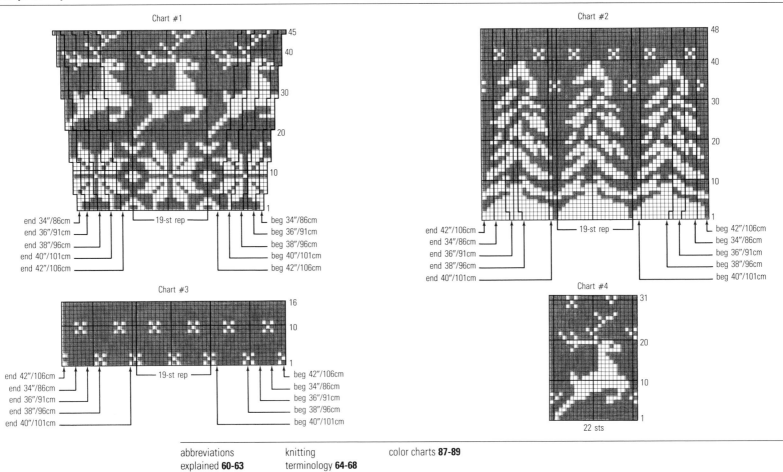

Chart #1

45
40
30
20
10
1

end 34"/86cm
end 36"/91cm
end 38"/96cm
end 40"/101cm
end 42"/106cm
— 19-st rep —
beg 34"/86cm
beg 36"/91cm
beg 38"/96cm
beg 40"/101cm
beg 42"/106cm

Chart #2

48
40
30
20
10
1

end 42"/106cm
end 34"/86cm
end 36"/91cm
end 38"/96cm
end 40"/101cm
— 19-st rep —
beg 42"/106cm
beg 34"/86cm
beg 36"/91cm
beg 38"/96cm
beg 40"/101cm

Chart #3

16
10
1

end 42"/106cm
end 34"/86cm
end 36"/91cm
end 38"/96cm
end 40"/101cm
— 19-st rep —
beg 42"/106cm
beg 34"/86cm
beg 36"/91cm
beg 38"/96cm
beg 40"/101cm

Chart #4

31
20
10
1

22 sts

abbreviations
explained **60-63**

knitting
terminology **64-68**

color charts **87-89**

Aran pattern pullover

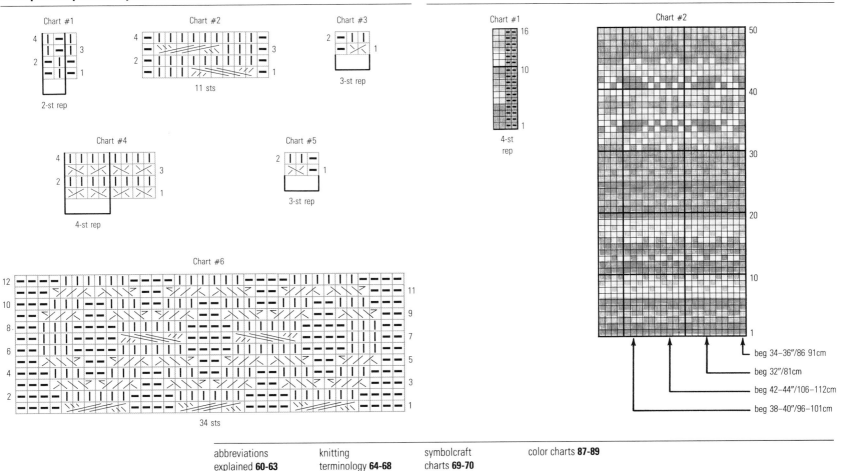

Fair Isle vest

Aran pattern pullover symbolcraft charts

Chart #1

2-st rep

Chart #2

11 sts

Chart #3

3-st rep

Chart #4

4-st rep

Chart #5

3-st rep

Chart #6

34 sts

Fair Isle vest color charts

Chart #1

4-st rep

Chart #2

beg 34–36"/86 91cm

beg 32"/81cm

beg 42–44"/106–112cm

beg 38–40"/96–101cm

| abbreviations explained **60-63** | knitting terminology **64-68** | symbolcraft charts **69-70** | color charts **87-89** |

Fair Isle pullover

Argyle pattern pullover

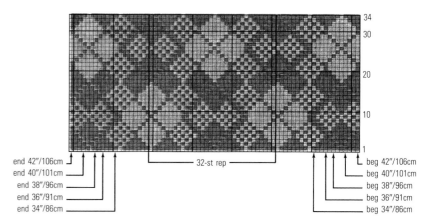

Fair Isle pullover color charts

Chart #1

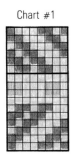

8-st rep

Chart #3

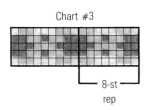

8-st
rep

Chart #2

5

1

8-st
rep

Chart #4

5-st
rep

Argyle pattern pullover color chart

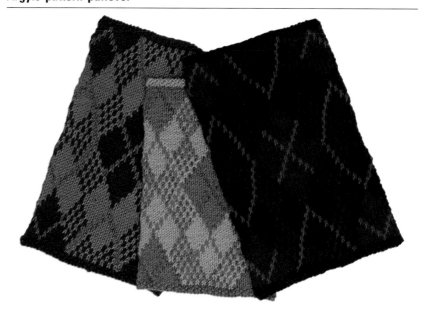

34
30

20

10

1

end 42"/106cm
end 40"/101cm
end 38"/96cm
end 36"/91cm
end 34"/86cm

32-st rep

beg 42"/106cm
beg 40"/101cm
beg 38"/96cm
beg 36"/91cm
beg 34"/86cm

Note: Each square represents 1 st and 2 rows.
Work all RS rows from right to left.
Work all WS rows matching colors.

abbreviations
explained **60-63**

knitting
terminology **64-68**

color charts **87-89**

Index

5×7 **Knitter's graph paper**

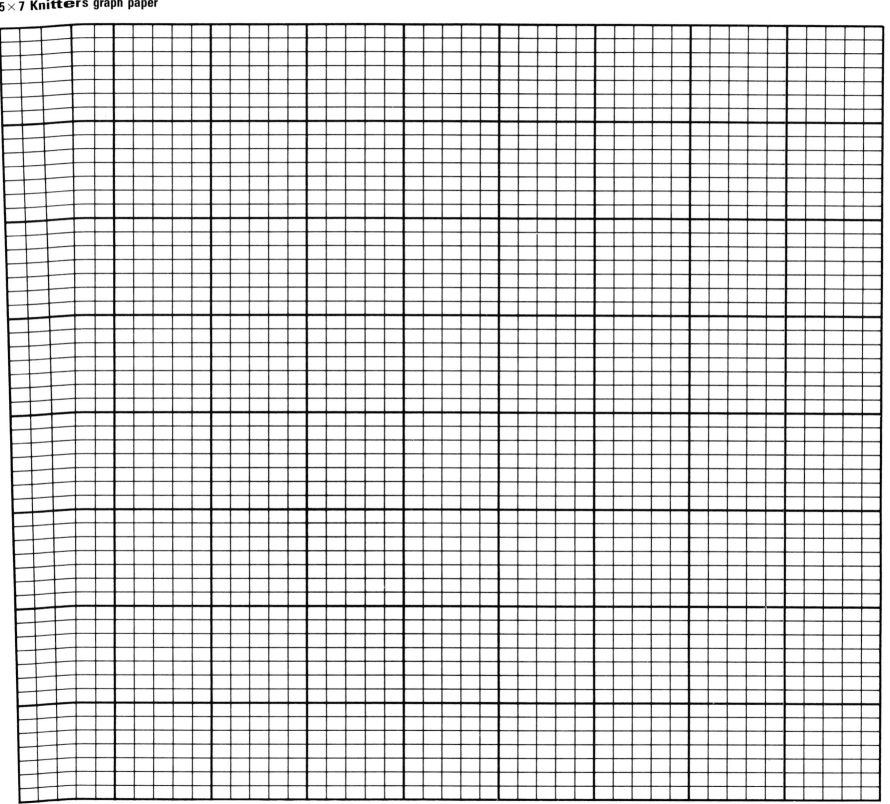

6 × 8 Knitter's graph paper